W9-AQD-255

ALSO BY NORMAN MAILER

The Naked and the Dead
Barbary Shore
The Deer Park
Advertisements for Myself
Deaths for the Ladies (and Other Disasters)
The Presidential Papers
An American Dream
Cannibals and Christians
Why Are We in Vietnam?
The Armies of the Night
Miami and the Siege of Chicago
Of a Fire on the Moon
The Prisoner of Sex
Existential Errands
St. George and the Godfather
Marilyn
The Fight
Genius and Lust
The Executioner's Song
Of Women and Their Elegance

Pieces and Pontifications

NORMAN MAILER

Pieces

and

Pontifications

LITTLE, BROWN AND COMPANY BOSTON · TORONTO

81354
Mai

c. 1

COPYRIGHT © 1982 BY NORMAN MAILER
INTRODUCTION TO "PONTIFICATIONS"
COPYRIGHT © 1982 BY J. MICHAEL LENNON
ALL RIGHTS RESERVED. NO PART OF THIS BOOK MAY BE REPRO-
DUCED IN ANY FORM OR BY ANY ELECTRONIC OR MECHANICAL
MEANS INCLUDING INFORMATION STORAGE AND RETRIEVAL SYS-
TEMS WITHOUT PERMISSION IN WRITING FROM THE PUBLISHER,
EXCEPT BY A REVIEWER WHO MAY QUOTE BRIEF PASSAGES IN A RE-
VIEW.

FIRST EDITION

Library of Congress Cataloging in Publication Data

Mailer, Norman.
  Pieces and pontifications

  1. Mailer, Norman—Interviews. 2. Authors,
American—20th century—Interviews. I. Title.
PS3525.A4152P5   813'.54   82-214
ISBN 0-316-54418-3   AACR2

MV

Designed by Janis Capone

*Published simultaneously in Canada
by Little, Brown & Company (Canada) Limited*

PRINTED IN THE UNITED STATES OF AMERICA

11/23/82
gift
$20.00

For my sister, Barbara

A Preface
to this Collection

❧

The book you hold in your hand is, critically speaking, two books, and the two do not have a great deal more relation to one another than any pair of works by the same author. If they are brought together here, it is at my request. I have an editor and publisher who would have been generous enough to publish *Pieces and Pontifications* as separate volumes, the first a collection of my favorite short writings from the Seventies, and the second a selection in the main of interviews from the same period. If the first part, "Pieces," dwells on a few closely related preoccupations — film, art, American literature, the long night of television, and the surrealism of espionage — the second, "Pontifications," by the rough and ready use of the interview, has a variety of remarks about marriage, sex, pornography, God, the Devil, rock, science, magic, violence, art, literary status, women's liberation, male identity, and even mentions a number of writers of our time with occasional comment on the craft of writing. Each part, therefore, might have made a book more easily by itself. Yet I am pleased that they are brought together. If I am as quick as any writer to present collections of short work, how can I pretend that such volumes have no value for me? Probably I feel as near to *Advertisements for Myself, The Presidential Papers, Cannibals and Christians,* and *Existential Errands* as a good short story writer toward his collections. So one looks for the fifth book to match the first four in one essential — that it have a grasp on its period. Since the pieces certainly show my shell-shocked despair of the Seventies, so do the interviews, of which the vast majority are given in the same decade, become essential for balance, even as the god Horus had the moon for one eye and the sun for the other. The interviews represent the more forceful side of all of us — that portion of our brain which attempts to cope with all we cannot bear. I am one writer who hated the Fifties, lived close to the Sixties, and was much out of step with the Seventies. Still, one does one's best. If my deepest instinct over the last decade has been to withdraw to serious writing, there has also been another part of myself that will not relinquish the idea — does it come with my mother's milk? — that one must be there to speak to one's time. And in these interviews this is what I tried — or such was the illusion while I spoke.

So I would say to the reader that you hold in your hand the work of a divided man. Not schizophrenic — divided. His personality is bicameral and built on two points of reference. (Perhaps this is why his body, whenever he eats too much, is shaped like an ellipse.) The reader, however, need feel no vast superiority. Metaphorically, all too many of us are, these days, kin to pregnant women, and feed not one person within us but two. Here, then, are two sides of myself as I survived the Seventies — my literary ghost looking for that little refinement of one's art which becomes essential as one grows older, and the cry of the street debater, front and center, who always speaks in the loudest voice.

Pieces

Contents

Pieces

❧

A Preface to This Collection   ix

Our Man at Harvard   1

An Advertisement Advertised   6

Are We in Vietnam?   9

Of a Small and Modest Malignancy, Wicked and
  Bristling with Dots   13

Two Letters from Frank Crowther   82

Miller and Hemingway   86

Papa & Son   94

My Friend, Jean Malaquais   97

Narcissism   106

Tango, Last Tango   115

The Faith of Graffiti   134

A Harlot High and Low   159

Our Man at Harvard

❧

Let me tell you about the Somerset Maugham party that we gave at *The Advocate* in the spring of 1942. The magazine was housed then in a dark gray flat-roofed three-story building across the street from the stern of *The Lampoon* (and indeed we were much aware of being in their wake — *Lampoon* editors usually went to *Time;* ours to oblivion). In those days *The Advocate* building was as ugly from the exterior as it is now. A few small and dingy stores occupied the ground floor; some mysterious never-seen tenants were on the second; and *The Advocate* offices took up the third. They were beautiful to me. One climbed a dull, carpeted staircase as dusty as a back road in Guerrero, used one's *Advocate* key to go through the door at the top, and opened the suite, an entire floor-through of five rooms, five mystical chambers full of broken-down furniture and the incomparable odor that rises from old beer stains in the carpet and syrup-crusted empty Coke bottles in the corners. It is a better odor than you would think, sweet and alcoholic and faintly debauched — it spoke of little magazines and future lands of literature, and the offices were almost always empty in late afternoon, when the sunlight turned the dust into a cosmos of angels dancing on a pin. Magicians would have felt a rush of aphrodisia amid all this pendant funk and mote. Maybe I loved the *Advocate* offices more than anyone who was taken in my competition — I spent the spring of sophomore year at Harvard drinking Cokes by a table at the window that faced on *The Lampoon*, and I read old issues of the magazine. Once I was an authority on the early published work in *The Advocate* of T. S. Eliot, Edwin Arlington Robinson, Van Wyck

Brooks, John Reed, Conrad Aiken, E. E. Cummings and Malcolm Cowley — it must have been the nearest I ever came to extracting genealogical marrow from old print. Occasionally Marvin Barrett, the president, or Bowden Broadwater, Pegasus, would come through the office, give a start at seeing me at the same chair and table where he had glimpsed me on the last visit and go off to do his work.

The following academic year, '41–'42, Bruce Barton, Jr., was elected president and John Crockett became Pegasus. We had troubles instantly. Barton, called Pete, was the son of Bruce Barton, Sr., an advertising magnate as well known in his period as was Nicholas Murray Butler, and for that matter one could find similarities. (Barton must have been the last of the advertising tycoons who believed passionately in a strenuous Jesus with muscles.)

His son, in compensation, was a gentleman. Pete Barton was the nicest guy a lot of us met at Harvard, and with his blond hair, good if somewhat pinched features and fundamental decency, he could have passed for Billy Budd if 1) he had not gone to Deerfield, which left him a little more patrician than yeoman in manner, and if 2) he had had more beef. But he was gentle, he was quietly literary, and his father had millions. Since *The Advocate* was in its usual cauldron of debt, no other man would have been so appropriate to serve as president. Barton might even have had a benign, well-financed and agreeable administration if not for the new Pegasus, John Crockett, a man as talented as Claggart and equally riven in his soul by detestation of our Billy Budd.

Being innocent of Crockett's propensities for literary evil, we were a happy group coming into the office. The magazine would be ours. We would print what we wished. Our first issue, therefore, consisted of each of us putting in his own story. Crockett then took our gems to a printer in Vermont. This was, I think, in November. By February we still did not have a magazine. Crockett kept assuring us the printer would soon deliver. None of us ever called him. Crockett had promised us that the inexpensive rate he had managed to extract from the Linotype mills of the Vermont woods would be ruined forever if we broke any of our voices on the printer's ear. Therefore, we waited. Nervously, impatiently, suspiciously, we waited for the issue with our stories.

Instead, Crockett came back with the seventy-fifth anniversary edition of *The Advocate*, a little work of love Crockett had gotten together by himself over the last year — in truth, a prodigious push of

Pegasus-manship — collecting poems, pieces and comment from the fine ranks of Wallace Stevens, Horace Gregory, Djuna Barnes, Marianne Moore, Robert Hillyer, Frederic Prokosch, Mark Schorer, John Malcolm Brinnin, Richard Eberhart, Bowden Broadwater, William Carlos Williams, plus a poem by John Crockett, "The Sulky Races at Cherry Park." It was a mammoth virtuoso literary crypto-CIA affair back in March of '42, and none of us on *The Advocate* had had the first clue as to what Crockett was cooking. As for the issue with our stories — Crockett promised to get to that next. The expression on his young but sour face told us what he thought of our stories. Crockett, incidentally, while not as well-featured as John Dean had a great resemblance to him — I remember his tortoiseshell glasses, high forehead and thin pale hair.

Pete Barton had been agitated for weeks at the long wait on our first issue. Painfully aware of his father's weight in the world, he was invariably overscrupulous never to push his own. He had suspended himself into a state of forbearance worthy of a Zen warrior considering the immense agitation the late appearance of the magazine had caused. When the anniversary issue appeared (to rich critical reception in the Boston papers, worse luck!) Barton finally demonstrated his father's blood. He called an emergency meeting where he calumniated himself for his derelictions of attention, took the full blame for the financial disaster of the issue (it had cost something like three times as much as more modest issues; our debt on the consequence had doubled overnight) and — Billy Budd to the last, absent even to intimations of a further notion to evil — stated that he would not ask for Crockett's resignation if he could expect his cooperation on future projects.

Crockett replied with a nod of his head and a profound turning of our collective head. Having heard, he said, that Somerset Maugham would be in the Boston area during April, he had sent an invitation to Maugham to come to a party that *The Advocate* would be happy to throw in his honor, and Maugham had accepted. Maugham had accepted.

This piece of news ran around the ring of Cambridge like a particle in a cyclotron. Nothing in four years at Harvard, not Dunkirk, Pearl Harbor or the blitz, not even beating Yale and Princeton in the same season for the first time in years, could have lit Harvard up more. Not to be invited to that party was equal to signifying that one had mismanaged one's life.

The literary grandees of the faculty sent their early acceptance:

F. O. Matthiessen, Theodore Spencer and Robert Hillyer in the van; the officers of *The Lampoon* sucked around; housemasters' wives asked how things were *going* at *The Advocate*. On the night of the party, four hundred souls in four hundred bodies as large as Patrick Moynihan's and as delicate as Joan Didion's came to the small rooms on the third floor and packed themselves in so completely that you ended by bringing your drink to your lips around the wrist of the strange forearm in front of your face. The noise of cocktail gabble anticipated the oncoming shapings of time — one would not hear the sound again until the first jet planes fired up their engines at an airport. Drinks were passed overhead. If you did not reach at the right time, another hand plucked the drink. It did not matter. More was on its way. Glasses bounced like corks over white choppy Harvard hands. From time to time, word would pass like wind through grass that Maugham had just entered the building, Maugham was having trouble getting up the stairs, Maugham was through the door. Maugham was in the other room. We formed phalanxes to move into the other room; we did not budge. A phalanx cannot budge a volume that is impacted. The lovely smile of resignation was on the lips of faculty wives: It is the establishment smile that says, "Life is like that — the nearest pleasures are not to be tasted." After a half hour of such smiling into the face of a stranger as one brought one's arm around her neck to get at one's drink, the wind came through the grass again. Maugham, we heard, was at the door. Maugham was slowly going down the stair. Somerset Maugham was gone.

Hands passed drinks above the impacted mass. Eyes flashed in that hard gemlike smile of pride retained when opportunity is lost. In another half hour, there was a lessening of pressure on one's chest, and bodies began to separate. After a while, one could walk from room to room. What was the point? Maugham was gone.

It was only on the next day, after the claims of liars had been checked against the quiet evidence of reliable witnesses who had found themselves analogously empretzeled in every room and on the stairs, that the news came back. By every sound measure of verification, Somerset Maugham had never been in *The Advocate* building that night. Crockett, now confronted, confessed. Out of his unflappable funds of phlegm, he allowed that he had known for weeks Somerset Maugham was not coming — the great author had been kind enough to send a telegram in answer to the invitation. "Certainly not," it said.

It was too late to ask Crockett to resign. Due to the war and an accelerated graduation, our term as *Advocate* officers was up; the new president and Pegasus were in. Because of the party, we left with a debt that had just doubled again. *The Advocate* has never been solvent since.

A postscript: Pete Barton became a Navy officer and commanded a ship, came home, worked as quietly for *Time* as if he had been a *Lampoon* man, and died before he was forty. The only time I saw John Crockett again was about ten years ago in New York on a reunion at the Harvard Club. He was now in the State Department and had been stationed for years in Yugoslavia. He told delicious stories about idiotic conversations with Madame Tito at banquets in Zagreb. He looked to be as wicked as ever. Our cause was being well served in Yugoslavia. It occurs to me that the mag across the street never knew what a talent it missed when *The Advocate* got Crockett. Rest in peace, Pete Barton.

An Advertisement
Advertised

❧

The *Deer Park* is the book which taught me how to write, but *Advertisements* followed, and it was the first book I wrote that had a style I thought I might be able to call my own. It was forged out of a continuing recognition of how difficult it was to put words together when writing about oneself.

Style, of course, is what every good young author looks to acquire. In lovemaking, its equivalent is grace. Everybody wants it but nobody seems to find it by working directly toward the goal. On the other hand, unless born with grace or style, nobody seems to get there without working hard in some direction or other.

Advertisements was written at the end of the slowest and most morale-disrupting kind of work. I didn't begin the book until 1958, ten years after *The Naked and the Dead* was published. In between had come *Barbary Shore* and *The Deer Park* and I never want to have two novels as hard again to write.

I did not know what I was doing. As I have explained now and again, I had been divorced by success from any intimate sense of my identity and had a hard time getting halfway back. Apart from that psychological vertigo which will attack any athlete, performer or young businessman who has huge early success, I had my own particular problem, a beauty — I did not know my métier. *The Naked and the Dead* had been written out of what I could learn from James T. Farrell and John Dos Passos with good doses of Thomas Wolfe and Tolstoy, plus homeopathic tinctures from Hemingway, Fitzgerald, Faulkner, Melville and Dostoyevsky. With all such help, it was a book that wrote itself. It had a style-proof style. That is to say it had a best-seller style, no style. Very few people failed to read that book with some interest.

I knew however it was no literary achievement. I had done a book in a general style borrowed from many people and did not know what I had of my own to say. I had not had enough of my own life yet. The idea could even be advanced that style comes to young authors about the time they recognize that life is out there ready to kill them, kill them quickly or slowly, but something out there is not fooling. It would explain why authors who were ill in their childhood almost always arrive early in their career as developed stylists: Proust, Capote, and Alberto Moravia give three examples; Gide offers another. This notion would certainly account for the early and complete development of Hemingway's style. He had had before he was twenty the unmistakable sensation of being wounded so near to death that he felt his soul slide out of him, then slip back.

The average young author is not that ill in childhood nor that ill used by early life. His little social deaths are overcome by his small social conquests. So he writes in the style of others looking for his own, and tends to love words more than rhythms. In his haste to dominate the world (rare is the young writer who is not a consummate prick) he tends to use words for their precision, their ability to define, their acrobatic action. His style often changes from scene to scene, from paragraph to paragraph. He knows little about creating mood and the essence of good style is that it sets a mood thick as a theatrical piece, and then alters that mood, enlarges it, conducts it over to another mood. Every sentence, precise or imprecise, vaulting or modest, is careful not to poke a hyperactive finger through the tissue of the mood, nor do the sentences ever become so empty of personal quality that the mood sinks to the ground of the page. It is an achievement which comes from having thought about one's life right into the point where one is living it. Everything that happens seems capable of offering its own addition to one's knowledge. One has arrived at a personal philosophy or has, at least, reached the rare plateau where irony rather than philosophy serves to sustain each day. At that juncture, everything one writes comes out of one mood, one's own fundamental mood.

Some such development may have gone on in me over the ten years from the publication of *The Naked and the Dead* to the commencement of work on *Advertisements For Myself*. Maybe I had come to realize that authors died from the reception of their books, literally began to die a little, and every dishonesty in oneself added gangrene to the wound. So *Advertisements* became the book in which I tried to separate my legitimate spiritual bile from my self-pity and maybe it was the hardest continuing task I had yet set myself. What aggravated every problem was that I was also trying to give up smoking, and as a corollary of kicking nicotine, I was thrust into the problem of style. In those days, my psyche felt as different without cigarettes as my body felt in moving from air to water. It was as if I perceived with different senses, and clear reactions were blunted. Writing without cigarettes, the word I looked for almost never came, not in quick time: in compensation I was granted a sensitivity to the rhythm of what I wrote and that helped to develop my style, no, rather say it proceeded to turn my nose in the direction of style. I began to learn how difficult it is for a prose writer to move from the hegemony of the word to the resonance of the prose rhythm. That can be a jump greater than a leap into poetry; maybe it is analogous to changing one's religion.

I suffered, anyway, prodigies of brain-curdling, and educated myself all over again how to write, write without cigarettes, and found the beginnings of a style that might begin to express the way my own mind (as opposed to other writers' minds) was ready to work. So, *Advertisements for Myself* was a book whose writing changed my life. Let us hope that is conceivably for the better.

Are
We in Vietnam?

❧

This is the only novel I ever finished under the mistaken belief I was writing not this kind of novel but another. Living in Provincetown on the edge of those rare, towering and windy dunes which give the tip of Cape Cod a fair resemblance to the desert of the Sahara, I had begun to think of a novel so odd and so horrible that I hesitated for years to begin it. I did not like the story; it came to me with fear. I imagined a group of seven or eight bikers, hippies and studs plus a girl or two living in the scrub thickets that sat in some of the valleys between the dunes. Only six feet high, those thickets were nonetheless forests, and if one could find a path through the thorns and cat briars, nobody could track you, not in a hurry. So I peopled the thickets with characters: my characters were as wild as anyone who ever came to Provincetown. It is not a tame place. Years ago, a First Lady was once told it was "the Wild West of the East," and that is not a bad description. The tip of Cape Cod curls in on itself in a spiral — the long line of the dunes comes around like the curve of one's palm and fingers as they close into a fist — it is one of the very few places in America where one comes to the end of the road for a more profound reason than real estate ceasing to be profitable. In Provincetown, geography runs out, and you are surrounded by the sea.

So it is a strange place. The Pilgrims landed there before they went on to Plymouth — America began here. The Pilgrims lost interest in scrub pine, mournful winds, and sand in the land. They moved on, left ghosts. Whaling captains settled in later, left ghosts. In winter the town is filled with spirits. One can go mad in that rainy climate waiting for March to end. It is a place for murderers and suicides. If decades went by without a single recorded homicide, that record ended abruptly with a crime of true carnage. A few years ago, a young Portuguese from a family of fishermen killed four girls, dismembered their bodies, and buried the pieces in twenty small and scattered graves.

That catastrophe was not a good deal worse than anything I had already contemplated for my gang, since I conceived of them making nocturnal trips from the dunes into town where out of the sheer boredom of an existence not nearly intense enough to satisfy their health, they would commit murders of massive brutality and then slip back to the dunes. Motiveless crimes. I saw a string of such crimes.

I was, as I say, in fear of the book. I loved Provincetown and did not think that was a good way to write about it. The town is so naturally spooky in mid-winter and provides such a sense of omens waiting to be magnetized into lines of force that the novel in my mind seemed more a magical object than a fiction, a black magic.

Nonetheless, I began the book in the spring of '66. It attracted me too much not to begin. Yet because I could not thrust Provincetown into such literary horrors without preparation, I thought I would start with a chapter about hunting bear in Alaska. A prelude. I would have two tough rich boys, each as separated from social convention as any two rich boys could be — Texans I would make them out of a reserve of memories of Texans I had served with in the 112th Cavalry out of San Antonio. The boys would be still young, still mean rather than uncontrollably murderous — the hunting might serve as a bridge to get them ready for more. They would come back from the Alaskan hunting trip ready to travel — Provincetown would eventually receive them.

Now, anyone who reads the book which this preface serves will see that nobody ever gets to Provincetown. The chapter on hunting becomes a half-dozen chapters, a dozen chapters, it ends up being all of the book. If I wrote those chapters wondering how long it would take to extricate myself with novelistic integrity from all the elaborations of the hunt I seemed more and more bound to get into, it was not until those boys were back in Dallas and I was getting ready to move them East that I realized two things.

(1) I had nothing further to say about them.

(2) Even if I did, I could no longer believe that Tex and D.J. could still be characters in the Provincetown novel. They had another quality by now.

So I lived with my manuscript for a few months and ended by recognizing that I hadn't been too bright. I had written a novel not a prelude. The book was done. Later, a number of readers would think *Why Are We in Vietnam?* was far and away my best book. I thought I had never written a funnier one.

In retrospect, I was less certain, however, of the humor. For when Sharon Tate was murdered in the summer of '69, and the world heard of Charles Manson, I could wonder what state of guilt I might have been in if I had written that novel of desert murderers. How then could I ever have been certain Manson had not been sensitive to its message in the tribal air?

But then writing has its own occult force. At its best, we never know where our writing comes from nor who gives it to us. If Jack Kennedy's name is invoked in the first sentence of *An American Dream*, nine lines farther down that page, a man named Kelly is mentioned. Later in the same chapter we learn Kelly's middle name is Oswald — Barney Oswald Kelly. That chapter appeared in *Esquire* about a month after the assassination, but it had been written three months earlier, a coincidence to force one to contemplate the very design of coincidence.

So, too, had I written in *Barbary Shore* about a secret agent named McLeod who had been, in his time, a particularly important Soviet agent. He lived in a cheap room on the top floor of a cheap rooming house just across the hall from the narrator. Writing the book, I always found it hard to believe that such a man would be found in such a place, and the simple difficulty of not quite believing what I wrote did not help to speed the writing of the book. A year after it was published, I rented a room in a dank old building with high ceilings called Ovington Studios on Fulton Street in Brooklyn not a half mile from the rooming house in *Barbary Shore,* and on the floor below during those ten years I kept the studio was Colonel Rudolph Abel, the most important Soviet spy in America — or, at least, so was he described by the FBI when the arrest was finally made.

We will never know if primitive artists painted their caves to show a representation, or whether the moving hand was looking to placate the forces above and the forces below. Sometimes, I think the novelist fashions a totem just as much as an aesthetic, and his real aim, not even known necessarily to himself, is to create a diversion in the fields of dread, a sanctuary in some of the arenas of magic. The flaws of his work can even be a part of his magical strength, as if his real intent in writing is to alter the determinations of that invisible finger which has written and moved on. By such logic, the book before you is a totem, not empty of amulets for the author against curses, static, and the pervasive malignity of our electronic air.

Of a Small
and Modest Malignancy,
Wicked and Bristling
with Dots

❧

This summer I took my family on a motor trip through the West, and left the highway for a one-hundred-mile jog to pick up some fossils for my boy. This took us to Hurricane, Utah ... around the Zion Park country. A great vastness, magnificent. ... It is three in the afternoon when we get there, to a house, the fossil-seller we read about in the Museum of Natural History magazine operating out of his cellar. It's a gorgeous day, just right, and we go in — into a small living room with about nine people in it, all staring at that square of light: they're watching a game show, three generations of them, the grandparents (American gothics, blooded, stolid) down to the near-infants, wired, a funny show, I guess it's supposed to be, at least "joyous," but no one is laughing, no one is smiling even; they're just fixed there in their places, staring (not looking, mind you, in the way that Sontag separates looking and staring: by God, this is "silent" art for the populace). Well, the feller sends us down to the cellar to pick around in his stuff and goes back into the living room. We're down there almost three hours; my boy can't make up his mind, and my wife is no help: and when we come back up, they're there, same postures, no change; a soap opera, I think it was, running. ... It leaves you feeling something about the force we are talking about, its power to de-nature.

— out of a letter from Gordon Lish

13

Channel 1

Limbo was a house of many mansions. Mailer's spirits, while hardly free — they whipped around his soul like electrons orbiting a ring — began, nonetheless, to awake. The telling monotonies of Limbo (all those faceless fornications that rang in the ears, those stupors that drifted like bad weather, apathies piling on apathies like old newspapers, the crackle of static, and the playback of cocktail gabble, the gluttony of red wine taken after white wine on top of harshly cooked food, or the holes in one's memory now plugged with electronic hum, plus the horror of contemplating drops from heights where one did not want to find oneself, and all the stations of the cross of feeling empty while waiting for subway trains and airline shuttles and waitresses in busy lunchrooms) all such items having been so far experienced in Limbo as direct punishment, now began to partake of ecological logic. It may be that Lish's letter had something to do with it.

Mailer began to believe that this enforced immersion in every sensation, episode, glut, glop, and repellent handle of experience (his vision filled with nothing but the faces of digital watches, the smell of pharmacies, the touch of polyester shirts, the wet wax-paper of McDonald's hamburgers, the air of summer when traffic jams, and shrieks of stereo as the volume is mis-laid, the little nausea that plastic highball glasses will give to the resonance of booze) were not necessarily items to scourge him around one eternity before dispatching him to another, but might be instead his own natural field of expiation. In place of his soul expiring, or suffering some whole damnation now, he might still be part of his own karmic chain and going through a purification of those misspent hours before being thrown back into the contest again. A joke resounded in his ears. "It's a great day for the race," said the elevator operator in the acrylic uniform in the Formica-paneled cage. "What race?" said the passenger. "The human race," said the elevator operator and laughed his way up the ascension.

All who died were guilty. In part, at least, they were guilty, and conceivably they were innocent in part, and Limbo, thought Mailer, might even be the charity to suppose that innocence, if it wanted to go back to the race, was in need of education. Limbo, on the consequence, took all those moral stances embedded in concrete, and wrenched them askew. In the mansion, there was that human, for instance, who held the award for the most faithful church attendance over two decades in the American Midwest; now, he was pissing and moaning up a storm at the injustice of being here. Still, he was guilty. The inhabitants were all judged by one fine measure: had they or had they not wasted more of the soul's substance than was required by the exigencies of their life? Since the first perception offered here was that the most consumable substance of the soul was nothing other than time; that Time, whole and mysterious bed of light, electricity, and force, was invested, like the true fund of the realm, in every soul, it followed as a consequence that Time was not to be wasted, but rather, whatever the warp of one's upbringing, was to be spent, all neurotic, psychotic, screwball, timid, stingy, spendthrift, violent or fear-filled habits taken into account, was still to be spent as wittily, cheerfully, and/or bravely as possible.

That was the standard of Limbo. Time was not to be wasted. It came over one, even on emerging from the first stupefying sleep (and therefore beginning to suffer monotony, apathy, and the boredom that comes from being out of Time) that this dreadful experience, these appalling emptinesses of the spiritual gut which now made up the hours — could one presume to speak still of hours: rather was one not living in seamless non-dark non-light units punctuated by no breath? — was, while a doleful experience, steeped in torpor, still a course in orientation over spiritual ills. For instance, the Midwestern churchgoer now inhabited a cell (in this penitentiary of the heavens) next to one of the world's worst cons, a man who had killed three prisoners before dying himself over the twenty years of his Lewisburg stretch. Yet the con was here for another kind of crime — he had put in more man-hours watching TV than any other convict in the federal system. All the same, the two were installed side by side — their crimes against the cosmos were apparently not dissimilar. They had both wasted their stuff, and egregiously. The churchgoer had perpetrated this by the brute sterility of his attendance: the complacency of his performance (that is to say, the spiritual stagnation at the center of his complacency) had been a powerful miasma to lay on the spirit of three young ministers who in succession grew old at accelerated rates looking into his professionally empty eyes — he had certainly spoiled more of existence than he sustained. The con, in his turn, had poisoned the livelier possibilities of many a young wolf and punk whose burgeoning shit-oriented libidos would somehow drain out of them after sauntering past that corner of the inmates' lounge where the con was ensconced by the set. Considering how immense was his potential violence, just so flattened had been the mood by that act of his will which chose to do time quietly, watch TV, and get out — at which, in fact, he failed, for he kept killing other convicts. The con's real mission in life, and he knew it, was to outwit guards, stifle alarm systems, and climb unclimbable prison walls. The logics of Limbo were not easily available, and yet the message, as one took it through the now non-corporeal equivalent of one's pores, was that something in the cosmos could have prospered more if the con had climbed the wall instead of imbibing TV, even as the churchgoer could have stirred beneficial forces in the universe by catching an X-rated movie or two.

Given the iron law of such logic, Mailer came to recognize that he would have done better in his life to go to church once in a while on Sunday (not even Limbo suggested a synagogue for him!) rather than increase the total of his appearances on television.

Indeed, it was this particular piece of moral knowledge he was obliged to ingest right after his emergence from the first stupefying sleep-out. It was to recognize that every dull thing one had done to the universe (filling out crossword puzzles one did not wish to fill, taking the Eastern Airline shuttle when other transportation was available) every hour one had voided thereby of its fresh and keen desire to be used, the air around one, in consequence, suffocated by psychic exhaust, had now to be breathed again, the air of the stifled past to be swallowed, digested, suffered, and then stuffed into the ongoing baggage of one's karma. This mansion of Limbo was here to bring you face to face with those sins for which there are no tears, even as a husband and wife cannot weep if they lose a potentially heartfelt piece of ass by watching TV all night; yes, this corner of Limbo (a clean and well-appointed place whose appurtenances were suggestive of the interior of a picture tube on a black-and-white set — that is, all curved, silver, and gray, an odorless impalpability of fluorescence in an eternity of flickering) was now apparently ready to teach him, that is, teach his soul, something new. That meant, on reflection, that he might still have a soul. Something in himself exactly like the Old Center seemed certainly not to have ceased, that part at least of himself he had always thought wiser than the rest of him (that part which took pains to mash an invisible egg on his head after a rotten remark) was coming to recognize that his tour through Limbo (if indeed a tour and not an ongoing punishment) would ask him to meditate at length and presumably to purpose on those yaws and palls of his life which had passed through TV. He was going to be obliged to regard his own wretched collaboration with the multimillion-celled nausea-machine, that Christ-killer of the ages — television. (Let us say it takes a Jew not wholly convinced of the divinity of Christ to see that is who the tube is killing.) And he shuddered through the now-familiar, if minimal, retchings of Limbo while remembering how on numerous occasions with each of his seven children he had closed the doors of his own resistance to TV and let the little fuckers keep looking at the screen because it *pacified* them, which is to say took the lividity of their five-year-old nerves and slowly (that is, faster than sight) and buzzingly, cauterized their nerve ends just the right bloody bit, no blood seen. Again the guilt that cannot be alleviated by tears stirred like sludge in his own small part of the great cosmic gut. Yes, there was a malignancy present in the bowels of communication, and it was video.

So could he meditate now for his next karma, or at least for this part of his next karma, by brooding over the nature of television. As soon brood over the nature of cancer gulch! Might they not be the same? A piece of plastic in the tissues of communing, a pollution in the avatars, good old anti-matter living next to matter.

He prepared therefore for the meditative journey that proves most excruciating in Limbo, a rounding through the past, a trip back! It is a venture full of perils. For the glassy sluggish surface of the past, once disturbed, would offer every encouragement to mosquitoes, insomnia, the rash which issues from deodorants, and more Limbo.

To meditate on TV would prove equal, however, to writing a recollection of an enemy one had never met and could not quite believe in. How can one conceive of an enemy who is without personal animosity? It is like writing a memoir on an oxymoron. Limbo set its tasks.

Channel 2

Mailer, nonetheless, had a few tricks. The virtue of having lived as a professional writer was that one's soul — much punched-out bag — had acquired a little craft for dealing with the peculiar properties of context. One knew what to guard against. Not all events were, for example, equally extricable from the past. It was not unlike hunting for odd-colored stones in tidal flats. Some would come up at the touch of one's fingers. Others stirred with a fury and threw off clouds of black sand full of anathema. A root of blatwort (or any weed with some such name) would be discovered beneath, embracing the stone. On the other hand, those attractive pebbles that came up free, tended also to be slick. Like good anecdotes that had no roots, they soon lost their charm. Whereas, a real piece of the past always seemed to connect to an underground creeper that went on forever.

Writing about what had happened, therefore, could put you into difficulties worthy of Proust or Einstein. Hoping to evoke an event, one could not expect that the act of finding the facts would fulfill the job. It was more elusive. The event might have a fine mood created by the facts that went into it, but it was another matter to get one's writing to prove equal to the mood. A poem does not describe a movement of a bird in flight so much as the unaccountable stir from one syllable to another will allow us to feel the thrust of a wing.

This glimpse of the intricate nature of his craft left Mailer, however, with only a small glow. Limbo was adept at dimming the rosier emoluments of reverie. There came the gloomier conclusion — a pure artifact of Limbo itself — that if his memories of TV were without roots, they were also without mood. The inner taste of his experiences on TV tasted like aspirin to him.

He might have a problem, therefore, equal to the size of this mansion of Limbo. It would be to take his soul through the leachings of its experience in fifty, or was it a hundred, or two hundred TV appearances (the promiscuous are not those who know too many lovers so much as those who no longer count them) and extract from the memory of these outings, not the moral lesson, but the way to absorb back into himself the excrementitiousness of his TV past.

Yet he could not even know that this was his task. He found, out of the thousand papers he might have managed to smuggle across with him, nothing in Limbo but a letter from Gordon Lish, an editor he hardly knew; on the evidence of this letter, Lish had a style whose carefree disjunctions were much like the author's own, and that was swell. That was company on a long trip.

On the other hand, Mailer had small trust in Limbo. There was no way of knowing the certifiability of what you could remember.

Lish's letter seemed to propose an immense essay: *"Treat television,"* Lish had written, *"as pure phenomenon, purest form ... open the eye onto television without comment, without attitude, without the particularities that constitute the content of the thing as it is."* So went a couple of the phrases. To the degree that Mailer thought he understood what this meant, he thought he understood it well: *". . . television will be displayed wholly in terms of its existence as the all-pervasive environment, the universally felt national experience . . . an awesome, omnipresent force, the object that has penetrated and now fused with its subject . . . a revelation of TV as gestalt, form, power."*

What if he had written the piece already? What if it had been a good piece, and he had only brought Lish's letter along to remind himself of a nice achievement. The most damnable property of Limbo (other than its nearness to Damnation itself) was how one's memory was more appalling than a hangover. It certainly felt as if he had written such a piece, or was it only that on every day in the past when he turned on a television set, he had felt the emotions Lish was exhorting him to put upon the page: *"the immense circuitry, something is beaming, beaming, beaming."* Yes, he thought of that every time he was near a set. It was a most unpleasant *something.* So unpleasant, that over the years he had virtually stopped looking at TV. Even the study of professional football games on Sunday afternoon in a room full of good friends and Bloody Marys had begun to pall. The company was good, the drinks were fine, but *something* was in the room, and he could feel its presence eating them all. Yes, you did not make love to your wife after watching TV for an evening. *Something* had entered the blood; *something* had been busy eating the sweetmeats out of the seed.

It was true. It was a personal phenomenon. He had stopped watching TV. He had no interest even in what was supposed to be good. Once he turned on *Mary Hartman, Mary Hartman* and could see what was being talked about, yes, it was tastefully written, it took chances, was offbeat, but *something* was right in there with it and he didn't like Mary Hartman enough to keep the taste of aspirin in his mouth. *Roots* went by; he never took a look. "It's a cultural phenomenon," friends argued with him. He was experiencing his own phenomenon. No more TV. Unlike cigarettes or booze, TV was the easiest habit in the world to give up — once it had leached you out. Every night, or almost every night, even three nights a week for twenty years, the vampire that lived at the center of *some-*

thing had come out of the set and sucked his blood; so it was small surprise that *something* had no interest left in him either, not after twenty years of getting his blood ready for Limbo. The vampire of video obviously preferred to live on young blood. TV was not the altar of modern medicine for nothing, bloodletting was still the secret agent in every debilitating cure.

There were, of course, no TV sets in Limbo. Indeed, how could there be, if it was understood that for the duration of one's stay in the mansion, one was supposed to gather back from the air those vibrations one's TV sets had once put into it!

Still, he would not have been above turning on a set for an instant now if only to give himself a clue as to whether he had written his detestation of TV already, or if the task was yet upon him, and if so, then it would never be done; he now had the misery of comprehending that he would do no writing in Limbo; nothing further to add to the ideational glut of the world. Instead he would rest here, a cow digesting and redigesting the waste he had injected into human stuff, that *"small living room with about nine people in it, all staring at that square of light . . . no one is laughing, no one is smiling even; they're just fixed there in their places, staring . . ."* It was part of the malice of Limbo that Mailer now began to brood on the possibility that these people in the little Utah ranch house were looking at himself, were stupefiedly studying his own electronicized limbs and lineaments in a replay of some godawful afternoon show ten years old — what else would they choose to replay for these black-and-white sets on the desert? "Norman," said Joey Franklin beaming in the midday sun of the TV lights, "you're a great writer I hear, he's a great writer, folks, he writes books! And I don't read books much, don't have the time, so tell me what's the name of a good book?" Into the silence, Joey says — he has a pipeline into *something* — Joey *asks:* "Is *Alice in Wonderland* a good book?"

It cannot be a put-on. Franklin's eyes bounce like marbles.

"Yeah," says Norman Mailer, "it is a good book."

"How about *Rebecca of Sunnybrook Farm*, Norm?"

"I would guess that's not as good." When this is over, Mailer tells himself, he will kill the publicity girl from New American Library who put him on this show in the first place. It will sell books, she had promised him.

Out in Utah, are they taking it all in?

Is he more guilty for having appeared on TV shows than those who only refused to turn off their sets?

Channel 3

In the years before he ever went on TV himself, he used to watch it religiously; after a while, sacrilegiously. It started in the winter he was first smoking marijuana. He smoked it with all the seriousness of what was then his profoundly serious heart. It was 1954, and the drug was more important than any love affair he had ever had. It taught him more. Making love to different women, he would attempt to find that place where marijuana had last left him. It was the arena of the particular sensation he chased, as though he had been given a lovely if ineluctable emotion while watching a bullfight, and so went to the Plaza the following week to look for the same emotion — it did not matter altogether who the bullfighter was.

Since he was then in the opening-out of a career that would later provide a false legend of much machismo, he was still timid. Being deep in pot, and relatively full of life, certainly full of every intimation about himself, he was nonetheless too timid to go out late at night and see what the bars would provide. Since his second wife, not unlike himself in her jangled relations to bravery and cowardice, had usually and prudently gone to bed, he would be up alone at night, his mind teeming, and he would watch TV till the stations shut down. In those days, he made monumental connections on pot. He had to see no more than one animated spiral inserted by a commercial into the guts of a washing machine, a lively spiral that would tunnel right up the tube, and he would try to explain to his friends next day that the advertising agency was promoting the idea that their washing machine was congenial to a housewife's cunt. His friends thought him mad. He examined automobile commercials by the same light and saw that they were no longer selling the car by way of the pretty girl sitting on the fender as once they did; now, they were selling the car itself. The car was the fuck. "Dynaflow does it in oil," the announcer would say of an automatic transmission. So, he would tell his friends. His friends would think him mad and try to dissuade him from smoking too much pot. Marijuana was regarded differently in those days; it offered echoes of *Reefer Madness*.

He would watch Ernie Kovacs and Steve Allen late at night and would recognize that they knew what he knew. They saw how the

spiral worked in the washing machine commercial, and why Dynaflow did it in oil. Years later when Motivational Research was presented to the world, and everybody was ready to tell everybody at a
party that an automobile was not used by a man to get a mistress,
but was the mistress; and a housewife liked to identify the health of
her washing machine with her own genito-urinary harmonies —
speak no ill of the bowels! — Mailer was merely glad that Vance
Packard had done the job. He was behind on too many of his own
jobs. Marijuana had flung the separate parts of his brain into too
many vivid places. In those days he had perceptions on every subject; was convinced, on the consequence, that he was a genius. He
was getting very little writing done.

Still, he clung to his set. It explained the world to him. He was
getting hip to everything, and the beauty was that he did not have to
venture out.

It would not occur to him until six years later, when he would
stab his wife, that it was not timidity which had been his first vice,
but violence, a murderous nest of feeling so intransigent that he did
not dare to go out at night for good cause, and did not know how to
sleep at night without Seconal for even better cause — there was too
much hatred at the distance between what he wished to do and what
he was able to accomplish. Since his wife, faced with the choice of
going to sleep early, or entering on a claustrophobic quarrel, would,
of course, go to sleep, he would sit by himself from midnight until
two in the morning when the last show would go off the air, the flag
would ripple in the wind, and The Star-Spangled Banner would be
played. In those days, he got to hate The Star-Spangled Banner all
over again. It sounded like the first martial strains of that cancer he
was convinced was coming on him, and who knows? If he had not
stabbed his wife, he might have been dead in a few years himself —
the horror of violence is its unspoken logic.

So, in those early mornings when television was his only friend,
he knew already that he detested his habit. There was not enough to
learn from watching TV. Some indispensable pieces of experience
were missing. Except it was worse than that. Something not in existence was also present, some malignancy to burn against his own
malignancy, some onslaught of dots into the full pressure of his own
strangled vision. Often, when the stations would go off the air and
no programs were left to watch, he would still leave the set on. The
audio would hum in a tuneless pullulation, and the dots would hiss
in an agitation of what forces he did not know. The hiss and the

hum would fill the room and then his ears. There was, of course, no clamor — it was nearer to anti-noise dancing in eternity with noise. And watching the empty video, he would recognize it was hardly empty. Bands of gray and lighter gray swam across the set, roll-overs swept away the dots, and something like sun-spots crackled forth. Then the set went back to the slow scan of the waves and the drone of the audio. He discovered at last that such use of TV was a species of tranquilizer and could deaden the sharpest edge of his nerve. Blunted, impalpably bruted by a half-hour of such odorless immersion, he would with the aid of his Seconal be a little more ready to go to sleep.

A few years later when McLuhan would torment the vitals of a generation of American intellectuals with the unremovable harpoon that "the media is the message," Mailer could give his agreement. The message of TV was the scan of gray on gray and the hum of the sound when there was neither music nor a voice. Much later, in the Fall of '72, he would set out to make audiences laugh by comparing President Nixon's then featureless but disturbing personality to a TV screen that is lit when nothing is on the air. Nixon was there, he would remark, to deaden the murderous mood of the Republic. In-deed, it was the best explanation for why a man so unpopular was going to win by so great a majority. If Nixon did not make anyone very happy, neither did the TV set. Its message was equal to Nixon's: I am here to deaden you — you need it!

Maybe America did need it. Brooding over America of the Six-ties, that insane expanding America where undercover FBI men were inspiring (wherever they were not committing) the most vio-lent acts of the Left, brooding on that rich and powerful country where puritanism was still as alive as every Baptist, that corporate land with no instinctive response to aesthetics engaged now in the dissemination throughout the world of the worst applied aesthetics in the history of the world, its superhighways the highest form of strip mining, its little buildings kin to shoeboxes, its big buildings scaled to the module of one cardboard carton piled on top of an-other, the U.S. skyline thereby deserting the high needles of Man-hattan for the Kleenex boxes of Dallas; that food-guzzling Republic that froze its food before it would overcook it, and liked to lick ketchup off French fries so soggy they dropped from your fingers like worms — the worst food in the history of the world! — that sex-revolutionary Republic where swinging singles were connecting up with like-units — every other Baptist! — that sadistically revolutionary Republic going into black leather, S-M, and knocking off gooks in rice paddies, defoliating the foliage, digging the hog-resonance of motors between one's legs, and flame-throwers and comic books, and Haight-Ashbury, hitting golf balls on the moon, yes, that America, full of dread, could certainly use TV — I am here to deaden you, you need it!

Those were legitimate feelings for 1972. One had had a large fraction of a life by then watching TV, and one had long ago had the education of putting oneself on shows. Back in '53 and '54, however, stoned on pot, wafted up and down on Seconal, jammed with ambition, terror, and the common lust to learn the secrets of the world some easy way, the immersion into TV was profound. By it, one could study the world, and the tricks of the world.

So, for instance, would he examine people as strange to him as Igor Cassini who had a show in those years for snobs and it was hard as fiberglass. TV proved to be more interesting then for you could see a genuine article regularly, well-groomed, Republican, rich enough to own horses, sexy enough to marry up, and empty enough to find any topic of conversation amusing provided it was void of content. Those were Igor Cassini's guests. Mailer would on such occasions peer right into the tube to get a little nearer to the novelistic wealth.

Or: studying the tourist, he learned much about American fellatio. TV was scintillating for that. Next to the oil of Dynaflow and the spiral in the washing machine, came the phallic immanence of the microphone. A twinkle would light up in Steve Allen's eye as he took the mike and cord down the aisle and in and out of impromptu interviews with his audience, snaking the rounded knob right up to the mouth of some starched skinny Middle West matron, lean as whipcord, tense as rectitude, a life of iron disciplines in the vertical wrinkles of the upper lip; the lady would bare her teeth in a snarl and show a shark's mouth as she brought her jaws around to face and maybe bite off that black dob of a knob so near to touching her tongue.

A high school girl would be next, there with the graduating class on a trip to New York, her folks watching back home. She would swoon before the mike. She could not get her mouth open. She would keep dodging in her seat, and Steve would stay in pursuit, mike extended. Two nights ago she dodged for two hours in the back seat of a car. My God, this was in public.

A young housewife, liberal, sophisticated, happy to present her congenial point of view, compliments Mr. Allen on the quality of his show. "We watch you regularly, Steve, and like to think we're not too far behind the times up in Norfolk, Connecticut. That's right, Norfolk, not Norwalk." Her mouth, which has regular lips, is held a regular distance from the microphone. She shows no difficulty with it, no more than she would have with a phallus; two fingers and a thumb keep the thing canted right. There can be nothing wrong, after all, in relations between consenting adults. So speaks her calm.

Then there is a big heavy-set man who owns a grain-and-feed store in Ohio. He prides himself on imperturbable phlegm, and some thrift with words. He is not quite aware of the mike. If a man came into his store and proceeded to expose himself, this proprietor would not see it right away. He might, after all, be explaining the merits and demerits of one feed-mix to another; since he chews no gum when he walks, neither does he offer attention to tangentia as he talks. Now, singled out from the audience to be interviewed, he is stiffnecked, and responds only from that side of his mouth adjacent to the cheek on which Steve is asking the questions; he allows, "New York is a good place to visit, but, yessir, I'll be glad to start up for home," then, bla-looh! he sees it, black blimp-like little object! he blinks, he swallows, he looks at Steve: "I guess I've had my say, Mr. Allen," he says, and shuts up shop. Later he will tell a pinochle partner about the crazy people in New York. "Yes," the friend will acknowledge.

"You bet, Steve," says the next fellow, "I'm awfully glad you selected me. I've always wanted to talk to you." He is fully aware of the mike and what it portends. "Yes, yes, I'm a male secretary, love the work." "It doesn't bother you," asks Steve, "if people say, 'What is that, a male secretary, isn't it supposed to be women's work?'" "Oh, Steve, that doesn't bother me a bit. Here," he says, reaching for the mike. "Do you mind? I'm much more comfortable when I hold it."

"Help yourself," says Steve.

"Oh, I intend to," says the guest. "Life is a feast, and I think we should all get what we can, don't you?"

Hip! Mailer, building dreams of future power in the darkness, saw it all. America was getting hip. In the center of marijuana was the secret of how to do it. You needed the audacity to take your step.

In those days his life was simple, if much debilitated. Exhausted from writing *The Deer Park*, frantic from trying to do his columns

for *The Village Voice,* used-up from the terror of his central political premise — he believed that the orgy was the salvation of
America (he still did not know that the average swinger was about
as militant as the average tennis player, and in an equal rush to save
the cosmos!) — he was, if three times exhausted, nonetheless a
demon of psychic r.p.m.'s. When his brain was not in torpor, it felt
like an immense dynamo running at top speed in an empty shed in
the middle of the woods. He knew what it was to feel like electricity,
and understood the profoundly depressing statement in *Being and
Nothingness* that consciousness was the nihilation of Being. For his
brain worked at a great rate (half as fast it must be on occasion as
Jean-Paul Sartre's) and he felt the full dimensions of the void his
consciousness was generating in his brain cage.

Still, he was also possessed of an idea. It would go through many
changes and verge on becoming the opposite of itself, but it would
remain the idea of his life — it was (to take it by the most dangerous
premise first) that criminals were nearer to God than cops; corollary: a good cop was therefore a work of art. It would also conclude
that love was as rich a mystery as death, and perhaps as indecipher-
able; you could hardly know more than whether you had a love that
was good or bad for your orgasm. In consequence, the idea would
state that fine justice could be found only once in one's life, and that
was in the hour after death; something quite the opposite of *something* looked at you then from the other side.

He had the confidence that ideas such as these would eventually
thrive, unless the liveliest nerve of the mind was doomed. If such
doom was a real possibility, and the totalitarianism of the twentieth
century was not the shadow but the reality, and one lived beneath
it, well, society was not yet dead, and he still saw a great mission for
himself: it was to save the nerve of Being.

Since he had also to recognize that nine-tenths of what went on in
television looked to kill the nerve, his sense of mission grew larger.
It was the backstretch of the Eisenhower years. There was not
much hope on any horizon. Not a clue on how to stir. Since he did
not know that a revolution was beginning in America which would
live for a little while on an exchange of consciousness between
blacks and whites, and a beat generation would yet poke holes in the
American middle class, and a civil rights movement shift the nature
of the laws, he thought in the measureless vales of his vanity that he
was obliged to do the job himself, and he had mental experiences
out on marijuana that were so harsh, so arrogant, so lonely, so tor-

mented, and so demon-ridden — as if twenty devils could pull his chariot when ordered — that he was left with the confidence for years to come that he could write about the inner states of men like Hitler and Napoleon, Lenin and Castro and Cortes. It is a vanity to keep a young writer alive.

Of course, it also made him look on every action as immense with consequence — the early steps of a great leader! He did not forgive friends lightly for failing to see the transmogrificational significance of his thought, nor would he forget, he told himself, their lack of alacrity to follow him. He felt like a general without any army; his attention when he watched TV was not for his pleasure, therefore, but his martial art. He studied Ernie Kovacs like Moltke read Clausewitz, certain his hour was coming. The first TV show on which he would ever appear would be a call to the first battle, and he would fire a shot to ring around global village.

Channel 4

The first show happened to be *Night Beat*, Mike Wallace the host. Mailer got ready like a Depression fighter going into the main bout at the Garden on Friday night. Since his anticipation of such experiences had been formed by films of the Thirties, and his wife would in fact have their first baby in two weeks; since he also saw his opponent as tough, the pressure might be immense, but, as he saw it, he had to win. On just such trinities as poverty, babies, and tough opponents had John Garfield's movies been built.

Two decades later, Norman would not bother to think about a TV show until he was on it. He had learned over the years that the inner condition for projecting a firm and agreeable presence for TV was to be bored. Ideally, it was best to feel no more desire than a prostitute toward the tenth client of the night. This abyss between the luminosity of the outer appearance and the void of the inner dark was a phenomenon unique to TV participants, and might be the very health of the malignancy; it was certainly what kept television such a formidable foe. How could one battle a process that accommodated the emptiest space in oneself?

Of course, on the afternoon before his first television appearance, Mailer was hardly in possession of such wisdom. Rather, he was as tight as a man going to the electric chair. Trying to relax on his bed, adrenaline would take the best of him, and he would pace the room, and proceed to interrogate himself, asking the worst questions Mike Wallace might dare to ask, then search himself for the best of eight possible answers, a true fever! Young fighters dropped fights by squandering adrenaline before they reached the ring; they, too, were overcome with the monumental significance of whether they won or lost. Mailer, possessed of all the innocence of a protagonist who had never been on TV, did not understand he was entering no main event, but seeing the floor plans for a future mansion of Limbo; how was there a way to comprehend that he would not make history, but probably stifle it a little more?

It was a natural error to make. He could not, after all, get beyond the idea that he would be on the virgin air. If one said what one had to say with wit, conviction, and passion, if one said the unsayable, if people therefore heard something for the first time, passions ought to commence, buried sentiments could take life. But first he must be able to hold his own with Mike Wallace, and given Mailer's massive incapacity to stay cool, that was not automatic.

Wallace had become a success by way of a personality considerably at contrast to other TV hosts. His manner was not friendly but adversary. His straight black hair and craggy face gave off a presence as formidable as an Indian in a gray flannel suit. To this he added a humorless mind of which he was utterly unashamed, and used therefore as a weapon — no wit could slow his attack. His badly pitted skin suggested the unremitting stubbornness of a district attorney bitten hard enough in his youth to offer little mercy now. He was obviously not, like other interviewers, full of the very lard of companionability. Instead, Wallace gave the impression of wanting to interrogate further than the family manners of television permitted. Something of solemn, even heavy, purpose came off him, a distrust of human nature that was ready to focus on the probable insincerities of his guest. It was therefore a show to attract jokes about the masochism of people who would accept invitations from Mike Wallace, but Mailer, having studied the format for months, saw it as a rite of passage. If one wanted to make an impact on TV, *Night Beat* was the proper test.

By now, his own approach was as humorless as Wallace. He had so fired up the household, that his wife, in her ninth month, also took it as a test and put on a low-cut black velvet dress, thereby mustering her best appearance. Her hair was as black as Mike Wallace's and being a real Indian (Peruvian) she did her best to help her

husband make a decent entrance. Indeed, she looked splendid and
sent out the beauty of her pregnancy like a promulgation of status.
Her mate might have been happier to come into a real ring with a
trainer to massage the back of his neck, and he certainly had the rav-
enous flare in his throat that only true desire for whiskey can bring,
but he also knew the happiness of the fighter — at long last, love!
even if love is the pow of a glove and the rocketing of the ring lights.
He felt equal to expectation itself — maybe he had never been as
aware before of all of America out there — a pregnancy in the night
itself equal to his awareness of a million homes tuning into *Night
Beat.* In later years, when everything was taped, he would not often
feel the sensation that everyone was listening as the sounds came out
of his throat.

Now, the program began, that is, they took seats that had been set
out facing each other, chatted a little — it was a false and most unnatural kind of chatting, like fighters meeting at a weigh-in — and
then with thirty seconds to air-time, to Wallace's small but somewhat superior annoyance, Mailer poured his water back into the
carafe, took a small flask of gin out of his pocket, and decanted half
of it into the empty glass.

He was sipping the gin as they went on the air. Since his mind
had been overworked for hours, the liquor did not relax his tongue
so much as disconcert his head and burn his stomach.

"*Life* magazine accuses your novel, *The Deer Park,*" said Wallace
in his opening and hortatory tones, "of dealing with immorality, al-
coholism, perversion, and political terror in Hollywood. Why do
you emphasize these themes?"

Mailer laid out the rights of a novelist to choose his subject, but
his answer went on too long, and Wallace merely looked quizzical,
self-centered, and superior in his lack of comprehension even as
Norman said, "Only hypocrisy and insincerity are dirty. *Life* magazine is a dirty magazine."

So he felt uncomfortable through the early questions, going too
long for one answer, too flippantly for another, only to be brusque
on the third reply. He was like a tight-muscled fighter and could not
seem to fake Wallace the least bit out. His voice began to grow dog-
ged. On the other hand, Wallace did not seem comfortable either.
Before one could expect it, the first commercial had come. One-
third of the show was over, and it wasn't going as he had hoped.

He raised the ante. Mailer had an instinct for the wicked. If evil
was to discover what was good, and proceed to destroy it, then how

many people could ever learn enough to be evil? Wickedness was more available. Wickedness would consist of raising the ante without knowing what the consequences might be. It was a way of asking for peril without a clue to who would be hurt. Wickedness was what he leaped into tonight. It was as if the only means for dealing with Mike Wallace's imperturbable certainty that the people who ran things knew more than the people who didn't was to keep raising the ante of his replies. Before long, he was saying, "America is a great and prosperous country, but it is not a brave or noble country. Our leaders are drowning in conformity and act like *women*."

(May it return a full sense of the Eisenhower period to recognize that our author was not near to suspecting a powerful movement would arise one day to banish men from public life for failing to refer to women as persons.)

Wallace, being equally ignorant of the future, looked awfully confident. "Who in high office," he asked in his deepest voice, "would you say is so feminine?"

Mailer came back with the first happiness he was ever to know on television. "President Eisenhower is a bit of a woman," he said into the ring of night around them, and was certain he could feel the instant when the heart of a million TV sets missed a beat.

Wallace never looked more like an Indian. His eyes grew as flat as the eyes of a movie Apache who has just taken a rifle bullet to the stomach.

"Come off it," he said. He, too, was listening to the silence in the living rooms.

"I mean just that," said Mailer.

They went on. The atmosphere was not dissimilar to the tension in a bar when a glass has been shattered and no apologies are made. They went through the half-hour to conclusion, and Mailer did a little better, and Wallace might have done a little less well, and the show came to its end. Mailer felt a great glow. He was immensely pleased with himself. In the elevator, going down to the street, his wife said, "Maybe we'll be dead tomorrow, but it was worth it." It is possible they never had a better moment together. They had been with each other for years, yet always fought in the animal rage of never comprehending one another. On this night, however, with the baby two weeks away, they were ready for one hour, at least, to die together. For once Mailer felt like a hero. In those days saying something bad about Dwight D. Eisenhower was a not great deal less atrocious than deciding Jesus Christ has something wrong with Him.

Our new TV talent waited therefore on large and scandalized results from this Wallace show. Nothing seemed to happen. Occasionally he would run into an old friend who had happened to see it, and would chuckle over his remark. Weeks later, he learned that James Hagerty, the Press Secretary to President Eisenhower, asked for a transcript. That was all he ever heard. The phone did not ring with invitations from network executives to discuss a new show built around his controversial personality. Indeed, he was not invited on other shows for a while. It was more than another year before he was asked by David Susskind to come on *Open End* with Dorothy Parker and Truman Capote.

Channel 5

In Limbo, it was becoming less difficult to understand why he always felt an instinctive distrust of the memoir. Part of one's share of anathema was to recollect the past in a style now analogous to the sentimental and streamlined details of the memoir. The final insult to one's life came by way of recognizing that one was here reduced to viewing the moral lessons of one's past through a film of slick. All the real, important, and (now that one was in Limbo) desperate meanings of one's acts slipped by, vague and smooth, almost without evaluation. The agreeable readability of the memoir (that property which made it perfect for the kind of magazines laid on airline passengers) was exactly what made it a torture now. Living among the glossy walls of Limbo, moral facts were hard enough to hold without the frictionless surface of a memoir.

Ergo, the author found himself shuddering — even if he did not know why — at the recollection, let us say at the reconstitution, of his experience on *Open End*, shivering indeed in that feverless ague where boredom is at last revealed as the ultimate protection against dread; yes, what better explanation for that family in the Utah desert staring at the video glass than precisely their awful if unstated decision, so gloomily made, that boredom was better than dread, that even an unpalatable mixture of boredom and dread was better than dread. Anything was better than that immense on-sliding

American dread. For here, on this northern half of the continent, where the uprooted had looked for every frontier that could be broken (since people without roots discover peace in the sound made by tearing up the roots of others — how else account for the glee of airplane designers at the sound of jet engines sucking up the promise of the nearby air, or the joy of a young criminal breaking into a home?) yes, here, dread was the ongoing uneasiness of those whose roots were cut (which automatically made America the country most possessed of dread, since how many in this country could find the house where they were born?) Yes, if dread was the communal American experience (how better account for the prodigious American fear of communism in those years after the Second World War when the USSR was at its weakest?) yes, if security against dread was the subtext behind every political movement in America, everything from right-wing fear of a conspiracy in high financial places to destroy Christianity forever, all the way over to the liberal terror that a violence was coming which would not be controlled by even the most sophisticated and enlightened social planning, then, given a dread so immense, it was easy to see why a man should be chosen for President so late as 1976 by way of a number of television debates that presented to the nation the first proposition of American politics: "When it comes to picking a President, Boredom is better than Dread!" So said the debates, and the power that was finally elected, the political movement whose real fortunes were advanced, was television itself, yes, television, with its silent radiating argument that it was the best political program yet found for the tranquilization of dread — "I will deaden you a little bit; you need it!"

Contrast these grim conclusions, arrived at in the bowels, that is to say in the glassy coils of Limbo, and compare them to the innocence of Norman's early assumption that television was a platform from which to incite an ideological riot, a God-given opportunity (offered by the complacency of the Establishment) to get the truth out; perhaps, we can learn, after all, why he shuddered at the recollection of his appearance with Dorothy Parker and Truman Capote. He was now suffering from the derision of Limbo; few souls offend it more than the actor who believes he is becoming a protagonist when he is only turning into a comedian, and this unpleasant thought now as unable to move out of his head as a jellyfish fixed on the sand, he was able for a space to feel the grit of reality, and thereby found himself thinking again, and with considerable pain, of the expression on Dorothy Parker's face when he first saw her standing on the studio floor in Newark waiting for the arrival of Capote and himself. She had earlier been picked up in Manhattan, as they had been later, by a dark Cadillac limousine, furnished by the studio, to carry them to New Jersey for a few hours, and the expression in her eyes suggested that that was outrage enough in itself — to be found in Newark!

Dorothy Parker was not to shine on this night. It was to be her first appearance on TV (and probably her last) and never may a video camera have been less disposed toward a talented writer. She was not, in person, a large woman, nor by the measure of her literary wit, a bold woman. Anyone who had read Dorothy Parker, and was expecting therefore a lady of immaculate wit and elegant savagery of tongue, would feel on the consequence when meeting her, a discernible shock. She was tiny, and she tended to be plump. She had bags under her eyes (from the fatigues of three good decades of drinking) and these bags touched the heart in a way few middle-aged women and only a very few middle-aged men with wondrously lugubrious bags can so touch us. (Perhaps it is by way of the sorrows they have bottomed out on while drinking.) Dorothy Parker looked like a bird at the mercy of every beast with teeth, a flurry of feathers up in a tree with wonderful bags under her eyes. And in the middle of her sad little face, sad as the ghost of tenderness itself, was her nose, the tip of which was always overpowdered. She would dust it once with a swipe to one nostril, and again with a swipe to the other, the overlay thereby suggesting the white painted button of a clown who is more lugubrious than his bulbous red-tipped colleagues.

She also wore a series of black shawls and garments to give her the appearance of a British witch. The garments looked to have come from an attic. Since Norman met her first in Los Angeles, seven or eight years before the evening they went on in Newark, he could not imagine at the time where she found her clothes. Los Angeles was a city whose homes were conspicuously without attics.

She also had a manner that was gentle, full of praise, and treacherous as a scorpion. The day he was introduced, an agent who would later be powerful enough to deal with the memoirs of presidents and kings was in Dorothy Parker's room at the Chateau Marmont, and she gave the agent nothing but compliments, sweet compliments in a tender threadbare little voice that spoke of his energy, (boundless!) his good-will (Christly) and his genius (large enough to sell one of her poor scripts; he, he alone, could do it!) and the agent having left in all the happiness of being given these compliments by a great American writer — he was still a young agent, pushy, and prematurely bald — she said, so soon as the door was closed, "Agggrhh" — a clearing of the throat in pure facsimile to that first blast of the interior when vomiting — and added, "What an awful man. What a dreadful dreadful man!"

After that meeting, Mailer always did his best to be the last to leave Dottie Parker's sitting room at the Chateau Marmont. Once, confessing to Lillian Hellman his concern at how Dorothy Parker might describe him in his absence, Miss Hellman laughed with the happiness she always felt in being generous, instructive, and superior to the innocence of her friends, and said, "Norman, everyone knows that Dottie will talk about you after you leave the room. It will amount to no more than the compliments she's just given you. Everybody who cares about Dottie knows that's the price to pay." And she laughed gaily.

Still, Norman wanted Dottie Parker's real affection. He wanted the lovely things she said to him on one side of the door to be repeated on the other. Since they got along very well, and he was always proud to invite her to his rented house, and pleased to be invited back to her poor suite at the Marmont (she had no money in those years — all the splendid short stories and no money!) he even entertained the illusion that she might offer a dispensation.

He would never find out, however, because of her dog. She had a Boxer, not a year old, named Bruce, who had been badly mistreated by his first owners, and now whimpered at harsh looks. Dottie did her best to give the dog more courage — she raised him like the child she had never had, ready to take Bruce up each rung of the mile-high ladder that climbs from abysmal cowardice to transcendental courage; she would tell her friends of each new advance Bruce and she had made. One would learn that Bruce had gotten up his nerve sufficiently one day to take a walk around the block with her.

These methods seemed intolerably slow to Norman. He kept telling her that she ought to bring Bruce over to meet his dog. Since Dorothy Parker had by now made friends with Karl, she was tempted. Timid people were invariably proud of such a friendship for Karl was a black German Shepherd, huge and ferocious to strangers. Since his first allegiance was to the house, his master became whoever lived in the house (and incidentally fed him). Norman, renting the place, was therefore the master and thus became the only man in Laurel Canyon who could drive up to the house, get out of his car, and not be attacked. No one else dared. Our best-selling young author used to run out to the driveway when guests came; otherwise visitors were obliged to cower inside their vehicle while the dog would lunge at the windows. Once Norman got out, however, and barked, "Karl!" the Shepherd immediately subsided. He could now recognize that these intruders would be acceptable to the house. After they were admitted to the living room, Karl would even go over, sit down on the floor, and make a point of shaking hands with them. Delighted that the dog had become well-disposed, the new arrival would make much of this. Karl would extend his paw for a second greeting. His tongue would loll and he would pant a little. After the third handshake, Karl would get a hard-on. "*Karl!*" his master would say, and the hard-on would go away. Under such circumstances, it became easy to think of him as an overrated danger.

So when Dorothy Parker finally decided that she might bring Bruce to the house, Mailer thought it was a terrific idea. He would take care of bringing them together peacefully, he promised. Good to his word, he put Karl away in the bedroom before Dorothy Parker arrived with Bruce. The Boxer, however, did not want to quit the car. He could hear the other beast.

"It'll be all right," said Mailer cheerfully, "once Bruce is inside. Karl is really lonesome."

Coaxed within the house, however, Bruce urinated on the carpet. It was not difficult to forgive him. In the bedroom, Karl was making that sound a cat will make when a dog is near, and she is ready to fight for her life. It is a more awesome sound when it comes from a large hound.

"Don't you think this is a mistake?" said Dottie Parker. "I can put Bruce in the car and go home now."

That would be a loss for Bruce, he answered. "Why don't I put Karl on a leash, and bring them together slowly? It'll be so good for Bruce if he and Karl can make friends."

This liberal and romantic expectation prevailed. Karl was brought out of the bedroom. The dog came quietly on his tether, and looked at Bruce without a sound. He sniffed the other's nose. A pause. Bruce peed. Karl's head went off in a roar as loud as a howitzer. His mouth opened into shark's teeth and flayed the air with strings of saliva; at this point his master was sufficiently outraged to yank him back by the neck, and manhandle him to the bedroom. In the space this took, Dottie Parker was out the door, and in her car. Before she could drive away, Norman came running out to find Bruce collapsed in the rear seat. The dog's limbs were vibrating. It was that quiver which will not cease until the nerve dies.

"I said it wouldn't work," said Dottie Parker face to face. She imparted this in a tone of whole reproach as if to tell him that the worst damage a friend can wreak is to convince you to be brave when you know you are right to be cautious, and then proceed to prove that indeed you were right. It throws you back even further upon yourself when that is no place to be.

As she drove off, he knew that he had wanted to bring Karl from the bedroom because he wished to show how well he could control the dog. Besides he had been curious on the outcome. He noticed that he did not feel very sorry. Only chagrined. But then the wicked are famous for offering small remorse.

Channel 6

He was not to see Dottie Parker again until this evening they would meet on *Open End* eight years later, and when he arrived at the studio in Newark, and saw her waiting, older, more fragile, close to desperately nervous and certainly not cordial, his feelings were only in a small way hurt that she was not happy to see him again, and showed an obvious preference for Truman Capote. He was, by his own measure, not the same writer she had known before. He had met her, after all, in the season after *The Naked and the Dead* when he went out to Hollywood, and much had been made of him. Now, after this early success, he had gone through a number of years in which people spoke of him as a failure. Since he had written two novels, *Barbary Shore* and *The Deer Park*, which he thought had received unfair reviews, he had a view of himself that was at odds with others, and he did not like to be snubbed by people who had been friendly to him ten years ago. All the same, it gave justification to his anger. So her unfriendliness left him in a well-balanced position. If it came to it, he would not have to be too friendly on the show.

David Susskind also gave small welcome. "We met a long time ago," Susskind said.

"I remember."

"I do, too," said Susskind in a chilly voice. It had been at a party on a very hot summer night in 1948, and they had talked on a Manhattan roof. Susskind was then a young agent, and he had wanted to sell *The Naked and the Dead* to the movies. Mailer had made fun of him. "Don't you understand?" he had said to Susskind, "*they* can't make it into a film, and I don't want it made."

Of course, years later, he sold it after all, and *they* had made a very bad film. So he felt at a disadvantage now with Susskind and said, "Maybe I should have listened to you."

Susskind's face showed what he thought of people who were rude years ago and ready to flatter now. Their relations for this night were certainly not off to a good start.

He had only Capote. They had gotten along well on the drive out to Newark, each — they had not met before — intensely curious of the other. Since Mailer's wife accompanied him again, and again was looking her best, he had made a point of having her sit between Truman and himself. Since she was twice Truman's size and had the overpowering sexuality, on occasion — this was such an occasion — of her burgeoning Latin blood, it had been an advantage equal to playing on one's home court.

Truman did much complaining on the trip out. "I didn't want to do this show," he said in a dry little voice that seemed to issue from an unmoistened reed in his nostril, "I told Bennett Cerf it was a mistake, but Bennett thinks television is going to be very important for selling our books. I hope he's wrong," said Truman Capote and laughed.

Once the show began, Norman thought himself splendid. Unlike the night with Mike Wallace, he felt at his best, thoughts came clearly, he was full of energy and the others seemed bewildered. Susskind labored in the early minutes to put Dorothy Parker at ease but he was not able to succeed; she simply would not trust him. She spoke in a pained and quavering voice, hardly able to make herself heard. Truman did not add much, and Mailer, pleased with his powers, began to take over. Soon he and Susskind were doing most of the talking, that is, most of the debating, for it was obvious Susskind was irritated by what he had to say. Whenever Norman would launch on a flight of what he considered well-stated criticism of society, Susskind would make a point of looking at his watch. Whenever he could, Susskind tried to give time to the others, but it did not work. The others seemed apathetic. Once, while executing a panegyric about politicians, Norman Mailer flew so high as to say, "They're all whores."

Dottie Parker interrupted then to say with a little real force, "That's a sweeping remark."

"Well," said Mailer, "it may be sweeping, but it certainly is true."

It put Dorothy Parker back into silence — who was she, after all, to defend politicians? — and it irritated Susskind more. After close to an hour of TV time that felt wholly enjoyable to Mailer, he began to grow irritated at Susskind's efforts to slow him up. Since his host seemed determined to shut off this most interesting part of the show, Norman could see no reason not to allow the host to hang himself, and so he ceased speaking. Susskind began immediately to draw upon Truman Capote, and Capote, having digested a few of the peculiar processes of this odd medium, and measured the possible fit for himself, began at last to speak, and was, Mailer thought, not unamusing. He laughed encouragingly at Truman's remarks; he offered attention. Truman was so tiny that something gallant came to you from the fact of his existence itself. Mailer felt generous indeed. Few moods are as charitable as this sensation of being physically superior to everyone in the room.

In such a state, feeling handsome, vital, and more interesting than anyone had a right to be, he got into a discussion with Truman about the merits of Jack Kerouac. Since Mailer was not without his jealousy of the large attention paid Kerouac that year, he gave a defense of *On the Road* that was built on the basis of calling Kerouac, Jack — that is, he was two-thirds for Jack's virtues and one-third against Jack's vices.

Capote detested Kerouac. As Mailer grew benign, Capote grew precise. He rose at last to his own peroration and invoked the difficulties of the literary craft in contrast to Mr. Kerouac's undisciplined methods of work. Finally, in a tone of fearless and absolute severity, Capote said: "It is not writing. It is only typing."

"I agree," said Dorothy Parker in a hoarse voice.

"Well, I don't," said Mailer, only to give a limp defense. He was empty of vast indignation at this dreadful put-down of Kerouac. He even decided it might look good to let Truman have his winning little moment, certainly better than trying to hog the show.

Open End came to a finish. As they walked off the set, a few technicians were studying the kinescope of what they had just done. Therefore, Parker, Capote, Susskind, Mailer and Mrs. Mailer stopped to watch a minute of it.

Dorothy Parker did not look good on TV. She took one peek at herself, gasped, and said to Susskind, "No, I really don't want to see another instant of it." Solicitous as St. Peter, Susskind led her away.

In contrast, Norman Mailer had the pleasure of seeing himself as he wanted to look. The kinescope caught him as he was making a point, and his face looked forceful, his language was good, yes, he appeared even better on TV, he thought, than in the mirror. "Didn't I tell you," said Truman, "that you're terrific on this? You're *telegenic!*" It was true. But then, in every intermission, Truman had been telling him how splendidly he was doing.

Truman groaned when the camera shifted to him. There was a medium shot of Truman looking a hint bewildered at the beginning of the show, and he winced as he heard his voice. "I told my publishers I shouldn't go on," he declared with annoyance.

In the limousine on the way back to Manhattan, Truman kept saying, "I shouldn't have done it. I didn't want to, I've never appeared on television, not once — even though I've had many invitations — and I certainly oughtn't to have been here tonight. What I can do is special, it's *very* literary, and I shouldn't attempt to *intrude* my personality. I'm not good at that like you, Norman. Television is good for you."

Mailer lay back in the limousine, enjoying a winner's ride, and his wife said encouragingly to Capote, "You were good, too, Truman. You really got better as it went on."

"Do you think so?" asked Truman. "Do you really think so?"

Now, both Mr. and Mrs. Mailer assured Truman Capote that he was better than he thought he had been.

"Well, at least," said Truman, "I was better than poor Dorothy Parker. When she looked at herself afterward . . ." He shuddered in sympathy. "Wasn't that *Disasterville?*" They laughed, but not in pleasure at her woe so much as in wonder at the clear lines of Judgment itself.

Truman could not quite get out of his bad mood, however. Before they said goodnight he suggested they have a drink with him at El Morocco. Before long, they thought to have supper. Despite all the sandwiches served on *Open End,* they were starved. Truman insisted on treating. A prince, he seemed to hint, must play the host after a sorry loss — it is the only way to come close to one's blood again.

It was late on Sunday night and they had the place to themselves. Under the solicitousness of the waiters and the captain, and finally the manager himself, who all came over to assure Capote of their unremitting attention, under the spell of this wholly superior service Truman was obviously accustomed to receiving whenever he went into El Morocco, his spirits not only revived but turned charming, and he began to offer an attention to Adele Mailer that had her believing in the unique properties of her attractiveness and her wit; yes, Truman was charming. Mailer saw why he had become the in-house author of the most important hostesses in New York, and envied him honestly, the way one good athlete will have respect for another. Just as a pitcher will think, "If I had as much stuff to my curve, I'd win more games because of my superior ball sense," so did Mailer think wistfully that if he could get to a few of the select parties Truman got to, why, boy, he'd have more to say about society. Of course, how could you be a radical yet intimate to the top drawer of the world — that was the iron warp of irony itself.

They had a fine time. They discovered unexpected points of agreement, and lively places to disagree; they had each had such curiosity about the other after all these years — their first novels had come out within a year of one another; both had been celebrated almost instantly. It was a grand evening, and at the end, Truman announced they would be great friends forever, and thanked them for taking him through what would otherwise have been a terribly depressing night — "God, was I awful on that show," he said as they parted, and he made a face to simulate the gargoyle of godawfulness.

There were not many nights when Norman Mailer went to bed so pleased with his wife, himself, and what they were able to do for each other as on this evening. He woke up early in the morning, enjoyed his breakfast, and could hardly wait for the phone to ring, and the praises of his friends to begin. But when he had heard from his parents (who loved the show) from an aunt and uncle (loved the show) from his sister who liked what he had done ("generally") and was somewhat taken with Truman, "what an interesting personality he has really," she said; and when he had gotten tired of waiting for friends to ring, and called up one instead, there was a pause at the other end, and then the friend said in sorrow, "Oh, man, did Truman take you!"

He called other friends. They seemed not to have seen the show and left a pall equal to the message of the medium itself. He went out on the street for a walk; since he was living in Greenwich Village, it was not hard to run into a few acquaintances. One stopped, saluted, and said: "It is not writing; it is *only* typing," and gave a long phlegmy laugh as he went on down the street. Another said, "Truman; too much!" A third said, "Could you get me to meet Capote?"

More serious friends were balanced. "In terms of polemical points, I think you made the most. Of course, Capote does suggest real authority."

He called Truman a couple of days later.

"Yes," said Capote, "isn't it the *strangest* thing? Everybody has been telling me how marvelous I was. I can't believe it. 'Norman Mailer is the one who was marvelous,' I say to them, and they reply, 'Truman, you were *wunderbar.* Don't sell yourself short.' 'Honey,' I told this friend, 'I been short all my life,' " Truman guffawed with pleasure even more profound than the night at El Morocco. "It certainly is a mystery," he said with complacency.

Mailer couldn't bear it. He finally called *Open End* and asked to see a kinescope. It became his first introduction to our hypothesis that television is not a technological process that reproduces images of real life by way of electronics, but is rather a machine (more or less cosmically operated) to anticipate the judgments and/or anathema of Limbo; the technicians pitch in with camera angles.

He discovered that the nice close-up he had seen of himself immediately after the show was one of the few close-ups they had chosen to give him. The more he talked, and the more Susskind looked at his watch, why the more they relegated him to medium shots and long shots. There is something pathetic about a man speaking at the bottom of a long shot: he does not sound convinced by himself. He is, after all, at the end of the tunnel.

In contrast, they gave many close-ups to Truman. Capote did not look small on the show but large! His face, in fact, was extraordinary, that young-old face, still pretty and with such promise of oncoming ugliness; that voice, so full of snide rustlings and unforgiving nasalities; it was a voice to knock New York on its ear. The voice had survived; it spoke of horrors seen and passed over; it told of judgments that would be merciless.

Watching the kinescope, Mailer realized at last what an impact Capote had made on the television viewers of New York. They had never seen anyone remotely like him. Once Truman finally opened his mouth, the camera never left his face. The camera would turn to Capote even as Norman was speaking.

His own arguments that sounded so forceful to him a few nights ago now seemed vague, and with his beard, pious. (He shaved off the beard a week or two later.) Talking about large matters on television with all the passion and all the lack of specific detail these immense theses encouraged, speaking in a voice that came out of the depths of a medium shot proved to be not nearly so exhilarating to a viewer as it had felt for him in the middle of articulating his thoughts. His obvious pride in his ideas now seemed fatuous. His physical superiority was gone. He was only intense, vague, and a bit out of focus. Whereas Capote took his unforgettable personality and added to it, practicality, common sense, and pride. In so misty a medium, the best gift a guest could provide was pearls. The certainty of a pearl! Yes, to light upon a problem and come up with a good one-line answer was to produce a pearl of the mind. How much interest could viewers have in a point that took five minutes to make? That was something they could not do. It spoke of too good a college education. So they preferred people with a one-line answer, barroom knockouts, one-punch pearls. There is no man or woman on the street whose mind will not produce a pearl from time to time. They loved Truman because he had given them "It is not writing. It is only typing."

From now on, thought Mailer, he would not try to show how intelligent he was; he would look for pearls. That became his latest hypothesis: the light from a TV screen was flattering to a pearl.

Of course, he was always miserable without an hypothesis. The hypothesis could later prove invalid, but it had to be interesting enough so that he could live with it for a while. That the orgy would benefit humankind more than the family was one of his early hypotheses, Bolshevist as hell. That the war in Vietnam was a bad war because rich boys should not fight poor boys unless there was equality in the weapons was another, and that offered the best of conservative principles: the rich had better be terrific. Whether the particular hypothesis was good or bad, however, he leaned on it. There was something so rigid in his upbringing that for reference he had great need of a straight line — a straight line is, after all, the very first of the hypotheses (and, according to Einstein, wholly incorrect, since no line can run straight in space given the curly route of a light wave and the oval field of magnetic force). Mailer sometimes wondered if he was one of the first to recognize that 186,000 miles a second was not the true speed of light, but only its calculated progress along a nonexistent straight line. If you measured the speed of light by the time it took to wind through the waves, then a beam might travel up to 1,000,000 miles a second in order to traverse 186,000 miles. That, doubtless, was one more reason why the sum of a million was magical to Americans.

Such were a few of Mailer's conclusions after his defeat by Capote.

The next time they met, Truman had a new assurance to put on top of the old one. In these few weeks, he confessed, there had been numerous invitations, all turned down, to appear on other shows; a difference in Truman's idea of himself had begun to appear. That personality he had presented, with all his early bravado, to a most special part of the world, was, it seemed, going to be accepted by all the world. He obviously felt stronger already. And Mailer, stunned as any confident contender who has been abruptly knocked out, now felt, measure to measure, weaker. It was obvious to him (for no one understands the future reactions of a snob so well as an unsuccessful snob) that never again would Truman spend a night trying to recoup the losses of his ego out of *this* Mr. and Mrs. Mailer.

Channel 7

Years later, Norman would decide that television was one of those hostesses who were most impressed if you were somewhat unimpressed to find yourself in her home, and that was easy enough to handle. It was just that on television, your real hostess had to be the spirit of the electrons. While nobody was in command of enough physics to explore the idea that some men and women tend to attract electrons, while others most certainly repulse them, it seemed reasonable to suppose that electrons might conduct relations with more than a few forces, satanic and divine, and so could be working in unseen harness to focus or ruin your TV appearance. Translated, that should be able to state: The telegenic have good bioelectric relations with the tube, and these relations may yet be measured. Of course, Norman, biased to the depths of his unexpected defeats, was convinced that zombies were the first to benefit from such relations.

These were conclusions he came to with reluctance. He was plagued in those years by the divide between his absolute, if somewhat improbable, sense of intellectual mission, and his incapacity to work at anything like the necessary pace to accomplish his wonders. He thought, without admitting it to himself, that television might be a way to express ideas that would otherwise never reach an audience, not if they had to wait for the writing. (Obviously, he wished to lift himself to heaven by the power of his speech — a little misapprehension of cosmic reality that he only came to recognize when his later writing, so well praised, raised him no higher than Limbo.)

Of course, he had an idea not easy to express under any quick circumstances, and hardly by way of the pearl: he saw a conspiracy in society to destroy existence. Being blessed with no ear for the finer sounds of nature, he did not hear the drip of pollution in the conduits; he only felt the stifling of his own existence. That, of course, is enough. It may be even a sign of health to sense danger to nature in every little death to oneself.

So he wanted to be on TV; so he told himself; he would be on it to shout the alarm. So he saw every appearance where he did well as a decent effort committed to his side of the gods; yes, he would do his best to get the great dialectic of society unfrozen once more — that was the dialectic where the people knew enough to affect even the most skillful manipulations of the establishment — he would, yes, try to get such a dialectic going. A mature democratic society was worth zero without it. He did not understand that *something* was calculating how to cancel more than one dialectic.

Still, these were the early years of TV. He had a few moments when he felt as if he broke through. It was not entirely a string of disasters. He had, after all, the illimitable freedom (in early 1960) of saying late one evening on Irv Kupcinet's show in Chicago that he thought J. Edgar Hoover had done more harm to America than Joseph Stalin, and so had the pleasure of being the center of attention one early morning in Chicago; Kup's show by 1960 was big news to the local audience, for it had an ability to gather all the visiting firemen passing through. An amazing number of people would therefore come home on Saturday night and go into four A.M. of Sunday morning watching *At Random*. This was March in 1960, after all, nine months before Jack Kennedy was inaugurated, and how many in Chicago had something better to do at that hour if they could not sleep?

"Yes," Norman repeated, "J. Edgar Hoover has paralyzed the imagination of this country in a way Joseph Stalin never could," and the other guests put their hands in the air to state that they were not opposed to J. Edgar Hoover. The former president of the B'nai B'rith was a guest, and the Lord Mayor of Dublin was another; a chief from the national police of Sudan made a third; a woman reporter who had traveled with Eisenhower in South America composed a fourth; they all were in a hurry to swear their allegiance to Hoover.

Later, after the show, he heard that a large number of calls had come in, forty-eight in fact. He had always assumed that thousands of calls came to such shows every night. He did not yet know that television did not send you to the telephone, let alone the barricades. Still, forty-eight calls had come at two in the morning. Twenty-eight had opposed what he said; twenty approved. Since no call was counted unless you left your name, it meant that twenty people (with whatever number of false names among them) had been ready to agree. That count was as agreeably astonishing to Norman Mailer on that night as Gene McCarthy's forty percent against Lyndon Johnson's forty-eight percent in New Hampshire would seem apocalyptic to the media in '68. Mailer felt an intimation for the first time that the Sixties might bring a few changes to the old game.

Eighteen years later, obtaining his FBI file by way of the Freedom of Information Act, he would discover that out of three hundred xeroxed and highly deleted pages sent to him, more than thirty were devoted to his single appearance on Kupcinet's show. Let us depart from Limbo long enough to see how language sounds in the real world.

TO: DIRECTOR, FBI
FROM: SAC, CHICAGO
SUBJECT: NORMAN MAILER, PANELIST
          IRVING KUPCINET
          "AT RANDOM" TV PROGRAM
          MARCH 20, 1960
          INFORMATION CONCERNING

NORMAN MAILER is an admitted "leftist." He is also an author, his most popular work being the novel "The Naked And The Dead." His remarks clearly reflect his animosity toward the Bureau.

The enclosed text clearly reflects that other noted panelists on the program definitely and specifically disagreed with and refuted his observations.

A number of persons in Chicago have personally commented to me that MAILER made an ass of himself on the program, and all such comments received have been definitely pro Bureau and anti MAILER.

RE: NORMAN MAILER

During the program, the participants engaged in a discussion relating to the Federal Bureau of Investigation. These remarks are being included below in summary form and at pertinent places verbatim.

MAILER talked of the United States as the most powerful nation in the world after World War II with the exception of Russia, and both these countries, who had no tradition of ruling, fought about who would rule. The United States began to ape the methods of Russia with the tactics of the Communists being taken by Madison Avenue, the term used to indicate the advertising agencies who run the mass media. MAILER went on to say:

> I said the other day in an interview that we have a very subtle totalitarianism here, a pleasant totalitarianism, in that we don't have concentration camps. We don't have a secret police everywhere. We do have an FBI which is one of the two religions left in America. There's the FBI and medical science.

ELAINE SHEPHERD: And hooray for the Federal Bureau of Investigation.

MAILER: Well, I would say three cheers against them. I am for putting them down. I say let's have no more of the FBI; they are running the country.

SHEPHERD: You can't be serious.

MAILER said he had only one more comment to make with regard to Miss SHEPHERD's saying the Communist aim is to make America soft.

MAILER: This country was softened up but not by the Communists. It was softened up by the FBI, by Joe McCARTHY, by the House Un-American Affairs (*sic*) Committee, by the peculiar, subtle psychological reign of terror that went on in this country five years ago. . . .

KLUTZNICK: People have abused J. EDGAR HOOVER, and there are times when I have been angry at him myself for some things he said, but let's put it this way. He has given us a kind of police administration that people like Inspector Hamid and others all over the world respect because of its efficiency, and more than its efficiency, its peculiar devotion to staying within that law which it is permitted to stay within and nothing more.

SHEPHERD: At really comparatively low salaries. These are dedicated men.

KLUTZNICK: This is very important to remember.

MAILER: This is marvelous, but I would like to say something. You speak of efficiency. You speak of the low salary the people have who work for it. . . . I will also say that the concentration camps at Buchenwald were run in exactly the same way; they were terribly efficient.

KLUTZNICK: This is not true.

MAILER: They were efficient. The people who worked there received low wages relatively, and they probably kept within the directives that were issued to them.

SHEPHERD: Now, that is beneath the dignity of sophistry.

There was a momentary digression with some remarks on the meaning of sophistry.

KLUTZNICK: No, but look. I read the records of Buchenwald —

MAILER: Now, I didn't say — I didn't say —

BRISCOE: You said they were efficient and with low salary.

MAILER: I didn't say that the FBI is a Buchenwald. I only said that the virtues you ascribe to the FBI can be ascribed to the concentration camps.

The discussion turned to the proposition of the police as a necessary evil.

MAILER: . . . the man in the street does not have a specific knowledge of the right things and the wrong things that the FBI does. He has a general knowledge of them and a general fear of them and a general respect for them which, I say, is too great. Because what I am getting at is this. There has been so much damn fear in this country for the last five or ten years . . . that people in this country are being worn down and they are being softened, and they are turning apathetic, and there's getting to be very little passion left in American life, and this was about the most passionate country in the history of the earth at one time, and the most adventurous and the bravest and the boldest, and it has become a cowardly, sleek, soft, fat country.

KLUTZNICK: I would agree with some of that.

MAILER: What I am saying is that this is exactly the climate which the Russians adore, and if they ever come over here, the first thing they would do is that they would have their secret police chief get together with the FBI, and you would be amazed at how little time it would take — We are exactly creating a totalitarian climate in this country which will make it possible for the Russians to come over and take us with no pain at all.

SHEPHERD: You are questioning the patriotic integrity of our federal agents?

MAILER: That they are patriotic I would not deny for a moment. I
am sure they are all passionately in love with America, and
maybe a little bit too much in love with America. The thing is
that I distrust it.

KUPCINET: I can agree with NORM that we should stand back
and take a look from a distance; don't be swelled up by anything you read about anything. Ask questions about everything, and this would be a better democracy.

In another part of his file, Mailer found a letter from SAC, New
York, to the Director of the FBI. It was dated March 25, 1960.

Information has been received that Mailer, in an appearance on
the Chicago television program, "At Random," on 3/20/60, ad-
vocated the abolition of the FBI. He said the FBI was too efficient
against communism and was connected with McCarthyism and
the House Committee on Un-American Activities. He also said
that the FBI's efficiency "created a psychological atmosphere on
the part of the public and that the public is being protected from
communism" and that the public, and not the FBI, should be allowed to decide for itself what is good for it.

You are requested to bring the investigation of Mailer up to
date.

Channel 8

He could hardly have known the FBI was taking such interest in
his few remarks — he did not really believe in his own paranoia —
yet somewhere in those market places of sleep where the knowledge
of one dreamer passes over to another, in those psychic flights that
lift from the mind and are on the air, maybe we reach another
human despite all the crackling and confusion and outright din of all
those amplified waves electronically induced by torture of the air itself, maybe our own thoughts, often so noble as to originate out of
the magnetism of human mood itself, also pass back and forth like
radio waves and come into our sleep despite the interference of
every electronically communicating machine, yes, come to us
through all the jammed air and defoliated fields of lost prayer. (Is
that any more difficult to believe than that one corporate machine

can pass a message to another when they do not touch?) So some obscure but real message may have come to him that the FBI had bit on his words and he had pricked their blood; afterward he was fortified in the notion that TV could be a forum for ideas, at least for ideas that came in the shape of pearls — J. Edgar Hoover has done more harm to the minds of America than Joseph Stalin — and you could change people's lives and give a shift to society; you need only be good enough to do it.

So, he kept the idea that he would yet learn to handle himself on the most obdurate and repellent medium in which he ever worked. He certainly kept appearing on TV shows. As the years went by and a little more literary work began to get done, there seemed always a new book for which it was natural to go on TV. Of course, TV did not help his books to sell — not with his personality! — but still he went on. He learned that an appearance on TV left you feeling as agreeable as a session with a doctor and an X-ray machine; he learned that the taste of aspirin (was it ashes?) would follow in the mouth; he learned that you formed no friendships with other guests on a show for everyone split the moment a program was done as if they had all been participants in a bloodless sexless and faintly disgusting orgy — some high whinny of sanitized shit was in the sniff of the air. He learned that the pioneer days of TV were indeed over, for only one experience on TV had been great, and that was to be on *live*, on to feel the unfelt oncoming reaction of millions of people all at once — that was gone. Now, every show was taped, which is to say ninety-nine out of a hundred shows were taped, and the others were either early in the morning, or news shows, and the anchor men read their texts. It meant that you were usually recorded at ten in the morning or six in the evening for a show that might go on at midnight that night, or on a night next week, or in half a year, and so you were skewed out of time. The subtle emotions of a previous day and another hour would go into the midnight perceptions of an audience who would be obliged to assume — even when they knew better — that you were speaking to them at that moment even though you were not, and that was a subtle poison to slip into the perceptions of anyone studying a TV set, not to speak of the chop laid into the waves on wherever was the sea of time.

Yet if nearly everything but the early morning shows were now taped, and even the *Today* show had a seven-second lag between what you said and the instant it reached the audience's ear, time precisely for fuck-the-President to come out as "Bleep the President" — sounds in any case that only a madman would be able to make at seven twenty-two A.M. — if you knew as you got on the air, therefore, that the air was not the air, no more than the last shiver of a transcendental act is going to pass through the lining of a condom; if some technician had his fingernails on a knob between you and the air, then you were not live, you were captive. Words good enough or conceivably great enough to move the doors of history in any future time of stress would never get into the transmitter. If a subtle totalitarianism or an outright fascism came to America, then the instrument to control TV had already been installed — your words were taped, and on occasion they were bleeped. Even a hero looked like a chicken when his words were bleeped.

Still, he went on shows. He could not rid himself of the notion that it was a technique worth learning. Besides it is pretentious to look for virginity in the midst of the promiscuous. So he went on Joey Franklin, and on Mike Douglas and David Frost and Cavett and Merv Griffin and Carson and even appeared on Steve Allen in a ghost of the old show. He went on CBS and NBC and ABC, he went early in the morning to be taped live, that is with a seven-second hitch, and went in the late afternoon to be seen in the middle of the night and he went on Channels 5 and 9 and 11 and 13, and station KNET in Los Angeles, some such letters, and other letters for Detroit and Houston and San Francisco and Cincinnati, New Orleans and Chicago, Denver and Atlanta and Toronto and Washington and Philly, he went on with athletes and singers and dress designers and comedians, with ingenues and the inventors of novelty products, with doctors who knew diets and doctors who could speak of sex, he went on with worthy and self-serving politicians and lawyers for newsworthy rights, and once he even went on with Mother Teresa and Malcolm Muggeridge; he took what was offered, seeking to refine a technique whose first lesson he might never have learned, yet something in his stubbornness insisted on keeping the idea; he must use every means to advance his idea, and rarely did. And over the years, his idea changed. For if in the beginning he had seen a conspiracy by society to stifle existence, he came in time to think there was a conspiracy in one part of the cosmos to destroy the existence of the rest of the cosmos, and how do you get such an idea across, when it involves a train trip to Philadelphia, a half-hour with Mike Douglas and Rocky Graziano, and back again? He could have been a wrestler working one night in Atlantic City, the next in Pittsburgh, he took falls that would have broken his back if he had

had a literary sensibility left, he listened to Joe Garagiola once on the *Today* show reading from *Why Are We in Vietnam?* "Bleep," said Garagiola pretending to read from the novel, "I want to bleeping tell you that that's bleeping bleep when the bleeps hit the bleep." It was proper payment for going on the *Today* show to try to advance the fortunes of *Why Are We in Vietnam?* On the other hand, it was just a wrestler's loss; he was supposed to lose that event.

He went on wherever they invited him. He would go on Bob Cromie's *Book Beat,* and act like a gentleman, he would go on Susskind again, and again, he was on with Buckley once in '64, and Buckley finally allowed that Russell Kirk was right in calling Norman Mailer a freak, and Mailer in simple pain (you weren't supposed to get hurt in wrestling) said, "If you think I'm a freak, why did you invite me to dinner?" and Buckley shrugged and said, "No matter," and Mailer never forgave himself for not throwing a punch at that moment (except he wanted to get over the reputation he threw punches at people). He waited for the next show they were on together — it was Les Crane who had the new interview show that year — and Mailer called Buckley a very bad word, and Buckley, as if he had been waiting a year for this, calmly raised his hand to Les Crane and said, "I assume you're cutting this out of the show," and Crane said of course he would, and a few hours later, since Buckley was drinking with Mailer in the best good-will, Norman apologized, for he knew the word he had called Buckley was not true, or in any case — how was one to know of anyone? — not fair, and finally probably not a sin, and Buckley accepted in good grace. Hours later, Mailer began to brood over the little fact that Buckley had not apologized in turn and then he began to wonder if one of the reasons for the Buckley family fortunes was that they did not go around exchanging apologies for too little. Buckley invited him once to *Firing Line* and he had the pleasure of telling Bill that he thought Fidel Castro and Charles de Gaulle were the only heroes he could find in the modern world, and Buckley may even have missed a breath on that remark. Mailer was beginning to take pleasure in his pearls. Like an old pederast who keeps warm with the memories of a few divine young phalluses he has seen, Mailer lived with the memory of a few of his remarks. Once, in London, on David Frost's *Saturday Night* show, on the night he met Frost, David had come at him like a British heavyweight mauler, no great skill, but plenty of shove, "All right, Norman Mailer, you've written that sex can be killing. What do you mean by that?"

"David, I don't think one should talk about sex on TV."

"Why don't you?"

"It's like talking about your wife."

"Now, Norman, you said sex is killing, you wrote that right here, and we want to know: What is so killing about sex?"

It was a live show. They still had live shows in London in 1970. He could feel half of Britain gathered around the hearth; the other half were right next to their TV sets. He was getting ready to speak to this other half.

"Tell us, Norman. Don't be coy. What is punishing about sex?"

"David, do you want me to unzip, and lay it on the table and show you the welts and the warts?"

It was his best shot to a TV interviewer's eye since he dropped Eisenhower-is-a-woman onto Mike Wallace. Frost looked like a British heavyweight who has just been tagged but somehow does not go down. His eyes blinked. They sat there looking at one another over the sputtering of the British hearth.

Frost went on to do the rest of his show and do it well, engaging in a dozen arguments with a panel of management and labor union men, he took a good punch, and Johnny Carson gave a good punch (in the clinches) as Mailer would also discover on the occasion in '72 when he announced he was for McGovern while sitting next to Carson. During the break, as the canned commercial went on, Carson leaned in and said, "You really like McGovern?"

"Yeah," answered Mailer.

"Nah," said Carson. He leaned in at the advanced angle of a slim man about to slip you a tip on a horse, "I was talking to six friends, and on an impulse, I don't know why, I stopped and said to them, 'Who does McGovern remind you of?' What do you think all six said?"

"What?" asked Mailer.

"Liberace," said Carson and leaned away. They were on the air again. "Norman," said Johnny, "you were about to give us your views on McGovern."

He did his best but Carson had taken two percent forever from his genuine respect for George McGovern.

Yes, in the middle of metaphorical visits to Dr. Something, our national radiologist, out of the sum of spiritual wrestling matches and invisible boxing-fests, out of that accumulation of hours over the years that felt like exposure to the subtlest cancer of them all (and had they ever done a correlation between the purchase of TV sets and the rise in cancer — no, *they* hadn't; no, *they* wouldn't!) he came, more and more (to his own embarrassment), to treasure his TV pearls. They took some of the taste of the aspirin away; they had to; nothing was so depressing as those predictable draws TV encouraged; you were polite, the host was polite, an idea went back and forth and died. All the while, out in the vast pall, *something* was coming out of the sets. In such a pass, pearls took on the luster of small and pleasurable drinking habits. He even came to think of pearls the way an Irishman will live with legendary put-downs of one protagonist by another; and that was sad because Norman knew pearls appealed best to people who couldn't bear questions that took longer than ten seconds to answer. He was catering to TV addicts.

He would discover this all over again in that place where one may always learn something — in the middle of an event that has gotten out of hand. One night on Merv Griffin, back in 1967, he attacked the war in Vietnam as an evil war that would bring every horror in this country up from the sewer, and went on to describe America as a huge drunk staggering down a road while covered with his own vomit. The studio audience began to hiss with real anger; he looked back in equal anger and said: "Did you all go to high school?" The remark came out faster than his mind, and it was cruel: it went to the heart of the secret. For this audience had a common denominator. Something in their faces spoke of high school as the summit of their lives, the end of their development. These lumpy, dull-necked, dead-eyed people with their flower print blouses and acetate shirts, their big-beamed slacks for the women, and pinch-cheeked slacks for the men, were living in the kind of torpor that encouraged spending three hours on line to get into a TV show, yes, high school had been the most exciting few years of their life, and just as they hated him for scoring such an unhappy secret, so did he hate them because he never had a good time in high school and felt deprived for thirty years afterward.

Merv Griffin had his work that afternoon. If a studio audience was normally a TV host's prize cow, the cow was acting on this occasion like a bull. The disturbance did not cease, and Mailer, hardly about to hush his views on Vietnam, kept answering the audience's gibes with his own, until he could feel the moment when Griffin must have wondered if the time had come at last when a few dozen people were going to leave their seats and charge on stage. They never did, they never would, but Griffin couldn't be certain that day, and so, for years, whenever he invited Mailer back on his show, he would introduce him as "one of America's best-known brawlers, although he's really a very nice man."

After a time, Dick Cavett began to do something of the same. Once, when Norman suggested he was not a brawler, Cavett gave his fine Venetian smile: "A brawler is a guy who's all marked up after a fight — is that what you object to?"

The audience laughed, and Mailer nodded. Cavett owed him one. Cavett, indeed, owed him more than one. Once, on Cavett's program, Norman said he thought David Frost was the best TV interviewer in America, and proceeded to explain to the studio audience that while he had been drunk when he said it, the remark had its merits. Carson, he would explain, left you feeling like a horse that has been taken through its paces by a no-nonsense jockey, and Griffin, while cordial and decent, was more comfortable with singers and comedians.

"What is my fault?" asked Cavett, as if hoping there might still be a joke at the end.

"You're fine."

"No, tell me my flaws. I only invite you on, after all, to give my masochism a fighting chance."

The audience laughed, and Norman was annoyed enough now to pass over Cavett's merits. So he did not say that he thought him the most literate of television hosts, and admired him for trying to keep wit alive in the Sludge (which is the name of the great TV river) but instead said next, "Well, Frost is a good listener." It was true. Frost's gifts were personal. He listened better than other hosts, and so left his guest feeling forceful. "Frost is fun to be on with," Norman concluded.

"I'm not?"

"Oh, I like you."

"I don't care if Frost is better than me," said Cavett, "just as long as you like me." The audience roared.

They moved on to other matters, and in the intermission, Cavett said, "Did you mean it?"

"I said it on Frost's show last night."

"Well, why do you tell me now?"

"This show will go on tonight, but David's won't be heard for another week. I thought it would be unfair to come here, have a good time, and then let you find out later what I said." He paused. "I was going to tell you in the intermission, but it seemed the cheap way to do it."

"Yes, you bet," said Cavett. "David Frost, Jesus Christ!"

The next afternoon crossing a street in Chicago — Norman was in Chicago to do more TV to promote the sales of a book that no one who watched TV would ever be likely to buy: could it have been *Of a Fire on the Moon?* — he heard a stranger yell out from across the street, "Hey, Norm, how could you ever do that rotten thing last night to Dick Cavett?"

It took years to recognize that he had uttered no little harm; across the seasons, whenever Cavett might have a fight with his network, one or another executive hostile for certain to Cavett's subtle superiority to TV itself, would be able to say, "After all, Dick, even your friend Norman Mailer thinks David Frost is better than you."

Still, he did not come to understand how often the entertainer could have thought about that remark until the night he was on the Cavett show with Janet Flanner and Gore Vidal. It would prove to be an evening where no one would come out well, unless it was Janet Flanner, but it was a night, nonetheless, to convince Mailer that he was incapable of learning how to conduct a feud on TV.

Channel 9

From a letter to *Women's Wear Daily:*

Sirs:

It has come to my attention that Gore Vidal has been speaking in your pages of my hatred of women. Let me present the following items.

Number of times married:	Mailer 5	Vidal 0
Number of children:	Mailer 7	Vidal 0
Number of daughters:	Mailer 5	Vidal 0

These statistics of course prove nothing unless it is to suggest that the reason Vidal may have married no lady and fathered no child is due perhaps to his love of women and his reluctance therefore to injure their tender flesh with his sharp tongue.

Yours sincerely,
Norman Mailer

Until this letter, Vidal and Mailer had managed to keep a public peace for years. They had each decided long ago there were more profitable wars in the literary world, and so maintained the professional pact not to speak ill of each other for too little.

Probably this peace had exacted its small price. It is difficult for certain authors not to say terrible and/or accurate things about each other in print. Mailer might hear occasionally of a nasty remark Vidal had made in private, but ignored it on the assumption that Gore, tuning up for a little writing, was once again confusing malice for precision.

Still, Mailer knew his own career had become too popular for the pact to continue. Sometime after *The Armies of the Night* won a couple of prizes, Vidal began to sour in public. Condescending and somewhat righteous references to Mailer began to appear in Vidal's interviews. That was a clue to the temper of the time. Vidal was one literary politician with an impeccable nose for ripe liberal issues, and he was now rushing into the most useful denunciations, politically speaking, against machismo, and was quick to attach to this theme the-hatred-of-Norman-Mailer-for-women as if that were a well-established fact known to most of the citizenry.

Since Mailer was fond of repeating that there were four stages to comprehending a woman's character, and you could not claim to know her until you had passed through the four, that is, living together, being married, having children, and going through divorce, since he might therefore like or dislike a lost mate in a given season, but finally thought that was equal to approving or disapproving of Paris or London after you have lived there for many years, a woman indeed equal to a culture, so that you could hardly pass through four such stages with her and be left with nothing, he thought (as we can see by his letter to *Women's Wear Daily*) that it was kind of gross of Gore to declare that Mailer hated women when (to be downright crass about it) it was not Vidal, dig! who had spent his life in the collective arms of the powerhouse.

Of course, in compensation, Gore had taken up a seat in the power of print. If people saw something in a magazine, they liked to believe it. That much, Vidal knew. Stupid people! So, some time after his letter to *Woman's Wear Daily*, Mailer picked up *The New York Review of Books* one summer day and read a review by Vidal of a book by an author named Eva Figes in which the young-old critic stopped long enough to say, "There has been from Henry

Miller to Norman Mailer to Charles Manson a logical progression. The Miller–Mailer–Manson man, or M3 for short, has been conditioned to think of women as, at best, breeders of sons, at worst, objects to be poked, humiliated, killed. . . ." Vidal, going on from here to speak of M3 as if the case were made — well, in truth, even as Mailer knew that Vidal was looking for just such a result, just so did something blow in his brain.

"Why," asked Mailer in his mind of Vidal, "didn't you have the simple literary decency to say, 'This literary progression, extreme as it may sound at first, will engage my best efforts to show that there are startling and frightening similarities between Manson and Miller and Mailer'?"

Instead, this arrogance! Vidal, with his insensitivity to nuance, would not even make a suitable valet for Henry Miller.

And then, there was himself! He had not been writing for thirty years to be called M3. Mailer could hardly wait to catch up with Gore Vidal.

Yet the opportunity, when it came, did not give good anticipation. Indeed, he hardly knew whether the meeting would take place. He had been invited to appear on Cavett, then he heard Vidal had also been invited, then was told Vidal had dropped off the show. Finally he was informed Vidal was back again. It seemed Cavett would now have one more guest: Janet Flanner. The assistant producer who offered this piece of news said she was formidable.

Mailer had never met Janet Flanner but was used to seeing her pen name, Genêt, in *The New Yorker*. She had been doing a column on Paris for as long as he could remember (for decades it seemed before the real Genet came along) a firm gossipy *feuilleton*. It is the kind of writing whose merit is not easy to evaluate unless you know as much about the subject as the author; ergo, he had been less impressed with Janet Flanner's literary abilities than by her power to keep a job for a lifetime.

"I assume she's Gore's friend," Mailer said.

"It's more like he's her doll," replied the assistant producer.

"Thank you very much," said Mailer.

It did not bother him. Formidable people were often not formidable under video. Indeed, there was never a reason any longer to be bothered with what was awaiting you. By just so much had Mailer's opinion of television's importance changed. By now, he saw no point in being splendid on a TV show — it did not contribute to the sort of meaningful career where every step was on the staircase, in fact one rarely had an idea of when one was good and when terrible. Mailer had appeared on shows where he felt splendid and full of energy, yet looked uncomfortable to himself, even agitated, when he watched it afterward; conversely, he had come into many a studio feeling lifeless and later looked a model of cool deportment. The secret on TV, if there was a secret, was not to do too much.

Yet it could never be as simple as that. Sitting next to Johnny Carson, for example, was like setting up camp next to an ant-hill. Carson never stopped fidgeting. None of his nervousness, however, passed through the tube. Finally, one was at the mercy, Mailer expected, of this as yet undiscovered psycho-electronic valve that filtered vices out of certain people only to distort enthusiasm into the appearance of hysteria for others.

Of course, if you could not control how you would appear, if it was up to the valve, then there was no point to getting charged-up for a show. Mailer had come to believe in the old Hindu saw: Do not spend time worrying about matters you cannot affect.

So he made other appearances that day, other radio or TV — he could no longer remember — it seemed from the vantage of Limbo where old dates were quietly curved (so that you slid in memory around one winter over to another) that he may have been making some kind of effort on *The Prisoner of Sex* — was it for the hardcover or the paperback? and had, in any case, done a show already, and gone to a cocktail party where he enjoyed three or four drinks to the hilt. Mailer had the operative definition of *to the hilt:* it was the state where a carelessly lit match sent you up in flames.

When he arrived at the studio, they rushed him to makeup. Vidal had been supposed to go on first, but hadn't arrived. Would Mailer object to taking his place? He had hardly given his assent before he was informed that Vidal had arrived after all. Would he now mind if Mr. Vidal went on as originally planned? Since Mailer had formed the little vice when appearing on Cavett, of comporting himself as the star, he could not pretend to happiness at finding himself on the shuttle. Still, he kept his mouth shut. He did not wish to jostle his liquor.

At this moment, alone in the Green Room, he felt a tender and caressing hand on the back of his neck. It was Vidal. Vidal had never touched him before, but now had the tender smile of a man who would claim, "It doesn't matter, old sport, what we say about each other — it's just pleasant to see an old friend."

Mailer answered with an open-handed tap across the cheek. It was not a slap, neither was it a punch, just a stiff tap.

To his amazement, Vidal slapped him back.

Norman smiled. He leaned forward and looked pleasantly at Gore. He put his hand to the back of Gore's neck. Then he butted him hard in the head.

"Are you crazy?" asked Vidal.

"Shut up," said Mailer.

"You're absolutely mad. You *are* violent," said Vidal.

"I'll see you on the show."

He was, after Vidal left (and that was quickly enough), obliged to pace about. Other people came into the Green Room, saw him, and went away. It was obvious; he did not feel like speaking.

The show began. Cavett did his monologue, and it was a good one. "A lot of critics knock television. They have a kind of snobbish attitude towards TV and they think it lacks culture," he said with a smile. He had the only smile that came through the valves of video looking wicked and angelic at once.

"Tonight," continued Cavett, "I have three people on who are important in writing; they've done other things too, but they're all well-known writers. Just to prove to them that television has figured in the thoughts and writings of people of some stature among the literary profession, I asked my research department to come up with a few things that have been written about this program from some prominent figures. In a couple of cases I have a tendency to do it in the voice of the well-known person. This is from an unpublished work of William F. Buckley, Jr. entitled, 'A Felicitous Discourse on Epistemological Incunabula,' subtitled, 'God: The Man and The Myth.' " The audience applauded his smile with laughter. "The quote is: 'One of the less onerous duties incumbent upon a quondam political journalist is the occasional appearance on sundry quotidian chat programs that proliferate these days like Liberals at a hundred dollar a plate dinner for the poor. Not the least in stature, though clearly the least in stature actually, is a jovial dwarf named Cavett,' " — they roared — " 'who fortnightly forays into — or nightly actually — all fields of erudition and these forays are unblemished by the slightest knowledge of any of them.' That's old Bill." There was laughter.

"Here," Cavett went on, "is a paragraph by women's liberationist Kate Millett entitled 'Little Pig, Big Mouth.' " (Laughter) " 'Let's look at the facts. In the past year, sexist talk-show host Dick Cavett has welcomed several hundred guests on his show. Why have these not included one woman Supreme Court justice, one woman admiral, one woman pro-football player,' " — he stopped for the laughter — " 'one woman-father, husband, king or rapist? I'll tell you, sisters. Because Mr. Cavett, like all arrogant, ignorant, hypocritical, selfserving, pompous, rotten male chauvinist pigs, is simply . . .' and then she goes on to become slightly insulting." The audience adored him. "I don't," said Cavett with his finest smile, "want to read that part to you."

A question period with the audience followed, and he was asked "Do you dye your hair?"

"No," Cavett replied, "I tint my body a little to set it off."

Vidal now came out, and was as sluggish as a club-fighter who is looking for his mother.

> VIDAL: You're looking very well. Do you tint your body? (*laughter*)
> CAVETT: Funny, that was going to be my first question to you.
> VIDAL: That was it exactly, yeah.
> CAVETT: You heard all that?
> VIDAL: I was overhearing the audience, yeah.
> CAVETT: The audience was giving me a bit of time there, as we say in America.
> VIDAL: As you say in America. Well . . . love it or leave it.
> CAVETT: I haven't seen you in a long time. Do they say that in other countries — love it or leave it?
> VIDAL: Well, yes. Amsterdam, love it or leave it. No, no, you're free to come and go.

Vidal, however, was not a professional for too little. After the commercial, he began to rally; indeed Mailer was finally obliged to admire how Gore was able (wonder of wonders) to recover from the head-butting. Having been taught this informal martial art by a retired black Light-Heavyweight named John Bates who worked for a spell in the late Fifties as a bouncer in the Cafe Riviera on Sheridan Square — Bates' head felt like a cannonball! — Mailer knew the aftermath; nausea, and an ongoing vacuum in the brain.

Still, Gore was only showing a few bad effects. Of course, his head had been somewhat harder than expected — writers' heads tended to be more rock-like, for example, than actors', who suffered disproportionately from even a tap: head-butting may be ultimately a question of how heavy an identity (authentic or false) one is able to support — but, even so! Mailer knew how hard he had hit him. (Between half and three-quarter throttle.) Of course, Gore had given his television routines on so many shows that he could probably recite the same lines, with the same wit, same timing, and same turn of delivery, under sodium pentothal. Moreover, Vidal was not one to forget an effective remark; he never used a new thought so long as the old one could still seem new; it was obvious he had no respect for Mailer's long-held belief that repetition kills the soul. On the contrary, if such a law was in force, Gore would decide it was best not to have a soul. The soul was most famous, after all, for getting in your way — this much cynicism had Vidal absorbed from world literature!

Therefore, the only evidence, at present, that young Gore had passed through a contretemps in the Green Room — that is, had his head smashed — was his gesture, repeated somewhat frequently, of bringing up several fingertips to gently massage the skin of his forehead, same fingers indeed that had so recently offered to caress the back of Mailer's stiff neck. Other than that, Mr. Vidal was getting around to presenting a first-rate picture of himself.

He was speaking of his friendship with Mrs. Roosevelt. He and she had interests in common, including the protection of the Hudson River from further pollution. For Cavett's liberal audience, there was no name, Mailer decided gloomily, more calculated than Eleanor Roosevelt's to give the wholly satisfactory sensation of having one's buttocks stroked with velvet. To be given intimate glimpses of the lady! Even though he sneered at such crowd-pleasing tactics, Mailer was as taken as anyone in the audience. His only contact, after all, with Mrs. Roosevelt had been at long distance in the Fifties when he saw her printed reaction to a statement he had made in Lyle Stuart's *Exposé* that white southerners did not wish to give the Negro his equality because — he had been quick to explain — Southern Whites felt they had their social superiority and Negroes had their sexual superiority, and that — thought Southern Whites — was fair enough. Eleanor Roosevelt's short statement read: "I think Mr. Mailer's remarks are horrible and unnecessary."

Vidal's life with Mrs. Roosevelt transpired, however, on less troubled waters. He spoke of their first meeting with tender éclat. "I drove down," he told Cavett's audience, "to Val-Kill Cottage where she lived. It was a summer afternoon. The place was absolutely empty. Front door was open, walked in, nobody there. 'Anybody home?' She was a little deaf. No answer. So I went to the — the nearest door was half open, so I opened the door and there to my horror was Eleanor Roosevelt — very tall woman — standing in front of the toilet bowl. And I thought, 'Oh, my God.' And she gave a terrible cry, and then she turned around and she said, 'Well, I suppose you'd better know everything.' And she had some gladiolas in the toilet bowl which she was arranging. She said, 'It keeps them fresh.' " The audience laughed happily. "So we began with perfect intimacy, Mrs. Roosevelt and I. I knew everything from then on that was in the bathroom."

Clever Vidal! Out of the twenty-eight routines suitable for an appearance on Cavett, Gore had chosen to disclose Eleanor Roosevelt's watercloset. How could the audience not believe they had divine relations?

> VIDAL: (*ruminatively*) What I liked about her was there was nothing human that she felt human ingenuity wouldn't sense and right action could fix it, and she really believed that, and many people found her very boring because of it. I found her very inspiring. Gosh, I've been with her four in the morning in Schenectady trying to get a bus someplace when we were out campaigning, and on and on she would go, this old woman, quite sick, because she felt it was worth doing. And what's gone wrong in the world now, I think a great many of us feel that things are now irreversible, you know. They're never going to make the rivers clear and clean again, they're not going to save the land, they're not going to do anything about Detroit, the American empire is not going to liquidate itself. And there's beginning a sense of despair. You cannot turn it back, and Eleanor was the last person really who said, "Oh, we can, and we must."

Janet Flanner now came on. She was not a large woman, but she was old and grand and had an air of giving short measure to fools. By the manner in which she sat down next to Vidal, and laid her white-gloved hand on his arm, it was also apparent that she was authoritatively fond of him.

Cavett began to say that the last time he had had Janet Flanner on his program, she had told of finding Ernest Hemingway in her bathtub.

"He was stealing my warm water, that's what he was doing. Sheer theft is what I called it," said Janet Flanner.

She had a nice crust to her personality. It was like the crust on good bread that lets out agreeable sounds when a piece is broken off for you. The audience was tittering to show their approval. It hardly mattered how much she said since she could give you a lesson in deportment by the clearing of her throat.

Cavett asked: "Can you bury once and for all the tired old myth of the Frenchman being the sexual marvelous athlete of all time? . . ." And she replied: "Well, I've only buried a few so I can't tell about all the rest of them." In the midst of the applause, it was now obvious that Cavett, in his turn, was certainly fond of her. His manner seemed to suggest that the only reason he had ever wanted to have his own show in the first place was for the honor of introducing a lady so splendid as herself. He was actually laughing with happiness at her remarks.

For that matter, Mailer was obliged to admit all three were getting on very well:

> VIDAL: Did you know that George Washington used to take his false teeth at night and put them in a bowl of Madeira wine?
> CAVETT: No.
> VIDAL: I thought you would like to know that, Dick.
> FLANNER: As they were made of wood they must have been quite tasty by breakfast. (*laughter*)
> VIDAL: It was his brunch that he would put in the next morning.
> CAVETT: Madeira wine. Why? What's the effect of that on the false teeth?
> VIDAL: I think he liked the taste and they were made out of elephant bone and wood.
> FLANNER: And out of bone. The elephant bone is a new trick to me.
> CAVETT: I thought they were always wood. I always wondered — I pictured his dentist saying, "I have bad news for you — termites," or something. (*laughter*)
> FLANNER: Oh, you're a wicked boy. (*laughter*)
> CAVETT: Am I? (*laughs*) Where are we going?

In the Green Room, Mailer — like that general he could never become — was contemplating the military chances for entering an ambush of such delicacy connected to such strength. The only answer was attack. Shatter all prepared positions. Go out, he said to himself, and smash that fucking tea-house.

Channel 10

Those watching would see Norman Mailer emerge on the screen in a dark and disheveled suit, bow heavily to Janet Flanner, shake hands with Cavett, and pointedly not shake hands with Vidal. People in the studio audience would comment audibly at this display of discourtesy. Mailer would glare at them. Cavett would ask why he did not shake hands. Mailer would reply that he did not approve of Vidal, and thought him shameless in intellectual argument.

The camera would cut to Vidal's face. He would look composed on occasion, less composed on other occasions. Occasionally, Janet Flanner would touch his arm in reassurance, as if to signify that she would protect him from ruffians. Vidal was obliged to simper at that. It takes real machismo to look stern when your protection is seventy years old.

Under these loads, the next minutes progressed unevenly. Mailer was wound-up, and Vidal was silent. Cavett did not seem to know whether to put Lanolin on a rash, or pull cocks' feathers. Given this sort of prompting, Norman managed to get in a few words he had written about Vidal in *The Prisoner of Sex.*

> MAILER: I said that the need of the magazine reader for a remark he could repeat at dinner was best satisfied by writers with names like Gore Vidal.
> FLANNER: All those writers called Gore Vidal.
> VIDAL: I know. There are thousands of them, yeah.
> CAVETT: Writers with names like Gore Vidal.
> MAILER: There are two or three, you see.
> CAVETT: Who are some of the others?
> MAILER: I don't know.
> CAVETT: Who wants to host the rest of this show for me? (*laughter*)

Who had butted who in the head? Mailer now asked himself. After this exchange, his ability to mount a sustained argument, never impressive at best, was hardly robust in the face of Cavett's wit, and Flanner's deft interruptions. In short time, the audience turned unmistakably against him. When he said that the contents of Vidal's stomach were "no more interesting than the contents of an intellectual cow," they began to boo. He turned to them, and said, "You boo before you know what the man has done." They booed him again. He knew that he must move the conversation over to how Vidal had characterized Miller, Mailer and Manson as M3, but there was nothing routine about scoring a point when you were debating one on three, or, since Gore was so silent, one on two-and-a-half. During each commercial, Mailer would sit heavily in his seat, staring with a dead eye at Vidal, but this time — air-time certainly racing away — he handed Cavett a page he had torn out of *The New York Review of Books* with Vidal's review, and asked him to pass it over to be read aloud. As the show proceeded, however, Vidal did not read it. Norman began to upbraid him further.

"You go in for intellectual adulteration," he said to Vidal, and then with no great display of coherence added that Vidal was welcome to rip apart any piece of his writing. "By God," Mailer vowed, "I may be writing on the floor, but if you taught me something about writing, I'd look up and I'd love you for having taught me something about writing. But when you only teach me something about the tricks of adulteration," Mailer shook his head. "You say the rivers will never be clean again and you pollute the intellectual rivers . . ."

"I wasn't," Vidal drawled, "setting myself up as the Famous Writers School, you know." He drew the chortles he must have anticipated for that.

> MAILER: Why don't you try to talk just once, Gore, without yuks? Why not just talk to me instead of talking to the audience?
> VIDAL: Well, by a curious thing we have not found ourselves in a friendly neighborhood bar, but both, by election, are sitting here with an audience, so therefore it would be dishonest of us to pretend otherwise. (*applause*)
> MAILER: All right, Gore, look. We are here with an audience by choice, but let us at least — let us at least —

He wanted to grapple with him in argument, get him to read his own words. In the confusion of trying to get to Vidal with one hand and keep Cavett and Flanner off with the other, he was planning to say, "At least, read your own words," when Flanner whispered half-audibly to Gore.

> MAILER: Hey, Miss Flanner. Are you workin' as the referee or as Mr. Vidal's manager? (*laughter*) I'm perfectly willing to accept you in either role . . .

CAVETT: Can we afford you both talking?

MAILER: But my mind is fragile and I find it very hard to think and if you're muttering in the background it's difficult.

FLANNER: I made only the slightest mutter. (*laughter*) You must be very easily put off center.

MAILER: It's true, you made only the slightest mutter.

FLANNER: A tiny mutter.

MAILER: Yes, yes. But I listen to you spellbound —

FLANNER: I won't bother you anymore.

Norman was beginning to wonder if anything would work. He made a small vow never to drink again before going on TV. That valuable paper with Vidal's invaluable comments on Manson, Miller and Mailer was now in Vidal's pocket, oh that fine review with such plums as "M3 is on the defensive, shouting names; he thinks that to scream dyke is enough to make the girls burst into tears. . . ." "It was in those years that M3 was born, emigrated to America, killed Indians, killed blacks, conned women. . . ." "Miller–Mailer–Manson. Women, beware. Righteous murder stalks the land. . . ."

In the absence of any substance to Mailer's attack, Vidal was taking on strength. The show was past the three-quarter mark and Gore was coming alive. Yes, Gore was now saying avuncularly, the good thing about Norman "is his constant metamorphosis. He does rebear himself like the phoenix, and what the next reincarnation will be, I don't know."

MAILER: You seem to have figured out that the next reincarnation for me is going to be Charles Manson.

VIDAL: Well, you left yourself —

MAILER: Why don't you read what you wrote?

VIDAL: You let yourself in for it, and I will tell you — I'll give you a little background here — that Mailer has —

MAILER: We all know that I stabbed my wife years ago, we do know that, Gore. You were playing on that.

VIDAL: Let's just forget about it.

MAILER: You don't want to forget about it. You're a liar and a hypocrite. You were playing on it.

VIDAL: But that wasn't a lie or a hypocrisy.

MAILER: The fact of the matter is that people who read *The New York Review of Books* know perfectly well — they know all about it and it's your subtle little way of doing it . . .

VIDAL: Oh, I'm beginning to see what bothers you now. OK, I'm getting the point.

MAILER: Are you ready to apologize?

VIDAL: I would apologize if — if it hurts your feelings, of course I would.

MAILER: No, it hurts my sense of intellectual pollution.

VIDAL: Well, I must say, as an expert you should know about such things. (*laughter*)

MAILER: Yes, well, I've had to smell your works from time to time and that has helped me to become an expert on intellectual pollution, yes.

VIDAL: Yeah, well . . . let's — I was going to say, I —

FLANNER: Not only do you insult each other, not only in public, but you act as if you were in private. That's the odd way —

MAILER: It's the art of television, isn't it?

FLANNER: It's very odd that you act so — you act as if you were the only people here.

MAILER: Aren't we?

FLANNER: They're here, he's here. *I'm* here, and I'm becoming very, very bored. (*laughter, applause*)

MAILER: You still haven't told me whether you're Gore's manager or the referee.

CAVETT: If you make history here by punching a lady . . . (*laughter*)

FLANNER: I won't have it! I won't have it!

MAILER: Now, look, you see the sort of thing that goes on. Now you say I make history by punching a lady. You know perfectly well — you know perfectly well that I'm the gentlest of the four people here. (*laughter*)

CAVETT: I just hope it lasts through the next whatever we have left. (*laughter*)

MAILER: I guarantee you I wouldn't hit any of the people here because they're smaller.

CAVETT: In what ways? (*laughter*)

MAILER: Intellectually smaller.

CAVETT: Let me turn my chair and join these three. (*laughter, applause as he moves his place*) Perhaps you'd like two more chairs to contain your giant intellect. (*laughter, applause*)

MAILER: I'll take the two chairs if you will all accept finger-bowls.

This remark was sufficiently gnomic for Cavett to chew it and get to no witty place.

CAVETT: Who wants to grab this on our team? (*laughter*) I nearly have it, it means something to me. Fingerbowls. Fingerbowls. Things you dip your fingers in after you've gotten them filthy from eating. Am I on the right track? Am I warm?

MAILER: Why don't you look at your question sheet and ask a question.

CAVETT: Why don't you fold it five ways and put it where the moon don't shine.

It was received as the remark of the evening. Boborygimous was the laughter. Mailer sat there, contemplating a region in the depth of his rectum. "Mr. Cavett," he said, "on your word of honor, did you just make that up or have you had it canned for years and were you waiting for the best moment to use it?"

"I have to tell you a quote from Tolstoy," said Cavett, and the laughter continued.

Mailer turned his chair away from the guests and toward the theater. "I want to ask all of you something," he said to the audience. "Are you all really truly idiots or is it me?"

The audience replied, "YOU!"

"Oh, that was an easy answer," said Cavett. The music came up. Another intermission was on them.

CAVETT: I just wonder what the people at home think happened during the break. The four of us sat here in stony silence and —

VIDAL: No, somebody in the audience shouted, "Your argument is immature," to all four of us.

CAVETT: To all four of us. Oh. So we can each take as much —

FLANNER: We can each take a bow.

CAVETT: — as we feel we deserve. I'm sorry, Norman, I did interrupt you, and you were talking to the assembled audience.

MAILER: Yes, I was going to ask the audience what I was doing that was making them cheer every time the other side connected with a pass from one to the other of my three opponents.

MAN IN AUDIENCE: You're rude.

WOMAN IN AUDIENCE: You're a snot.

MAILER: That's fair. Someone said I'm rude and someone said I'm being a snot.

WOMAN IN AUDIENCE: You're a pig.

MAILER: Ohhh, the joint is loaded with libbies, ohhh. (*applause*) Gore, my God, it wasn't enough to trundle Janet Flanner along, the most formidable presence in the history of television, but you had to load the balcony with your libbies, your little libbies.

CAVETT: Well, now, wait a minute. There was only one lady's voice that rang out. Do you consider that loaded?

MAILER: It was the voice of legions. (*laughter*)

WOMAN IN AUDIENCE: Why do you have to argue so negatively and insulting to your guests?

MAILER: They're not my guests. They're not my guests any more than they're your guests.

CAVETT: It seems it's your show now.

WOMAN IN AUDIENCE: Why do you have to answer them with insults and nasty statements and they're answering you maturely and with dignity? (*applause*)

MAILER: That's because they're mature and full of dignity and they'd cut my throat in any alley and I answer rudely because I'm crude and a lout and a clod, that's why. (*applause*) Now have we progressed at all? Can I reach you, can I talk to any of you, or is it hopeless? I mean, if you care to listen, I do have a thing or two to say, believe it or not.

MAN IN AUDIENCE: Why are you bellyaching so much?

MAILER: Well, I'm bored with being misrepresented, you see. I've been misrepresented, by my own paranoid lights, for twenty-five years in this country, something like that, and to find an older litterateur like Gore Vidal, who knows his way around, you know . . . knows the ropes, and then suddenly, after all these years, he's suddenly developed a particularly dirty literary game. Well, it inflames me, you know. I've been so bold as to pretend to be the presumptive literary champ, you know, whether I deserve to be or not. The reason people always talk about me in relation to Hemingway is just that Hemingway at a certain point said to himself with his huge paranoia, "They're going to kill me for this but I'm going to be the champ, it's all I care about." And he shifted the course of American letters because up to that point people who wrote books were men of letters, they were gentlemen, they wrote books, and Hemingway said, in effect, "No, people who write books take as much punishment as prizefighters and one of them has to be a champion." Now, we've had a time that has not been interesting in terms of champions. In Hemingway's time there were great writers: there was Faulkner, there was Hemingway, and there were many other writers like Steinbeck and Farrell and Dos Passos and Thomas Wolfe, many, many really wonderful writers. Our time has been much more complicated and there hasn't been that many really extraordinary writers around, and I have presumed with all my extraordinary arrogance and lout-

ishness and crudeness to step forth and say, "I'm going to be
the champ until one of you knocks me off." Well, fine, but, you
know, they don't knock you off because they're too damned
simply yellow, and they kick me in the nuts, and I don't like it.

That was perhaps the most impassioned speech he had ever delivered on television. It said little but it was full of feeling, and it con-
tained the cardinal virtue of television (for any ambitious performer) which is that it kept attention on himself. It suggested that
his close-up in the scheme of things would demand more minutes
than the others. The audience, obedient to these conditioned re-
flexes of television, actually gave him a hand, a powerful hand of
applause. But, of course, he was hardly finished.

The time had now come to give his peroration on Women's Liberation. He was not opposed to it, he wished to tell the world, he even
honored it. It would free the best of women to discover how brave
they were; a world in which women were maintained systematically
in cowardice had to be a bad world. But, look, he wanted to say, as
in all revolutions, the worst are running with the best, and there is
an evil loose in Women's Liberation. It is the idea that the male
search for bravery is mean and ridiculous, and that it is easier to be a
man than a woman. Destroy the difference in the sexes, he would
tell this audience, and a world of asexual human units, ready to fit
the computers of a future totalitarianism, would also be prepared;
these were the questions Vidal was polluting with his use of M3.

It might have been worth giving, but the commercial came before
he was half-launched, and what he had to say was unsaid.

During the intermission, they argued on how to proceed. Vidal
now wanted time to reply. Cavett indicated that it was Cavett's
place to decide; he decided Vidal was entitled to equal time. Mailer
offered to accept if Vidal would at least read from his review. With
nothing agreed, the music came up.

> CAVETT: Gore, the aim narrowed down to you and we have three
> and a half minutes left. I insist that you get them.
> VIDAL: Well, I'll begin to answer Norman's charge about what a
> bad person I am. The attack on him, really, if you want to
> know, Norman, is simply what I detest in you — and I like
> many things in you, as you know, I'm a constant friend despite
> this — but your violence, your love of murder, your celebra-
> tion of rage, of hate ... "American Dream" — what was the
> dream? A man murders his wife and then buggers this woman

afterwards to celebrate an American man's dream. This violence, this knocking people down, this carrying on, is a terrible thing. Now, it may make you a great artist —

MAILER: I demand one minute at the end —

VIDAL: It may make you a great artist —

MAILER: I'll listen, but I demand one minute at the end . . .

VIDAL: It may make you an interesting artist, I don't say that, but to the extent that one is interested in the way the society is going, there is quite enough of this stress, quite enough of this violence, without what I think are your celebrations of it, your attitude towards women in this thing, which I thought really horrible, and you said I compared you to Charles Manson. I said Henry Miller in his way, Norman in his, and Manson in his far out mad way, are each reflecting a hatred of women and a hatred of place.

One person was applauding loudly. At that moment, Norman got up from his chair, took a few steps over to Vidal's chair, flipped the review from *The New York Review of Books* out of his hand (for Vidal had been waving it as he spoke) and then returned to his seat. Vidal had been in the thick of saying, "And frankly if I may say so," when he saw Norman's bulk looming above, and he flinched. Vidal flinched discernibly: a monumentally high number of electrons were thereby shifted in millions of TV sets.

Back in his seat, Mailer began to read from Gore Vidal's review:

MAILER: "There has been from Henry Miller to Norman Mailer to Charles Manson a logical progression." Period. "The Miller–Mailer–Manson man, or M3 for short, has been conditioned to think of women as, at best, breeders of sons, at worst, objects to be poked, humiliated, killed," and from there on in the piece you speak of Miller, the great writer Henry Miller, the greatest writer alive in America — if we're going to talk like muckers, I'll talk too like a mucker — Henry Miller, the greatest writer alive in America, and myself, and Charles Manson, a hugely complex and contradictory figure, are spoken of, lumped together as M3, and if you call that good intellect working, to lump together three people as curious as Henry Miller, Norman Mailer and Charles Manson?

VIDAL: Well, you must read the piece. You can't —

MAILER: I read it.

VIDAL: You happened to read it but the audience has not. You are selecting this one passage as representative of the whole. I made my case very carefully. But I will say, giving you a few minutes more on the program, you will prove my point. So, it is — I come back to what I said. I detest this violence in you. You have actually written that "murder is never nonsexual."

MAILER: Well, is it ever nonsexual?

VIDAL: Well, I'm —

MAILER: Don't you know, Gore?

VIDAL: Not having murdered anybody lately, no, I don't know.

MAILER: You bragged about what you did to Jack Kerouac, after all.

VIDAL: He didn't die.

MAILER: Well, he did.

VIDAL: Oh, come on.

MAILER: Don't you remember the stories you used to tell about him —

VIDAL: I'm going to give you a line that Degas said to Whistler — two celebrated painters — and Whistler was a great performer, like Norman, and Degas said, "You know, Whistler, you act as if you had no talent." You represent yourself as though you really had no talent at all and, of course, you are one of our best writers.

MAILER: I read it in the same place you read it, which is Edmund Wilson's answer to Vladimir Nabokov in last week's *Times.*

VIDAL: So what? What's that got to do with it?

MAILER: I thought it was marvelous.

VIDAL: Good. I'm happy that we both agree that the sentiment is correct.

MAILER: The difference is that I savor the remark and you throw it into the battle.

VIDAL: Oh, Norman.

MAILER: Now, may I have my one minute for rebuttal?

CAVETT: There is one minute remaining.

MAILER: There is one minute. All right. He speaks of a character in a book of mine murdering his wife and then buggering a woman as a celebration of American manhood. Now I throw myself upon your court, hanging judge. I say that's intellectual muckerism of the worst sort because the character I have there was a particularly complex character and, in fact, he did not simply bugger a woman, he entered her the other way as well and there was a particularly complicated —

FLANNER: Oh, goodness sake. (*laughter*)

MAILER: I know you've lived in France for many years, but believe me, Janet, it's possible to enter a woman another way as well.

FLANNER: So I've heard. (*laughter*)

CAVETT: On that classy note . . . (*laughter*)

FLANNER: I don't think it's restricted to French information, dear.

CAVETT: She said she doesn't think that's restricted to the French.

FLANNER: Practically international.

MAILER: Are we quitting on that classy note?

CAVETT: On that classy note, we have a brief message from our local stations and we will be back.

Cavett and Mailer were not looking at each other. Vidal was looking off into space. Flanner was grinning at Mailer as if he were a most curious fellow. What a way to use his last minute!

The music came up.

CAVETT: Well, this has been an interesting evening around the old table and, Miss Flanner, I'm glad to see you got that box of cookies that you wanted. And you other two fellows —

FLANNER: It's the only solace.

CAVETT: Yeah. (*laughter*) Could you two come back New Year's Eve and maybe we can — (*laughter*)

MAILER: That's the night.

CAVETT: Christmas Eve. Well, let us know who you think won. That'll be interesting, and we'll see you next time we're on the air. If. (*laughter, applause*)

The goodbyes were short. Mailer turned around and Vidal was gone.

Channel 11

Afterward, long after the mail stopped coming (which took a time in itself) after the magazine accounts were finished, and he no longer heard students ask, "Were you really mad at Mr. Vidal?" every time he gave a lecture, long after he had lost every last bit of interest in the evening and remembered the program only because accounts kept coming back to him of Vidal saying on one network that Mailer-is-finished-as-a-writer, and Norman-is-bad-news on another, a string of claims that was now in its sixth year (and would never end since he knew he would never run into Vidal for an accounting — once when Norman was in Rome for a month to work on a movie script, Vidal managed to leave for New York) he finally had time to recognize that this Dick Cavett show, if it was one of the few occasions when television had come alive, had also been killing to the last of his hopes that television might be a forum for those curious ideas with which he lived.

Hundreds of letters came in, ten times more, or maybe it was fifty times more letters than he had ever received from any other show, and as many he was certain came to Vidal — all those lovers of Eleanor Roosevelt! His mail was favorable to him, even as Vidal's mail must in turn be favorable, but the letters, if they brought a sense of his real audience, were not in response to any triumph he had had over the medium, but more a note, even a chorus of outrage, at the restraints of television, the villainy of Cavett in choosing sides, the inanity of the audience, and much on Vidal's little flinch — hardly a letter did not pride itself on seeing that Vidal had flinched.

In turn he hardly had to speculate how other letters must be describing him: a boor, a drunk, an incoherent and unworthy opponent for Mr. Vidal.

It had been Bullshit Bisque when all was said. He had not only failed to dramatize his ideas, but had dramatized himself — it was himself rather than any idea that had come through the tube. He had succeeded at best in evoking sympathy for his own lack of taste and polish; yes, when it was all done, and psychic horizons could be glimpsed again, he knew that he had wasted another fierce piece of Time, and Limbo was by that measure more advanced on him, even knew at last from the vantage of Limbo, from the intimacy of this observation into the interstices of his past that it did not matter on how many TV shows he would yet appear, on Cavett again and Carson and Griffin and Douglas and Susskind and *Today* and *Tomorrow, Sixty Minutes,* no past and no future, no antipathy and no forgiveness, no, it did not matter, he had crossed over to the other side on this night of the Dick Cavett show, and now saw that television was an addiction whose pleasure (since every addiction has its pleasure) was to give a small sense of manners to the mannerless and pass a hint of style over to those who are hungry with some unfulfilled vision of themselves (even as he had once studied TV). Yet, as an addiction, it would exact, like any drug, its own cruel price. That took many a form, but for our purposes the price may be equal to the power to destroy the virility and fecundity of ideas. TV was not with us to make history but to leach the salts of history right out of our cells.

Since Mailer came to know this in his life, and yet continued to go on TV, he advanced from a wicked man to the beginnings of an evil figure, at least to his own eyes which here were unhappily congruent to the eyes of Limbo. If it was wicked to up the ante, it was evil to come to know the good and defy it, and the good in this case was to keep the hell off TV, which he did not. So he came to know his place in Limbo before he was even there. That is our story and we could be done if it were not demoralizing to cease at such a point, blanked in Limbo and empty of hope.

Since it is also the work of such a place, however, to cleanse the choked-up rivers of one's life and thereby enable us to voyage out to a more adventurous plane (where the walls are rough and the ascents are vertical) not every meditation in the mansion need brood over the hopelessness of the past. There is also the memory of odd and mysterious instants when hope is in the air, even if comprehension is dim. So Mailer, sentenced by Limbo to remember no experiences that were altogether separate from television, was nonetheless able to think fondly of two events he saw from the spectator's side of the tube and was agreeably overcome with the suspicion — suspicion being tonic to the dull recognitions of Limbo — that even in the middle of *something* there might be a force devoted to the extinction of *something*. If the Devil always appeared in the most splendid intentions of the Lord, the Devil being the most beautiful creature God ever made (in those days when the Lord was young and still vain in His vision and therefore wicked enough to create beauty before prudence) so, too, had God been obliged in His turn to enter all those baleful and Satanic mediums where the air is destroyed and electromagnetism chases its tail and shatters frequently, yes, maybe God was now as grim as the glimpse of defeat in the center of television when the set goes off, and yet was also ready if no longer young, to chase the Devil into every void, live in every static, and go to war on each bleak field. So there might be hope. Mailer did not know — Limbo gave no final purchase on the eschatological structure of things, but, still! Mailer remembered the night he invited friends to his house in Provincetown back in the summer of '66 because his great friend José Torres was defending the Light-Heavyweight Championship against Eddie Cotton in Las Vegas, and the fight was on TV. That was an occasion to remember in Limbo, and see again in Limbo, yes.

Torres was a strong favorite that night, but Cotton gave him trouble. Eddie Cotton was an old black fighter with a thousand tricks and more than a hundred fights, and being near the end of a distinguished and rugged career, he was ready to steal the championship if he could put it all together, and Cotton put it together. He fought the fight of his life. Before half of the fifteen rounds were gone, he was clearly ahead of José Torres.

There were eight guests in Mailer's living room and they were quietly drinking and commenting on the action. About this time, Norman began to go out of his mind. He did not really know a lot about boxing, not so much as he was reputed to know, but he knew Torres' style and had an insight into Torres' strengths, and on this night he felt as if he knew what Torres was not doing right. "Stick him," he began to shout at the set. "Get your jab working." Torres' vice, if he had one as a fighter, was vanity, and Torres was being beaten on combinations by Cotton. Since José's vanity was that nobody was better at combinations than Torres, he had been trading his best combinations against Cotton, and for one round after another, Cotton had been beating him by just a little. What a fight! One was seeing some of the finest combinations ever to come out of a war between Light-Heavyweights, fantastic combinations indeed for Light-Heavyweights, it was a great fight, but Torres was not using his jab, that jab off his long arm that had been finer even than the jab of Willie Pastrano on the night Torres took the championship from him, and so Norman began to scream at the set in a purple and apoplectic voice, "Stick him! Stick him! Get it going! Stick him!" And as if he had been in Torres' corner, and Torres was listening to him, so Torres began to pop Cotton with his jab, there in the middle of the fight, Torres shifted his pattern, and began to jab, and this threw Cotton off just a hair on his combinations, and the jab began to take the edge from Cotton and give it back to Torres, and Norman, watching the action, swallowed bourbon like gasoline, and screamed instructions, "Keep it up, keep it up. Keep the pressure!" to what must have been the *peculiar* horror of his guests; now more rounds were going to Torres than to Cotton, and Norman screamed him home, eight rounds to seven, and José kept his championship. Norman was never to get over the impression that somewhere in the depths of Torres' attention the message had come back through the tube. "Stick him!" A miracle in communication had occurred. A TV set, that malign corporate mechanism of valves that allow communication to pass in one direction only, had been transcended for half an hour, and managed to take messages back, or to say it real, the heart of Mailer's insanity that night was to think he had passed through the heart of *something* and was talking success-fully to the tube.

Insanity has its rewards. Later that night, convinced he had bro-ken through some encircling ring of the Devil, and was now out of his box, that is to say, alive in his life rather than sequestered in a psychic coffin, Norman began to run amok at a dress rehearsal of his play, *The Deer Park*, which would have its premiere the following night at the Art Association in Provincetown. He had kept his mouth shut at rehearsals when he wished to interfere, he had al-lowed, he thought, his director to take *The Deer Park* down lanes the play should not travel, and on this night, after the Torres–Cotton fight, having come to the rehearsal late, and lately filled with a sense of power few humans could know — he could talk back to the tube! — saw no reason why he should not talk back to his actors, and did. Sitting at the back of the hall, hardly able to hear their voices, he began to shout, "Louder!"

"Norman, will you please be quiet," said the director.

"I will not be quiet. I cannot hear the actors."

They had a quarrel in front of the cast. It grew worse, and the director, in a rage, called the rehearsal off. It was only on the next day that Mailer found out he had been witnessing not a dress re-hearsal, but a walk-through for light cues, and that was why he could not hear the actors. They were saving their voices.

"When it comes to theater, you are an ignorant man," said the director, Leo Garen, next day, and since he was a young director and had no money at the time, and this play, if it went on to Off-Broadway, was his best prospect, Mailer knew the courage it re-quired for Garen to tell him off, and shook his hand on the spot — it was somehow relaxing to hear in the middle of his fearsome hang-over that he was ignorant; he had not been called ignorant in many a year; some insults come like a blow on the head the morning after, but a few are balm — and he later hired Garen to take *The Deer Park* to New York, and thus began a short career in theater and soon invested his own money in making and directing three films, and by way of them proceeded eventually to lose all his money and more, and so was obliged to keep writing fast for the rest of his life, a blessing to those who liked his stuff, a curse to those who didn't, but much change had certainly come to his life by daring to go up through the tube.

If this pale reminiscence of the rehearsal of *The Deer Park* was as far as he had been able to stray in Limbo away from grim recollections of television, still it cheered him, even if the new images were still of himself as a fool; at least they were recollections free of video. If such memories continued, he might even recall a happy copulation or two. Of course, he did not have the hope that Limbo would permit any rounded view of one's powers of compassion and detachment, fear and greed, strength and responsibility, as a good friend and a bad one, a lover and a monster of love, as egocentric and selfless, no, Limbo was strict, Limbo repaid you for dabbling in television by making you live in it; these walls like the inside of a TV tube were equal to the insomnia that got you up at two in the morning to peer into the box. He had never expected that the scale of payment would be as intimate as your worst enemy's judgment on your hopes.

Channel 12

Yet, as his mind went on, and he came to retrace every episode on this avenue of his sins, an itinerary for which he did not have to move a step, since the curved walls of Limbo served splendidly as a screen, he was at last entitled to move out of his most intolerable punishment (which here for the Narcissist, paradoxically, is constant and enforced contemplation of the self) and begin to consider the merits of others.

So he came at last to the one night on TV in many years that had given him real pleasure, and he thought often about it. In his partial comprehension of television, in his researches into the mystery of that hum in its void, he had always centered his hypotheses around the familiar certainty that Richard Nixon owned the human personality closest to the persona of the television set. Mailer had even built his distrust of TV and Nixon on their similarity to one another, their incorporation of baleful disregard for the finer possibilities of human attention.

Yet, when he replayed in his mind, that is on the curved walls of the mansion, Nixon's first appearance before David Frost, where the ex-President spoke of Watergate, Mailer was cheered by that ninety minutes. In later years, his detestation of TV close to complete, ninety minutes had become an immense dose of video, and left Mailer feeling like a canceroid (that is, like someone who could not justify why he should not bear the disease). Yet Nixon's ninety minutes were of another order; on the scale of video, they were alchemy itself: the American with the least charismatic personality of the twentieth century, the American most ready to be emitted from the tube and infiltrated into your pores had become for a few minutes a personality capable of moving multitudes, and had done it by the refractory art of the actor.

He had always believed Richard Nixon was the most untalented actor he had ever witnessed, and Mailer had often brooded on the first meeting decades ago of Richard and Pat Nixon in an amateur theatrical company, and wondered whether Nixon, if he had been somewhat better in those early years as an actor, would have become in later life a politician more like Ronald Reagan. Instead, his acting career had been given over to the practice of law, and Nixon had become one of the few politicians who was a consummately abominable actor on the American scene. His lack of conviction vibrated through the diodes, triodes, and later the transistors of every American set; the message he gave was profoundly depressing. Even as a district attorney who speaks in too-righteous tones to a jury will depress us on questions of law and order and their relation to justice (since the fact that a D.A. can prosper on such hypocritical terms has either to speak ill of the jury or of a system that encourages us to believe that phony voices carry the real tones of avenging authority) so Nixon's inability to act had always, by reflection, intimated that something in the American public must be atrocious if millions were ready to accept his transparent lack of sincerity, his push-button smile, and his simple lack of ability to offer even that resonance of the throat which is a ham actor's emotion.

Yet in the interview with Frost that Mailer witnessed, a miracle was visible — Richard Nixon had become not merely a good actor but a great actor, great by the measure of actors like Bogart, and Fonda and old Spencer Tracy, great — good God! — like Edward G. Robinson, like Edward G. Robinson playing Richard Nixon full of woe at what had come to him from Watergate, and after thirty or forty minutes of watching Nixon, it did not matter what the truth might be, any more than one would find fault with a great stage actor for bringing life and splendor and passion and the monumental echoes of tragic woe to lines that were not his own and that he could say in his sleep or while shaving, he had practiced them so

well, yes, Nixon struck America with a miracle — a talentless actor
had become a splendid actor — yes, Nixon now went to the root of
good acting, where before he had lived in the center of bad acting.
In his political years, Nixon used to comport himself as if acting
were a set of semaphores and you frowned if you wished to look
stern, and glanced heavenward to demonstrate that your motives
were benign; now, face to face with Frost, he was an actor from the
guts out, which is that he got his words out through every effort to
control himself. The great actor does not play a drunk by staggering; rather, he plays a man whose stomach is raw and whose head is
whirling, but a man who nonetheless believes he is sober and so will
make every effort to convince others he is sober. The power of his
drunkenness comes over the audience by his attempts to conceal it
from us. That was Nixon's power on this night. What a mighty
emotion he was seeking to hold like a man. It did not matter after a
while that a part of one's brain could still remember many an intri-
cacy of Watergate that Nixon was debauching once again; that was
like saying of Olivier in *Marathon Man* that he might be playing an
ex-Nazi, but actually was still Olivier and born British, what indeed
did the truth of Nixon's guilt have to do with the higher truth that a
talentless man had become a powerful actor? A fact such as this was
kin to a miracle and warmed the heart. So as Richard came forth
with those beautiful and unforgettable lines, beautiful, that is, and
unforgettable, as examples of the actor's, not the playwright's, art, as
he said: ". . . it was springtime. The tulips had just come out . . . it
was one of those gorgeous days when, you know, no clouds were on
the mountain. And" — his voice went husky here from the effort
not to be husky — "I was pretty emotionally wrought-up, and I remember that I could just hardly bring myself to tell Ehrlichman
that he had to go. . . . I said, 'I hoped, I almost prayed I wouldn't
wake up this morning.' Well, it was an emotional moment. I think
there were tears in our eyes, both of us. He said, 'Don't say that.'
We went back in." Then he said goodbye to Haldeman and Ehrlichman, and took their resignation. ". . . It was late, but I did it."
No actor alive, not Ralph Richardson, Jack Nicholson, or John
Gielgud could have given a better reading than he gave on the next
line. "I cut off one arm," Nixon said manfully, and in partial control
of great pain, "and then cut off the other arm." He nodded. ". . . You
could sum it all up," he said to Frost, "the way one of your British
Prime Ministers summed it up, Gladstone, when he said that 'the
first requirement for a Prime Minister is to be a good butcher.' Well,

I think . . . I did some of the big things rather well. But I . . . have to admit, I wasn't a good butcher."

It would come out later that Nixon's version of these events was not necessarily accurate; first Ehrlichman, then Haldeman, would dispute what he had said. He was not cutting off his own arms so quickly, it seemed, as he was cutting off their legs.

Yet with what a difference did he lie! In the past, a deadening actor and a lifeless politician, Nixon had lied with every dull light in his eye; now, his eye was bright, he had learned to act; his lies partook of art.

The impact upon Limbo was immense. Limbo had many mansions and took many shapes, but the rock on which Limbo was founded would state: men like Richard Nixon are not redeemable.

Nixon had shattered the rock. Reflecting on Nixon's Ode to the Prime Minister and the Art of Butchery, Mailer felt the breaking of the rock. Nixon had demonstrated that if one's suffering were great enough, even a hopeless actor could learn to act, and that meant millions of Americans dragged into the pit by Nixon and forced to believe that bad acting, and/or transparent hypocrisy, are the main road to success, would now be obliged to stare into the true pit: life demanded that one improve. Even a hypocrite was wise to sin with a light in his eye. So the fundament of Limbo cracked. It could not decide whether Richard Nixon was still the avatar of video, a TV set with a head and limbs, and video itself was altering into a higher form of the maligant; or, whether Nixon, having betrayed all other gods, had now betrayed the Devil as well, and would try to make a last career for himself good enough to bring Broadway back.

Mailer did not have time to care. He knew only that Limbo was looser now, and he was getting ready to move from the mansion; to go on — where to, he did not know, a curiosity or a horror could await him next. He hoped only that tomorrow — in the long tomorrow of Limbo — would lead to autumnal places where the record of his sins might reek of wood-smoke rather than the insulation of all those TV wires charring in the night.

It was on this note that he was allowed to think of a poem, but the irony was that it was by a poet named James Elroy Flecker he could hardly have read before, and only the last two lines would stay in mind. "O, is it," said Mailer to himself,

"Is it the mist or the dead leaves?
"Or is it the dead men — November eves?"

Two Letters from Frank Crowther

❧

Dear Norman,

I just wrote Joe Flaherty a note, and he'll probably call you.

But, at the last minute (and this is surely that), I couldn't check out without sending you a last note.

I've been reading Baudelaire's Last Poems (1859–63), and stopped after Le Voyage and Anywhere Out Of The World. They mean different things to different people (especially the author), but I saw some of myself in them. I sure as hell wish I'd written at least one or two things as good. . . .

Before checking out, I merely wanted to say a personal farewell and wish you all the best. If there's some way you can sneak the big novel over to the 'other side,' give it a try. It would be something fine to carry off into eternity.

So long, old man. Keep giving them hell.

Good luck and God bless,
Frank Crowther

P.S. One final thought. If you wouldn't mind, when you have a chance, I'd appreciate your dropping my father a note. I worry, as would any son, how he's going to take this. I had a good life, a good shot at things, and I leave with almost no regrets. It wasn't anything to do with my *parents. God knows. They were always loving and kind to me. I just had some bad luck, that's all, and chose this way of departure rather than lingering and getting worse by the day. It might help him through what will undoubtedly be a bad time. . . .*

He wrote other letters that day to Wes Joyce, proprietor of the Lion's Head where he drank, and to Joe Flaherty, the writer who lived in the same house as himself. The letters were all postmarked at three in the afternoon. That evening he went to the Lion's Head, drank quietly, said little, and studied the faces of Joyce and Flaherty who were also at the bar and would receive his letters in the morning. Then he went home and took an overdose of pills and died in his tidy apartment, dead before he was forty-four. A number of us went to his funeral. Being asked to speak, I read aloud from his letter. I confess I had read the letter twice before I realized what it said, and so I tried to explain that Crowther lived, more than any friend I knew, by an idea of style. When style is a way of life rather than a literary act, it has only the modern fundament on which to base itself — grace under pressure. It is probable that Frank had more pressure in the last two years of his life than anyone I know, and he was not necessarily prepared for it; his early career had been an easy and attractive one. He had four years in the Marine Corps with two of them at the American Embassy in Paris, followed by a good campus career at the University of North Carolina, and then a stretch of nine years in the Kennedy and Johnson administrations and with Roger Stevens on the White House staff for the National Endowment for the Arts. He was that rarest of career men, a literary functionary on the national level, and it gave him a certain blandness. He was, in the years I first knew him — we would run into one another at Plimpton's parties — a well-built, pleasant-featured slightly round-faced acquaintance, with a half-agreeable, half-promiscuous heartiness, and a great knowledgeability of the activities of everyone in the literary world. I doubt if he missed reading a single issue of any magazine relevant to those times and those people. He was up on every bit of gossip. It was easy not to take him seriously, and I remember my surprise at discovering in 1971 when he came to visit in Provincetown, that Crowther was more of a literary man than I had realized, and had the passionate love of good writing you expect to find in people who have high literary ambitions but know agonies in trying to set it down.

After that, we were friends of a sort, and came closer when he managed my Fiftieth Birthday Party at the Four Seasons (where I announced the need for a Fifth Estate in a sixth-rate speech) and if the affair had any success at all, it was in Frank's skill at getting people to believe that my birthday party was the place you wanted to be seen on that night, a piece of social legerdemain when you consider the not wholly cordial reputation of the principal.

A year later, more or less, he was ill. Sick with a most mysterious and maddening disease. His skin turned red, peeled, and itched intolerably. He lived in the cauldron of a body that itched for twenty-four hours a day. The skin of his hands turned as red as the shell of a boiled lobster. His weight went down. His round face turned thin, and his gray eyes had the imploring light of a man who dwelt in unremitting torture. He was in and out of hospitals. They tested him for every cancer they could find — they found none; for every common and exotic disease of the skin — they found none. He managed to write during this period and did a screenplay which came close to a good sale and then fell through and he was living now on next to no money. It ought to have been unendurable to see a man with such misfortunes, but the suffering brought an expression close to beauty in what had been once an almost dough-shaped face. I think the first horror for him was that he did not know if his suffering was attached to the mystery of pain itself, or whether he was a sport, his illness a fluke, and himself a protagonist of the absurd.

That horror breaks through the reserve he usually managed to maintain in his letters. Let me quote from another written six and a half months before his death. He says it there better than I can, and I think he was enough of a literary man to be pleased that I would say so:

> *I came across the following in Kierkegaard's* Diary (*p. 19, Entry 18*): *"All of existence intimidates me, from the tiniest fly to the enigmas of incarnation; as a whole it is inexplicable, my own self most of all; all of existence is pestiferous, my own self most of all. . . ."*
>
> *I have no pleasure in these days, as well you know, I feel wasted and useless, although in clear moments, there is so much I wish to say, so much I would wish to write were I capable thereof. I remember your saying: "I'm a pro. I can work on a bad day."* I'm not a pro, and therefore must *try*

to work on both *bad* and *good* days. But the raging of the flesh too often burns away all energy, all motivation. And God knows how terribly difficult it is even to sit down at the typewriter, much less write coherently and well. Ideas abound, but I am unable to capture them. . . .

Finally, although I have both fear and disdain for death (*the latter possibly being the greatest mistake of all*), I smell its stench approaching, and hear the snicker of that jackal somewhere in the night. I feel useless and, worst of all, irrelevant. My strengths, whatever they were, have waned, and my weaknesses are beginning to overwhelm me. And I feel dirty (*not only physically*). My circle of 'friends' recedes, and I withdraw more and more. I drink more and more. Although before my illness I hardly ever took so much as an aspirin, I fall back on pills of all nature, knowing they are of no use other than a temporary sop. I loathe my body, and have little faith in whatever I might achieve were I not physically afflicted and mentally depressed. Life still has its light moments of frivolity, and I do have a well-developed sense of detachment, but the harsh realities have become a bad film. . . .

. . . I may soon disappear, or I well may hang about a while longer, but these are some things I wanted to say, sooner rather than later.

I send you my love and good wishes,
Frank Crowther

Miller and Hemingway

Henry Miller, his work embraced, which is to say swallowed in four or five weeks, and then re-read over another month or two, can sit in one's mind with all the palpability of a huge elm lying in your back yard. The nobility of the trunk is on the ground for you to examine, not to speak of the rich nightmare of the roots and crawlers. To read Miller in that short a period reopens the old question which is always too large: What is a man? Just as our uprooted elm would take on constellations of meaning as it lay in the yard, until finally it could be reminiscent of a battleship, or a host of caverns in Hieronymus Bosch, so might you be forced to ask: What the devil is a tree? Just so does Miller return us to the first question of humanism. What, finally, is a Man? Nothing is settled after all. We have been given the illusion that we know Miller, know every one of his vices, peccadilloes, hustles, horrors, cadges, gifts, flaws, and transcendent generosities, are, yes, familiar with that man who is by his own description "confused, negligent, reckless, lusty, obscene, boisterous, thoughtful, scrupulous, lying, diabolically truthful ... filled with wisdom and nonsense." Nonetheless, when we are done reading, we wonder if we know anything. It is not that he bears no relation to the Henry Miller who is the protagonist of his books. (That Henry Miller is, indeed, the ultimate definition of the word protagonist.) No, the real Henry Miller, which is to say, the corporeal protean Miller a few writers knew intimately and wrote about well, Anaïs Nin being the first, is not very different from his work, but more like a transparency laid over a drawing, copied, and then skewed a degree. He is just a little different from his work. But in that difference is all the mystery of his own personality, and the paradoxes of a great artist. And the failure. For it is impossible to talk of a great artist without speaking of failure. The greater they are, the more they do not fulfill their own idea of themselves. Dostoyevsky failed to write The Life of a Great Sinner, and Tolstoy never brought a religious metamorphosis to man. Miller was never able to come to focus on the one subject which cried out to him: D. H. Lawrence's old subject — what is to be said of love between a man and a woman? Miller saw that Lawrence had come to grips with the poetry of sex but none of the sewer gas. Miller would strike matches to the sewer gas, and set off literary explosions, but he never blew himself over to the other side of the divide. While nobody can be more poetic than Miller about fornication itself — two hundred beer-hall accordions might as well be pumping away as he describes the more heavenly engagements he has played — the writing becomes an evocation of some disembodied but divine cunt and what it is doing to him — his appreciation equal to the enjoyment of a great symphony, yet he still cannot write about fucking with love. (Of course, it is fair to ask, who can?) Miller nonetheless pounds away on the subject like a giant phallus trying to enter a tiny vagina — in the pounding is one simple question: How the hell do you get in?

Miller has not lacked for adulation. A small but accountable part of the literary world has regarded him as the greatest living American writer for the last four decades and indeed, as other American writers died, and Hemingway was there no longer, nor Faulkner and Fitzgerald, not Wolfe, not Steinbeck, nor Dos Passos, and Sinclair Lewis long gone, Dreiser dead and Farrell in partial obscurity, who else could one speak of as the great American author? Moreover, Miller provided his considerable qualifications. One had to go back to Melville to find a rhetoric that could prove as noble under full sail. Miller at his best wrote a prose more overpowering than Faulkner's — the good reader is revolved in a farrago of light with words heavy as velvet, brilliant as gems; eruptions of thought cover the page. You could be in the vortex of one of Turner's oceanic holocausts where the sun shines in the very center of the storm. No, there is nothing like Henry Miller when he gets rolling. Men with literary styles as full as Hawthorne's appear by comparison stripped of their rich language; one has to take the English language back to

Marlowe and Shakespeare before encountering a wealth of imagery equal in intensity.

Yet it can hardly be said that the American Establishment walks around today thinking of Henry Miller as our literary genius, or one of the symbols of human wealth in America. Born in 1891, he will be eighty-five by December 26 of 1976, an artist of incomparably larger dimensions than Robert Frost, yet who can conceive of a President inviting him to read from his work on Inauguration Day, no, the irony is that a number of good and intelligent politicians might even have a slight hesitation over whether it is Arthur Miller or Henry Miller being talked about. "Oh, yes, *Henry* Miller," they might say at last, "the guy who writes the dirty books."

Even in the literary world, however, Miller's reputation survives in a vacuum. It is not that he lacks influence. It is not even excessive to say that Henry Miller had influenced the style of half the good American poets and writers alive today: Would books as different as *Naked Lunch, Portnoy's Complaint, Fear of Flying,* and *Why Are We in Vietnam?* have been as well received (or as free in language) without the irrigation Henry Miller gave to American prose? Even a writer so removed in purpose from Miller as Saul Bellow shows a debt in *Augie March.* Miller has had his effect. Thirty years ago, young writers learned to write by reading him along with Hemingway and Faulkner, Wolfe and Fitzgerald. With the exception of Hemingway, he has had perhaps the largest stylistic influence of them all. Yet there is still that critical space. Miller has only been written about in terms of adulation or dismissal. One does not pick up literary reviews with articles entitled "Ernest Hemingway and Henry Miller — Their Paris Years," or "The Social Worlds of F. Scott Fitzgerald and Henry Miller," no comments on "The Apocalyptic Vision of Henry Miller and Thomas Wolfe as Reflected in Their Rhetoric." Nor is there bound to be a work titled "Henry Miller and the Beat Generation," or "Henry Miller and the Revolution of the Sixties." Young men do not feel they are dying inside because they cannot live the way Henry Miller once lived. Yet no American writer, not even Hemingway, necessarily came closer to the crazy bliss of being alone in a strange city with no money in your pocket, not much food in your stomach, and a hard-on beginning to stir, a "personal" hard-on (as one of Miller's characters nicely describes it).

The paradox therefore persists. It is a wonder. To read *Tropic of*

Cancer today is to take in his dimension. He is a greater writer than one thought. It is one of the few great novels of our American century, a revolution in style and consciousness equal to *The Sun Also Rises.* You cannot pass through the first twenty pages without knowing that a literary wonder is taking place — nobody has ever written in just this way before, nobody may ever write by this style so well again. A time and a place have come to focus in a writer's voice. It is like encountering an archaeological relic. Given enough such novels, the history of our century could never be lost: there would be enough points of reference.

It is close therefore to incomprehensible that a man whose literary career has been with us over forty years, an author who wrote one novel that may yet be considered equal to the best of Hemingway, and probably produced more than Thomas Wolfe day by day, and was better word for word, and purple passage for purple passage, a writer finally like a phenomenon, has somehow, with every large acceptance, and every respect, been nonetheless ignored and near to discarded.

We must assume there was something indigestible about Miller which went beyond his ideas. His condemnations are virtually comfortable to us today, yet he is not an author whose complexities are in harmony with our own. Hemingway and Fitzgerald may each have been outrageous pieces of psychic work, yet their personalities haunt us. Faulkner inspires our reverence and Wolfe our tenderest thoughts for literary genius. They are good to the memories we keep of our reading of them — they live with the security of old films. But Miller does not. He is a force, a value, a literary sage, and yet in the most peculiar sense he does not become more compatible with time — he is no better beloved today than twenty, thirty, or forty years ago — it is as if he is almost not an American author; yet nobody could be more American. So he evades our sense of classification. He does not become a personality, rather he maintains himself as an enigma.

The authors who live best in legend offer personalities we can comprehend like movie stars. Hemingway and Fitzgerald impinge on our psyche with the clarity of Bogart and Cagney. We comprehend them at once. Faulkner bears the same privileged relation to a literary Southerner as Olivier to the London theatregoer. A grand and cultivated presence is enriching the marrow of your life. Nobody wishes to hear a bad story about Olivier or Faulkner.

Henry Miller, however, exists in the same relation to legend that anti-matter shows to matter. His life is antipathetic to the idea of legend itself. Where he is complex, he is too complex — we do not feel the resonance of slowly dissolving mystery but the madness of too many knots; where he is simple, he is not attractive — his air is harsh. If he had remained the protagonist by which he first presented himself in *Tropic of Cancer* — the man with iron in his phallus, acid in his mind, and some kind of incomparable relentless freedom in his heart, that paradox of tough misery and keen happiness, that connoisseur of the spectrum of odors between good sewers and bad sewers, a noble rat gnawing on existence and impossible to kill, then he could indeed have been a legend, a species of Parisian Bogart or American Belmondo. Everybody would have wanted to meet this post-gangster, barbarian-genius. He would have been the American and heterosexual equivalent of Jean Genet. But that was not his desire. Paradoxically, he was too separate from his work.

In fact, he could never have been too near to the character he made of himself in *Tropic of Cancer*. One part never fits. It is obvious he must have been more charming than he pretends — how else account for all the free dinners he was invited to, the people he lived on, the whores who loved him? There had to be something angelic about him. Anaïs Nin when describing the apartment in Clichy that Miller kept with Alfred Perles made the point that Miller was the one tidying the joint. "Henry keeps house like a Dutch housekeeper. He is very neat and clean. No dirty dishes about. It is all monastic, really, with no trimmings, no decoration."* Where in all of *Tropic of Cancer* is this neat and charming man?

The novel must be more a fiction than a fact. Which, of course, is not to take away a particle of its worth. Perhaps it becomes even more valuable. After all, we do not write to recapture an experience, we write to come as close to it as we can. Sometimes we are not very close, and yet, paradoxically, are nearer than if we had a photograph. Not nearer necessarily to the verisimilitude of what happened, but to the mysterious reality of what can happen on a page. Oil paints do not create clouds but the image of clouds; a page of manuscript can only evoke that special kind of reality which lives on the skin of the writing paper, a rainbow on a soap bubble. Miller is

---

* *The Diary of Anaïs Nin* (*Vol. 1*) (New York: The Swallow Press and Harcourt, Brace & World, Inc., 1966), p. 62.

forever accused of caricature by people who knew his characters, and any good reader knows enough about personality to sense how much he must be leaving out of his people. Yet, what a cumulative reality they give us. His characters make up a Paris more real than its paving stones until a reluctant wonder bursts upon us — no French writer, no matter how great, not Rabelais, nor Proust, not De Maupassant, Hugo, Huysmans, Zola or even Balzac, not even Céline, has made Paris more vivid to us. Whenever before has a foreigner described a country better than its native writers? For in *Tropic of Cancer* Miller succeeded in performing one high literary act: he created a tone in prose which caught the tone of a period and a place. If that main character in *Tropic of Cancer* named Henry Miller never existed in life, it hardly matters — he is the voice and spirit which existed at the time. The spirits of literature may be the nearest we come to historical truth.

For that matter, the great confessions of literature are apart from their authors. Augustine recollecting his sins is not the sinner but the pieties. Stendhal is not Julian Sorel, nor Kierkegaard the seducer. *On the Road* is close to Jack Kerouac, yet he gives a happier Kerouac than the one who died too soon. Proust was not his own narrator, even as homosexuality is not heterosexuality but another land, and if we take *The Sun Also Rises* as the purest example of a book whose protagonist created the precise air of a time and a place, even there we come to the realization that Hemingway at the time he wrote it could not have been equal to Jake Barnes — he had created a consciousness wiser, drier, purer, more classic, more sophisticated and more graceful than his own. He was still gauche in relation to his creation.

The difference between Hemingway and Miller is that Hemingway set out thereafter to grow into Jake Barnes and locked himself for better and worse, for enormous fame and eventual destruction, into that character who embodied the spirit of an age. Miller, following, had only to keep writing *Tropic of Cancer* over and over, refining his own personality to become less and less separate from his book, and he could have entered the American life of legend. But Henry, eight years older than Hemingway, yet arriving at publication eight years later, and so sixteen years older in 1934 than Hemingway was in 1926, chose to go in the opposite direction. He proceeded to move away from the first Henry Miller he had created. He did not wish to be a character but a soul — he would be various. He was.

The cruelest criticism ever delivered of Henry James is that he had a consciousness (and a style) so hermetic that his pen would have been paralyzed if one of his characters had ever entered a town house, removed his hat, and found a turd on his head (a matter we would hope of small moment to Tolstoy or to Dostoyevsky or to Stendhal). Hemingway would have been bothered more than he liked. Miller would have loved it. How did his host react to the shit? How did our host's wife? My God, the way she smacked her nostrils, you can be sure her thighs were in a lather.

In fact, Hemingway would have hated such a scene. He was trying to create a world where mood — which Hemingway saw as the staff of life — could be cultivated by the scrupulosity with which you kept mood aloft. Mood surviving through the excellence of your gravity, courage, and diction, that is to say, your manners.

Hemingway's dreams must have looked down the long vista of his future suicide. So he had a legitimate fear of chaos. He never wrote about the river — he contented himself with the quintessentially American aesthetic of writing about the camp he set up each night by the side of the river: That was the night we made camp at the foot of the cliffs just after the place where the rapids were bad.

Miller became the other half of literature, an *espontaneo* without fear of his end, a literary athlete at ease in air, earth, or water. I am the river, he was always ready to say, I am the rapids and the placids, I'm the froth and the scum and the twigs — what a roar as I go over the falls. Who gives a fart? Let others camp where they may. I am the river and there is nothing I can't swallow.

Hemingway's world was doomed to collapse so soon as the forces of the century pushed life into a technological tunnel; with Hemingway, mood could not survive grinding gears, surrealist manners — here's shit in your hat — static, but Miller took off at the place where Hemingway stopped. In *Tropic of Cancer* he was saying — and it is the force of the book — I am obliged to live where mood is in the meat grinder, so I know more about it. I know all of the spectrum that runs from good mood to bad mood, and can tell you — a stinking mood is better than no mood. Life has been designed to run in the stink.

Miller bounces in it. We read *Tropic of Cancer*, that book of horrors, and feel happy. It is because there is honor in the horror, and metaphor in the hideous. How, we cannot even begin to say. Maybe, mood is vastly more various, self-regenerative, hearty and sly than Hemingway ever guessed. Maybe mood is not a lavendar lady, but a barmaid. Without stoicism or good taste, or even a nose for the nicety of good guts under terrible pressure, Miller is still living closer to death than Hemingway, certainly he is closer if the sewer is nearer to our end than the wound.

History proved to be on Miller's side. Twentieth-century life was leaving the world of individual effort, liquor, and tragic wounds, for the big-city garbage can of bruises, migraines, static, mood chemicals, amnesia, absurd relations, and cancer. Down in the sewers of existence where the cancer was being cooked, Miller was cavorting. Look, he was forever saying, you do not have to die of this crud. You can breathe it, eat it, suck it, fuck it, and still bounce up for the next day. There is something inestimable in us if we can stand the smell. Considering where the world was going — right into the world wide sewer of the concentration camps — Miller may have had a message that gave more life than Hemingway.

Papa & Son

❧

What characterizes every book about Hemingway I have read is
the way his character remains out of focus. Even a writer with an
edge as hard as Lillian Ross did not seem able to catch him properly
in her famous *New Yorker* piece. Hemingway was there, but much
too precise in his portrait, as if he had sat for one of those neo-realis-
tic paintings where the pride of the artist is to make the subject look
as if he has been photographed, not painted.

For contrast, there is Carlos Baker's monumental biography and
it gives us an immense amount of day-to-day material somewhat
modestly undigested. It is nonetheless an invaluable book which
every ambitious biography to come will evaluate detail by detail, a
necessary task, for Baker's book was written with a determinedly
soft focus as if the author felt his literary mission was not so much to
present the man as to cover every year of Hemingway's existence in
the recollections of his friends.

There is also A. E. Hotchner's book which gives a portrait, and
most readable it is, but askew. Hotchner is using a wide-angle lens;
the very nostrils of the great man are distorted. Sadly we learn there
is reason to believe the materials are transposed. A long and marvelously articulated speech which Hemingway makes once to
Hotchner turns out in fact to have been taken from a letter. It is a
minor literary peccadillo of the sort professional magazine writers

commit often, since their skills mature in a school that demands you tell your story fast and make it track (and a quotation from a letter comes off slower than a man talking), but such methods breed distortion with their speed.

Now, we have here a book* written by a son about his father, written by a son who is not a professional writer as he is quick to tell you (although he can write interestingly enough — it may even be a book which will be read at one sitting by more than half the readers who pick it up). That is because it is unlike most books written by sons about great fathers. There is nothing slavish here. The son lies to the father, and the father pays him back, meanly; the son loves the father and the father loves him back, but in his own style, and it is remote enough for the son to hate him a little as well. If it is a portrait written in love, it is with all the sweets and sours of love. What characterizes love when not wholly blissful is how damnably sweet and sour it gets. It kills any man or woman if they have the bad luck to be deeply in love with a veritable son of a bitch, and every bad thing we have ever heard about Hemingway can find its echo in this book. You do not have to wonder when you are done why any number of men and women could know Hemingway well and hate him. Yet everything fine, noble, attractive, and splendid in the man comes in with its echo as well. For once, you can read a book about Hemingway and not have to decide whether you like him or not. He is there. By God, he exists. He is a father, good and bad by turns, even sensational and godawful on different days of the year, and his contradictions are now his unity, his dirty fighting and his love of craft come out of the same blood. We can feel the man present before us, and his complexes have now become no more than his moods. His pride and his evasions have become one man, his innocence and sophistication, his honesty and outsize snobbery, his romantic madness and inconceivably practical sense of how to be outrageously romantic, it all comes through as in no other book about Hemingway, and for the simplest reason — the father was real to the son. Whereas those of us who approach Hemingway from without have been in the position of trying to find the reality behind the legend, and that is an especially contemporary form of analysis which tends to come out wrong. Hemingway, when all is said, was a Midwestern boy seized by success and ripped out of every root, and

---

* *Papa* by Gregory H. Hemingway, M.D.

he spent the rest of his life in trying to relocate some of his old sense of terra firma by following each movement of the wind (and there were many) through his talent and his dread. What a remarkable achievement, that the sense of that talent and dread, while hardly ever referred to in these pages, is nonetheless in every paragraph of this unassuming and affective memoir.

My Friend,
Jean Malaquais

♪

I did not like this book* twenty years ago, and thought it disappointing. Since I had learned as much about writing from the author as from anyone alive, large demands were put upon the manuscript. Jean Malaquais was not only my good friend, perhaps even my best friend, but my mentor, more — he had had more influence upon my mind than anyone I ever knew from the time we had gotten well acquainted while he was translating *The Naked and the Dead* into French. Part of the friendship rested on his candor. He is hardly rich now, and he was poor then, as only a French intellectual who teaches an evening course at the New School can be bread-crust poor in New York, and he made no pretense — he was not in love with *The Naked and the Dead.* No, he was doing the translation because he needed the work. It proved a munificent sum. The publisher was giving him $2,000, and in the course of the year, I added another $1,000 out of shame. I had never seen a man work so hard at a job for which he did not have respect. In the year it took him to make that translation, he must have worked eight hours a day, five or six days a week; he was a perfectionist and a French stylist, and hated my prose in that book with much detailed justice: he would draw vectors across the pages to show how sloppily I had repeated words, or worse, *ideas* — how he detested anything slovenly in literature! He had, after all, fashioned the style of his own French prose out of the hungriest inner disciplines. Like Conrad, he was Polish, and also began to learn the language in which he would write

---

* (From an introduction to *The Joker.*)

only after he was out of his adolescence. Conceive of such hungry disciplines when he was a young emigrant from Warsaw who worked in French mines and came to clarify the literature of his new tongue by spending fourteen hours a day in the Bibliothèque Nationale in order to keep warm — it was cold on the winter streets of Paris in the years of the Depression — yes, learned his French by reading and writing in that library with all his imagination, ambitions and privations going into it, and took a post-graduate course in the hierarchical elegance of the tongue by being secretary to André Gide for a period, indeed met his future employer by composing a furious letter on the spur of reading a casual piece the author had done for a literary review.[1]

In those pages, Gide had written that he sometimes wondered if poverty might not have deepened his art. We can imagine the irony with which he would surround so direct a sentimentality. Malaquais, however, pulled up the barbarism and shook it in the air. *You ought to get down on your knees and pray to that God you occasionally pretend to believe in that He has let you be a comfortable bourgeois so you can make your art.* Such was the note of the letter, a howl of ferocity torn right out of the bitterness of trying to write at the maximum of one's possible talents when there was no money in the pocket and no food in the belly. Gide wrote back to apologize. He confessed he had not been thinking of the situation of young writers like Malaquais for whom such words had to be naturally and justifiably intolerable, no, he feared he had been playing too inconsiderately with a conceit; he had wished to startle a number of his confreres who were overconcerned with their sensibility and so had been cushioning themselves against too much shock. He hoped to pose the possible stimulations of shock. But it had been unfeeling to ignore the situation of penniless young men like Malaquais and their sentiments on reading his words.[2] To the letter, Gide pinned a bill,

---

[1] I think it is worth printing Malaquais' corrections (by way of a recent letter) to a few of my biographical facts.

"The library was la bibliothèque Sainte-Genevieve, the only one in Paris that stayed open till 10 P.M. I'd remain there all day long (10–12 hours), often without a meal. At closing time I'd go to Les Halles where, with some luck, I'd be unloading crates of cackling poultry or frozen cabbage. Still, job or no job, I could always grab there an apple or a couple of carrots to keep the man alive."

[2] *From Malaquais' letter:* "Gide's piece, an excerpt from his *Journal* dated March 1935, appeared in the October issue of la Nouvelle Revue Française. I think it was December when I happened to read it. Had you a chance to look it up (cf. Justin O'Brien's transl., Knopf), I am sure you'd agree it was plain sentimental gibberish, and not in the least ironic. Idiocy was the price one had to pay for going along — even for a while — with the Stalinists."

something like ten pre–World War II francs. Let us say the sum might bring back twenty dollars' worth of groceries today. Malaquais tore up the money and mailed the scraps back to Gide. "Do not think," he wrote, "that you can buy a postage stamp for your soul. If you wish to do something for me, do something real, give me a job! Do not throw me crumbs!"

Now came another letter. Would Malaquais come and visit?[3]

"C'est toi, Malaquais?" asked Gide on the day he appeared.

"Oui, c'est moi. C'est toi, Gide?"

Could fifty years have gone by since a younger man had said "toi" to him? Still, it was the period of Gide's growing sympathy for the USSR. How characteristic to be intrigued, therefore, with a young Pole who was both an intellectual and a worker, not only a Marxist, but — perverse prize to esteem — a species of rare Marxist from some rarefied splinter group, the absolute antithesis, therefore, of all those Soviet bureaucrats with whom Gide was now trying to find tillable intellectual ground. All the more intoxicating to listen then to the concentrated polemic of a Marxist who was altogether anti-Soviet — that was in the grain for Gide. He could hardly move toward atheism without encouraging the friendship of every cleric he knew.

So began an intellectual relationship which would continue intermittently for years. If Gide was to absorb little of Marx from Malaquais (which may have been Gide's fault!) the new secretary was to learn a great deal about writing from the master.[4] A decade and a half later during the winter and spring of 1949 while Malaquais was translating *The Naked and the Dead* and we became friends despite his aforesaid abomination of my writing (with which I secretly

---

[3] *From Malaquais' letter:* "G. pinned to his letter a postal order for 100.00 francs (20.00 doll. is about right). I mailed it back, telling him he couldn't buy himself a piece of real estate in paradise at my expense. Not that I was beyond bribery. Had he sent 1.000.00 francs, I might have considered. But for 100.00 francs I'd rather have him stay in hell. That's when he wrote, would I come and visit."

[4] *From Malaquais' letter:* "I was not G's secretary or otherwise in his pay. He did ask me from time to time to do this or that for him — read and comment upon the hundreds of letters (mostly insulting) he had received as a sequel to his two books on Russia; or he'd want me to put some order in his voluminous archives; or call on me at any odd hour for a game of chess; or drag me along the streets through lengthy aimless errands; or drop in my lap a manuscript of his and out of the corners of his eyes watch me as I sniffed over it, and so on. But there was never a question of employment or salary. Yet, it is true that he gave me a helping hand. He had me examined by his doctor, saw to it that I put on a few badly needed pounds of flesh, that I was taken care of when in the hospital, in short possibly kept me from spitting my lungs. And he supported me intermittently when I was writing my first book, and it was he who secured for Galy and myself the Mexican visa which saved our hides."

agreed — was I the first to think that *The Naked and the Dead* was a good novel in spite of its style?) I would be obliged in my turn to pick up Malaquais' literary precepts, live with them, wrestle with their intent, and even absorb one or two while hearing Gide's example cited so repeatedly during debates on style that I came to feel at last as if I knew him, or at least knew something of his taste and how his strictures were formed.

There was nothing slavish about Malaquais, least of all his mind. He was an intellectual sultan, still is, and so my ongoing education in the niceties of good writing was not a simple concert of homage to Gide — Malaquais had for his old employer the comfortable respect we offer a writer whose virtues are prominent but whose lacks are clear in our estimate. After any harangue by Malaquais designed to reduce my truculence toward elegance, severity, and restraint (which virtues were elevated through all of my friend's dialectic in order to purify the quality of *surprise* in one's work — a traditional Gallic presentation under the very shadow of the great literary chef, André G., himself) my mentor was also perfectly capable of saying in an aside, "Of course when it comes to an analysis of history, Gide is like a schoolboy. He has every gift for seizing the paradox of character — he is virtually the first to comprehend that character *is* paradox — but give him a social context and he will lose all instinct for the dialectic."

On reflection, it was true. Gide did not live with dialectic. His mind was singularly particular just where Malaquais' was marvelously abstract. Malaquais had the most powerful ability to move from any particular offered him into the Leviathan of his general theory — he was not a Marxist for nothing! — and trying to argue in his presence was analogous to being drawn with one's brain along a magnetic field of the intellect. Willy-nilly was one's mind reoriented along one Polish Frenchman's poles. Nothing vulgar or bullying about it. Malaquais loathed formula, propaganda, or any variety of thinking which deprived a situation of its nuance. So he was capable of advancing a new thesis, anticipating your objections, stating them with clarity (like Freud disarming his critics) and then would overtake his own verification of your position in the return swing of the dialectic. He would do this with such power that when he argued, the veins in his forehead would throb as though to demonstrate that the human head was obliged to be the natural site if not the very phallus of Mind. Malaquais would have at such times a remarkable resemblance to Picasso — the same noble vault of forehead and workingman's knob of a nose, same characterological determination of chin, same cleft. (Of course, Malaquais might detest the comparison. "What a stinker!" I heard him say once of Picasso.)[5] Still, speaking of genius, I heard Malaquais give a lecture once at the New School. I never heard a better one. For fifty minutes he spoke (without a note) exploring into the recesses of a novelist's unique relation to his time — memory across the years suggests the lecture may have been on Stendhal, or was it Proust? — I only remember the sensation of feeling my intelligence conducted through exercises I might not ordinarily have been able to follow. He had the same intense application of energy upon a given point that one finds only in those few great athletes who bring absolute concentration to every instant of a contest and so reveal to you by their body movement some meanings of the sport. When Malaquais lectured, it was inconceivable that his mind and tongue could separate. To cerebrate was to speak. Once at a party, he went on for hours, dominated the conversation. When his wife later remonstrated, "Jean, you talked nine-tenths of the time," he grunted and said, "I had ten times as much to say." It was not arrogance. Merely his grim estimate of the proportions, grim because this small French Pole with his rugged face and mighty brow, his virile purchase on any question to come his way, this prodigy of debate, this behemoth of orality — he spoke out of the same gusto with which a good appetite devours steak — was a man locked in chains when it came to writing. No author ever had more to be grim about.

With no belief in karma, one might still have to postulate a phenomenon like reincarnation to explain the enormity of Malaquais' woes when he tried to write — only a soul paying in this life for outrages it had performed in another could pass through such suffering. So Malaquais may once have been Gilles de Rais. In the late Forties and the early Fifties when Jean was writing *The Joker*, just those years when I first came to know him well, he would sit at his desk for ten or twelve or fourteen hours a day, every day. It was his boast that he would not get up, not pace around, not break for a meal, no, he would sit, contemplate his page, and would write ... to the tune of two or three hundred words a day. Two hundred words in ten hours! It is twenty words an hour, or a new word every three minutes. Can any torture be more horrifically designed for a man who

---

[5] *From Malaquais' letter:* "Did I ever say of Picasso, 'What a stinker!'? If so, it must have been in relation to some concrete occasion, perhaps his drawing a 'dove of peace' in Stalin's honor."

could deliver an extempore lecture complete in thought, example, and syntax, a work of seven or eight thousand words in less than an hour, to be reduced now, down now, with a pen in his hand, to twenty words in sixty minutes? The culture of the past must have sat on his mind like Gibraltar. How could he dare to write about anything? Given his profound contempt for authors who rushed to place their shoddy artifacts into that small temple where only a few perfect works ought to be installed, how presume to add to the excrementa? So this flame-thrower of a mind (when free at its own unrecorded speech) was now confined to one burning wire which sought to drill a tiny hole into the rock of his weighty regard for the value of literature. A man who sat twelve hours at his desk in meditation might have enjoyed such a life even with no more than two hundred words a day, but Malaquais, like many an author before him, labored in depression and whole fatigue. "Yes," he said once, "if you want to do good work, you must *pisser le sang,*" and he must have pissed the blood of every disappearing ambition into the hours he chained himself to that desk. What an effort! Over two years, then three years of just such work, slowly *The Joker* bored its little hole into the great rock of his resistance to himself, and Malaquais emerged at last with this novel.

2.

I was aghast when I read it. So much had happened in his life. He had escaped from the Germans after being a prisoner of war, then as a man without a passport had slipped out of Occupied France, only to become metamorphosized into a Jew again, obliged still to hide from the Nazis in Cadiz, while haunting visa factories like a character in *The Consul,* then a penniless émigré living by his wits in Venezuela and Mexico for the rest of the war. He had also been a movie-script writer with respectable credits and an award winner of a major literary prize, the Prix Renaudot, as well as the post-war author of a major novel, *Planete Sans Visa,* and a much-lauded war diary, an ideologist, a romantic, a Marxist, a man with a charmingly demonic wife as well as a critic with every elevated instinct for the kill. He had now written a book so empty of the novelistic riches of

his life, that I was in a fury as I read. I had wanted something I was
not receiving. *The Joker* seemed bizarre and unlovable — a tract on
the bureaucratic horrors of the future written in a nineteenth-
century style, an inconglomerate, an *incondominium* of Kafka,
Alice in Wonderland, some TV afternoon laugh-snort, and *Mission
Impossible*. I thought it indigestible; worse, some of the dialogue
was guaranteed to grate your teeth. Perhaps it was the fault of the
translation I suggested in desperation. No, it was a fine translation,
Malaquais insisted. He had worked closely with the translator, a
most intelligent woman.

What was one to do with passages like this?

> "I'm called Bomba," he said, "and she's called Kouka. What's
> your name?"
> I took his hand absent-mindedly and said nothing. He had a
> grip of iron.
> "You're a oner," he said.
> A radio was blasting away on the mantel of a dummy fireplace.
> Mistress Kouka unstoppered one of my jars and plunged her nose
> into it with delight.
> "Oner, punner," she said.

No, Malaquais liked it fine. Nothing wrong with, "You're a
oner."

It was obvious this intellectual conquistador had no feeling for the
little rhapsodies of the English tongue. I told him what I thought of
his book — he had hardly been gentle in his earlier turn on *The
Naked and the Dead* and *Barbary Shore* whose imperfections were
left forever mortal to me by his critique. What unconscious anger
must have been stored in my own reactions; with what an unwitting
hostility I must have gone through his pages. The recognition that
Malaquais was not one of the world's greatest living writers exploded in me a critical response akin in judgment to a slave rebellion. I was obviously trying to forge my escape from all influence;
Malaquais took it like a master. Indeed, it was his turn; if I had been
one attentive student through every severity he visited on my work,
so he absorbed everything I had to say on the faults of *The Joker*,
listened with a half-smile on his face, that painful touch of merriment we feel when good friends are an abyss of agreement apart,
and shook his head gloomily from time to time as if it were all too
possible that what I had to say might even be true.

Still, he always recovered the private heat of that private and indispensable arrogance which had enabled him to drill the wire into the rock. No, he would always finish by saying, it was a modest book and doubtless had its serious flaws; *quand même*, it had its irreducible little value — he thought finally there was something to it. That was to prove a small consolation in the face of his ongoing poverty, and the modest reception when it came out, its even more modest sale, hardcover for a couple of thousand and no paperback, its quick disappearance. Even in France, where the reviews were good, the book did little.

None of that could have offered him much, and in fact he has not published another novel over all these twenty years — perhaps we keep writing fiction until the pressure of everything in the scheme of things which does not desire novels squeezes us back. It could be said that civilization will enter hell when no more good novels are written and the hum of the TV set is the only resonance in our ear — certain enough, at any rate, a novelist feels that void of substance in his soul (which saints refer to as hell) about the time all urge to write a novel has deserted him. Just as it is the human fate to die, so it may be the novelist's fate to stop writing novels — it comes finally out of the baggage of disappointment in one's life, a species of cumulative nothingness, and Malaquais' fictional talents have indeed been silent.*

Still, it was also part of the character, part of the dignity of a master, that my intense dislike of *The Joker* never affected our friendship, in fact may have improved it, for in coming to revere him less and comprehend him a little more, I came also to understand that he was made of the noble material from which the best friendships are formed.

For he was utterly without rancor at my dislike of his work, and it was a soup of good marrow for any friendship to know that the intensity of the critical standard he imposed on others was applicable to himself. Literary criticism had to exist for itself. This is what this good Marxist, full of his own paradox, proceeded to teach me: that there were more important things than vanity or self-expression. One of them was art. Critical standards were the praetorian guard of that most perishable majesty, art. It is, as an original insight, equal to the claim that one has discovered the wheel, but then every artist

---

* He has published a book: "Kierkegaard: Faith and Paradox" which must surely be one of the most extraordinary studies ever done on the Dane. Unfortunately it has not been translated from French to English.

may have to discover this wheel for himself, and I never knew another writer who was as impersonal about his own work and the work of others, friends or enemies, than Malaquais. If we are buddies we must naturally be ready to die for one another on the barricade, was his unspoken premise, but do not ever ask me to approve of a literary performance I cannot respect. Could anything be less American than to be ready to die for friends if they do not agree with you?

It is the last of my debts to Malaquais and far from the smallest. For whenever I cannot write with ease, whenever the weight of the stone I drag up the ramp of my own pyramid becomes onerous, and I wish for any other occupation than the heavy hours of a writer, the example of my good friend Jean is before me, and I bow my head and go to work again. "Start to pity yourself," says the little voice within, "and you will end up working as hard as Malaquais." How many friends can one count on to set examples for a life?

Narcissism

❧

June Edith Smith, Henry Miller's second wife, became a figure of obsessive importance in his work. Seen first as Mara in *Tropic of Cancer*, she is called Mona in his trilogy, *The Rosy Crucifixion*, and that novel covers exhaustively (through sixteen hundred pages) the day-to-day movement of their five years together in New York. If the first book, *Sexus*, was begun in 1940 it was not finished until 1945, and *Plexus* took from 1947 to 1949. *Nexus*, the final volume, was not even started until 1952 nor done before 1959. Close to twenty years is spent on this magnum opus! Of course, he has written other books in the same time, *The Air-Conditioned Nightmare*, *The Time of the Assassins*, *The Books in My Life*, *Big Sur and the Oranges of Hieronymus Bosch*, but he is not far from seventy when he is done. The mysteries of his relation with June-Mara-Mona have so beguiled him that he has spent thirty-six obsessive years first living with her, then writing about her, and he never succeeds, never quite, in making her real to us, that is, novelistically real, like Anna Karenina or Emma Bovary. Instead, she hovers in that tricky space between the actual and the fictional where everything is just out of focus. Indeed, Anaïs Nin in one page of her diary succeeds in making the lady as vivid as Miller ever can. (Yet, no more real.)

> Henry came to Louveciennes with June. As June walked toward me from the darkness of the garden into the light of the door, I saw for the first time the most beautiful woman on earth. A startlingly white face, burning black eyes, a face so alive I felt it would consume itself before my eyes. Years ago I tried to imagine

a true beauty; I created in my mind an image of just such a woman. I had never seen her until last night. Yet I knew long ago the phosphorescent color of her skin, her huntress profile, the evenness of her teeth. She is bizarre, fantastic, nervous, like someone in a high fever. Her beauty drowned me. As I sat before her, I felt I would do anything she asked of me. Henry suddenly faded. She was color and brilliance and strangeness. By the end of the evening I had extricated myself from her power. She killed my admiration by her talk. Her talk. The enormous ego, false, weak, posturing. She lacks the courage of her personality, which is sensual, heavy with experience. Her role alone preoccupies her. She invents drama in which she always stars. I am sure she creates genuine dramas, genuine chaos and whirlpools of feelings, but I feel that her share in it is a pose. That night, in spite of my response to her, she sought to be whatever she felt I wanted her to be. She is an actress every moment. I cannot grasp the core of June.

By the end of the evening I felt as Henry did, fascinated with the face and body which promises so much, but hating her invented self which hides the true one.

Curious! If we fix on Miller's mind rather than June's beauty, Nin could be giving a description of Henry's talent: *startling, burning, phosphorescent, bizarre, fantastic, nervous, in a high fever,* full of *color, brilliance,* and *strangeness,* but possessed of an *enormous ego, false, weak, posturing,* and finally *lacking the courage of* (*its*) *personality,* leaving behind *chaos* and *whirlpools of feelings.* Yet it may be all a *pose.* One *cannot grasp* the core of Henry Miller, and one can come near to *hating* (his) *invented self which hides the true one.*

It works. If one is to judge Miller's talent by the vices of his mind, the result is not unequal to the flaws in June's beauty. No wonder they spend seven years together. It is a relation which proves compulsive yet is stripped of roots; as emotional as blood but as insecure as emotion itself. She will take him a long way in seven years from the hard-nosed Brooklyn hard-on he pictured himself to be when they met. More enterprising than he, wiser about the world, a better hustler, she convinces him to quit work and try to write while she makes their living. If ever there is an inner movement in his life, it is here. We are witness to his first metamorphosis. He changes from a promoter of bad debts and riotous Brooklyn nights, to a faithful and tortured young writer helplessly in love with a voluptuous woman whose maddening lack of center leads him into an awareness of his own lack of identity. He comes to discover all those modern themes that revolve around the difficulty of discovering oneself. Soon he will dive into the pit of recognizing that there may not be any geological fundament in the psyche that we can call identity. Like June, he will have to re-create himself each morning. Soon, he realizes he has been doing it all his life. He has never had to look back in moral guilt because whatever act he committed yesterday could be looked in the eye today. The man who did it was no longer himself. In the act of doing it, he had become another man, free to go in a new direction. It could be 180 degrees away from yesterday's attempt. Tomorrow he may be close again to the man he was day before yesterday, but it will never be the same. Since he has a life full of adventure, mishaps, and constant lack of funds, since June brings in their living as irregularly as changes in the weather, so there is no nicety to his liberation. Miller's new psychic life is more like a scatback scampering upfield on a punt return. He can lose ten yards as easily as gain them. And his head is forever ringing from the last concussion.

His confusion, however, is great; his passivity feels pervasive. He has changed from a stand-up hallway-fucker to an indolent husband-pimp. His wife is having the adventures. He is home doing the writing, sometimes the cooking. The wife is a consummate liar, and makes money off men to the tune of hundred-dollar bills dropped in from the sky, never tells him how, a woman even more changeable than himself, and vastly more bisexual — their love will crash finally when she brings home a girl to live with them, and becomes hooked on the girl. Sixteen hundred pages of *The Rosy Crucifixion* will founder on Miller's inability to penetrate these bisexual depths, or even come near them. He was brought up by a moral code that taught love was attached to the living room; one's family was one's house. The living room carpet was one's rock. Now he floats in a fluid as limitless as amniotic fluid. He has no limbs and his feet are over his head, his eyes smell sounds and his nose feels colors, he is in the confusion of living with a woman even more unpredictable than himself. He will not use the word, it is not in the vein of his literary blood, but our present temperament can have less difficulty in seeing him as a narcissist awash in the uncategorizability of such experience.

Let us look at the word with fresh interest, however. It is too simple to think of the narcissist as someone in love with himself. One can detest oneself intimately and still be a narcissist. What characterizes narcissism best is that the fundamental relationship is with oneself. That same to-and-fro of love and hate which mates feel for one another is experienced within the self. A special kind of insanity always underwrites the narcissist, therefore. The inner dialogue almost never ceases. Each half of oneself is forever scrutinizing the other. Two narcissists in love are not like two lovers who may feel a visceral need holding them together. Narcissists, rather, are linked up into themselves. They do not attach to each other so much as they approach like crystals brought into communication. They have a passionate affair to the degree that each makes it possible for the other to resonate more fully than when alone. Two narcissists might live together for fifty years in every appearance of matrimonial solidity (although it probably helps if money is present) but essentially, no matter how considerate they may be to one another, the mutual courtesies come more from the decision to be *loving* rather than issuing forth from a love which will express itself whether one wishes it or not. The narcissistic relation insists that the mate be good for one's own resonance. In the profoundest sense, one narcissist is never ready to die for the other. It is not love we encounter so much as fine tuning. Small wonder that the coming together of narcissists is the natural matrimony of the Stereo Century. Small wonder that Henry Miller, the last great American pioneer, is first to boff and bang his way across this last psychological frontier, there first with the most. No love in literature is so long recounted as his sixteen-hundred-page affair and marriage and separation from Mona. *The Rosy Crucifixion* becomes a literary cake as large as the Himalayas. Across half at least of its sixteen hundred pages are peaks and avenues and haunches and battlements and aretes and basins and summits and valleys of writing so good one shakes one's head. Pity the poor aspiring mediocrity of a writer who reads Miller without protection — he will never write another word if he has any decency left. Pity for that matter the good writer. At times Miller is too good.

Yet *The Rosy Crucifixion* is one of the monumental failures in the history of the novel. For those sixteen hundred pages, Miller knocks on the door of ultimate meaning, and it never opens a crack. By the end he is where he was at the beginning, at least so far as sexual satori is concerned. I-got-laid-and-it-was-wondrous is the opening theme of the book. By the end not one new philosophical connection has been laid onto that first lay. Miller and the reader know no more of the wonders beneath the first wonder.

An obvious critical impulse is to decide the work is too long. But on examination it cannot be cut. Rather, as it stands, it is too fragmentary. Perhaps it should be a novel of four thousand pages. What Miller has bogged into (precisely because he is the first American to make the attempt) is the uncharted negotiations of the psyche when two narcissists take the vow of love. Yet it is finally his own true novelistic terrain. He has always eschewed politics as a literary subject (he merely issues calumnies against it). He has also been indifferent to the finicky if invaluable literary task of trying to place people in society, indeed, he never really writes about society except through metaphor. Since he is a great writer, however, his metaphors can occasionally draw the whole of society over one's brain like an incubus. He does this with his vision of the Cosmodemonic Telegraph Company and the unforgettable metaphor in *Tropic of Cancer* when Miller and Van Norden are exhaustedly fucking a worn-out whore like men standing up in the trenches.

His preference, however, is to create his literary world through the dreams and myths that are appropriate to his use. That has to be a perfumed and farty literary game unless there is real novelistic meat on each mythic tendon. So Miller naturally goes to sex for his meat. He is not a social writer, but a sexual writer. Even Lawrence never let go of the idea that through sex he could delineate society; Miller, however, went further. Sex, he assumed, was a natural literary field for the novel, as clear and free and open to a landgrab as any social panorama. One could capture the sex-life of two people in all its profundity and have quite as much to say about the cosmos as any literary plot laid out the other way with its bankers and beggars, ladies and whores, clerks and killers. The real novel, went Miller's assumption, could short-circuit society. Give it to us by way of a cunt impaled on a cock.

That is a herculean assumption. Because you need the phallus of Hercules to bring it off (and conceivably the brain of Einstein). A writer works with what he is given, and in Miller's case, for cosmic blast-off, he had a narcissistic cunt on a narcissistic cock and thirty-six years of bewilderment from the day of meeting his love to the hour he finished writing of her. She was so *changeable* went his everlasting lament.

It is hard enough for a man twisting a pencil through the traps and loops of his handwriting to get a character onto an empty page, but to create someone who shifts all the time! As soon teach one's spine to wind like a snake. The narcissist is always playing roles. If there is any character more difficult for an author to create than a writer more talented than himself, it must be a great actor. We do not even begin to comprehend the psychology of actors. Yet the narcissist not being obliged to conform to the severe discipline of the stage or the camera, is, in effect, on the measure of complexity, a great actor without a stage, a Hamlet without a sea of faces to listen to what is nobler.

The narcissist suffers from too much inner dialogue. The eye of one's consciousness is forever looking at one's own action. Yet — let us try to keep the notion clear — a narcissist is not self-absorbed so much as one self is immersed in studying the other. The narcissist is the scientist and the experiment in one. Other people exist, have value to the narcissist because of their particular ability to arouse one role or another in oneself. And are valued for that. May even be loved for that. Of course, they are loved as an actor loves his audience.

Since the amount of stimulation we can offer ourselves is obviously limited, the underlying problem of the narcissist is boredom. So there are feverish, even violent, attempts to shift the given. One must alter that drear context in which one half of the self is forever examining the stale presence of the other. That is one reason why narcissists are forever falling in and out of love, jobs, places, and addictions. Promiscuity is the opportunity to try a new role. The vanity gained from a one-night stand is an antidote to claustrophobia. That is, if the gamble of the one-night stand turns out well! Miller complains bitterly of June's lack of center, her incapacity to tell the truth or even recognize it. "I want the key," he says once to Anaïs Nin, "the key to the lies." Blind to himself — does not every artist have to live in partial and self-induced blindness, or he could never find a foundation for his effort? — Miller does not want to recognize that the key may be simple. Every day is a scenario for June. On the best of days she creates a life into which she can fit for a few hours. She can feel real love and real hate for strangers, and thereby leave the circle of her self-absorption. Through scenarios, she can arrive in an hour at depths of emotion other people voyage toward for years. Of course, the scenario once concluded, so, too, is

the love for the day. The passing actor she played with is again a
stranger. It is useless to speak of whether she loves or does not love
Miller. It depends on whether he is in her scenario that day. So it is
also useless to speak of her lies. They are no more real to her than
yesterday's role. It is today's scenario that is her truth and her life.
That is her liberty from the prison cell of the narcissist.

Of course, it is not all that bad. Part of Miller's continuing literary
obsession with June is due to the variety of her roles. Each, after all,
offers its new role for Miller. He does play opposite the leading lady.
If one day he is a detective, and the next, a criminal, that keeps interest in one's personality alive.

Narcissists, after all, induce emotion in one another through their
minds. It is not their flesh which is aroused so much as the vibrancy
of the role. Their relations are at once more electric and more
empty, more perfect and more hollow. But the hollow seems never
to fill, experience is poured into no vessels of the psyche, but seems
to drain away. So, narcissism may be a true disease, a biological displacement of the natural impulse to develop oneself by the lessons
of one's experience, which could bear the same relation to love that
onanism does to copulation, or cancer to the natural growth of tissue. Can we come a little nearer to the recognition that there may be
a base beneath all disease, an ultimate disease, a psychosomatic
doom, so to speak, against which all the other illnesses, colds, fevers,
infections, and deteriorations are bulwarks to protect us against a
worse fate? Which is none other than that irreversible revolt of the
flesh or the mind into cancer or insanity. That is psychosomatic
doom — to follow the growth of the flesh or the mind into hideous
anomaly. But if that is the case, how can we not suppose that for the
narcissist — always so aware that something is wrong within —
there is a constant unconscious terror: his or her isolation, if unre-
lieved, will end in one arm or the other of the ultimate disease.

The paradox is that no love can prove so intense, therefore, as the
love of two narcissists for each other. So much depends on it.
Each — the paradox turns upon itself — is capable of offering de-
liverance to the other. To the degree that they tune each other superbly well, they begin to create what before had been impossible — they begin to acquire the skills that enable them to enter the
world. (For it is not love of the self, but dread of the world outside
the self, which is the seed of narcissism.) Narcissists can end, therefore, by having a real need of each other. That is, of course, hardly

the characteristic relation. The love of most narcissists tends to become comic. Seen from the outside, their suffering manages to be equaled only by the rapidity with which they recover from suffering.

The reality, of course, is considerably more painful. Given the delicacy of every narcissist, and the timidity which created their detachment, we can see again that the intensity of their relations is for good cause with themselves. For their own self-protection, they need an excess of control over external events. (Not too removed in analogy is that excess of control which technology is forever trying to exact from nature.)

To the degree, however, that narcissism is an affliction of the talented, the stakes are not small, and the victims are playing a serious game right in the midst of their scenarios. For if one can break out of the penitentiary of self-absorption, then there may be artistic wonders to achieve.

Miller could have been playing, therefore, for the highest stakes. He had the energy, the vision, the talent, and the outrageous individuality to have some chance of becoming the greatest writer in America's history, a figure equal to Shakespeare. (For Americans.) Of course, to invoke such contrasts is to mock them. A writer cannot live too seriously with the idea that he will or will not beat Tolstoy — he has rather some sense of a huge and not impossible literary destiny in the reverberations of his own ambition; he feels his talent, perhaps, as a trust; so he sees his loves as evil when they balk him. He is living, after all, with his own secret plot. He knows that a writer of the largest dimension can alter the nerves and marrow of a nation; no one, in fact, can measure what collective loss would have come to English people if Shakespeare had failed to write. (Or, for that matter, conceive how the South would be subtly less interesting without Faulkner.)

In those seven years with June, Miller was shaping the talent with which he would go out into the world. It is part of the total ambiguity of narcissism (despite the ten thousand intimate details he offers of his life) that we do not know by the end of *The Rosy Crucifixion* whether she breathed a greater life into his talent or exploited him. We do not know whether Miller if he had never met Mona could have become something like equal to Shakespeare and capable of writing about tyrants and tycoons (instead, repetitively, of his own liberation) or — we are left wide open — the contrary is the true possibility and he might never have written at all if he had not met her. All we know is that after seven years of living with her, he went off to Paris alone and learned to live by himself, having come into that confluence of his life where he could extract a clean and unforgettable aesthetic from ogres and sewers. It is kin to the nightmare of narcissism that we are left with this question and no answer.

Tango, Last Tango

⚘

To pay one's $5.00 and join the full house at the Translux for the evening show of *Last Tango in Paris* is to be reminded once again that the planet is in a state of pullulation. The seasons accelerate. The snow which was falling in November had left by the first of March. Would our summer arrive at Easter and end with July? It is all that nuclear radiation, says every aficionado of the occult. And we pullulate. Like an ant-hive beginning to feel the heat.

We know that Spengler's thousand-year metamorphosis from Culture to Civilization is gone, way gone, and the century required for a minor art to move from commencement to decadence is off the board. Whole fashions in film are born, thrive, and die in twenty-four months. Still! It is only a half year since Pauline Kael declared to the readers of *The New Yorker* that the presentation of *Last Tango in Paris* at the New York Film Festival on October 14, 1972, was a date that "should become a landmark in movie history — comparable to May 29, 1913 — the night *Le Sacre du Printemps* was first performed — in music history," and then went on to explain that the newer work had "the same kind of hypnotic excitement as the *Sacre*, the same primitive force, and the same jabbing, thrusting eroticism. . . . Bertolucci and Brando have altered the face of an art form." Whatever could have been shown on screen to make Kael pop open for a film? "This must be the most powerfully erotic movie ever made, and it may turn out to be the most liberating movie ever made. . . ." Could this be our own Lady Vinegar, our quintessential cruet? The first frigid of the film critics was treating us to her first public reception. Prophets of Baal, praise Kael! We had obviously no ordinary hour of cinema to contemplate.

Now, a half year later, the movie is history, has all the palpability of the historic. Something just discernible has already happened to humankind as a result of it, or at least to that audience who are coming in to the Translux to see it. They are a crew. They have unexpected homogeneity for a movie audience, compose, indeed, so thin a sociological slice of the New York and suburban sausage that you cannot be sure your own ticket isn't what was left for the toothpick, while the rest of the house has been bought at a bite. At the least, there is the same sense of aesthetic oppression one feels at a play when the house is filled with a theater party. So, too, is the audience at *Tango* an infarct of middle-class anal majesties — if Freud hadn't given us the clue, a reader of faces could decide all on his own that there had to be some social connection between sex, shit, power, violence, and money. But these middle-class faces have advanced their historical inch from the last time one has seen them. They are this much closer now to late Romans.

Whether matrons or young matrons, men or boys, they are *swingers*. The males have wife-swapper mustaches, the women are department-store boutique. It is as if everything recently and incongruously idealistic in the middle class has been used up in the years of resistance to the Vietnamese War — now, bring on the Caribbean. Amazing! In America, even the Jews have come to look like the French middle class, which is to say that the egocentricity of the Fascist mouth is on the national face. Perhaps it is the five-dollar admission, but this audience has an obvious obsession with sex as the confirmed core of a wealthy life. It is enough to make one ashamed of one's own obsession (although where would one delineate the difference?). Maybe it is that this audience, still in March, is suntanned, or at the least made up to look suntanned. The red and orange of their skins will match the famous "all uterine" colors — so termed by the set designer — of the interiors in *Last Tango*.

In the minute before the theater lights are down, what a tension is in the house. One might as well be in the crowd just before an important fight commences. It is years since one has watched a movie begin with such anticipation. And the tension holds as the projection starts. We see Brando and Schneider pass each other in the street. Since we have all been informed — by *Time* no less — we know they are going to take carnal occupation of each other, and very soon. The audience watches with anxiety as if it is also going to be in the act with someone new, and the heart (and for some, the bowels) shows a tremor between earthquake and expectation. Maria Schneider is so sexual a presence. None of the photographs has prepared anybody for this. Rare actresses, just a few, have flesh appeal. You feel as if you can touch them on the screen. Schneider has nose appeal — you can smell her. She is every eighteen-year-old in a mini-skirt and a maxi-coat who ever promenaded down Fifth Avenue in the inner arrogance that proclaims, "My cunt is my chariot."

We have no more than a few minutes to wait. She goes to look at an apartment for rent, Brando is already there. They have passed in the street, and by a telephone booth; now they are in an empty room. Abruptly Brando cashes the check Stanley Kowalski wrote for us twenty-five years ago — he fucks the heroine standing up. It solves the old snicker of how do you do it in a telephone booth? — he rips her panties open. In our new line of *New Yorker*–approved superlatives, it can be said that the cry of the fabric is the most thrilling sound to be heard in World Culture since the four opening notes of Beethoven's Fifth.[1] It is, in fact, a hell of a sound, small, but as precise as the flash of a match above a pile of combustibles, a way for the director to say, "As you may already have guessed from the way I established my opening, I am very good at movie making, and I have a superb pair, Brando and Schneider — they are sexual heavyweights. Now I place my director's promise upon the material: you are going to be in for a grave and wondrous experience. We are going to get to the bottom of a man and a woman."

So intimates Bertolucci across the silence of that room, as Brando and Schneider, fully dressed, lurch, grab, connect, hump, scream, and are done in less than a minute, their orgasms coming on top of one another like trash cans tumbling down a hill. They fall to the floor, and fall apart. It is as if a hand grenade has gone off in their entrails. A marvelous scene, good as a passionate kiss in real life, then not so good because there has been no shot of Brando going up Schneider, and since the audience has been watching in all the som-

---

[1] John Simon, as predictable in his critical reactions as a headwaiter, naturally thought *Last Tango* was part of the riff-raff. Since it is Simon's temper to ignore details, he not only does not hear the panties tearing (some ears reside in the music of the spheres) but announces that Schneider, beasty abomination, is wearing none.

ber awe one would bring to the first row of a medical theater, it is like seeing an operation without the entrance of the surgeon's knife.

One can go to any hard-core film and see fifty phalluses going in and out of as many vaginas in four hours (if anyone can be found who stayed four hours). There is a monumental abstractedness about hard core. It is as if the more a player can function sexually before a camera, the less he is capable of offering any other expression. Finally, the sexual organs show more character than the actors' faces. One can read something of the working conditions of a life in some young girl's old and irritated cunt, one can even see triumphs of the human spirit — old and badly burned labia which still come to glisten with new life, capital! There are phalluses in porno whose distended veins speak of the integrity of the hardworking heart, but there is so little specific content in the faces! Hard core lulls after it excites, and finally it puts the brain to sleep.

But Brando's real cock up Schneider's real vagina would have brought the history of film one huge march closer to the ultimate experience it has promised since its inception (which is to re-embody life). One can even see how on opening night at the Film Festival, it did not matter so much. Not fully prepared for what was to come, the simulated sex must have quivered like real sex the first time out. Since then we have been told the movie is great, so we are prepared to resist greatness, and have read in *Time* that Schneider said, " 'We were never screwing on stage. I never felt any sexual attraction for him . . . he's almost fifty you know, and' — she runs her hand from her torso to her midriff, 'he's only beautiful to here!' "

So one watches differently. Yes, they *are* simulating. Yes, there is something slightly unnatural in the way they come and fall apart. It is too stylized, as if paying a few subtle respects to Kabuki. The real need for the real cock of Brando into the depths of the real actress might have been for those less exceptional times which would follow the film long after it opened and the reaction had set in.

Since *Tango* is, however, the first major film with a respectable budget, a superbly skilled young director, an altogether accomplished cameraman, and a great actor who is ready to do more than dabble in improvisation, indeed will enter heavily into such near to untried movie science, so the laws of improvisation are before us, and the first law to recognize is that it is next to impossible to build on too false a base. The real problem in movie improvisation is to

find some ending that is true to what has gone before and yet is sufficiently untrue to enable the actors to get out alive.

We will come back to that. It is, however, hardly time to let go of
our synopsis. Real or simulated, opening night or months later, we
know after five minutes that, at the least, we are in for a thoroughgo-
ing study of a man and a woman, and the examination will be close.
Brando rents the empty apartment; they will visit each other there
every day. His name is Paul, hers is Jeanne, but they are not to learn
each other's names yet. They are not to tell one another such things,
he informs her. "We don't need names here . . . we're going to forget
everything we knew. . . . Everything outside this place is bullshit."

They are going to search for pleasure. We are back in the existential confrontation of the century. Two people are going to fuck in a
room until they arrive at a transcendent recognition or some death
of themselves. We are dealing not with a plot but with a theme that
is open range for a hundred films. Indeed we are face to face with
the fundamental structure of porno — the difference is that we have
a director who by the measure of porno is Eisenstein, and actors
who are as gods. So the film takes up the simplest and richest of
structures. To make love in an empty apartment, then return to a
separate life. It is like every clandestine affair the audience has ever
had, only more so — no names! Every personal demon will be
scourged in the sex — one will obliterate the past! That is the huge
sanction of anonymity. It is equal to a new life.

What powerful biographical details we learn, however, on the instant they part. Paul's wife is a suicide. Just the night before, she has
killed herself with a razor in a bathtub; the bathroom is before us,
red as an abattoir. A sobbing chambermaid cleans it while she
speaks in fear to Paul. It is not even certain whether the wife is a
suicide or he has killed her — that is almost not the point. It is the
bloody death suspended above his life like a bleeding amputated existence — it is with that crimson torso before his eyes that he will
make love on the following days.

Jeanne, in her turn, is about to be married to a young TV director. She is the star in a videofilm he is making about French youth.
She pouts, torments her fiancé, delights in herself, delights in the
special idiocy of men. She can cuckold her young director to the
roots of his eyes. She also delights in the violation she will make of
her own bourgeois roots. In this TV film she makes within the

movie she presents her biography to her fiancé's camera: she is the daughter of a dead Army officer who was sufficiently racist to teach his dog to detect Arabs by smell. So she is well brought up — there are glimpses of a suburban villa on a small walled estate — it is nothing less than the concentrated family honor of the French Army she will surrender when Brando proceeds a little later to bugger her.

These separate backgrounds divide the film as neatly between biography and fornication as those trick highball glasses which present a drawing of a man or a woman wearing clothes on the outside of the tumbler and nude on the inside. Each time Brando and Schneider leave the room we learn more of their lives beyond the room; each time they come together, we are ready to go further. In addition, as if to enrich his theme for students of film, Bertolucci offers touches from the history of French cinema. The life preserver in *Atalante* appears by way of homage to Vigo, and Jean-Pierre Léaud of *The 400 Blows* is the TV director, the boy now fully grown. Something of the brooding echo of *Le Jour Se Lève* and Arletty is also with us, that somber memory of Jean Gabin wandering along the wet docks in the dawn, waiting for the police to pick him up after he has murdered his beloved. It is as if we are to think not only of this film but of other sexual tragedies French cinema has brought us, until the sight of each gray and silent Paris street is ready to evoke the lost sound of the *Bal musette* and the sad near-silent wash of the Seine. Nowhere as in Paris can doomed lovers succeed in passing sorrow, drop by drop, through the blood of the audience's heart.

Yet as the film progresses with every skill in evidence, while Brando gives a performance that is unforgettable (and Schneider shows every promise of becoming a major star), as the historic buggeries and reamings are delivered, and the language breaks through barriers not even yet erected — no general of censorship could know the armies of obscenity were so near! — as these shocks multiply, and lust goes up the steps to love, something bizarre happens to the film. It fails to explode. It is a warehouse of dynamite and yet something goes wrong with the blow-up.

One leaves the theater bewildered. A fuse was never ignited. But where was it set? One looks to retrace the line of the story.

So we return to Paul trying to rise out of the bloody horizon of his wife's death. We even have some instinctive comprehension of how he must degrade his beautiful closet-fuck, indeed we are even given the precise detail that he will grease her ass with butter before he buggers her family pride. A scene or two later, he tricks forth her fear of him by dangling a dead rat which he offers to eat. "I'll save the asshole for you," he tells her. "Rat's asshole with mayonnaise."[2] (The audience roars — Brando knows audiences.) She is standing before him in a white wedding gown — she has run away from a TV camera crew that was getting ready to film her pop wedding. She has rushed to the apartment in the rain. Now shivering, but recovered from her fear, she tells him she has fallen in love with somebody. He tells her to take a hot bath, or she'll catch pneumonia, die, and all he'll get is "to fuck the dead rat."

No, she protests, she's in love.

"In ten years," says Brando looking at her big breasts, "you're going to be playing soccer with your tits." But the thought of the other lover is grinding away at him. "Is he a good fucker?"

"Magnificent."

"You know, you're a jerk. 'Cause the best fucking you're going to get is right here in this apartment."

No, no, she tells him, the lover is wonderful, a mystery . . . different.

"A local pimp?"

"He could be. He looks it."

She will never, he tells her, be able to find love until she goes "right up into the ass of death." He is one lover who is not afraid of metaphor. "Right up his ass — till you find a womb of fear. And then maybe you'll be able to find him."

"But I've found this man," says Jeanne. Metaphor has continued long enough for her. "He's you. You're that man."

In the old scripted films, such a phrase was plucked with a movie composer's chord. But this is improvisation. Brando's instant response is to tell her to get a scissors and cut the fingernails on her right hand. Two fingers will do. Put those fingers up his ass.

"*Quoi?*"

"Put your fingers up my ass, are you deaf? Go on."

No, he is not too sentimental. Love is never flowers, but farts and flowers. Plus every superlative test. So we see Brando's face before us — it is that tragic angelic mask of incommunicable anguish

---

[2] Dialogue from *Last Tango in Paris* was not entirely written in advance, but was in part an improvisation. In other words, a small but important part of the screenplay has in effect been written by Brando.

which has spoken to us across the years of his uncharted heroic depths. Now he is entering that gladiator's fundament again, and before us and before millions of faces yet to come she will be his surrogate bugger, real or simulated. What an entrance into the final images of history! He speaks to us with her body behind him, and her fingers just conceivably up him. "I'm going to get a pig," are the words which come out of his tragic face, "and I'm going to have a pig fuck you," — yes, the touch on his hole has broken open one gorgon of a fantasy — "and I want the pig to vomit in your face. And I want you to swallow the vomit. You going to do that for me?"

"Yeah."

"Huh?"

"Yeah!"

"And I want the pig to die while," — a profound pause — "while you're fucking him. And then you have to go behind, and I want you to smell the dying farts of the pig. Are you going to do that for me?"

"Yes, and more than that. And worse than before."

He has plighted a troth. In our year of the twentieth century how could we ever contract for love with less than five hundred pounds of pig shit? With his courage to give himself away, we finally can recognize the tragedy of his expression across these twenty-five years. That expression has been locked into the impossibility of ever communicating such a set of private thoughts through his beggar's art as an actor. Yet he has just done it. He is probably the only actor in the world who could have done it. He is taking the shit that is in him and leaving it on us. How the audience loves it. They have come to be covered. The world is not polluted for nothing. There is some profound twentieth-century malfunction in the elimination of waste. And Brando is on to it. A stroke of genius to have made a speech like that. Over and over, he is saying in this film that one only arrives at love by springing out of the shit in oneself.

So he seeks to void his eternal waste over the wife's suicide. He sits by her laid-out corpse in a grim hotel room, curses her, weeps, proceeds to wipe off the undertaker's lipstick, broods on her lover (who lives upstairs in the hotel), and goes through some bend of the obscure, for now, off-stage, he proceeds to remove his furniture from the new apartment. We realize this as we see Jeanne in the empty rooms. Paul has disappeared. He has ordered her to march into the farts of the pig for nothing. So she calls her TV director to look at the empty apartment — should they rent it? The profound practicality of the French bourgeoisie is squatting upon us. She appreciates the value of a few memories to offer sauce for her lean marriage. But the TV director must smell this old cooking for he takes off abruptly after telling her he will look for a better apartment.

Suddenly Brando is before her again on the street. Has he been waiting for her to appear? He looks rejuvenated. "It's over," she tells him. "It's over," he replies. "Then it begins again." He is in love with her. He reveals his biography, his dead wife, his unromantic details. "I've got a prostate like an Idaho potato but I'm still a good stick man. . . . I suppose if I hadn't met you I'd probably settle for a hard chair and a hemorrhoid." They move on to a hall, some near mythical species of tango palace where a dance contest is taking place. They get drunk and go on the floor. Brando goes in for a squalid parody of the tango. When they're removed by the judges, he flashes his bare ass.

Now they sit down again and abruptly the love affair is terminated. Like that! She is bored with him. Something has happened. We do not know what. Is she a bourgeoise repelled by his flophouse? Or did his defacement of the tango injure some final nerve of upper French deportment? Too small a motive. Must we decide that sex without a mask is no longer love, or conclude upon reflection that no mask is more congenial to passion than to be without a name in the bed of a strange lover?

There are ten reasons why her love could end, but we know none of them. She merely wants to be rid of him. Deliver me from a fifty-year-old, may even be her only cry.

She tries to flee. He follows. He follows her on the Métro and all the way to her home. He climbs the spiraling stairs as she mounts in the slow elevator, he rams into her mother's apartment with her, breathless, chewing gum, leering. Now he is all cock. He is the memory of every good fuck he has given her. "This is the title shot, baby. We're going all the way."

She takes out her father's army pistol and shoots him. He murmurs, "Our children, our children, our children will remember . . ." and staggers out to the balcony, looks at the Paris morning, takes out his chewing gum, fixes it carefully to the underside of the iron railing in a move that is pure broth of Brando — culture is a goat turd on the bust of Goethe — and dies. The angel with the tragic face slips off the screen. And proud Maria Schneider is suddenly and most unbelievably reduced to a twat copping a plea. "I don't know who he is," she mutters in her mind to the oncoming *flics*, "he followed me in the street, he tried to rape me, he is insane. I do not know his name. I do not know who he is. He wanted to rape me."

The film ends. The questions begin. We have been treated to more cinematic breakthrough than any film — at the least — since *I Am Curious, Yellow*. In fact we have gone much further. It is hard to think of any film that has taken a larger step. Yet if this is "the most powerful erotic film ever made" then sex is as Ex-Lax to the lady. For we have been given a bath in shit with no reward. The film, for all its power, has turned inside out by the end. We have been asked to follow two serious and more or less desperate lovers as they go through the locks of lust and defecation, through some modern species of homegrown cancer cure, if you will, and have put up with their modern depths — shit on the face of the beloved and find love! — only to discover a peculiar extortion in the aesthetic. We have been taken on this tour down to the prostate big as an Idaho potato only to recognize that we never did get into an exploration of the catacombs of love, passion, infancy, sodomy, tenderness, and the breaking of emotional ice, instead only wandered from one onanist's oasis to another.

It is, however, a movie that has declared itself, by the power of its opening, as equal in experience to a great fuck, and so the measure of its success or failure is by the same sexual aesthetic. Rarely has a film's value depended so much on the power or lack of power of its ending, even as a fuck that is full of promise is ready to be pinched by a poor end. So, in *Tango*, there is no gathering of forces for the conclusion, no whirling of sexual destinies (in this case, the audience and the actors) into the same funnel of becoming, no flying out of the senses in pursuit of a new vision, no, just the full charge into a blank wall, a masturbator's spasm — came for the wrong reason and on the wrong thought — and one is thrown back, shattered, too ubiquitously electrified, and full of criticism for the immediate past. Now the recollected flaws of the film eat at the pleasure, even as the failed orgasm of a passionate act will call the character of the passion into question.

So the walk out of the theater is with anger. The film has been in reach of the greatness Kael has been talking about, but the achievement has only been partial. Like all executions less divine than their conception *Tango* will give rise to mutations that are obliged to explore into dead ends. More aesthetic pollution to come! The performance by Brando has been unique, historic, without compare — it is just possible, however, that it has gone entirely in the wrong direction. He has been like a lover who keeps telling consummate dirty jokes until the ravaged dawn when the girl will say, "Did you come to sing or to screw?" He has come with great honor and dignity and exceptional courage to bare his soul. But in a solo. We are being given a fuck film without the fuck. It is like a Western without the horses.

Now the subtle sense of displacement that has hung over the movie is clear. There has been no particular high passion loose. Brando is so magnetic an actor, Schneider is so attractive, and the scenes are so intimate that we assume there is sexual glue between their parts, but it is our libido which has been boiling that glue and not the holy vibration of the actors on the screen. If Kael has had a sexual liberation with *Tango*, her libido is not alone — the audience is also getting their kicks — by digging the snots of the celebrated. (Liberation for the Silent Majority may be not to attend a fuck but hear dirty jokes.) So the real thrill of *Tango* for $5.00 audiences becomes the peephole Brando offers us on Brando. They are there to hear a world-famous actor say in reply to "What strong arms you have,"

"The better to squeeze a fart out of you."
"What long nails you have."
"The better to scratch your ass with."
"Oh, what a lot of fur you have."
"The better to let your crabs hide in."
"Oh, what a long tongue you have."
"The better to stick in your rear, my dear."
"What's this for?"
"That's your happiness and my ha-penis."
Pandemonium of pleasure in the house. Who wants to watch an act of love when the ghost of Lenny Bruce is back? The crowd's joy is that a national celebrity is being obscene on screen. To measure the media magnetism of such an act, ask yourself how many hundreds of miles you might drive to hear Richard Nixon speak a line like: "We're just taking a flying fuck at a rolling doughnut," or "I went to the University of the Congo; studied whale fucking." Only liberal unregenerates would be so progressive as to say they would

not drive a mile. No, one could start mass migrations if Nixon were to give Brando's pig-and-vomit address to the test of love.

Let us recognize the phenomenon. It would be so surrealistic an act, we could not pass Nixon by. Surrealism has become our objective correlative. A private glimpse of the great becomes the alchemy of the media, the fool's gold of the century of communication. In the age of television we know everything about the great but how they fart — the ass wind is, ergo, our trade wind. It is part of Brando's genius to recognize that the real interest of audiences is not in having him portray the tender passages and murderous storms of an unruly passion between a man and a woman, it is rather to be given a glimpse of his kinks. His kinks offer sympathetic vibration to their kinks. The affirmation of passion is that we rise from the swamps of our diapers — by whatever torturous route — to the cock and the cunt; it is the acme of the decadent to go from the first explosive bout of love in *Tango* down to the trimmed fingernails up his rectum.

Then follows the murder. Except it does not follow. It has been placed there from the beginning as the required ending in Bertolucci's mind, it has already been written into the screenplay first prepared with Trintignant and Dominique Sanda in mind. But complications and cast changes occurred. Sanda was pregnant, et cetera. Brando appeared, and Schneider was found. Yet the old ending is still there. Since it did not grow convincingly out of the material in the original script, it appears, after Brando's improvisation, to be fortuitous altogether.

In the original screenplay, the dialogue is so general and the characters so vague that one has to assume Trintignant, Sanda, and Bertolucci planned to give us something extraordinary precisely by overcoming their pedestrian script. It is as if Bertolucci purposely left out whole trunklines of plot in order to discover them in the film. Only it was Brando who came along rather than Trintignant to make a particular character out of a general role, to "superimpose" — in accordance with Bertolucci's desire — his own character as Marlon Brando, as well as something of his life, and a good bit of his private obsessions. As he did that, however, the film moved away from whatever logic the script had originally possessed. For example, in the pre-Brando treatment, we would have been obliged to listen to the following:

LEON (alias Paul): I make you die, you make me die, we're two
murderers, each other's. But who succeeds in realizing this is
twice the murderer. And that's the biggest pleasure: watching you die, watching you come out of yourself, white-eyed,
writhing, gasping, screaming so loud that it seems like the
last time.

Oo la la! We are listening to a French intellectual. It is for good
cause that Bertolucci wants to superimpose Brando's personality.
Anything is preferable to Leon. And Brando most certainly obliter-
ates this mouthy analysis, creates instead a character who is half
noble and half a lout, an overlay drawn on transparent paper over
his own image. Paul is an American, ex-boxer, ex-actor, ex-foreign
correspondent, ex-adventurer, and now with the death of his wife,
ex-gigolo. He is that character and yet he is Brando even more. He is
indeed so much like Brando that he does not quite fit the part of
Paul — he talks just a little too much, and is a hint too distinguished
to be the proprietor of a cheap flophouse at the age of fifty — let us
say that at the least Paul is close enough to the magnetic field of
Marlon for an audience to be unable to comprehend why Jeanne
would be repelled if he has a flophouse. Who cares, if it is Marlon
who invites you to live in a flophouse? On the other hand, he is also
being Marlon the Difficult, Marlon the Indian from the Underworld, Marlon the shade of the alienated, Marlon the young star
who when asked on his first trip to Hollywood what he would like
in the way of personal attention and private creature comfort, points
to the nerve-jangled pet he has brought with him and says, "Get my
monkey fucked."

Yes, he is studying whale-pronging in the Congo. He is the rau-
cous out-of-phase voice of the prairie. Afterwards, contemplating
the failure, we realize he has been shutting Schneider off. Like a
master boxer with a hundred tricks, he has been out-acting her
(with all his miser's hoard of actor's lore), has been stealing scenes
from her while she is nude and he is fully dressed, what virtuosity!
But it is unfair. She is brimming to let go. She wants to give the
young performance of her life and he is tapping her out of position
here, tricking her there — long after it is over we realize he does not
want the fight of the century, but a home town decision. He did not
come to fuck but to shit. To defecate into the open-mouthed wonders of his audience and take his cancer cure in public. It is the fast-
est way! Grease up the kinks and bring in the pigs. We'd take a

stockyard of pigs if he would get into what the movie is about, but he is off on the greatest solo of his life and artists as young as Schneider and Bertolucci are hardly going to be able to stop him.

So he is our greatest actor, our noblest actor, and he is also our national lout. Could it be otherwise in America? Yet a huge rage stirs. He is so great. Can he not be even greater and go to the bottom of every fine actor's terror — which is to let go of the tricks that ring the person and enter the true arena of improvisation? It is there that the future of the film may exist, but we won't find out until a great actor makes the all-out effort.

But now we are back to the core of the failure in *Last Tango*. It is down in the difficulty of improvisation, in the recognition that improvisation which is anything less than the whole of a film is next to no improvisation. It has diminished from the dish to a spice that has been added to the dish (usually incorrectly). Bertolucci is a superb young director, adventurous, steeped in film culture, blessed with cinematic grace. He gives us a movie with high ambition, considerable risk, and a sense of the past. Yet he plows into the worst trap of improvisation — it is the simple refusal of film makers to come to grips with the implacable logic of the problem. One does not add improvisation to a script that is already written and with an ending that is locked up. No matter how agreeable the particular results may be, it is still the entrance of tokenism into aesthetics: "You blacks may work in this corporation, and are free to express yourselves provided you don't do anything a responsible white employee won't do." Stay true to the script. It reduces improvisation to a free play period in the middle of a strict curriculum.

The fundamental demand upon improvisation is that it begin with the film itself, which is to say that the idea for the film and the style of improvisation ought to come out of the same thought. From the beginning, improvisation must live in the premise rather than be added to it. The notion is not easy to grasp, and in fact is elusive. It may even be helpful to step away from *Tango* long enough to look at another example of possible improvisation. An indulgence is asked of the reader — to think about another kind of film altogether, a distracting hitch to the argument, but it may not be possible to bring focus to improvisation until we have other models before us.

So the following and imaginary film is offered: Orson Welles to play Churchill while Burton or Olivier does Beaverbrook in the week of Dunkirk. Let us assume we have the great good fortune to find these actors at the height of their powers, and have for *auteur* a film maker who is also a brilliant historian. To these beginnings, he adds a company of intelligent English actors and gives them the same historical material to study in order to provide a common denominator to everyone's knowledge. At this point the *auteur* and the company agree upon a few premises of plot. The *auteur* will offer specific situations. It will help if the episodes are sufficiently charged for the actors to lose their fear first of improvisation — which is that they must make up their lines.

Then a narrative action can begin to emerge out of the interplay of the characters, in much the way a good party turns out differently from the expectations of the hostess, and yet will develop out of her original conception. With a script, actors try to convince the writer, if he is present, to improve their lines — with improvisation they must work upon their wits. Why assume that the wits of this company of intelligent English actors will have less knowledge of manner and history than an overextended script writer trying to work up his remote conception of what Churchill and Beaverbrook might have been alike? Why not assume Welles and Burton have a better idea? Are they not more likely to contain instinctive knowledge in their ambulating meat? Isn't the company, in its steeping as good British actors into their own history, able to reveal to us more of what such a week might have been like than any but the most inspired effort by a screenwriter?

We all contain the culture of our country in our unused acting skills. While Clark Gable could probably not have done an improvisation to save himself, since he had no working habits for that whatsoever, the suspicion still exists that Gable, if he had been able to permit himself, could have offered a few revelations on the life of Dwight D. Eisenhower, especially since Ike seems to have spent a good part of his life imitating Gable's voice. If violence can release love, improvisation can loose the unused culture of a film artist.

The argument is conceivably splendid, but we are talking about *historical* improvisation where the end is still known, and it is the details that are paramount. How simple (and intense) by comparison become the problems of doing a full improvisation for *Tango*. There we are given a fundamental situation, a spoiled girl about to be married, a distraught man whose wife is a suicide. The man and the girl are in the room to make love. We are back at the same beginning. But we can no longer project ahead! If the actors feel nothing for one another sexually, as Schneider has indicated in several interviews was the case for Brando and herself — she may even have been telling the truth — then no exciting improvisation is possible on sexual lines. (The improvisation would have to work on the consequences of a lack of attraction.) Actors do not have to feel great passion for one another in order to give a *frisson* to the audience, but enough attraction must exist to provide a live coal for improvisation to blow upon. Without some kernel of reality to an improvisation only a monster can continue to offer interesting lines. Once some little attraction is present, there is nothing exceptional about the continuation of the process. Most of us, given the umbilical relation of sex and drama, pump our psychic bellows on many a sensual spark, but then most affairs are, to one degree or another, improvisations, which is to say genuine in some part of their feeling and nicely acted for the rest. What separates professional actors from all of us amateur masses with our animal instinct for dissembling, our everyday acting, is the ability of the professional to take a small emotion in improvisation and go a long distance with it. In a scripted piece of work, some professionals need no relation to the other actor at all, they can, as Monroe once said, "wipe them out" and substitute another face. But improvisation depends on a continuing life since it exists in the no-man's-land between acting and uncalculated response, it is a *special* psychic state, at its best more real than the life to which one afterward returns, and so a special form of insanity. All acting is a corollary of insanity, but working from a script offers a highly controlled means of departing from one's own personality in order to enter another. (As well as the formal power to return.)

What makes improvisation fertile, luminous, frightening, and finally *wiggy* enough for a professional like Gable to shun its practice is that the actor is doing two things at once — playing at a fictitious role, while using real feelings, which then begin to serve (rather than the safety of the script) to stimulate him into successive new feelings and responses, until he is in danger of pushing into emotional terrain that is too far out of his control.

If we now examine *Tango* against this perspective, the risks (once there is real sexual attraction between the man and the woman) have to multiply. They are after all not simply playing themselves, but have rather inserted themselves into highly charged creatures, a violent man with a blood-filled horizon and a spoiled middle-class girl with buried tyrannies. How, as they continue this improvisation, can they avoid falling in love, or coming to hate one another? With good film actors, there is even every real danger that the presence of the camera crew will inflame them further since in every thespian is an orgiast screaming to get out.

So murder is the first dramatic reality between two such lovers in a continuing film of improvisation. They progress toward an end that is frighteningly open. The man may kill the woman, or the woman the man. For, as actors, they have also to face the shame of walking quietly away from one another, a small disaster when one is trying to build intensity, for such a quiet ending is equal to a lack of inspiration, a cowardice before the potential violence of the other. Improvisation is profoundly wicked when it works, it ups the ante, charges all dramatic potential, looks for collision. Yet what a dimension of dramatic exploration is also offered. For the actors can even fall in love, can truly fall in love, can go through a rite of passage together and so reach some locked crypt of the heart precisely because they have been photographed fucking together from every angle, and still — perhaps it is thereby — have found some private reserve of intimacy no one else can touch. Let the world watch. It is not near.

So the true improvisation that *Tango* called for should have moved forward each day on the actors' experience of the day before; it would thereby have offered more aesthetic excitement. Because of its danger! There is a very small line in the last recognitions of the psyche between real bullets in a gun, and blanks. The madness of improvisation is such, the intensities of the will become such, that one hardly dares to fire a blank at the other actor. What if he or she is so carried away by excitement that they will refuse to fall? Bring on the real bullet, then. Bite on it.

Of course, literal murder is hardly the inevitable denouement in improvisation. But it is in the private design of each actor's paranoia. Pushed further together in improvisation than actors have gone before, who knows what literal risks might finally have been taken. That is probably why Brando chose to play a buffoon at a very high level and thereby also chose to put Schneider down. Finally we laugh at those full and lovely tits which will be good only for playing soccer (and she will choose to lose thirty pounds after the film is done — a whole loss of thirty pounds of pulchritude). Brando with his immense paranoia (it is hardly unjustified) may have concluded like many an adventurous artist before him that he was adventuring far enough. No need for more.

Still he lost an opportunity for his immense talent. If he has been our first actor for decades, it is because he has given us, from the season he arrived in *Streetcar*, a greater sense of improvisation out of the lines of a script than any other professional actor. Sometimes he seemed the only player alive who knew how to suggest that he was about to say something more valuable than what he did say. It gave him force. The lines other people had written for him came out of his mouth like the final compromise life had offered for five better thoughts. He seemed to have a charged subtext. It was as if, whenever requested in other films to say script lines so bad as, "I make you die, you make me die, we're two murderers, each other's," the subtext — the emotion of the words he was using behind the words — became, "I want the pig to vomit in your face." That was what gave an unruly, all but uncontrolled, and smoldering air of menace to all he did.

Now, in *Tango*, he had nothing beneath the script, for his previous subtext was the script. So he appeared to us as a man orating, not improvising. But then a long speech can hardly be an improvisation if its line of action is able to go nowhere but back into the prearranged structures of the plot. It is like the aside of a politician before he returns to that prepared text the press already has in their hands. So our interest moved away from the possibilities of the film and was spent on the man himself, his nobility and his loutishness. But his nature was finally a less interesting question than it should have been, and weeks would go by before one could forgive Bertolucci for the aesthetic cacophony of the end.

Still, one could forgive. For, finally, Bertolucci has given us a failure worth a hundred films like *The Godfather*. Regardless of all its solos, failed majesties, and off-the-mark horrors, even as a highly imperfect adventure, it is still the best adventure in film to be seen in this pullulating year. And it will open an abyss for Bertolucci. The rest of his life must now be an improvisation. Doubtless he is bold enough to live with that. For he begins *Last Tango* with Brando muttering two words one can hardly hear. They are: Fuck God.

The unmanageable in oneself must now offer advice. If Bertolucci is going to fuck God, let him really give the fuck. Then we may all know a little more of what God is willing or unwilling to forgive. That is, unless God is old and has indeed forgot, and we are merely out on a sea of human anality, a collective Faust deprived of Mephisto and turning to shit. The choice, of course, is small. Willy-nilly, we push on in every art and every technology toward the re-embodiment of the creation. It is doubtless a venture more demented than coupling with the pig, but it is our venture, our white whale, and by it or with it shall we be seduced. On to the Congo with sex, technology, and the inflamed lividities of human will.

The
Faith of Graffiti

❧

1.

Journalism is chores. Journalism is bondage unless you can see yourself as a private eye inquiring into the mysteries of a new phenomenon. Then you may even become an Aesthetic Investigator ready to take up your role in the twentieth-century mystery play. Aesthetic Investigator! Make the name A-I for this is about graffiti.

A-I is talking to CAY 161. That is the famous Cay from 161st Street, there at the beginning with TAKI 183 and JUNIOR 161, as famous in the world of wall and subway graffiti as Giotto may have been when his name first circulated through the circuits of those workshops that led from Masaccio through Piero della Francesca to Botticelli, Michelangelo, Leonardo and Raphael. Whew! In such company Cay loses his name, although he will not necessarily see it that way. He has the power of his own belief. If the modern mind has moved from Giotto who could find beatitude in a beheading as well as the beginnings of perspective in the flight of angels across the bowl of a golden sky, if we have mounted the high road of the Renaissance into Raphael's celebration of the True, the Good and the Beautiful in each succulent three-dimensionality of the gluteus maximus on out to our own vales and washes in Rothko and Ellsworth Kelly, why so, too, have we also moved from the celebration to the name, traveled from men and women who wrested a degree of independence from Church and God down now to the twentieth-century certainty that life is an image.

A couple of stories:

The first is a Jewish joke. Perhaps it is *the* Jewish joke. Two grandmothers meet. One is pushing a baby carriage. "Oh," says the other, "what a beautiful grandchild you have." "That's nothing," says the first, reaching for her pocketbook. "Wait'll I show you her picture!"

The second seems apocryphal. Willem de Kooning gives a pastel to Robert Rauschenberg who takes it home and promptly erases it. Next he signs his name to the erasure. Then he sells it. Can it be that Rauschenberg is saying, "The artist has as much right to print money as the financier?" Yes, Rauschenberg is giving us small art right here and much instruction. Authority imprinted upon emptiness is money. And the ego is capital convertible to currency by the use of the name. Ah, the undiscovered links of production and distribution in the psychic economy of the ego! For six and a half centuries we have been moving from the discovery of humanity into the circulation of the name, advancing out of some primitive obeisance to dread so complete that painting once lay inert on the field of two dimensions (as if the medieval eye was not ready to wander). Then art dared to rise into that Renaissance liberation from anxiety. The painterly capacity entered the space-perspective of volume and depth. Now, with graffiti we are back in the prison of two dimensions once more. Or is it the one dimension of the name — the artform screaming through space on a unilinear subway line?

Something of all this is in the mind of our Aesthetic Investigator as he sits in a bedroom on West 161st Street in Washington Heights and talks to CAY 161 and JUNIOR 161 and LI'L FLAME and LURK. They talk about the name. He has agreed to do a centerpiece for a book of photographs on graffiti by Jon Naar, has agreed to do it on the instant (in a Los Angeles hotel room) that he has seen it. The splendid pictures and his undiscovered thoughts on the subject leap together. There is something to find in these pictures, thinks A-I, some process he can all but name. The intellectual hedonism of an elusive theme is laid out before him. So, yes, he accepts. And discovers weeks later that his book has already been given a title. It is *Watching My Name Go By*. He explains to the pained but sympathetic ears of his collaborators that an author needs his own title.

Besides, there is a practical reason. Certain literary men cannot afford titles like *Watching My Name Go By*. Norman Mailer may be first in such a category. One should not be able to conceive of one's bad reviews before writing a word.

But then he also does not like *Watching My Name Go By* for its own forthright meaning. These young graffiti writers do not use their own name. They adopt one. It is like a logo. Moxie or Socono, Tang, Whirlpool, Duz. The kids bear a not quite definable relation to their product. It is not MY NAME but THE NAME. Watching The Name Go By. He still does not like it. Yet every graffiti writer refers to the word. Even in newspaper accounts, it is the term heard most often. "I have put my name," says Super Kool to David Shirey of the *Times*, "all over the place. There ain't nowhere I go I can't see it. I sometimes go on Sunday to Seventh Avenue 86th Street and just spend the whole day" — yes, he literally says it — "watching my name go by." But then they all use it. JAPAN I, being interviewed by Jon Naar and A-I in a subway, grins as a station cop passes and scrutinizes him. He is clean. There is no spray can on him today. Otherwise he would run, not grin. Japan says, with full evaluation of his work, "You have to put in the hours to add up the names. You have to get your name around." Since he is small and could hardly oppose too many who might choose to borrow his own immortal JAPAN I, he merely snorts in answer to the question of what he would do if someone else took up his name and used it. "I would still get the class," he remarks.

Whether it is one's own interviews or others, the word which prevails is always the name. MIKE 171 informs *New York Magazine*, "There are kids all over town with bags of paint waiting to *hit* their names." A bona-fide clue. An object is hit with your name, yes, and in the ghetto, a hit equals a kill. "You must kill a thing," said D. H. Lawrence once, "to know it satisfactorily." (But then who else could have said it?) You hit your name and maybe something in the whole scheme of the system gives a death rattle. For now your name is over their name, over the subway manufacturer, the Transit Authority, the city administration. Your presence is on their presence, your alias hangs over their scene. There is a pleasurable sense of depth to the elusiveness of the meaning.

So he sits with Cay and Junior and the others in the bedroom of Junior's parents and asks them about the name. It is a sweet meeting. He has been traveling for all of a wet and icy snowbound Sunday afternoon through the monumental drabs of South Bronx and Washington Heights, so much like the old gray apartment house ranks of Eastern Parkway in Brooklyn near where he grew up, a trip back across three generations. The Puerto Ricans in this apartment may not be so different from the poor ambitious families of relatives his mother would speak of visiting on the Lower East Side when she came as a child up from the Jersey shore to visit. So little has changed. Still the-smell-of-cooking-in-the-walls, a single word, and the black-pocked green stucco of the halls, those dark pits in the plaster speaking of the very acne of apartment house poverty. In the apartment, entering by the kitchen, down through the small living room and past the dark bedrooms in a file off the hall, all the shades drawn, a glimpse has been had of the television working like a votive light in some poor slum church chapel (one damp fire in the rainforest) while the father in shorts sleeps on the sofa, and the women congregate — the kitchen is near. The windows are stained glass, sheets of red and yellow plastic pasted to the glass — the view must be on an air shaft. No light in this gray and late winter day. It is all the darkness of that gloom which sits in the very center of slum existence, that amalgam of worry and dread, heavy as buckets of oil, the true wages of the working class, with all that attendant fever for the attractions of crime, the grinding entrapments of having lost to the law — lawyers' fees, bondsmen, probation officers, all of it.

Yet now there is also a sense of protection in the air. The mood is not without its reverence: CAY 161 has the face of a martyr. He looks as if he has been flung face first against a wall, as if indeed a mighty hand has picked him up and hurled him through the side of a stone house. He is big, seventeen, and almost six feet tall, once good-looking and may yet be good-looking again, but now it is as if he has been drawn by a comic strip artist, for his features express the stars, comets, exclamation points, and straight-out dislocation of eyes and nose and mouth that accompanies any hero in a comic strip when he runs into a collision. SOCK! ZAM! POW! CAY 161, driving a stolen van, fleeing the cops in an old-fashioned New York street chase, has gone off the road on a turn, "and right on 161st Street where he was born and raised, he hit a hydrant, turned over a few times, and wound up inside a furniture store. . . . When the police looked inside the car," — description by José Torres in the N.Y. *Post* — "Cay lay motionless in the driver's seat, and another youth, a passenger, sprawled unconscious outside, hurled from the car by the impact." The friend had a broken leg, and Cay had part of his brain taken out in a seven-hour operation. The doctor gave warning. He might survive. As a vegetable. For two months he did not make a move. Now, six months later, Cay is able to talk, he can move. His lips are controlled on one side of his face but slack on the other — he speaks as if he has had a stroke. He moves in the same fashion. Certain gestures are agile, others come up half-paralyzed and top-heavy, as if he will fall on his face at the first false step. So his friends are his witness. They surround him, offer the whole reverence of their whole alertness to every move he makes. There is all the elegance of good manners in the way they try to conceal that he is different from the others.

But Cay is happy now. He is in Junior's house, JUNIOR 161, his best friend. They used to go out writing together for years, both tall, a twin legend — when one stands on the other's shoulders, the name goes up higher on the wall than for anyone else. True bond of friendship: they will each write the other's name, a sacramental interchange. Junior has a lean body, that indolent ghetto languor which speaks of presence. "I move slow, man," says the body, "and that is why you watch me. Because when I move fast, you got to watch out." He is well dressed, ghetto style — a white turtleneck sweater, white pants, a white felt hat, white sneakers, nothing more. Later he will step out like this into the winter streets. You got to meet the eye of the beholder with class. Freezing is for plants.

A-I interviews them. Yes, they started three years ago and would hit four or five names a day. Junior liked to work at least an hour a day. So go the questions: Cay liked to use red marker, Junior blue. Hundreds of masterpieces to their credit. Yes, Junior's greatest masterpiece is in the tunnel where the track descends from 125th Street to 116th Street. There, high on the wall, is JUNIOR 161 in letters six feet high. "You want to get your name in a place where people don't know how you could do it, how you could get up to there. You got to make them think." It is the peril of the position which calls. Junior frowns on the later artists who have come after Cay and himself. The talk these days is of SLY and STAY HIGH, PHASE 2, BAMA, SNAKE, and STITCH. The article by Richard Goldstein in *New York* (March 26, 1973) has offered a nomenclature for the styles, Broadway, Brooklyn and Bronx, disquisitions on bubble and platform letters. Perhaps his source is BAMA, who has said to another reporter in his full articulate speaking style, "Bronx style is bubble letters, and Brooklyn style is script with lots of flourishes and arrows. It's a style all by itself. Broadway style, these long slim letters, was brought here from Philadelphia by a guy named Topcat. Queens style is very difficult, very hard to read."

Junior is contemptuous of this. The new forms have wiped out respect for the old utilitarian lettering. If Cay likes the work of STAY HIGH, Junior is impressed by none. "That's just fanciness," he says of the new. "How're you going to get your name around doing all that fancy stuff?"

Cay speaks into this with his deep, strangled, and wholly existential voice — he cannot be certain any sound he utters will come out as he thinks. "Everybody tries to catch up to us," he says.

"You have to put in the hours?"

A profound nod.

Of course, he is not doing it any longer. Nor is Junior. Even before the accident, both had lost interest. On the one hand, the police were getting tough, the beatings when you were caught were worse, the legal penalties higher, the supplies of paint getting to be monitored, and on the other hand something had happened to the process itself. Too many names had grown — a jungle of ego creepers.

A-I queries them about the prominence of the name. He hesitates how to pose the question — he fears confidence will be lost if he asks straight-out. "What is the meaning of the name?" but, indeed, he does not have to — Cay speaks up on what it means to watch the name go by. "The name," says Cay, in a full voice, Delphic in its unexpected resonance — as if the idol of a temple had just chosen to break into sound — "The name," says Cay, "is the *faith* of graffiti."

It is quite a remark. He wonders if Cay knows what he has said. "The name," repeats Cay, "is the *faith.*" He is in no doubt of the depth of what he has said. His eyes fix on A-I, his look is severe. Abruptly, he declares that the proper title is "The Faith of Graffiti." So it is.

A Sunday afternoon has come to its end. A-I walks downstairs with Junior, Cay, Lurk and Li'l Flame, and is shown modest examples of their writing on the apartment house walls. Cay has also used another name. At times he has called himself THE PRAYER 161. They say goodbye in the hall. Cay shows A-I the latest 161st Street sequence of thumb-up finger-curled handshakes. The pistol-pointed forefinger and upraised thumb of one man touch the thumb and forefinger of the other in a quick little cat's cradle. Cay's fingers are surprisingly deft. Then he and Junior spar a bit, half-comic for he lurches, but with the incisive tenderness of the ghetto, as if his moves also say, "Size don't come in packages. A cripple keeps the menace." It is agreeable to watch. As he attempts to spar, Cay is actually moving better than he has all day.

The name is the faith of graffiti. Was it true that the only writing which did not gut one's health lay in those questions whose answers were not known from the start? A-I still had no more than a clue to graffiti. Were the answers to be found in the long war of the will against the power of taboo? Who could know when one of the gods would turn in sleep as images were drawn? Was that a thought in the head of the first savage to put the silhouette of an animal on the wall of a cave? If so, the earliest painting had been not two dimensions but one — one, like graffiti — the hand pushing forward into the terror of future punishment. Only later would come an easier faith that the Lord might be on the side of the artist.

2.

No, size doesn't come in packages, and the graffiti writers had been all heights and all shapes, even all the ages from twelve to twenty-four. They had written masterpieces in letters six feet high on the side of walls and subway cars, and had scribbled furtive little toys, which is to say small names without style, sometimes just initials. There was panic in the act for you wrote with an eye over your shoulder for oncoming authority. The Transit Authority cops would beat you if they caught you, or drag you to court, or both. The judge, donning the robes of Solomon, would condemn the early prisoners to clean the cars and subway stations of the names. HITLER 2 (reputed to be so innocent of his predecessor that he only knew Hitler 1 had a very big rep!) was caught, and passed on the word of his humiliation. Cleaning the cars, he had been obliged to erase the work of others. All proportions kept, it may in simple pain of heart have been not altogether unequal to condemning Cézanne to wipe out the works of Van Gogh.

So there was real fear of being caught. Pain and humiliation were implacable dues, and not all graffiti artists showed equal grace under such pressure. Some wrote like cowards, timidly, furtively, jerkily. "Man," was the condemnation of the peers, "you got a messed-up handwriting." Others laid one cool flowering of paint upon another, and this was only after having passed through all the existential stations of the criminal act, even to first *inventing* the paint, which was of course the word for stealing the stuff from the stores. But then, an invention is the creation of something which did not exist before — like a working spray can in your hand. (Indeed, if Plato's Ideal exists, and the universe is first a set of forms, then what is any invention but a theft from the given universal Ideal?)

There was always art in a criminal act — no crime could ever be as automatic as a production process — but graffiti writers were opposite to criminals since they were living through the stages of the crime in order to commit an artistic act — what a doubling of intensity when the artist not only steals the cans but tries for the colors he wants, not only the marker and the color, but steal them in double amounts so you don't run out in the middle of a masterpiece. What a knowledge of cops' habits is called for when any Black or Puerto Rican adolescent with a big paper bag is bound to be examined by a Transit cop if he goes into the wrong station. So after his paint has been invented a writer has to decide by which subway entrance it is to be transported, and once his trip is completed back to the station which is the capital of his turf, he still has to find the nook where he can warehouse his goods for a few hours. To attempt to take the paint out of the station is to get caught. To try to bring it back to the station is worse. Six or seven kids entering a subway in Harlem, Washington Heights, or the South Bronx are going to be searched by Transit cops for cans. So they stash it, mill around the station for a time painting nothing, they are, after all, often in the subways — to the degree they are not chased, it is a natural clubhouse, virtually a country club for the sociability of it all — and when the cops are out of sight, and a train is coming in, they whip out their stash of paint from its hiding place, conceal it on their bodies, and in all the wrappings of oversize ragamuffin fatigues, get on the cars to ride to the end of the line where in some deserted midnight yard they will find their natural canvas which is of course that metal wall of a subway car ready to reverberate into all the egos on all the metal of New York, what an echo that New York metal will give into the slapped-silly senses of every child-psyche who grew up in New York, yes, metal as a surface on which to paint is even better than stone.

But it is hardly so quick or automatic as that. If they are to leave the station at the end of the line, there is foreign turf to traverse which guarantees no safe passage, and always the problem of finding your way into the yards.

In the A-train yard at 207th Street, the unofficial entrance was around a fence that projected out over a cliff and dropped into the water of the Harlem River. You went out one side of that fence on a narrow ledge, out over the water, and back the other side of the fence into the yards "where the wagons," writes Richard Goldstein, "are sitting like silent whales."

We may pick our behemoth — whales and dinosaurs, elephants folded in sleep. At night, the walls of cars sit there possessed of soul — you are not just writing your name but trafficking with the iron spirit of the vehicle now resting. What a presence. What a consecutive set of iron sleeping beasts down all the corrals of the yard, and the graffiti writers stealthy as the near-to-silent sound of their movements working up and down the line of cars, some darting in to squiggle a little toy of a name on twenty cars — their nerve has no larger surge — others embarking on their first or their hundred-and-first masterpiece, daring the full enterprise of an hour of living with this tension after all the other hours of waiting (once they had come into the yard) for the telepathic disturbance of their entrance to settle, waiting for the guards patrolling the lines of track to grow somnolent and descend into the early morning pall of the watchman. Sometimes the graffiti writers would set out from their own turf at dark, yet not begin to paint until two in the morning, hiding for hours in the surest corners of the yard or in and under the trains. What a quintessential marriage of cool and style to write your name in giant separate living letters, large as animals, lithe as snakes, mysterious as Arabic and Chinese curls of alphabet, and to do it in the heart of a winter night when the hands are frozen and only the heart is hot with fear. No wonder the best of the graffiti writers, those mountains of heavy masterpiece production, STAY HIGH, PHASE 2, STAR III, get the respect, call it the glory, that they are known, famous and luminous as a rock star. It is their year. Nothing automatic about writing a masterpiece on a subway car. "I was scared," said Japan, "all the time I did it." And sitting in the station at 158th and St. Nicholas Avenue, watching the trains go by, talking between each wave of subway sound, he is tiny in size, his dark eyes as alert as any small and hungry animal who eats in a garden at night and does not know where the householder with his varmint gun may be waiting.

Now, as Japan speaks, his eyes never failing to miss the collection of names, hieroglyphs, symbols, stars, crowns, ribbons, masterpieces and toys on every passing car, there is a sadness in his mood. The city has mounted a massive campaign. There was a period in the middle when it looked as if graffiti would take over the world, when a movement that began as the expression of tropical peoples living in a monotonous iron-gray and dull brown brick environment, surrounded by asphalt, concrete, and clangor, had erupted to save the sensuous flesh of their inheritance from a macadamization of the psyche, save the blank city wall of their unfed brain by painting the wall over with the giant trees and petty plants of a tropical rain-forest. Like such a jungle, every plant, large and small, spoke to one another, lived in the profusion *and* harmony of a forest. No one wrote over another name, no one was obscene — for that would have smashed the harmony. A communion took place over the city in this plant growth of names until every institutional wall, fixed or moving, every modern new school which looked like a brand-new factory, every old slum warehouse, every standing billboard, every huckstering poster, and the halls of every high-rise low-rent housing projects which looked like a prison (and all did) were covered by a foliage of graffiti that grew seven or eight feet tall, even twelve feet high in those choice places worth the effort for one to stand on another, ah, if it had gone on, this entire city of blank architectural high-rise horrors would have been covered with paint. Graffiti writers might have become mountaineers with pitons for the ascent of high-rise high-cost swinger-single apartments in the East Sixties and Seventies. The look of New York, and then the world, might have been transformed, and the interlapping of names and colors, those wavelets of ego forever reverberating upon one another, could have risen like a flood to cover the monstrosities of abstract empty techno-architectural twentieth-century walls where no design ever predominated over the most profitable (and ergo most monotonous) construction ratio implicit in a twenty-million-dollar bill.

The kids painted with less than this in view, no doubt. Sufficient in the graffiti-proliferating years of the early Seventies to paint the front door of every subway car they could find. The ecstasy of the roller coaster would dive down their chest if they were ever waiting in a station when a twelve-car train came stampeding in and their name, HONDO, WILDCAT, SABU or LOLLIPOP, was on the *front!* Yes, the graffiti had not only the feel and all the super-powered whoosh and impact of all the bubble letters in all the mad comic strips, but the *zoom*, the *aghr*, and the *ahhr* of screeching rails, the fast motion of subways roaring into stations, the comic strips come to life. So it was probably not a movement designed to cover the world so much as the excrescence of an excrescence. Slum populations chilled on one side by the bleakness of modern design, and brain-cooked on the other by comic strips and TV ads with zooming letters, even brain-cooked by politicians whose ego is a virtue — I am here to help my nation — brained by the big beautiful numbers on the yard markers on football fields, by the whip of the capital letters in the names of the products, and gut-picked by the sound of rock and soul screaming up into the voodoo of the firmament with the shriek of the performer's insides coiling like neon letters in the blue satanic light, yes, all the excrescence of the highways and the fluorescent wonderlands of every Las Vegas sign frying through the Iowa and New Jersey night, all the stomach-tightening nitty-gritty of trying to learn how to spell was in the writing, every assault on the psyche as the trains came slamming in. Maybe it was no more than a movement which looked to take some of the excrescence left within and paint it out upon the world, no more than a species of collective therapy of grace exhibited under pressure in which they never dreamed of painting over the blank and empty modern world, but the authority of the city reacted as if the city itself might be in greater peril from graffiti than from drugs, and a war had gone on, more and more implacable on the side of the authority with every legal and psychological weedkiller on full employ until the graffiti of New York was defoliated, cicatrized, Vietnamized. Now, as A-I sat in the station with Jon Naar and Japan and they watched the trains go by, aesthetic blight was on the cars. Few masterpieces remained. The windows were gray and smeared. The cars looked dull red or tarnished aluminum — their recent coat of paint remover having also stripped all polish from the manufacturer's surface. New subway cars looked like old cars. Only the ghost-outline of former masterpieces still remained. The kids were broken. The movement seemed over. Even the paint could no longer be invented. Now the cans set out for display were empty, the misdemeanors were being upped to felony, the fines were severe, the mood was vindictive. Two hideous accidents had occurred. One boy had been killed beneath a subway car, and another had been close to fatally burned by an inflammable spray can catching a spark, yes, a horror was on the movement and transit patrols moved through the yards and plugged the entrances. The white monoliths of the highrise were safe. And the subways were dingier than they had ever been. The impulse of the jungle to cover the walled tombs of technology had been broken. Was there a clue to graffiti in the opposite passion to look upon monotony and call it health? As A-I walked the streets with Jon Naar, they passed a sign: DON'T POLLUTE — KEEP THE CITY CLEAN. "That sign," the photographer murmured, "is a form of pollution itself."

3.

Since the metaphor of plant life had climbed all over his discussion of graffiti he went with profit to the Museum of Modern Art for it confirmed the botanical notion with which he began: that if subway graffiti had not come into existence, some artist might have found it necessary to invent, for it was in the chain of such evolution. Art had been rolling down the fall-line from Cézanne to Frank Stella, from Gauguin to Mathieu. On such a map, subway graffiti was an alluvial delta, the mud-caked mouth of a hundred painterly streams. If the obvious objection was that you might interview a thousand Black and Puerto Rican kids who rushed to write their name without having ever seen a modern painting, the answer, not quite as obvious, was that plants spoke to plants.

Famous plant-man Backster, attaching the electrodes of his polygraph to a philodendron one night, wonders in the wake of this passing impulse how to test the plant for some emotional reaction. Abruptly, a current courses through the philodendron at the horror of this thought. (When Backster cuts or burns the leaf, however, the polygraph registers little: now, the plant is numb. Its sensitivity seems to be its life, its suffering an abstention from life.) By the new logic of the experiment, plants must be a natural species of wireless. (What, indeed, did Picasso teach us if not that every form offers up its own scream when it is torn?) Radio is then no more than a prosthetic leg of communication, whereas plants speak to plants, and are aware of the death of animals on the other side of the hill. Some artists might even swear they have known this from the beginning, for they would see themselves as stimulants who inject perception into the blind vision of the century. (And like a junkie, does the century move into apathy from the superbrilliance of its injections?)

Still, when it comes to a matter of who might influence the writers of graffiti, one is not obliged to speak only of neon signs, comic strips and TV products, one has the other right to think the kids are enriched by all art which offers the eye a resemblance to graffiti. Which might enable us then to talk of Jackson Pollock and the abstract graffiti of his confluences and meanderings, of Stuart Davis' dramatization of print as a presence that grows in swollen proportion to its size, even include Hans Hofmann's *Memoria in Aeter-*

num where those red and yellow rectangles float like statements of a name over indistinct washes beneath, or Matisse's blue and green *Dance.* (Matisse's limbs wind onto one another like the ivy-creeper calligraphies of New York graffiti.) So might one refer to work which speaks of ghetto emotion in any place, of Siqueiros' *Echo of a Scream,* or Van Gogh's *Starry Night.* If the family histories of the most messed-up families have all the garbage-can chaos of de Kooning's *Woman,* no wonder the subway writers prided themselves on style and eclat — "you got a messed-up handwriting" being the final term of critical kill.

But on reflection, was A-I trying to slip in some old piety on the distribution of art down from the museums through media to the masses? — these subway children may never have seen *Memoria in Aeternum* at the head of the stairs at MOMA, but it filtered through to them by way of advertising artists. Fell crap! Rather say art begot art, and the migrations were no one's business. For if plants were telepathic, then humans lived in a psychic sea where all the forms of art also passed through the marketplace of the dreamer in his sleep, and every part of society spoke to every other part, if only with a curse.

So he had the happy thought during his visit to the Modern Art to decide that some paintings might be, by whatever measure, *on the air* — leave it to the engineers of some future techno-coven to try to determine the precise migrations of Miró's *Plate 8 from Series One, 1953, "The Family"* into the head of an espontaneo with a spray can looking over his shoulder for the black mother in a uniform who will beat his own black blue.

4.

Like a good reporter he goes to see the Mayor. It is ten days to Christmas and the last two weeks of the Lindsay administration on that Saturday morning he has his appointment to visit, nearly a week from the previous Sunday when he talked to Junior and Cay. Again the weather is iron-gray and cold. At Gracie Mansion, the wind is driving in from the East River, and the front porch looks across its modest private lawn to the Triboro Bridge in the north. (To the west apartment houses rise like the sheer face of Yosemite.)

It is not a large lawn in front of the Mayor's residence nor even a large house. Old white Gracie Mansion might be no exceptional residence on any wealthy road in Portland, Oregon or Portland, Maine — there is even a basketball hoop on a backboard not far from the front door, a political touch dating from recent years when the Knicks became the most consistently successful team in New York — yet with all its limited grandeur, Gracie Mansion is still one fine Federalist of a house (built in 1799) and if the spirit of an age could have been captured by a radio, then where better to measure this magic mean if not in the proportions of the Mansion's living room and dining room? They speak in their harmony of some perfect period of Arcadian balance between the early frontier being settled to the West and the new sense of democratic government forging itself in the state capitals of the East. How better to characterize the decorum, substance, grace, and calm center of such architecture if not to think that the spirit and style of the *prose* of the American Constitution is also in it (even to the hint of boredom in prose and buildings both), yet, why not precisely these high ceilings, paucity of curves, and all the implicit checks and balances of the right angle? Lindsay, it may be said, is at home in such surroundings. They seem built to his frame. Only a tall lean man could look well-proportioned in so *enlightened* a set of rooms. Nothing like a Gothic arch is present to suggest any mad irreconcilable opposites of God and man, no Corinthian columns to resonate with praetorian tyrannies (and orgies at the top), nor any small and slanted ceilings to speak of craft and husbandry, just government here in Federal style without the intervention of Satan or Jehovah (and next to nothing of Christ), just a fundament of Wasp genius, a building style to state that man could live without faith if things were calm enough. Perhaps the economy of balance is the true god of the Wasp.

His appointment is at eleven, but it is an unusual morning for the Lindsay family since they have been up until five the night before at a farewell party given the Mayor to honor the eight years of his administration. Lindsay has worked as hard as any man in New York for eight years, and can afford the luxury of being hungover before a reporter this Saturday morning. What a nice relaxation. Lindsay chuckles at the memory of each unexpected rejoinder of party dialogue and laughs at the expression on Tom Morgan's face, press secretary to the Mayor, a tall man with a dark brush mustache who recapitulates in the sardonic gloom of his hungover eyes the incandescence of all those good drinks at that good party. Watching them all, studying Lindsay's face with its patrician features so endowed with every purchase on the meaning of handsome that he could be not only a movie star but there at the front, right ahead of Burt Lancaster and Steve McQueen, on a par with Robert Redford, and hardly a millimeter of profile behind Paul Newman, it occurs indeed that no movie star could be more convincing than Lindsay if it came to playing some very important American politician in the quiet American years from 1800 to 1825. Even his eroded teeth — Lindsay's one failing feature — speak with authenticity of the bad teeth of those English ruling classes who became the American ruling classes in that Federalist era one hundred and seventy years ago. So sitting in such a dining room, and a little later adjourned to a living room with Lindsay and Morgan to bring up the subject of his interview, he is thinking that Gracie Mansion never had a Mayor nearly so perfectly suited to itself; if there were some divine renting agency in the halls of karma, then come soon or late the post of Mayor of New York would have had to be found for John Vliet Lindsay or the house would feel unfulfilled.

For Lindsay, however, the question may have been whether an ambitious man had ever come to power at a time less promising for himself. He had labored in his two terms, innovated and negotiated, explored, tinkered, tampered, and shifted the base of every municipal machine of government upon which he could work his cadres. He had built a constituency in the ghetto. Mailer-Breslin running for the mayoralty in '69 also ran into one argument over and over in Bedford-Stuyvesant, Harlem and the South Bronx. It was, "What do we want with you? Lindsay's our man." Lindsay had walked the streets in summer riots, and held some kind of line for decontrol, which is to say, local control, in the ghetto schools. That had taken political courage. Yet make him no saint! He had also worked with the most powerful real estate interests in the city. No question that in his eight years, the ugliest architecture in the history of New York had also gone up. The new flat tops of the skyline now left New York as undistinguished in much of its appearance as Cleveland or Dallas. It is possible Lindsay had bought ghetto relief at the price of aesthetic stultification. Call it desecration. The view of New York's offices and high-rise apartments proved sacrilegious to the mood of any living eye — Wasp balance had done it again.

Still, with all this effort, New Yorkers hated him. For every intolerable reason, first of which was his defense of the ghettos. "If I wanted a nigger for Mayor, I'd have voted for a nigger," said every archetype of a cab driver to any tourist who would listen. And yet this Federalist movie star, this hard-working mayor for ghetto rights, had been the first and most implacable enemy of subway graffiti. So there was a feather falling through the mood when he told Lindsay and Morgan why he had come.

But A-I had his speech. If he thought the Mayor had done an honorable job, and was prepared to say so, he still could not comprehend how a man who worked so hard to enter the spirit of ghetto conditions had been nonetheless so implacable in his reaction to graffiti. "Insecure cowards," Lindsay had called the kids. "A dirty shame." Others in his administration offered civic blasts: "graffiti pigs," "thoughtless and irresponsible behavior." It was surprising. While the management of a city required you to keep it clean — where would a mayor hide if he could not get the garbage out? — there was a difference between political necessity and the fury of this reaction. How could he call the kids cowards? Why the venom? It seemed personal.

Lindsay grinned. He had heard enough preambles from reporters to know when an interview was manageable. "Well, yes," he said, "I did get hot under the collar, and I suppose if we had to go through it again, I would hope to lose my temper a little less, but you have no idea what a blow that graffiti was to us." He shook his head at the memory. "You see, we had gone to such work, such ends, to get those new subway cars in. It meant so much to people here in the city to get a ride for instance in one of the new air-conditioned cars. On a hot summer day their mood would pick up when they had the luck to catch one. And you know, that was work. It's hard to get anything done here. You stretch budgets, and try to reason people into activities they don't necessarily want to take up on their own. We were proud of those subway cars. It took a lot of talking to a lot of committees to get that accomplished."

Morgan nodded. "And then," Lindsay said, "the kids started to deface them."

A-I put his demurrer. "Deface," after all, was the core of the argument. Some people might think subway graffiti was art. He suggested in passing Claes Oldenburg's classic remark, ". . . You're standing there in the station, everything is gray and gloomy and all of a sudden one of those graffiti trains slides in and brightens the place like a big bouquet from Latin America."

Lindsay smiled as if recalling the screams, moans, epithets, and agonized squawks of every bright college intellectual on his staff when Oldenburg's quote first came riding in. Grand division in the Establishment! Aesthetic schism! "Yes, we remember that quote," Lindsay's grin seemed to say. He had the most curious quality of personality. One did not know if he were secretly more or less decent than his personality. While the personality itself was decent enough, it was also patently not the man, nor, unhappily for him, characteristic at all of New York. He seemed now like a Westerner, full of probity, rawhide and something buried in the personality, a man you might not get to know at all even after a night of drinking together. He wasn't in the least like Richard Nixon except to share one quality. Lindsay was out of focus. He had always been out of focus. Part of his political trouble.

Well, Lindsay suggested, they had never really wondered whether it was anything but defacement. "People would come into new cars and suddenly they'd see them all marked up, covered inside and out, and it depressed people terribly. You know, we have to be a kind of nerve center to the city. Reports came in from everywhere. This graffiti was profoundly depressing — it truly hurt people's moods. The life would go out of everybody when they saw the cars defaced, they felt it was defacement, no question of that. And we kept hearing one request over and over, 'Can't you do something about it?' Then, too, we had our own pride in these matters. You know, you get to feel after you've put through a new municipal building that it's yours in some way. As Mayor I'd get as angry when a city building got marked up as if I owned it personally. Oh, it's easier to talk about it now, but I must say it was hard at times not to blow up."

"Actually," Morgan observed, "the Mayor would go around calming some of us down. 'Remember,' he would tell us, 'they're only kids.' "

Yes, in the framework of that time in the Summer of '71 and the Winter and Spring of '72 when Lindsay was looking to get the Democratic nomination for President, what an upset to his fortunes, what a vermin of catastrophe that these writings had sprouted like weeds all over the misery of Fun City, a new monkey of unmanageables to sit on Lindsay's overloaded political back. He must have sensed the presidency draining away from him as the months went by, the graffiti grew, and the millions of tourists who passed through the city brought the word out to the rest of the nation: "Filth is sprouting on the walls."

Of course, where was the tourist who could distinguish between men's-room and subway graffiti? Who was going to dare to look long enough to see that it was a name and not an obscene thought in the writing. Today, just before he had come to Gracie Mansion, he had stopped in the lavatory of a York Avenue bar for a minute, and there on the john wall was drawn a pure old-fashioned piece of smut graffiti. A balloon of dialogue issued out of a girl's mouth. No art in the lettering, no style. "Did you know," said her balloon, "that your clit is in your ass?" Some lost shred of fecal communion now nailed to the wall. Was there a public comfort station in America which did not have a dozen such insights, "Suck me," "Fuck you"? That was what people expected to see on the subways. They assumed the full mad explosive shithouse of America was now erupting in their faces. So they did not look but rode in the cars with their heads down, and brought the news out to the rest of America that Lindsay could not keep the city clean. No wonder he called it a dirty shame. And labeled the aplomb of the graffiti writers cowardice. That was his attempt to soothe the terror in the heart of every subway citizen who looked at the graffiti and put his head down so his eye would not meet any eye that might be connected to a hand which held a knife, yes, that was one side of the fear, and the other was fear of the insane graffiti writer in the self. For what filth would burst out of every civilized office worker in New York if ever *they* started to write on moving public walls, my god, the feces to spread and the blood to spray, yes, the good voting citizen of New York would know that the violent ward at Bellevue was opening its door to him on the day he would take a spray can to a subway. So, New York citizenry saw all the children as mad — and therefore saw madness, instability, and horror in the New York Transit. No wonder Lindsay had gone to war against graffiti. The city would tolerate junk, graft, insanities of traffic, mugging, every petty crime of the street, and every major pollution, but it could not accept a towering rain-forest of graffiti on all the forty-story walls. Yes, build a wall and balance a disease. For the blank wall of the new architecture was a deadening agent to balance the growing violence beneath. (Could it be said that the monotony of modern architecture increased all over the world in direct relation to the volcanic disturbances of each society it would contain?) Plastic above, dynamite below.

In the face of such questions the interview was effectively over. They chatted for a while, and got up to say goodbye. On the way out, A-I noticed there was a Rauschenberg on the wall.

Lindsay, in his courtesy, walked with him to the gate. Wearing a blue windbreaker he looked in the gray outdoor light like a veteran big league ballplayer, tall, weathered, knowledgeable. They took leave not uncordially, and he complimented the Mayor on eight good years, even meant it.

"I wish I had the talent to write," Lindsay said in parting. Was that a politician's gift? A-I pulled back the reply that he wished he could have been Mayor.

Outside the fence, a policeman was standing with a drawn gun. It was a simple measure of the times: be forever ready at the Gracie gate.

And indeed a ten-year-old boy on roller skates cried aloud, "That's him, that's him, that's the Mayor," and promptly took out a cap pistol and fired a number of bang-bangs at the back of John Lindsay going back into his house.

For a while, A-I walked, and had a little fantasy of how impossible it would have proved if the miracle worked and he had been elected in the campaign of 1969. What would he have done about graffiti? Would he have tried to explain its virtues to the people of New York — and laughed in all the pain of absolute political failure. The answer was simple — nobody like himself would ever be elected Mayor until the people agreed bad architecture was as poisonous as bad food. No, graffiti as a political phenomenon had small hope for life. His faith in the value of the question would have to explore in another place. Did the final difficulty lie in the meaning of graffiti as art? There the inquiry might become as incomprehensible as the motives of the most advanced artists. On then to the rim of the enigma, to the Sea of Vortices where the meanings whirl with no meaning.

5.

Years ago, so much as twenty years ago, A-I had conceived of a story he was finally not to write, for he lost his comprehension of it. A rich young artist in New York in the early Fifties, bursting to go beyond Abstract Expressionism, began to rent billboards on which he sketched huge, ill-defined (never say they were sloppy) works in paint chosen to run easily and flake quickly. The rains distorted the lines, made gullies of the forms, automobile exhausts laid down a patina, and comets of flying birds crusted the disappearing surface with their impasto. By the time fifty such billboards had been finished — a prodigious year for the painter — the vogue was on. His show was an event. They transported the billboards by trailer-truck and broke the front wall of the gallery to get the art objects inside. It was the biggest one-man exhibition in New York that year. At its conclusion, two art critics were arguing whether such species of work still belonged to art.

"You're mad," cried one, "it is not art, it is never art."

"No," said the other, "I think it's valid."

So would the story end. Its title, Validity. But before he had written a word he made the mistake of telling it to a young Abstract Expressionist whose work he liked. "Of course it's valid," said the painter, eyes shining with the project. "I'd do it myself if I could afford the billboards."

The story was never written. He had assumed he was proposing a satire, but it was evident he had no insight into how painters were ready to think. Some process had entered art and he could not discern it out.

Let us go back to the pastel by de Kooning which Rauschenberg erased. The details, when further inquiry is made, are less impromptu. Rauschenberg first informed de Kooning of what he would do, and de Kooning agreed. The work, when sold, bore the inscription "A drawing from Willem de Kooning erased by Robert Rauschenberg." Both artists are now proposing something more than that the artist has the same right as the financier to print money, they may even be saying that the meat and marrow of art, the painterly core, the life of the pigment, and the world of technique with which hands lay on that pigment are convertible to something other. The ambiguity of meaning in the twentieth century, the hollow in the heart of faith, has become such an obsessional hole that art may have to be converted into intellectual transactions. It is as if we are looking for stuff, any stuff with which to stuff the hole, and will convert every value into packing for this purpose. For there is no doubt that in erasing the pastel and selling it, art has been diminished but our knowledge of society is certainly enriched. An aesthetic artifact has been converted into a sociological artifact. It is not the painting that intrigues us now but the lividities of art fashion which made the transaction possible in the first place. Something rabid is loose in the century. Maybe we are not converting art into some comprehension of social process, but rather are using art to choke the hole, as if society has become so hopeless, which is to say so twisted in knots of faithless ideological spaghetti, that the glee is in strangling the victims.

But take the example further. Let us imagine a show at the Guggenheim. It will be like many we have seen. Let us make it a plausible modern one-man show. Nothing will be exhibited but computer read-out sheets from a statistical operation. Hundreds of such sheets tacked to the wall. Somewhat irregularly. Attempts at neatness will be contradicted by a confusion in the style of placing them on the wall of the Guggenheim as it spirals up the ramp. Checkerboards alternate with ascending bands, then cul-de-sacs, paper stapled up every way.

We try to digest the aesthetic experience. Of what do the computer read-out sheets consist? What is the subject of their inquiry? we ask. And what is the motive of the artist? Is he telling us something about the order and disorder of the mind in relation to a technological world? Has he presented us with an ongoing composition of exceptional cunning? Is it possible he even has set the problem for the computer himself? Maybe the endless numbers on these computer sheets reflect some analogue to the tension of major themes in his brain. Do we then have here an arithmetical display whose relation to art is as complex as *Finnegans Wake* to literature?

Bullshit, responds the painter. The computer sheets were selected at random. Because the artist did not even wish to bear an unconscious responsibility for the selection, he chose an acquaintance with whom he shared no great psychic identity to pick up the computer sheets for him. Neither he nor the acquaintance ever inquired into the subject of the statistical problem, and he never took a look at what was brought back. Rather, he spoke to the janitor at the Guggenheim by telephone and told him to tack up the pages any way at all. The checkerboards and bands and cul-de-sacs of stapled paper were merely a reflection of the personnel: the janitor worked with two assistants. One was neat, the other drunk. And the painter never came to see the show. The show was the fact that people came, studied the walls, lived for an uncertain hour in the Guggenheim and went out again, their minds exercised by a question that not only had no answer, but may not even have been a question. The artist had done his best to have no intent. Not unless his intent was to demonstrate that most of the experience of viewing a painting is the context of the museum itself. We are next to one of John

Cage's compositions in silence. Art has been saying with more and more intensity: The nature of the painting has become less interesting than the relation of painting to society — we can even erase Rauschenberg's erasure. Get the artist out of it altogether, and it is still art. The world is turning inside out.

What step is left to take? Only one. A show that offers no object at all. The last reference to painting or sculpture is the wall on which something can be hung, or the floor on which a piece can sit. That must now disappear. The art-piece enters the artist: the work can only be experienced within his psyche.

From the New York *Times*, September 2, 1973, by Peter Plagens:

> a marksman-friend shot Chris Burden in the upper left arm with a .22 long-jacket before an audience of 12 intimates. He (Burden) figured on a graze wound with a Band-Aid slapped on afterward, but it "felt like a truck hit my arm at 80 miles per hour"; he went to the hospital, nauseous, and filed the requisite police report ("accident").

Plagens goes on to describe other "pieces." Burden chooses situations for their possibility of danger, pain, humiliation, or boredom. There is:

> "Movie on the Way Down," in which Burden, hanging by his heels, nude, six feet off a gym floor with a movie camera in his hands, is summarily chopped loose.

The movie is presumably taken on the way down (is it filmed in slow motion?) and he ends with a cut lip. There are other pieces where he rockets flaming matches "at his nude supine wife" or sets ablaze two 16-foot wooden crosses on Laguna Canyon Road at 2 A.M. — "the intended audience for that piece," says Burden, "was the one guy driving down the road who saw it first." Ah, Los Angeles! For "Endurance/real time," he 1) stays in a locker for five days, 2) does 1600 tours of a gallery on his bicycle and 3) remains in bed for three weeks and a day. He also pretends to be a dead man lying under a tarpaulin on the street and is arrested by the police for creating a traffic hazard. He gets a hung jury at his trial and the case is dismissed but "one of the nine votes for conviction, a stewardess, told Burden if she ever saw him under a tarp again, she'd run over him herself." He even does a study in the shift of identity. For "I Became a Secret Hippie," Burden cuts his hair short and dresses in

FBI clothes. "If you want to be a heavy artist nowadays," Plagens, reporting on Burden, concludes, "you have to do something unpleasant to your body, because everything *else* has been done. . . . [Burden] may be a product of art-world art history — backed into some untenable masochistic corner because all the other novelty territory has been claimed."

At the least, Burden is fulfilling the dictum of Jean Malaquais that once there are enough artists in the world, the work of art will become the artist himself. Burden is refining his personality. Through existential tests. Burden is not exploring his technique, but his vibrations. The situations he chooses are, as Plagens describes, "edgy." They have nothing remotely resembling a boundary until they are done. In "Movie on the Way Down," Burden can hardly know if he will cut his lip or break his neck, feel a live instant on the descent or some dull anxiety. When he shoots lighted matches at his nude wife the areas defined are empty before the action begins. Given every variable from Women's Liberation to the sadomasochistic tales of Wilhelm Stekel, Burden can know in advance only that a psycho-dramatic enterprise will be commenced. But where it may end, and what everybody might feel — will the matches burn her skin? — will the marriage be fortified or scorched? — no, there is no confidence which question is going to offer an answer. Perhaps he is not refining his personality so much as attempting to clear a space in his psyche free of dread. But isn't that the fundamental operation of the primitive at the dawn of civilization, the establishment of the ego? For what is the human ego but a clearing in the forest of the psyche free of dread? Money, held in one's hand, is free of time. Cash has no past; its future is assignable. It is powerful and empty. So, too, is the ego. It bears the same relation to the psyche as cash bears to the security or comfort of the body. The ego is virtually separate from the psyche even as money is still separate from every organic communicating logic of nature.

We are back to the cave man and his cave painting. His hand draws the outline of the animal in defiance of those gods who watch him. Burden is smashing his nose on the floor or displaying his wife in defiance of the last gods of conventional art. They are that audience remnant of a once-leviathan bourgeois culture. They still trickle out to see Happenings, the desire of the middle class to preserve its last religion: the world of the artist, palette, museum and gallery wall. Middle-class passion is to appreciate the work of art.

But art may be the little ball rolling off the table. Perhaps art now signifies some unheard reverberation from the subterranean obsession of us all: Is civilization coming to an end? Is society burning? Is the day of the cave man returning? Has our search for ego which was once so routine — a useful (somewhat heartless) ego to be fashioned for a useful (if heartless) society — now gone past the measure of our experience so that we no longer try to construct a control center at the core of the mind, but plunge instead into absurdities which offer us that curious calm we find in the art of the absurd, even as the cave man, defying his gods, discovered he was not always dead on the next day.

But we are at the possible end of civilization, and tribal impulses start up across the world. The descending line of the isolated artist goes down from Michelangelo all the way to Shoot. But Chris Burden is finally more comfortable to us than the writers of graffiti. For Burden is the last insult from the hippie children of the middle class to the bourgeois art-patron who is their spiritual parent, but graffiti speaks of a new civilization where barbarism is stirring at the roots.

If at the beginning of Western painting, man was small and God was large; if, in the Renaissance, man was mysteriously large in his relation to God; now, in our times man has disappeared into God. He is mass-man without identity, and he is God. He is all the schizophrenia of the powerless and all-powerful in one psyche.

As we lose our senses in the static of the oncoming universal machine, so does our need to exercise the ego take on elephantiasistical proportions. Graffiti is the expression of a ghetto that is near to the plague, for civilization is now closed off from the ghetto. Too huge are the obstacles to any natural development of a civilized man. In the ghetto it is almost impossible to find some quiet identity. No, in the environment of the slum, the courage to display yourself is your only capital, and in the streets crime is the only productive process that converts such capital to the modern powers of the world, ego and money. Art is not peace but war, and form is the record of that war.

Yet there is a mystery still. From which combat came these curious letters of graffiti, with their Chinese and Arabic calligraphies? Out of what connection to the past did these lights and touches of flame become so much like the Hebrew alphabet where the form of the letter itself was worshipped as a manifest of the Lord? No, it is not enough to think of the childlike desire to see one's name ride by in letters large enough to scream your ego across the city, no, it is almost as if we must go back into some more primeval sense of existence. If our name is enormous to us, it is also not real — as if we have come from other places than the name, and lived in other lives.

Perhaps that is the unheard echo of graffiti, the vibration of that profound discomfort it arouses. Can the unheard music of its proclamation and/or its mess, the rapt intent seething of its foliage, be the herald of some oncoming apocalypse less and less far away, and so graffiti lingers on our subway door as a memento of all the lives ever lived, sounding now like the bugles of gathering armies across the unseen ridge.

A Harlot
High and Low

There are no answers. There are only questions.
— Jean Malaquais

A Harlot High and Low was the English title given to *Splendeurs et misères des courtisanes,* one of Balzac's best novels. The book was concerned as much with secret police as with the prostitutes who passed through its pages, but then whores and political agents made a fair association for Balzac. The harlot, after all, inhabited the world of *as if.* You paid your money and the harlot acted for a little while — when she was a good harlot — *as if* she loved you, and that was a more mysterious proposition than one would think, for it is always mysterious to play a role. It is equal in a sense to living under cover. At her best, the harlot was a different embodiment of a fantasy for each client, and at those moments of existence most intense for herself, the role she assumed became more real than the reality of her profession.

A harlot high and low. The pores of society breathe a new metaphor — the enigma of Intelligence itself. For we do not know if the people who make our history are more intelligent than we think, or whether stupidity rules the process of thought at its highest level. Is America governed by accident more than we are ready to suppose, or by design? And if by design, is the design sinister? Are the actors

"A Harlot High and Low" uses excerpts from nineteen sources. A bibliography is therefore appended. Three of these sources required permission to reprint. They are: *The Rolling Stone* for excerpts from "Strange Bedfellows — the Hughes-Nixon-Lansky Connection: The Secret Alliances of the CIA From World War II to Watergate" by Howard Kohn from *Rolling Stone* No. 213, May 20, 1976. By Straight Arrow Publishers, Inc. © 1976. All rights reserved. Reprinted by permission. *The Washington Post,* 6/21/72 issue. *At That Point In Time, the Inside Story of the Senate Watergate Committee.* Copyright © 1975 by Fred D. Thompson. Reprinted by permission of Times Books, a division of Quadrangle/The New York Times Book Co., Inc.

playing roles more intricate than we expect? Trying to understand whether our real history is public or secret, exposed or — at the highest level — underground, is equal to exploring the opposite theaters of our cynicism and our paranoia.

For instance, we may be getting ready to decide that the CIA was the real producer of Watergate (that avant-garde show!) but where is the proof? We have come to a circular place. The CIA occupies a region in the modern mind where every truth is obliged to live in its denial; facts are wiped out by artifacts; proof enters the logic of counterproof and we are in the dream; matter breathes next to antimatter.

There are Americans whose careers are composed of fact. One does not begin to comprehend certain men without their collections of fact. It would probably be crucial to know if Harry S. Truman had been happy or angry on a given day since that would enter the event of the day. He lives on an elementary level of biography. There are personalities, however, like Marilyn Monroe, for whom there are no emotional facts. It does not matter on any particular occasion if she was pleased or annoyed, timid or bold, even successful or unsuccessful. Her mood did not matter on a given day since she would as easily be feeling the opposite five minutes later. Moreover, she was an actress. She was able to simulate the opposite of what she felt. Since she was surrounded by people in show business who felt no need to be accurate if that interfered with a good story, one could not begin to discover the facts about such a woman, only the paradoxes. It may be that the difficulties in coming to know Marilyn Monroe offer a modest model for our penetration of Central Intelligence.

1.
A Skew in Sociology

Questions of social class and snobbery have always been very important in the CIA. With its roots in the wartime Office of Strategic Services (the letters OSS were said, only half-jokingly, to stand for "Oh So Social"), the agency has long been known for its concentration of Eastern Establishment, Ivy League types. Allen Dulles, a former American diplomat and Wall Street lawyer with impeccable connections and credentials, set the tone for an agency full of Roosevelts, Bundys, Cleveland Amory's brother Robert, and other scions of America's leading families. There have been exceptions, to be sure, but most of the CIA's top leaders have been white, Anglo-Saxon, Protestant, and graduates of the right Eastern schools. While changing times and ideas have diffused the influence of the Eastern elite throughout the government as a whole, the CIA remains perhaps the last bastion in official Washington of WASP power, or at least the slowest to adopt the principle of equal opportunity.

— Victor Marchetti and John D. Marks,
The CIA and the Cult of Intelligence

What a baby! Known affectionately as the Company, it was delivered to America by the Central Intelligence Agency Act of 1949, and grew from 5,000 employees in 1950 to 15,000 by 1955. Because the old OSS was not nearly large enough to make up its cadres, the CIA raided the FBI to obtain some of its first agents (thereby commencing an immense feud with J. Edgar Hoover) and also did its best to strip the army, the navy, the air force, the State Department, and virtually every other government bureau of good personnel. There was, after all, a vision. The potential functions of the CIA were calculated to become immense. They became immense. All intelligence was the purview. There was no reason, for instance, why the best long-term weather forecasts in America should not derive from CIA weather experts — knowledge of the weather helped crops; large crops were an instrument of foreign policy. No vein, therefore, of American business or culture was independent of Intelligence — not finance, media, economic production, labor-management relations, cinema, statistical theory, fringe groups, Olympic teams. There was no natural end to topics the CIA could legitimately interest itself in.

Since we live in an age of general systems, where all knowledge is assumed to live ultimately in the same field as other knowledge, so, from its inception, the CIA looked to draw its experts from every field: bankers, journalists, lobbyists, colonels, professors, commodores, soil-erosion specialists, diplomats, business consultants, students, lawyers, doctors, poison specialists, art experts, public-relations men, magazine editors, movie technicians. Out of every occupation in American life, men and women were drawn to make up the first cadres of the CIA, and they were often the best in their field.

Because the CIA, like other government bureaus, had a table of organization which limited the rank and salary of its employees, the Company had from the beginning an army of officers serving as privates. There was not room for the amount of ambition in its ranks.

People moved out of the CIA almost as quickly as they went in and returned to universities, businesses, other government departments, and major foundations, or back to their previous occupations in American life. Of course, a banker who had been a CIA man and was now in finance again was hardly the same banker. Nor had he necessarily left the CIA. If it had been the most exciting experience of his life and/or the most patriotic, he had sentimental loyalties to the Company. He was out of the CIA but still an effective member of it. Sometimes he might even be on call for special jobs or be asked for privileged information on the movements of his financial community.

Like the breaking out of a virus from the host cell, the metastasis of a cancer colony, or the leavening of yeast in bread — depending on one's point of view — the CIA offered a suffusion into the joints and pores of American life so complete that no master list of its active and reserve members (not to speak of its devoted sympathizers) was ever available. One CIA man could never know for certain whether a CIA man who had left the CIA did not still belong to it, and if he did, there were often excellent reasons no record should exist, particularly if he belonged to the Company as to a club, and took no salary. Some agents who left the CIA but were still in it, or of it, might have given reports every week of their life. Others may never have reported once. Like "moles" — it is the CIA word — they waited underground through the seasons working at their private career in order to be of eventual use. Some old agents might still be reliable, some might not — some might report only to one old friend in the Agency. No one would be certain finally who belonged and who did not. In places like the State Department, one could begin to guess, but never know, whether the first allegiance of many a foreign-service officer was to the State desk or to the Company's cover. Since the leaders of the CIA came from a social, financial, and corporate elite, it could be said that the Agency was the militant arm of the Establishment, an order of potential martyrs to Henry Luce's American Century.

The CIA is currently the owner of one of the biggest — if not *the* biggest — fleets of "commercial" airplanes in the world. Agency proprietaries include Air America, Air Asia, Civil Air Transport, Intermountain Aviation, Southern Air Transport, and several other air charter companies around the world . . . [but] CIA headquarters . . . has never been able to compute exactly the number of planes flown by the airlines it owns, and personnel figures for the proprietaries are similarly imprecise. An agency holding company, the Pacific Corporation, including Air America and Air Asia, alone accounts for almost 20,000 people, more than the entire work force of the parent CIA. For years this vast activity was dominated and controlled by one contract agent, George Doole, who later was elevated to the rank of a career officer. Even then his operation was supervised, part time, by only a single senior officer who lamented that he did not know "what the hell was going on."

— *The CIA and the Cult of Intelligence*

One cannot follow the CIA's use of funds: Nobody is meant to know where all the Company's sources of money originate nor how they begin to end. At the core of many a CIA operation is the need for secrecy in the use of money. Some foreign official has to be bought, or expensive military equipment must be left as a gift in another country. If spies are to be paid, and foreign companies infiltrated, if Central American troops are to be trained for invasion forces, and drug traffics infiltrated for the information they will supply on Indochinese troop movements, if a hundred semilegal or near-to-criminal patriotic activities need to be lubricated without congressional grit in the bearings, then money has to pass down to active operative levels in the middle regions of the Company without scrupulous bookkeeping. It was better for the Director of the CIA not to know what his agents were up to, not if he had to testify on oath before congressional committees. What one did not know, one could not tell. It was therefore the essence of policy for no one to be in command of more information than he needed — a cellular society has to have waterproof compartments, enclaves. Money, therefore, did not always have to be accounted for; indeed, it often was put into an activity on no more than the word of the good character (and/or good family) of the agent who requisitioned it. No word needed to come back on what had been done with the bread, who was bought, who was killed, who made a profit.[1]

Since inside information on foreign currencies, or the domestic commodities market and gold market, or advance warning of a de-

---

[1] The Pike committee in Congress had a withheld report (published in the *Village Voice*, February 16, 1976) which decided that the real intelligence budget is not $3 billion, the estimate given to Congress, but is "closer to $10 billion," the missing $7 billion being buried in the appropriations of other departments. Ten billion dollars is roughly equal to the annual budget of New York City.

valuation in the dollar, was as available on occasion as money, it is unthinkable that some of the Wall Street men in the CIA did not make secret investments for the Agency (that is, for their enclave in the Agency) which soon brought back huge profits by virtue of the secret information which had first encouraged the investment. That kind of surplus could now be used for ultrasecret operations or for even more resplendent financial investments. It is novelistically intoxicating to contemplate the pyramiding of wealth which must have gone on in some enclaves of the CIA. What a congeries of friendly and competitive financial empires may have begun to exist within the agency! For all we know, and we will not soon know, half the Swiss banks are now controlled by agents, facets, wings, arms, committees, councils, operators, and officers of the CIA. Contemplating the mix of real names and false names, actual companies and fronts, declared and secret investment, legal and illegal accounting, fair and flawed computers, it is doubtful that we will ever be able to measure the wealth manipulated by the CIA. Add to this the inevitable intimacies and financial interrelations of such prime possibilities as Hughes, Vesco, and J. Paul Getty, plus the covert investments of the Agency in any number of multinational corporations (with the Mafia and without) — lo, it is not so difficult to think that the economic history of the Arab nations may yet be seen to shine by the secret light of the Company's resources. One cannot, of course, know. It is just that it is easier to believe in such a scenario than to assume that all those proud, powerful Company patriots with their comprehensive information and financial skills never used CIA money to make money that did not have to be accounted for.

Besides, it would be interesting to guess the magnitude of the CIA's secret funds. Out of the real $10-billion Intelligence budget would come the seed money for concealed investments; if the process has been going on for twenty-five years with continuous reinvestment, then these secret investments could total by now anywhere from $25 billion to $100 billion, not an impossible sum for the twenty-five years it has been burgeoning if we compare it to the income of the CIA's senior partner, the Mafia — but we anticipate.

I have worked on projects with many CIA men so unaware of the entire operation that they had no realization and awareness of the roles of other CIA men working on the same project. I would know of this because inevitably somewhere along the line both groups would come to the Department of Defense for support. I actually designed a special office in the Pentagon with but one door off the corridor. Inside, it had a single room with one secretary. However, off her office there was one more door that led to two more offices with a third doorway leading to yet another office, which was hidden by the door from the secretary's room. I had to do this because at times we had CIA groups with us who were not allowed to meet each other, and who most certainly would not have been there had they known that the others were there. (For the record, the office was 4D1000 — it may have been changed by now; but it stayed that way for many years.)

— L. Fletcher Prouty,
The Secret Team

It is inevitable that there should be a loss to CIA agents of a clear boundary to their identity. A man may work in the CIA for twenty years and never perform the role his title suggests he is performing. Two men may work side by side in the same office for ten years and never learn the other's real work, or to the contrary may know the work intimately but not have a clue on what it is designed to cover. A man's wife may only guess at his real activities. Old moles who have been working at a separate career for years might find themselves suddenly activated as agents and have to deal with CIA men who are present under a new cover themselves.

After years of such work, one may no longer be certain of one's own function, loyalty, or sanity — one can hardly be certain of the identity of one's friends, and one can never be sure the CIA has or has not made a new piece of history. It is impossible, for example, for anyone in the Company ever to be positive the Agency had absolutely nothing to do with the assassinations of the sixties. In such a medium of existence, paranoia is equal to logic itself, and an infinite number of scenarios may dance on the head of a pin. There is always the unforgettable paradigm of the double agent Azev, who, in the years before the Russian Revolution, spied on the Bolsheviks for the czarist police, but in the course of his false Bolshevik duties murdered czarist police with such daring that Azev rose high in Bolshevik circles and became one of Lenin's most trusted men. Indeed, Lenin could not at first believe the captured files of the czarist police although they gave unimpeachable evidence that Azev was a double agent. Where is the root of identity in that kind of man?

The human brain is divided: into a right lobe and a left lobe; a bold side and a cautious one; a moralist and a sinner; a radical and a conservative; a live lover and a dead one; a wit and an idiot; a hard worker and a sloth. We are all ourselves, and to some degree we are the opposite of ourselves. Consider the overlays of personality which accompany these shifts of identity when a cover story is added — there must be an actual need to function as double agents now that the psyche has been already once divided! Then contemplate the variety of political activities which take place within the Company: from the right-wingers of the John Birch Society to the social engineers who brood in private over *The New York Review of Books;* consider the ideological wars which go on between cold warriors and lovers of détente, between those who would presumably die for more government and those who wouldn't mind killing for less. If we take into account the functional need of the agency to have its enclaves cut off from responsibility or accountability, and in turn the national propensity of these enclaves to become — in compensation for the dirtiness of the work — political, that is, to fight for political ends within the CIA and maneuver for power at the top, as well as engage in capers *on their own* to affect the internal history of the United States, how then can they not use every tool ranging from straight financial manipulation to Syndicate involvement to assassination? Yes, try to keep up (if you are the Director) with the movements of agents in the CIA attempting to infiltrate rival enclaves. The mind reels. The scenarios do a dervish. To live with a role is to live as an actor — so soon as the role is more satisfying than the life, all clear boundaries of identity are lost. All the more reason, then, for the CIA man to try to find an identity within his false identity by way of some enclave that satisfies his political needs. It is a way of saying he looks for a secret political action which will seem authentic to him — an action that can cut through the confusion of enigmatic projects and multiple identities in order to give the country what it really needs, that is, what he believes America secretly desires.

It is against the background of this mammoth of shuffled identities, concealed fortunes, fever-hot enclaves, secret killers, paranoid visions, osmotic bureaucratic walls, pervasive unaccountability, double agents, infiltrated capers, and cross capers that we attempt to look at Watergate. If what has been proposed already is valid at all, then we can be certain no clear picture will come to us soon. It is better to recognize that we are blind and can only try, through the distorted reverberation of the echo, to improve our knowledge of the mood. Of course, that is the true perception of the blind.

2.
A Hitch in Historiography

Haldeman ordered an exhaustive investigation into O'Brien's relationship with billionaire Howard Hughes. Caulfield reported back in a Jan. 25, 1971, memo that the investigation could bubblegum in Nixon's face.

The Hughes organization's "tentacles touch many extremely sensitive areas of government," cautioned Caulfield, "each of which is fraught with potential for Jack Anderson type exposures."[2]

— Jack Anderson, the Washington *Post*,
June 6, 1974

The phantom billionaire repeatedly insisted upon total secrecy. He didn't want "the most microscopic chance of the slightest hint being accidentally dropped to *anyone*," stressed a typical memo. Another time, he declared that his informants "put their very lives in jeopardy with some of the disclosures they make to me, and if they thought this information went to anybody — no matter whom — they would not continue to inform me."

— Jack Anderson, May 23, 1974

Howard Hughes has not been interviewed or photographed by any pressman since 1958.

— Stephen Fay, et al., *Hoax*

By the end of his life, Hughes satisfies some idea in us of the giant amoeba or master spider. If he first appeared on the screen of the American media as a rich and prodigiously eccentric young man, reminiscent of Orson Welles at the beginning of *Citizen Kane*, he ended as one of the wealthiest recluses and most mysterious right-wingers of history (that is, assuming it was Hughes who just died and not one of his — more than one — legendary doubles). He is at once the principle of total invisibility in public life and a gargoyle out of *The Day of the Locust*. We think fondly of young Hughes, his racing planes, and his movies: *Scarface, The Front Page*, and

---

[2] The memo actually said "Maheu's tentacles. . . ." We will meet Maheu before long.

Hell's Angels; his stars: George Raft, Jean Harlow, Bob Mitchum, Jane Russell; and then we read of the old gink who abhors bacteria as Dracula fears the cross.

> Hughes kept his last wife, movie actress Jean Peters, on a yo-yo string. He would disappear for long stretches and send her endearing but false messages. . . .
> In 1965, he promised to have Thanksgiving dinner with her. But because of his fear of germs, he told her to sit across the room from him. She walked out in a huff.
> The following year, he persuaded her to join him in Boston where he promised they would settle down. But again, he kept her at across-the-room distance. She put up with it for three days.
> — Jack Anderson, May 23, 1974

Since secrecy was his antiseptic, the media are often tempted to portray his ventures as absurd. The story of the $350-million CIA contract for the Glomar Explorer came out in the press as a huge and peculiar sum for the CIA to pay Hughes to design a boat that could "retrieve military codes and nuclear warheads from a Soviet submarine sunk three miles deep in the Pacific . . . [especially] since the codes were outdated and the value of the other information was negligible."[3]

Of course, the Soviet submarine might only have been the cover. Maybe, it was wiser to assume the CIA had grown concerned with finding a new source of minerals to compete with Third World cartels. They could have "awarded Hughes the $350 million to develop an advanced technology for underwater mining — thereby giving Hughes a head start toward a bonanza with more potential than oil. . . ."[4]

The Glomar bonanza could leave Hughes, by some counts already the wealthiest man in the world, an order of magnitude wealthier. But then for two decades Hughes must have been suffering something like the psychosis of a heavyweight champion. (Every heavyweight champion has to be a fraction insane since he cannot know if he is the greatest fighter alive or if some unseen maniac of the martial arts is getting ready to destroy him in an alley.) So Hughes had to wonder whether he was making history or was only a servant of the history the CIA might be making through him.

---

[3] Howard Kohn, "Strange Bedfellows — The Hughes-Nixon-Lansky Connection," *Rolling Stone.*
[4] "Strange Bedfellows."

He could not know, and no one looking on from the outside could know, how much of the CIA was part of his operation or how much of his operation was directed by the CIA. Indeed, was there even a live man named Hughes at the center of it all, or was there a Special Committee?[5] Suffice it that whatever entity was comprised by his name, Hughes had properties. Since we don't know what we are dealing with, let us designate it HUGHES.

HUGHES's corporations earned more than half a billion dollars a year from government contracts alone and thirty-two such contracts were with the CIA. That was the largest number held by any corporate entity with the Company. *Time* fortified such figures: "During the past ten years Hughes Aircraft, which relies almost exclusively on Government work, has won nearly $6 billion in Government contracts. . . . There was also about 6 billion dollars more in secret contracts with the CIA over this period. . . . Asserts one former Pentagon official, 'Their interests are completely merged.' "[6] So, HUGHES, whoever HUGHES was, might begin to look like the pope of Avignon to any director of the CIA. If an enclave needed funds for a special caper, who was better than HUGHES to fund it? HUGHES was Daddy Warbucks to the CIA. HUGHES owned half of Las Vegas. HUGHES, by way of various intermediaries, had absorbed it from Meyer Lansky. Since the CIA already had associations with Lansky, easily as old as their mutual attempts to assassinate Castro, the Company could now, by way of HUGHES and Las Vegas, enter into another majestic interface with the Mafia, that is, with half the labor unions of America, and nearly all of the entertainment industries, the construction industries, the highway, travel, and tourist industries, not to speak of the more celebrated nonlegal industries like prostitution, porny, narcotics, and — the finest operation yet discovered for laundering huge sums of money and evading the IRS — gambling. (If the Mafia had detested the very mood and atmosphere of gambling casinos, it would still have been obliged to get into the business for the legerdemain it offered to heavy sums.) In turn, the high-potential money in the CIA would want to discharge into the great sea of Syndicate wealth. There the take — voices fill in awe — came to $50 billion a year, and

---

[5] The body of the Hughes who died in April of this year had its fingerprints checked "against genuine Hughes prints on file with the FBI in Washington. It was," *Time* says cheerfully (April 19, 1976), "Hughes, all right." Of course that assumes no one in the mills of identification has ever been able to switch a set of prints.

[6] *Time* also says: "Not until 1971 did the IRS subject the Hughes holdings to an overall audit; the results of that audit have been kept secret."

that was twice General Motors' if only half the size of the defense budget.

> CIA officials asked Maheu to enlist Syndicate men for the Castro murder ... and authorized him to pay $150,000 for the hit. Maheu told the Church committee he hesitated initially because he feared the project might interfere with his work for Howard Hughes,[7] who also had retained Maheu's services. But Maheu said he agreed to the assignment after informing Hughes of the murder plot — and, according to one source, gaining the billionaire's approval. For the project Maheu called on John Roselli, Sam Giancana and Santo Trafficante.
> — Howard Kohn, *Strange Bedfellows*

We could speak of Maheu, an ex-FBI agent on special retainer to the CIA since 1954, as a man of variety and dimension, a veritable fixer, but such words do not elucidate the physics implicit in his personal forces. Rather, Maheu is known in Intelligence as a "pivotal" figure — the roads go through his tollbooth. We will learn for instance from the Pike committee that pornographic movies were sometimes made with CIA funds to blackmail people and "one of these was titled 'Happy Days' with Mr. Robert Maheu as casting director, make-up man, cameraman and director." The detail is cited not to offer us the opportunity to rise in moral height above Maheu so much as to loosen our imagination. He was also for a time the most visible HUGHES representative in public life. "You are me to the outside world," reads one memo to Maheu.[8] "Go see Nixon as my special confidential emissary," says another in the spring of '68. "A Republican victory this year ... could be realized under our sponsorship and supervision every inch of the way."[9] HUGHES even had a $600,000 French colonial mansion built for Maheu on the Desert Inn grounds.

> The first time he entertained for lunch the casino managers ... Maheu tapped his water glass for attention. Then, to the astonishment of his Las Vegas colleagues, Robert Maheu said grace.[10]

---

[7] In excerpt, out of respect for the source's punctuation, *Hughes* will appear in lowercase.
[8] David Tinnin, *Just About Everybody vs. Howard Hughes.*
[9] Ibid.
[10] Ibid.

"O'Brien and Maheu are longtime friends from the Boston
area.... During the Kennedy administration there apparently
was continuous liaison between O'Brien and Maheu."
— Memo from John Dean to H. R. Haldeman,
January 26, 1971[11]

There was, of course, the delicate matter that Hughes wanted
to hire me but didn't want to meet me face to face. Maheu raised
the issue — he said that was simply Hughes's style of operation,
that he, Maheu, had worked for the man for years, and was his
chief executive officer, but had never met him.
— Larry O'Brien, *No Final Victories*

After Hubert Humphrey's defeat in 1968, Larry O'Brien was
relatively at liberty. The new administration might be Republican,
but O'Brien had not worked as postmaster general and chairman of
the Democratic National Committee nor managed the presidential
campaigns of Kennedy, Johnson, and Humphrey for too little. Nobody had more contacts in Washington than Larry O'Brien. From
early in 1968 on, even as Maheu was being confidential emissary to
Nixon, so was he also being instructed to hire O'Brien as HUGHES's
Washington representative; but it was only in October, 1969, after a
stretch for O'Brien on Wall Street, that the consulting firm O'Brien
Associates was formed and given a HUGHES contract at $15,000 a
month. The arrangement, however, soon faced complications. By
late 1970, HUGHES had decided to replace Maheu with Intertel.

Although this is not widely known, an increasing number of big
corporations in recent years have either established private intelligence units or hired intelligence consultants from the CIA, the
FBI, the DIA, the Internal Security Division of the Justice Department, the Treasury, the Secret Service, or the Internal Reve-
nue Service. The purpose is, basically, to protect a corporation's
own secrets or acquire other corporations' secrets in the ever-
competitive business world. A whole underworld of corporate
intelligence has thus developed.
Several organizations in the United States openly offer corporate intelligence services. The most important is Intertel....
— Tad Szulc, *Compulsive Spy*

[11] J. Anthony Lukas, *Nightmare — The Underside of the Nixon Years.*

It could be said that Intertel had better CIA connections than Maheu. In fact, they were socially superior. Intertel's owner was James Crosby, good friend and host of Rebozo and Nixon. Crosby was also the chairman of Resorts International, an immense gambling-and-tourist complex in the Bahamas which (with many a camouflage) had been taken over from Meyer Lansky by the CIA. (Brave men grow bold in the Caribbean and gentlemen turn into pirates.) Resorts International came right out of the Crosby Miller Corporation, in which a controlling interest had been acquired in 1958 by Mary Carter Paint, a corporation originally gotten up by Allen Dulles and Thomas E. Dewey.

If the CIA hierarchy had icons analogous to the Mayflower, they were Allen Dulles, Thomas E. Dewey, and the Mary Carter Paint Company. By such cachet James Crosby of Intertel was to Maheu's CIA pornies and assassination capers as Louisburg Square to Scollay Square. In addition, Intertel may also have been in position to offer HUGHES the Glomar Explorer contract if he would take them on. That meant letting Maheu go. Since Maheu knew a lot about HUGHES, it was a big payment for a real peril.

The changeover in 1970 was accomplished with the maximum of mystery. The man, Hughes, six feet four inches, reported to weigh 97 pounds and, by a Las Vegas doctor's report, next to death, gave over his authority to Maheu's most determined enemies with a proxy which enabled these enemies to bring Intertel's security force into the casinos and drive out Maheu's troops, a dramatic night for Las Vegas, whose citizens were learning about this time that a tall thin man, claimed by his proxy-holders to be Howard Hughes, had been smuggled out of his sanctuary in the penthouse of the Desert Inn and been flown to the Bahamas (even though he was next to death and swore he would never fly again). There were some, Maheu among them, who offered the mordant suspicion that HUGHES was now a karmic transplant, but then there were others who had been supposing the same since 1958, when the man, Hughes, stopped seeing anyone but a few Hughes Tool Company executives and/or his rotating male nurse-secretaries (five), who received all messages for him. Maybe, by the time of the move to the Bahamas, HUGHES was going into his second karmic transplant; maybe HUGHES was now a computer not unrelated to OCTOPUS at Langley.

But such speculations take us too fast down the stream. Let us keep to what we may suppose we know. It seems clear that HUGHES, now divested of Maheu, would not necessarily want to keep Maheu's friend in his employ. Of course, dropping O'Brien would hardly be fail-safe. It was not comfortable to estimate how much O'Brien had learned about the CIA from Maheu (if for that matter O'Brien had had a great deal to learn about the CIA).

Nonetheless, the transfers were made. Some time after Intertel took over from Maheu, HUGHES replaced O'Brien with Bob Bennett. The son of Senator Wallace Bennett (R), from Utah, Bob Bennett was a churchgoing Mormon; in fact, he was part of the three-man bishopric of the Church of Jesus Christ of Latter-Day Saints in Arlington, Virginia, a detail of dubious interest until it is fortified with the knowledge that a large number of HUGHES aides, assistants, and top executives were Mormons; indeed, Maheu's most devoted enemies in HUGHES were Mormons. We might wonder how such religious fellows would comport themselves in Las Vegas, but there is always a tendency to underrate the sects we know least. It seems, consulting the *Encyclopaedia Britannica*, that a secret Mormon society called the Danites was organized for Joseph Smith in October, 1838. They had "the avowed purpose of supporting Smith at all hazards, of upholding the authority of his revelation and decrees as superior to the laws of the land, and of helping him to get possession, first of the state, then of the United States, and ultimately of the world."

It would be an investigator's pleasure to now reveal that there is a modern-day Danite enclave in the CIA reaching out to the Danites in HUGHES, but we shall have to content ourselves with the only Mormon we have — Bob Bennett — and his relations to Chuck Colson and Howard Hunt.

Bennett had been a director of congressional relations at the Department of Transportation, to wit, a public-relations man and lobbyist. Needless to say, both are splendid positions for a mole. In addition, any work Bennett could find concerning highway construction might bring him, if he chose, close to the Mafia; he was thereby twice-connected to voyage out from his one third of a bishopric. Since he had also been friends with Chuck Colson since 1968, and lately of quiet service as the White House contact (that is, informer) in the Department of Transportation, Bennett was on his way to being his own pivotal figure. Consequently, he was in a position to try to do a favor for HUGHES. The good deed (seeking to divert the dumping of nerve gas from the Bahamas ocean floor — a way of protecting future HUGHES investments in the Bahamas) could not be accomplished, but Bennett left a good impression and was hired by his fellow Mormons.

Then "Colson called Bennett to say that Robert Mullen wanted to sell his company. Colson urged Bennett to buy the company and said he would help him find clients."[12] Bennett bought into Mullen & Company, and in one month rose from executive vice-president to president; after nine months he completed the purchase. Earlier than this, sometime "during his first months with the company . . . Robert Mullen told him about the company's relation with the CIA."[13]

This small account of a purchase is invaluable for what it teaches of how to detect a cover story by the incriminating anemia of its narrative. For it asks us to tolerate the idea that a useful CIA front was sold to a non-CIA man who was then kindly informed of the CIA's relation to the company he bought; in return for such courtesy, he proceeded without ado to labor for the agency. Since Bennett will labor long hours, it is comfortable to suspect he has been with the CIA before we have met him.

> It is in the political agent's interest to betray all the parties who use him and to work for them all at the same time, so that he may move freely and penetrate everywhere.
>
> — Galtier-Boissière[14]

Enter Hunt. He has been with Mullen & Company since May, 1970, a little better than six months, before Bennett has arrived, and according to his account, he is furious with Mullen because Bennett came as a surprise. "The switch was as unexpected as it was unwelcome."[15] Hunt had seen himself as eventually taking over Mullen & Company. Accordingly we are encouraged by his account to believe Hunt moved over to the White House out of disgust with his situation at Mullen & Company rather than as part of a more or less orchestrated plan to bring Bennett and Hunt nearer to the administration. It was, in any case, not a shift that was difficult to make, for Hunt was also a friend of Colson's. They had met at the Brown University Club of Washington in 1966. Later, Colson became president of the club and Hunt, vice-president. They met frequently for

---

[12] *Nightmare.*
[13] Ibid.
[14] E. Howard Hunt, *The Berlin Ending* (epigraph).
[15] E. Howard Hunt, *Undercover.*

lunch all through 1969 and 1970, and at one time Colson even thought enough of Hunt to try to make him director of a conservative think-tank, the Institute for Informed America, which would provide intellectual opposition to the Brookings Institution. The scheme lapsed (since Hunt frightened off Jeb Magruder by a proposal to use the think-tank for covert action), but now that Hunt was working for Colson in the Plumbers and Colson was also friends with Bennett, maybe Colson could be forgiven for thinking the prospects seemed fair for a happy family. As early as the beginning of 1971, he even sent a confidential memo to an aide of Agnew's:

> Bob is a trusted loyalist and a good friend. We intend to use him on a variety of outside projects. One of Bob's (new) clients is Howard Hughes. I am sure I need not explain the political implications of having Hughes' affairs handled here in Washington by a close friend. . . . Bob Bennett tells me that he has never met the Vice President, and that it would enhance his position greatly if we could find an appropriate occasion for him to come in and spend a little time talking with the Vice President. The important thing from our standpoint is to enhance Bennett's position with Hughes because Bennett gives us real access to a sort of power that can be valuable, and it's in our interest to build him up.
>
> — *Compulsive Spy*

It is enough to remind us of Tolstoy's opening sentence in *Anna Karenina:* "Happy families are all alike: every unhappy family is unhappy in its own way." Colson's gang, we know in advance, will be unique.

But we can get a look into how closely Hunt is working with Bennett. A couple of years later, it was found out by way of the minority staff of the Ervin committee that Bennett "suggested to Hunt that Hank Greenspun, publisher of the Las Vegas *Sun*, had material in his safe that would be of interest to both Hughes and the Committee for the Re-election of the President," and Bennett also arranged "a Hunt interview with Clifton Demotte [about] the episode at Chappaquiddick. . . . Furthermore . . . Bennett learned of [Dita Beard's] whereabouts from a Hughes Tool Company executive . . . [and] acted as an intermediary between Howard Hunt and Gordon Liddy after the Watergate break-in. . . ."[16]

---

[16] Fred D. Thompson, *At That Point in Time.* The author was chief minority counsel for the Ervin committee.

This encourages the minority staff to the following conclusions:

(1) While Hunt was at the White House on Charles Colson's payroll, Bennett was, at least, suggesting and coordinating many of Hunt's activities; (2) Bennett obviously enjoyed a close and confidential relationship with some of Howard Hughes' top people at a time when they were furnishing cover for the CIA; and (3) Bennett was acting as a go-between between Hunt and Liddy immediately after the Watergate break-in, and during all of these activities he was undoubtedly reporting periodically to the CIA case officer.

— At That Point in Time

We are even offered a bona fide side-bar. An inquiry came in from HUGHES. The Mormons (we may as well assume it is specifically the Mormons) wanted to know "the cost of bugging the home of Clifford Irving at the time he was writing the spurious Howard Hughes biography. Hunt got an estimate from James McCord and reported back to Bennett." The project proved to be too expensive, but HUGHES, whether the man or the karmic transplant, announced by way of a telephone interview with seven reporters that he had suspicions about the origins of the hoax. "To assume that it's all an accident certainly takes a lot of assuming." It seems HUGHES had decided the genius behind Clifford Irving was Maheu. Dare we say that every unhappy family is happy in its own way?

3.
An Exercise in Epistemology

In an ironic twist, the White House's high priest of snoopery, Charles Colson, was himself bugged recently as he uttered some of the Watergate scandal's most indiscreet confessions.

Colson, when he was the top White House hatchet man, was fond of flipping a switch and tape-recording friends and enemies alike. A few days before he went to prison for obstructing justice, however, he was secretly recorded as he bared his soul to Washington businessman and sometime private eye Richard Bast. . . .

Beside Bast's swimming pool, whose fountain made background water music over a "mike" secreted among poolside flowers, the two men discussed how Nixon could rid himself of CIA and military spying on the White House.

— Jack Anderson, July 15, 1974

If we have been entertaining ourselves until now with the illusion that we are pursuing a narrative, or hovering over a picture that will soon come to focus, we may as well recognize that we can count, at best, on no more than a glimpse of a narrative — enough perhaps to give us hope this is a narrative which exists and not a chaos. But it is a curious endeavor. The best details often lead nowhere. Nixon, for example, received campaign contributions in 1972 which were as large as $2 million from W. Clement Stone and $1 million from Richard Mellon Scaife of Pittsburgh. Nonetheless, the Nixon administration reacted with excessive anxiety to the disclosure of a gift of $100,000 in 1970 from HUGHES by way of Richard Danner to Bebe Rebozo; in fact Nixon fired Archibald Cox only two days after he had indicated to Elliot Richardson how displeased he was about Cox's zealous investigation of Rebozo. The break-in at Watergate was even explained in some scenarios as the measure of Nixon's need to know how much O'Brien knew about HUGHES's gift.[17] It made no sense. Rebozo had an explanation which was legally impeccable. He told investigators that he was worried about the "appearance" of the gift and so did not give it to the President but put it in his own safe-deposit box, and later, in June, 1973, sent it back to HUGHES. One did not have to believe the story, but in the absence of evidence that the cash had been passed, why did Nixon react so powerfully?

> "They must certainly know something very heavy on Nixon," commented Bast. . . .
>
> Colson . . . replied, "They must."
>
> "I mean, if he knows this stuff is going on and he's not doing anything about it . . ." began Bast.
>
> "You know what I think?" interrupted Colson. "You want to know what I really think? . . . I'm loyal to the guy (Nixon) 'cause he's my friend . . . I think Bebe used that ($100,000) for himself and for the President, for the family, and the girls. I think that the President figures — this is my worst suspicion — that if he really blows this, Hughes can blow the whistle on him." . . .
>
> . . . Bast asked whether the only thing the CIA had hanging over Nixon's head was the $100,000.

---

[17] That would assume it was worth $250,000 to CREEP to find out a little more about $100,000.

Replied Colson morosely:
"Who knows that that's the only $100,000?"
— Jack Anderson, July 16, 1974

It is a fascinating detail. It is just that nothing comes of it. We still don't know if it is the only $100,000 or no more than the tail of the mouse left in the trap. Since much that we examine will appear, then tend to disappear, it is nice to think there is something iridescent about a view seen for an instant in the fog.

Perhaps it is the effect of such glimpses to leave us with an afterimage. On reflection, Nixon's reaction to the $100,000 does not have to be political. Even a political man is entitled to a private emotion. Fighting the attack on Rebozo, Nixon could be expressing the outrage he felt at attacks against himself. Or, maybe the gift just gave him an uneasy feeling from the moment it was proposed. Of course, the hard chancre of an inflamed in-house scandal could also have been sitting beneath the money. We simply do not know to which corner the mouse has gone.

The nature of the difficulty begins to disclose itself. We cannot house an explanation because we do not know which of our facts are bricks and which are papier-mâché painted to look like bricks. We can only watch the way the bricks are handled.

It is painful, nonetheless, to relinquish one's hope for a narrative, to admit that study of the CIA may not lead to the exposure of facts so much as to the epistemology of facts. We will not get the goods so quickly as we will learn how to construct a model which will tell us why we cannot get the goods. Of course, that will never be enough — willy-nilly, the habit will persist to look for a new narrative (and damn the papier-mâché bricks).

In the meantime, however, a short course:

Epistemological Model I:
If half the pieces in a jigsaw puzzle are missing, the likelihood is that something can still be put together. Despite its gaps, the picture may be more or less visible. Even if most of the pieces are gone, a loose mosaic can be arranged of isolated elements. The possibility of the real picture being glimpsed under such circumstances is small but not altogether lost.[18] It is just that one would like to know if the few pieces left belong to the same set.[19]

---

[18] Larry Rivers has taught us as much.
[19] Is this what Robert Rauschenberg is up to?

Epistemological Model II:
Maybe it is the splinters of a mirror rather than the scattered pieces of a jigsaw puzzle that provide a superior ground for the metaphor. We are dealing not with reality, after all, but that image of reality which reaches the surface through the cracked looking glass of the media.

Epistemological Model III:
What is most crucial is that we do not forget that we are interpreting curious actions. Men who seem to be honest are offering cover. We are obliged to remind ourselves that a life lived under cover produces a chronic state of mind in the actor which is not unlike those peculiar moments when staring in the mirror too long we come to recognize that the face looking back at us must — inescapably — be our own. Yet it is not. Our vicissitudes (but not our souls) stand revealed in the mirror; or, given another day, and another mirror, there we are, feeling wretched, looking splendid.

Epistemological Model IV:
Doubtless the difficulty is analogous to writing a poem with nothing but names, numbers, facts, conjecture, gossip, trial balloons, leaks, and other assorted pieces of prose.
For example:

> When we interviewed him in my office on December 10, 1973, he struck all of us as a highly intelligent, highly motivated person.... Finally I asked him, "Mr. Martinez, if in fact you were a CIA plant on the Watergate team and were reporting back to the Agency, would you tell us?" He broke into a broad smile, looked around the room, and laughed. He never answered the question; no answer was necessary.
> — *At That Point in Time*

Let us go back to the facts, to the false facts, distorted facts, concealed facts, empty facts, secretly rich facts, and unverifiable speculations of our narrative.

In this connection, nothing we have read about Gordon Liddy explains his long silence in jail so well as the supposition that he is an agent of real caliber. Of his biography we know he was in the FBI in the early Sixties, an assistant district attorney in Dutchess County, ran for Congress on the Conservative party ticket, and got a job with the Treasury Department high up in a Customs Bureau drug campaign called Operation Intercept. It was not a position to leave him alien to certain intimacies of the CIA, the Mafia, and the flow of profits in the drug trade. Liddy came to the White House to work for Egil Krogh, who was trying to organize the Nixon administration's war on drugs with a projected team of CIA men, FBI men, narcs, and private detectives, an undertaking some would see darkly as a most ambitious cover for Nixon's real intent, which was to commence his own Intelligence on a competitive level with the CIA and the FBI — in other words, his unspoken follow-up to the Huston Plan. It is worth mentioning that during this period, Liddy wrote a memo for Nixon in criticism of the FBI, which Nixon described to Krogh as "the most brilliant memorandum" to come his way "in a long time."[20] It is with this background that Liddy comes to CREEP. There is nothing in these details to suggest he could not be a career agent.

We read of how he burns his hand in a flame to impress a girl and threatens to kill Magruder if Jeb touches him on the shoulder again. John Dean describes to us how Liddy offers to commit suicide if that will protect the administration. Liddy offers a lecture on how to kill a man with a finely sharpened pencil. There is nothing in these details to suggest he could not be a career agent.

> "The master who instructed me in the deadliest of the Oriental martial arts taught me that the outcome of a battle is decided in the minds of the opponents before the first blow is struck."
> — G. Gordon Liddy[21]

We have the habit to look on the Watergate burglars as ignorant Cubans led by clowns. Being scorned as ridiculous is, of course, a cover in itself; the CIA can count on such a disguise being provided by the wire services. Simple declarative sentences make curious actions appear automatically absurd.

Under examination, the burglars look better. Gonzales had been a bodyguard for Batista, and fought in the Bay of Pigs. Martinez had been a CIA boat captain and made 354 illegal runs to Cuba. Barker was a member of Batista's secret police, and an FBI contact in Cuba, then an informer against Castro. By Hunt's own description, Barker

---

[20] These details are given in a forthcoming book impressively researched by Edward Jay Epstein, *An American Coup D'Etat* (Putnam's).

[21] As quoted in *Nightmare*.

became his "principal assistant" during the Bay of Pigs, and Hunt was chief of political action.

The fourth Cuban happens to be Italian — Frank Sturgis, an ex-Marine born Frank Angelo Fiorini. He served with Castro in the Sierra Maestra — and would later claim he was already an agent for the Company. In any case, he was good enough to be working as Fidel's personal supervisor in the Havana casinos until the day gambling was eliminated. Then Sturgis decided to defect. To the Mafia and to the CIA. (Or is it simpler to say the Mafia wing of the CIA?) It is a not inconsiderable defection.

Before the Bay of Pigs, Sturgis would act as contact for Santo Trafficante, who with his son Santo Jr. "controlled much of Havana's tourist industry," and was alleged to have received "bulk shipments of heroin from Europe and forwarded them through Florida to New York."[22] During this period, Sturgis joined a CIA unit called Operation Forty, which had been set up to kill Castro and a number of important Fidelistas. Involved in this training were Trafficante and E. Howard Hunt,[23] Frank Sturgis,[24] and Robert Maheu. Maheu and Sturgis must have been reasonably well met, since Sturgis is still pivotal enough eleven years later to be chatting with Jack Anderson in the lobby of Washington National Airport on the morning he arrives from Miami with Barker, Martinez, and Gonzales for the last break-in at Watergate, but then it would be difficult to name an investigative reporter in America more pivotal than Anderson.

> "I don't know if I told you before," Sturgis wrote to his wife [while in jail], "but William F. Buckley used to work for CIA and I don't know if he still does. When he found out that Howard (Hunt) was going to work in the White House, he told Howard it was good that he could be so close to the President but Howard told him that he was there to take orders and not to influence anyone. That was a good answer!"
>
> . . . Buckley frankly admitted he was a "deep cover agent" for the CIA from July, 1951, to March, 1952, but said he had not worked for them since.
>
> — Jack Anderson, September 18, 1973

[22] Alfred W. McCoy, et al., *The Politics of Heroin in Southeast Asia.*

[23] "Strange Bedfellows."

[24] In *Undercover*, Hunt mentions in passing that he did not meet Sturgis until shortly before Watergate. Of course, he also does not mention that there was a plot to assassinate Castro. Nor does he bother to inform us that Hank Sturgis is the name of a character in Hunt's early novel, *Bimini Run*, which Frank Angelo Fiorini liked well enough to modify into an alias.

It was apparent from the documents that in November 1971, a month after he took part in the Fielding break-in, Martinez mentioned his association with Hunt to his case officer who, in turn, took Martinez to the CIA's chief of station in Miami.

We immediately requested that the chief of station be brought from Florida for an interview. The chief, a heavyset man who appeared rather nervous, told us that in March 1972, Martinez had asked him if he "really knew all about the Agency activities in the Miami area." Martinez had dropped hints about Hunt's activities, the chief said, which had concerned him so much that he wrote a letter to CIA headquarters inquiring about Hunt's status. The answer, we were told, was that the chief should "cool it" and not concern himself with Hunt's affairs.

— *At That Point in Time*

One does better not to rely on that comfortable picture we have of E. Howard Hunt as an unhinged undercover man in a wild red wig impotently badgering Dita Beard on her hospital bed — the wig may have been chosen to make him startling to a fearful woman.

By the rank of the posts he occupied in his career, it is obvious that Hunt, for a long time at least, was well regarded in the Agency. For that matter, he has so many credentials we can wonder how close he came in his own mind to becoming director of the CIA. In his autobiography, *Undercover*, he remarks, "Obviously I was never going to be director of Central Intelligence, nor did I particularly want to be," but the year is 1966 and he says it after more than fifteen years of service and such prime positions as deputy chief of station in Mexico (which is where William F. Buckley, Jr. worked for him); chief of covert operations for southeastern Europe — Albania, Yugoslavia, Bulgaria, Greece, and Turkey; chief of political action for the Guatemala operation which overthrew Arbenz; chief of covert operations for the north Asia command — China, Korea, Japan; chief of station in Uruguay; chief of political action for the Bay of Pigs; chief of Domestic Operations Division (the United States); and chief of covert action for Western Europe.

Before joining the CIA Hunt had been an English major at Brown, served in the navy, the OSS, had been a war correspondent for *Life*, published novels, worked in Hollywood, had a Guggenheim Fellowship for one of his novels, and was in Europe for the ECA under Averell Harriman. Later, within the CIA, he collaborated with Allen Dulles in the writing of *The Craft of Intelligence*. He also worked closely with Frank Wisner, Allen Dulles,

Dick Helms, Richard Bissell, Track Barnes, Tom Karamessines —
there are no larger names in the CIA. If his autobiography fails to
mention Cord Meyer or James Angleton there is no reason we cannot speculate on his concealed relations with them, particularly
from 1966 to 1970, when Hunt neglects to describe what he is doing
for the Company, and the assumption, since he is stationed in
America, is capers, domestic capers.

> A Dutch manufacturer of electronic gadgetry was demonstrat-
> ing some ultrasophisticated electronic "sneakies." The Dutch
> salesman announced that over twenty items of gadgetry had been
> hidden in the exhibition room and invited his CIA guests to find
> them. Then the Dutchman set about to uncover them, and *he*
> couldn't find them. Jim McCord had sneaked into the room be-
> fore the demonstration, found them all, and removed them. "Jim
> is one fine operator," said Helms. . . .
> — Miles Copeland, *National Review,*
> September 14, 1973

McCord was in the CIA for twenty years but he seems like nothing so much as an FBI man. A devout Methodist, abstemious, soft-
voiced in his right-wing opinions, his personality speaks of law and
order rather than espionage or counterespionage. With the CIA
from the first years of its inception (those years when it was raiding
the FBI, and Hoover did not like it, and may for all we know have
been casting about for a career agent who could infiltrate the CIA
for the rest of his working life), McCord worked for the Company
from 1951 to 1970 and became chief of the Physical Security Division of the Office of Security.

As we know, his work had in part to do with finding concealed
bugs and dealing with advanced eavesdropping equipment. He was
good enough to receive a Distinguished Service Award from Helms,
and Allen Dulles once referred to him as "my top man."[25] We do
not know what he was top man in, but it is not mean praise.

His performance during the Watergate break-in is on the consequence fascinating for its incompetence. McCord, according to
Hunt's account, bought only four walkie-talkies where six had been
needed. He delayed charging the batteries. He neglected to discon-
nect a burglar-alarm system. In the course of the first break-in, he

---

[25] Lewis Chester, et al., *Watergate.*

removed his men from the Democratic National Committee offices before the job was done. Then for several days he was unable to process the two rolls of film the Cubans did manage to take because McCord's "man" was out of town. In addition, according to Liddy, McCord "bugged the wrong telephone line. He was supposed to tap O'Brien's."[26] So a second attempt was necessary. On the next try, two of McCord's walkie-talkies had uncharged batteries. McCord retaped the locks after the guard had removed the tapes. He then insisted to Liddy on going ahead with the operation. He also retaped the locks horizontally instead of vertically; the tape was therefore visible at a glance. Hunt would finally decide that McCord was a double agent for the Democrats. A double agent he may have been — for the CIA — and a triple agent for the FBI, but a Democrat? McCord?

Whoever he was, McCord broke the Watergate case by his letter in March, 1973, to Judge Sirica: "There was political pressure applied to the defendants to plead guilty and remain silent. Perjury occurred during the trial. . . ."

He also said, "The Watergate Operation was not a CIA operation. . . . I know for a fact that it was not." It is a retired CIA operative speaking, which is to say, a man who may or may not be retired. Authoritative disclaimers by CIA officials bear the same relation to fact that the square root of minus one bears to a real number. The net effect of McCord's remark, therefore, is to make us more suspicious of the CIA. The possibility that he is an FBI man thereby increases an iota.

The second break-in took place in order that the tap on Larry O'Brien's phone that McCord had not put in well enough to function after the first break-in should now be put in again. Hunt thought the project was odd. "O'Brien's in Miami," he said to Liddy. "Why in hell should we tap the phone in his Washington office? . . . What's the rationale? As a friend, colleague and fellow professional, I'm asking you to go back to Mitchell, Dean and Magruder and reargue the case."[27] Liddy replied, "Okay, I'll try again, but I hate to do it. They look to me to get things done, not argue against them."

---

[26] *Undercover.*

[27] Quoting from Hunt is biting the bullet. Still, it is tempting to quote. From *Undercover.*

Since Liddy is the conspirator who has remained silent, we do not know his "principal," that is, we do not know who told him to break into Democratic headquarters the first time, nor — it may be more interesting — who insisted on a second time when Hunt thought the only logic was to call it off. It is not impossible that Magruder, Mitchell — or could it be Dean? — had an undisclosed relation to the CIA. Let us spin on the vertigo of that thought.

> Mr. Haldeman said he had never understood why Alexander P. Butterfield, the aide who disclosed the existence of the White House tapes to the Senate Watergate committee, wanted to join the White House staff. . . .
>
> "He was soon to become an Air Force General. I have never understood why he insisted, against my advice, on dropping his commission or why he suddenly wanted to be part of the Nixon team.
>
> "In view of his subsequent role," Mr. Haldeman went on, "these actions seem even more curious today. Was Butterfield a CIA agent? Maybe. I just don't know."
>
> — The New York *Times,* June 23, 1976

> In the early Sixties he [Haig] ran a CIA-financed Bay of Pigs rehabilitation program, preceding Alexander Butterfield in the job.
>
> — "Strange Bedfellows"

> Colson complained to Bast that the President was always on the verge of coming down hard on the CIA. But, Colson groused, Nixon was talked out of it by presidential staff chief, Al Haig, who feared it would "take down the whole intelligence community."
>
> — Jack Anderson, July 15, 1974

> Haig told us there was "no way" he was working for the CIA.
>
> — Jack Anderson, July 15, 1974

> Paul F. Hellmuth, the managing partner of St. Clair's Boston law firm, has been associated over the past decade with . . . Anderson Security Consultants, Inc . . . a CIA front. . . .
>
> Mysterious checks, written for large amounts, would frequently arrive at the office of the firm's secretary-treasurer, Virginia lawyer L. Lee Bean, who would . . . disperse it upon instructions.

The secret instructions often came, say our sources, from James St. Clair's quiet law partner. Some of the mystery money was dispatched to Miami banks and was used allegedly to support the CIA's anti-Castro activities. . . . [Hellmuth] insisted . . . that James St. Clair didn't know "the first thing about the security firm."

— Jack Anderson, July 22, 1974

[Leon] Jaworski had been . . . a director of a private foundation that laundered funds for the CIA.

— "Strange Bedfellows"

We also learned that Paul O'Brien, who had served as counsel to the Committee to Re-elect the President after the Watergate break-in, was a former CIA operative.

— *At That Point in Time*

Among the officers of OSS Detachment 101 was Clark MacGregor, later a Congressman, a White House staffer, and, after the Watergate break-in, the replacement for John Mitchell as head of the Committee for the Re-Election of the President.

— *Compulsive Spy*

"Bob Woodward interviewed me on numerous occasions. I have told Woodward everything I know about the Watergate case, except the Mullen company's tie to the CIA. I never mentioned that to him."

— Robert Bennett: House subcommittee testimony[28]

Because Robert Bennett's CIA ties were exposed by the Watergate scandal, he has closed down the Mullen Agency. He now works for the Hughes organization as a vice-president and CIA liaison.

— "Strange Bedfellows"

During the Bast interview, Colson would name Bennett as Deep Throat. At one point, he would say in pain, "Every story that Woodward won the Pulitzer Prize for was fed to him by the CIA."

An observer of the Company, hearing of this, shook his head. "Deep Throat is a cover in itself. Where is the casual reader who will argue with so agreeable a story — one man's revelation pulling down the entire Nixon administration? If Deep Throat told all, it was only because the information had already been neatly collected

---

[28] As quoted in "Strange Bedfellows."

for Deep Throat to tell." The observer shook his head. "Learn the law of reversal. The victims can be the agents in these affairs. There is as much need to remain suspicious of Colson as to feel sorry for him, since in attacking the CIA, Colson creates good cover for them. The reaction of the newspaper reader who dislikes old Chuck is to think, 'Even if it is true (and I must say I have had my suspicions of the CIA) I won't believe the story if it comes from Colson.' The Bast interview, you see, bothers me. Colson visits Bast, a private investigator, sits down by the pool next to the shrubbery and never wonders if he is being taped? Colson? Pit-bull Colson?

"By the same guideline, the heroes can be the villains. Beware of the heroes of Watergate. I look at the Washington *Post* and think, 'Isn't it a brave paper? Isn't that a heroic editor who dares what no editor of no other major paper will dare? Isn't that right in the vein of major newspaper editors as we have come to know them?'"

On publication of this piece, the editor of the Washington *Post* emphatically denied that he had ever been, or was now, a member of the CIA.

"Never allow yourself," the observer says, "to think you have a fixed platform from which to measure these motions. We're out in the stars with Einstein, I assure you. For instance, you speak of McCord as being inefficient, when what you relate is no more than Hunt's description of how McCord acted in the break-in. Hunt's book could have been written by an enclave."

"Were they wishing to suggest that McCord was dealing with the Democrats?"

"Never look for the answer. Pursue the question into the next question. The answer is invariably smudged, but the questions are beautiful. There is the rapture of the depths descending into the questions."

I also suspected, but could never prove, that the Nixon crowd tapped my telephones. I was only slightly surprised, therefore, by a letter mailed to me on April 15, 1972. It was written by William Haddad, a New York entrepreneur who, until a dozen years ago, had been a prize-winning investigative reporter. Haddad told me he had learned from a private investigator of plans to tap the telephones of the Democratic National Committee. Haddad understood the plot had been hatched by a group of advertis-

ing men, known as the November Group, who had been re-
cruited for the Nixon campaign.

— Jack Anderson, *Parade*, July 22, 1973

A letter from William Haddad to Larry O'Brien, March 23, 1972:

"I am hearing some very disturbing stories about GOP sophisticated surveillance techniques now being used for campaign purposes and of an interesting group here in New York where some
of this "intelligence" activity is centered. The information comes
from a counter-wiretapper ... who had come to me highly recommended. ... Can you have someone call me so you can get the
info first hand and take whatever actions you deem necessary."

— *At That Point in Time*

O'Brien sent the director of communications for the Democratic
National Committee to visit Haddad and there was a meeting with
the counter wiretapper whose name proved to be Woolston-Smith.
He was "a short paunchy bald man who spoke with a pronounced
British accent and smoked a pipe." In October, 1973, a year and a
half later, two members of the minority staff of the Ervin committee
took a deposition from Woolston-Smith.

He testified that he was a private investigator in New York City,
a citizen of New Zealand with experience in British intelligence,
and a permanent resident of the United States. He acknowledged
that he had excellent contacts in the intelligence community and
said his New York offices had been used by the CIA, after the
Bay of Pigs, as a clearinghouse for those returning from the invasion brigades. This information was consistent with what we had
determined from other sources. Woolston-Smith was a most mysterious person; there were indications that he had connections
with both British and Canadian intelligence, although we could
never determine the exact relationship.

Woolston-Smith said he had told William Haddad of the possibility of Republican media control through the November Group
as early as December 1971, and that they had discussed the
Group many times before the meeting of April 26, 1972. He
knew enough about the operation, he said, to know that Gordon
Liddy "ran the show."

— *At That Point in Time*

Since Gemstone, Liddy's first ambitious plan to tap the Democratic National Committee and wire Miami for the Democratic con-

vention, was not even presented to John Mitchell until January 27, 1972, it seems that some undisclosed scheme was already being developed by Gordon Liddy and the November Group in the fall of 1971. Such a probability hardly diminishes the hypothesis that Liddy is an agent of stature. (In fact, the November Group will even be given a million dollars by CREEP before the famous April 7 deadline for campaign contributions. While the majority of this is ostensibly for the November Group's stated purpose, which is advertising, not espionage, the figure is nonetheless interesting. It is equal to the sum Liddy tried to get for Gemstone.)

At any rate, we are left with the following additions:

(1) The Democrats were well aware of the November Group and the possibility that their offices would soon be bugged.

(2) British and Canadian Intelligence can now be added to the soup. Let us think of them as herbs.

(3) Maybe the Democrats were putting in the garlic. Haddad "sent his entire file to Jack Anderson in April 1972" and now "could not remember what was in it. In fact, Haddad said, he sent material to Anderson twice, but had kept no copies." Jack Anderson "had acknowledged receipt of the material from Haddad concerning plans for the break-in, but he said he had since lost it."[29]

Of course, the CIA had infiltrated the FBI, and the FBI had unknown men working for it in the CIA. We must assume both had agents in the Bureau of Narcotics and Dangerous Drugs, the IRS, the National Security Council, the 40 Committee, the Atomic Energy Commission, the Special Operations Division, Naval Intelligence, Air Force Intelligence, the Defense Intelligence Agency, the National Security Agency, the Council on Foreign Relations, HUGHES, plus a number of private intelligence companies whose work extended from military-industrial security to private detectives' offices. In turn, these companies, bureaus, groups, and agencies had to the best of their ability infiltrated the CIA and the FBI. Since the CIA, the FBI, and other major intelligence also had had their authority infiltrated by their own unknown enclaves, it is, in certain circumstances, meaningless to speak of the CIA as a way of differentiating it from the AIA, the DIA, the NSC, HUGHES, or the SOD — let us use the initials CIA therefore like a mathematical symbol which will, depending on the context in which it is employed, usually offer specific reference to a CIA located physically

---

[29] *At That Point in Time.*

in Langley, Virginia, with near to 18,000 employees, understanding that under other circumstances CIA may be no more than a general locus signifying an unknown factor whose function is intelligence and whose field is the invisible government. Students of Einstein's work on tensor calculus may find it comfortable to deal with these varieties of unknowns. In the world of social theory, however, we are at the point where a special and general theory of relative identity in social relations would be of inestimable use since the only situation for which there can be no cover is *anguish*, and the operation of the twentieth century may be to alienate us from that emotion in preparation for the ultimate destruction of the human soul as opposed to the oncoming hegemony of the technological person.

Generally, his enemies and friends agreed that Nixon was a fool not to destroy the tapes. They may not have understood the depth of the pot in which he was boiling. There was reason to believe there were copies of the tapes. If Butterfield would reveal their existence, he could be an agent; if one agent was near those tapes, then more than one; what reason to assume duplicates of the damaging tapes were not being systematically prepared all the while he was being set up? Impeachment was certain if he burned the evidence and a copy appeared.

"You do not understand. This man stood at the threshold of his own idea of greatness. He was going to write the peace with Communism. He was going to be immortal. Now, as he loses respect, it is slipping away from him inch by inch." Kissinger smiles sadly over his salad. Across the city, the Ervin committee is holding a hearing in the hot summer afternoon. "People criticize Nixon for being irresolute about Watergate. Why does he not confess what is wrong and end it? they ask. They do not understand that he cannot make a move because he is not in possession of all the facts. He does not know what is going to happen next. He does not know what is going to break upon him next." Kissinger sighs. "Nobody will ever know how close that man was to getting the foreign situation he wanted."

Nixon is not only a Shakespearean protagonist in the hour of his downfall, but Macbeth believing that Birnam Wood will never come to Dunsinane. Of course, he is as appealing in his travail as Ronald

Reagan might be playing Lear, but the echo nonetheless of a vast anguish comes back — who else has known such anguish and managed to live in the American world? Birnam Wood will come back to Dunsinane as the tapes one by one get to be taken.

Epistemological Model V:
"Sometimes," said the wise observer, "I think of that story of Howard Hughes being so fearful of bacteria that he kept Jean Peters across the room from him, and then I think, what if the fear of bacteria is the cover, and the double dare not get too close to Jean Peters?"

Epistemological Model VI:
There is hardly an episode in Watergate which was not presented to us in a way that makes it seem more stupid than it ought to have been. Or, is it closer to say that what we hope to perceive is more brilliant than the level at which we have been encouraged to perceive it?

The tapes, for example. If a tape can be made, a copy can be made. Until we brood upon the matter, it is natural to assume the copy is equal to the original. We do not stop to think that the poor tapes we thought were the originals could in fact have been inferior copies. The remarkably bad quality of the tapes might have been produced by design. There are advantages to a tape which can hardly be heard: The affair is downgraded, and seems less sinister. No cover is more comfortable to a clandestine operation than the appearance of ineffectuality. Let us remind ourselves of how inept the Secret Service seemed in its taping operation. Possessing all that White House power, all those funds, all that available electronic equipment — yet the product sounds like it was recorded in the glove compartment of a moving car. Admittedly, there were technical difficulties to the taping, but the product still seems inadequate. Nixon must have suffered another turn of the screw. Since he cannot know if the tapes he hears are the unique, original, and only tapes, or a debased copy prepared by his enemies, he cannot even be certain whether it is a trap to encourage him to take advantage of the garbled sound and rephrase the transcripts in his favor. He takes the plunge. But his emendations are discovered later by the House Judiciary Committee. A corrected transcript is presented to America.

How can Nixon not wonder whether somebody substituted a subtly clearer version of the tapes to John Doar's staff?

All the while, Nixon has to confront another question. If he evades every snare, pit, impressment, and delusion, if he even manages to work his way through the Senate to the edge of being declared not guilty in the impeachment, how can he be certain that in the last minute after the very last of all these abominably unexpected breaches in his cover-up, the missing eighteen minutes will still not appear? Then he can envision how America will spank the horse, and he will twist forever in the wind.

4.
A Crisis in Criminology

I received a telephone call from L. Patrick Gray, the Acting Director of the FBI — a man I had never met. Gray told me he was disturbed by reports suggesting the FBI was not conducting a thorough investigation. "That is simply not true," Gray told me. "I assure you this matter will be pursued wherever it leads, regardless of my position in the Administration. Let the chips fall where they may." I told Gray I appreciated his call, and he concluded our talk with an unexpected comment: "Mr. O'Brien, we Irish Catholics must stick together."

On July 7, following Gray's call, I was visited by two Secret Service agents. . . . They told me they had been instructed to report to me that the FBI's exhaustive examination of the National Committee offices had uncovered no telephone bugs or other electronic devices — that "the place was found to be clean." I accepted their report without question. I knew the FBI had torn the place apart — removing ceiling panels, dismantling radiators, and the like — and if they said there were no bugs, then I assumed there were no bugs. Later evidence, of course, revealed that bugs had been placed on my phone and that of Spencer Oliver, Executive Director of the Association of State Democratic Chairmen. To this day I cannot explain the discrepancy between those facts and the report I was given.

— No Final Victories

When Hunt's team was caught, McCord had already removed a few panels from the ceiling of O'Brien's office. It is not so very well known that an excellent and advanced kind of eavesdropping can be achieved by driving a nail into the flooring of the office you wish to monitor from the ceiling of the office below. A listening device is then attached to the nail. The sophistication of this method is that it is not possible to detect the bug from the office being taped, since the listening device attracts no more attention than *any* nail in the floor. The first question to ask of many a break-in is not therefore which office was entered, but who is working in the office above. By this logic, a real interest in O'Brien's conversations could best have been satisfied by a break-in on the fifth floor — in order to tap the sixth. Since we are already on the sixth, who inhabits the seventh?

That part of the seventh floor of the Watergate Office Building, which rested unmistakably over Larry O'Brien's quarters, was occupied at the time by no less than the office of the secretary of the Federal Reserve Board. Can matters be this simple? It is not seemly that great financial secrets should be discussed in an office of a building which looks to have been designed by an architect with a degree in Mafia Modern, but interest augments when we learn that one of the computers of the Federal Reserve Board is located in the basement of the same Watergate Office Building. If, on a given day, the Federal Reserve Board had sealed itself in to discuss a change in the discount rate, is it wholly inconceivable that a CIA man (a veritable Grand Mole of a banker) installed for years on the Federal Reserve Board might have phoned in to the computer in the Watergate Office Building basement an apparently routine question that would yet manage to tell his undercover assistant in the basement what the shift would be in the discount rate? Assuming that this assistant has been sequestered with the computer to maintain his discretion during these important deliberations of the board, the question is whether the basement assistant could not manage to make an innocent phone call to somebody on the seventh floor. Since we are assuming the man on the seventh floor is not part of the team to which the man in the basement belongs, the conversation would have to go something like this:

> BASEMENT: I hear Vida Blue is pitching today.
> SEVENTH FLOOR: Impossible! He pitched two days ago.
> BASEMENT: (Indignantly) Who did?
> SEVENTH FLOOR: (Triumphantly) Vida Blue!

That was what the basement wanted to hear said on the seventh floor and said loud enough for the nail in the ceiling of the sixth floor to pick it up — the names of baseball pitchers having been geared to the rise and fall in the discount rate. Now, whoever monitored that conversation could pass the information along. Since more than one team would presumably be working to get advance information on the change in the rate, let us assume our team got the word out with a possible lead of three hours over all the others.

"How much would such information be worth?" a banker was asked.

"Conservatively," he replied, in the rich and pompous voice which is privy to large sums, *"billions."*

"For just a few hours' lead?"

"That is time enough."

The possibility is now open that the CIA was using the break-in to the Democratic National Committee as its elegant cover to the real operation, which was to tap privileged Federal Reserve Board information. Elegance offers its exquisite use of resources, so one would not claim the CIA had no interest in O'Brien nor in Oliver. O'Brien and Oliver had had their propinquity with the CIA, after all. While we know they cannot be in Intelligence — since how may we conceive of a good liberal Democrat who is? — nonetheless, they might attract an enclave in the CIA (if, of course, it is an enclave performing the break-in under the auspices of CREEP and not just a burglary by red-hot amateurs executed at the third rate of CREEP stupidity). Yes, some enclave might legitimately have been curious to know more about what O'Brien and Oliver knew of Chappaquiddick, or Eagleton's secret medical file, or HUGHES in relation to Maheu, Lansky, Rebozo, and Nixon on one side, or HUGHES, Bennett, Hunt, and Helms on the other. Name the teams; HUGHES is on all of them. Recognize that with the Democratic Committee break-in as cover, the operation has power over CREEP — which is to say ultimately over Nixon — even if its burglars are caught. That is elegance. Obtaining neither their first objective — the Federal Reserve tap — nor the second — lines on O'Brien and Oliver — the entrepreneurs still end with more power over the presidency than before. Once everybody made certain the election was won in spite of Watergate, there would be even more power.

Of course, a risk was taken. If Watergate had broken too early, McGovern might have been able to get his campaign turned around (although the thought does not ring loud in the lost ether) but then

Watergate never burst until the election was safe and the operators could begin to apply that wrenching pressure on the bones of the Nixon administration.

It must, however, be immediately visible that while this last scenario violates no facts, it is only a literary fancy — not an iota of proof. Just another model. Perhaps we can modernize William of Ockham's razor by saying: The simplest model which satisfies all the facts is likely to lead us to inexplicable facts.

> Four of the five men arrested in the bugging attempt at the Democratic National Committee headquarters Saturday morning were registered as guests at the Watergate Hotel on April 28, the same night that two other firms in the Watergate building were broken into. . . .
>
> The firm of Freed, Frank, Harris, Shriver and Kampelman, located on the 10th floor of the Watergate Building, 2600 Virginia Ave. NW, was broken into on May 18, but officials of the firm did not report the incident to police until yesterday. . . .
>
> A spokesman for the Freed law firm said yesterday that the burglary was not immediately reported to police because nothing appeared to be missing, and employees did not associate the incident with political espionage until disclosure of Saturday's break-in. . . .
>
> On April 28, the night four of the five bugging suspects were registered at the Watergate Hotel, according to police, the 11th-floor offices of the Sterling Institute, a management consulting firm, were broken into and $1,100 worth of typewriters and calculating machines was stolen. . . .
>
> The same night, police records show, the law firm of Boykin and DeFrancis, located on the eighth floor of the Watergate, was forcibly entered and $525 worth of office equipment was stolen.
> — The Washington *Post*, June 21, 1972

Maybe if our scenarios have had a purpose, it has been to flavor our reading with the temperament of an agent, a way of saying that we have become sufficiently paranoid to see connections where others see lists. So let us look at a list of the offices in July, 1973, on the seventh and eighth floors of the Watergate Building, and take the pleasure of wondering how many of those names and corporations have no relation to Intelligence.

701 Defense & Aerospace
Center of Sterling
Institute, Inc.
H. F. Dean
Human Factors Re-
search Associates,
Inc.
Inst. for Psychiatry &
Foreign Affairs
704 Harris Intertype Corp.
Harris Shire, Con-
ductor
Radiation, Inc.
R. F. Communications,
Inc.
707 EDP Technology
Systemed Corp.
711 Federal Reserve Board
Office of Sec'y

805 Division of Federal
Reserve Bank
Operations
808 Foreign Banking
Authorities
Office of Defense
Planning
Securities
Stat Methodology &
Procedures Section
811 Interstate General
Corp.
L. E. Steele
812 Armistead I. Selden, Jr.
Boykin & De Francis
815 Perkin Elver Corp.
Joseph Dixon,
Manager

When we add the three robberies in the last news story and include the possibility of break-ins to other offices we know nothing
about by burglary teams who were removing taps that others had
been putting in, there is now posed to our brand-new agent-type
brain a further question: What part of the Watergate Office Building
was not being tapped?

Our procedure has conducted us to the point where we have to
recognize that we have used up our last scenario in order to bring us
to a place where we have no scenario to replace it. Now, we know
less than before of what might possibly be going on.

5.
A Tension in Teleology

Said the CIA:
Authority imprinted upon emptiness
　　　is money,
　　　honey.
Bang bang Howard.
We don't need you.
We need
The space where you were.
　　　　　　　　— Anonymo L'Rivera

Like a main gear in the clockwork is Nixon's anguish. As we hear the tick, we dwell in the fascination of the inexorable.

Next to Nixon, Hunt is an idler gear. His anguish is all of his existence, but it moves us less. The main gear goes until the last of the tension in the spring runs down, but the idler gear never runs down — it is merely attached to the alarm. So its end is not inexorable but catastrophic — as when the clock is dropped and the idler gear is broken.

Hunt was broken. The style of *Undercover* has that numbness of affect which comes from a fall. He writes without feeling more for one period in his life than another as though he is saying it is costly enough to locate the episodes. He is like a semiconscious victim who senses that coming awake will be equal to crawling up a slope of broken glass. The horrors to come will be greater than the ones he has known already.

Yet, as with Nixon, there is no danger of getting to like Hunt too much. We can decide that Nixon was set up by Watergate and feel no great pity because we can also remember the war in Vietnam he kept going for four years in order to assure his reelection. One can always recall the voice Nixon used when he spoke of the North Vietnamese as "my enemy," on the day he ordered the Christmas bombing. He had always wanted to be an actor and he ended by playing the classic role of the criminal who is convicted for the wrong crime. So one does not have to feel an overcharge of compas-

sion for Nixon — just enough to water our imagination. Your enemies succeed after all when they dry up your imagination.

By the same token, there is a built-in limit to how much compassion we can feel for Hunt. We have only to read his account of his
own methods on a caper in the early Fifties:

> The Mexican Communist leader was then visiting Peking. On the
> day of his departure Bob North airmailed me a copy of a Chinese
> newspaper announcing his departure, sending a duplicate copy to
> CIA headquarters. To replace the departure announcement I fab-
> ricated a story in which the Mexican Communist was quoted as
> deprecating fellow Mexicans and saying, among other things, that
> Mexican peasants could never hope to achieve the cultural level of
> the superior Chinese. I cabled the fabrication to headquarters,
> where a special type font had been made by reproducing samples
> from the local paper. My fabricated story was set in this duplicate
> type and the entire front page of the local paper re-created by
> technical means. A dozen copies were pouched to me and were
> received before the target Communist returned to Mexico.
>
> The fabricated newspapers were made available to local jour-
> nalists who published facsimiles of the offensive interview to-
> gether with a translation into Spanish. The target's protestations
> of innocence gained no credence whatever, for technical tests
> conducted on the duplicated Chinese paper affirmed that the type
> in which the story was printed perfectly matched other type
> samples in the same newspaper and so had to be authentic.[30]
>
> — *Undercover*

A footnote says, "It was this sort of technical assistance from CIA
that I lacked when I undertook to fabricate two State Department
cables in 1971."

No, we do not have to like him too much. Self-pity is Hunt's
companion, and bitterness is his fuel. He writes with the tightly
compressed bile of a disappointed man; the reader is to be reminded
that his early prospects were happier than his later ones. Photographs taken of him on the beach at Acapulco a few months out of
OSS show the would-be screenwriter looking well built in bathing
trunks. He bears a bit of resemblance to Hemingway, and is at pains
in *Undercover* to show pictures of himself skiing and hunting. For
that matter, he is also adept at fishing, squash, golf, tennis, riding,
boxing, and screwing — so the autobiography suggests.

---

[30] This story is a perfect example of how a fact can be wiped out by an artifact.

It would be a bet Hemingway is his hero, and that Hunt in the late 1940s was torn between a life as a great novelist and a social life as a spy. We can guess how he chooses. He is, with everything else, a social climber, and drops on the reader every big name he knows from Eisenhower and Nixon down, making a show of his good WASP family origins (Hunt's Point in the Bronx is named after a relative who goes back to the Revolutionary War, and Leigh Hunt is on the family tree) as well as his wife's sterling ancestry ("In addition to being descended from the Presidential Adams and Harrison families, my wife was one-eighth Oglala Sioux . . ."). Before Hunt, she has been married to the Marquis de Goutière. No matter that her maiden name is Wetzel and Hunt is from Brown, not Princeton (a full demerit in the early CIA), he will still look to climb high into the good life of Oh So Social. "The service plates were Revere gadroon, the crystal was an opaline . . ." is a line from one of his novels, and he will make a point of asking Bill Buckley to be godfather to his children. At the end, when tragedy strikes, he and his family are living in a house called Witches Island in Potomac, Maryland, in "what was to be our final family home. On its ample acreage were paddocks, a stable, outbuildings and woods." He is the perfect reader for the magazine edited by the godfather of his children.

Still, he is not just one more anti-Communist with nothing but the righteous moral equivalent of tunnel vision. He has also had a life. It is almost an appealing life. He has had dyslexia as a boy and played trumpet in a high-school dance band. What is most irritating about Hunt is that he is nearly large enough to be a protagonist in a good and solid novel, and yet — hatred has certainly dried his imagination — he is never large enough. No moment of wit will ever separate his soul from his disasters.

All the heavier must those disasters sit on him. Those disasters pose insoluble questions. Their lack of an answer promises insanity.

What, for instance, can he make of that list of offices on the seventh and eighth floors of the Watergate Office Building? Or of those extra break-ins he may now be hearing about for the first time? With his sophistication in the infiltration of one group of Intelligence by another — he has after all been chief of covert action in the Domestic Operations Division — how could Hunt not entertain the hypothesis that a species of trench warfare in bugging and counterbugging had been going on in the Watergate Office Building long before his operation ran into its peculiar trap? Let us even assume

that everything he has told us is only a cover story for the more serious job he assumed he was doing. After the arrests, how can he be
certain he was told anything accurate?

There is a tool of inquiry provided by Lenin. He suggested that
when a political event occurred whose origin or motive seemed incomprehensible, then ask the question: "Whom?" Whom does this
benefit? Whom did Watergate benefit? Hunt would ask the question. And he would have to face the nightmare that the Nixon-Kis-
singer wing of the CIA, which by now for practical purposes could
be described as the Rockefeller-Détente wing, had been mangled at
Watergate by the Cold War wing. If so, however, then he, Hunt had
also been set up in the process, had been sacrificed by his own people to implicate Nixon. There was a centrality to such a hypothesis
no agent could ignore.

There are not only dimensions to paranoia but degrees. Cold paranoia can serve as the assistant to brilliance, but fevered paranoia
(where the heat comes from the thought that one is being done in
by one's friends) is the true hellion of hysteria. All panics are loose,
all proportions are lost. In such a fry, how can one ignore the smallest detail?

Hunt could even begin to brood over people like R. Spencer
Oliver, whose phone happened to be the other line tapped at the
Democratic National Committee. Hunt could remember a dinner
with a young Democrat named Spencer Oliver who had been out
with Mullen, Bennett, and himself back in 1970 or 1971. During the
meal, Oliver had made a point of mentioning the names of a few
CIA officers Hunt knew personally. Oliver had been surprisingly
knowledgeable. Mullen and Bennett had even wanted to take Oliver
into Mullen & Company as a partner! But Hunt had disapproved.

Now, he had been caught on an operation which had for one of
its tasks the tapping of Oliver's phone. Hunt could mention Oliver
casually in his book and make no connection between the Spencer
Oliver with whom he had dinner and the R. Spencer Oliver whose
phone was tapped. He does not ask if they are not most certainly the
same man. Such calm, however, is for his book. From Hunt's point
of view, Oliver might have little or a great deal to do with Watergate. In the ongoing crisis of trying to solve the mystery of his life
with all the working experience of his career, how is Hunt to measure the relevant importance of that detail, or of McCord and Fensterwald? McCord, for instance, has taken Bernard Fensterwald for
his lawyer to go before the Ervin committee, Fensterwald who is

chairman of the Committee to Investigate Assassinations. The unspoken shock to the media would not be small. It is a way of saying Watergate is related to Dallas. Which enclave now wanted the media to think that way? Dallas and Watergate. That would be the scoop of the century. The people behind McCord might be serving some kind of notice.

We are trying to live in the measure of Hunt's anguish, but it is impossible to speculate here. We do not know, after all, whether he had anything to do with Dallas. The photograph of the two bums arrested by the police in Dealey Plaza shortly after the murder does show a resemblance to Hunt and Sturgis but there is an indigestible discrepancy in the height. On the other hand, Hunt was chief of covert action in the Division of Domestic Affairs at the time; that is a perfect desk from which to have a hand in such an assassination (especially if it has been brought off by some variant of a Mafia and anti-Castro Cuban team). At the least, we have to assume that Hunt would have been in position to pick up enough to embarrass the CIA profoundly. But then it is staggering to contemplate how much Hunt may have found out about matters he had not necessarily been active in himself. If no one in the CIA could locate to a certainty the details of other operations, still a tremendous amount might be learned through gossip, or by reconnaissance through those more or less secret files which would be more or less available on long, dull office afternoons. And he was a writer of suspense novels, no less. What material might be at hand! To the degree the CIA is bureaucratic and not romantic there would be formal procedures in getting to the files which could be winked at, breached, circumvented, or directly betrayed. To the degree the CIA was a culture, then Hunt was a living piece of inquiring matter, and in the years from 1966 to 1970 as his career in the CIA was ostensibly winding down, he had time to do a little research on some of those hundred and more murders in Dallas supposedly connected to witnesses of the assassination, time to get a line on who might be doing the job. For the CIA, whether implicated or not, could hardly be without interest in a mop-up operation of such magnitude. Over a hundred murders to keep the seepage of information under control!

So Hunt may have known a great deal about Dallas. We have to hold this in our attention when we begin to think of the nightmare within Hunt's nightmare — the death of his wife in the crash of United Air Lines Flight 553 from Washington to Chicago on December 8, 1972. The plane had crashed on landing at Midway and she was one of forty-five people who were killed. We do not know how much Hunt knew nor how much he had told his wife. We know that she was making payments to the Cubans with White House money, but that is hardly a piece of information worth silencing by the risk and carnage of sabotaging an airplane. An investigator, Sherman Skolnick, in Chicago, would lay the claim that twelve people in one way or another connected with Watergate were on the plane, and he would remind us that White House aide Egil Krogh, Gordon Liddy's old White House boss, was appointed under secretary of transportation the next day and would supervise the National Transportation Safety Board and the Federal Aviation Administration in their investigations of the crash. That is not an automatically insignificant detail. On December 19, Alexander Butterfield would be appointed the new head of the F.A.A.[31]

If Hunt and Dorothy Hunt had known a great deal about Dallas and were threatening to tell the world, then Hunt would not have to brood over such details. He could assume his wife's plane had been encouraged to crash. Of course, we would no longer be talking about anguish, but masterplots and last-reel peril. The likelihood is that Hunt and Dorothy Hunt were trapped in a smaller game, and the crash was a mixture of inefficiency, cynical maintenance, and who knows? — some overload of psychic intensity among the passengers. (Why else do great athletes live in such fear of traveling by air but that psychic intensity is also a species of physical charge and can even distort the workings of an electronic system?)

No, it is more likely Hunt was living with the subtle horror that attends every inexplicable crash — is there a psychology to machines? Had there been an intervention of moral forces, a play of the dice from the demiurge? At the least, Dorothy Hunt's death was evidence of the raised law of coincidence in dramatic and dreadful events. Great or livid events could indeed be peculiar in their properties, and maybe no perfect conspiracy ever worked, since people were so imperfect — only imperfect conspiracies succeeded and then only when a coincidence drove the denouement home. Was it possible that Hunt was finally obliged to look over the lip of tragedy itself — a view which leaves us, the Greeks were certain, babbling and broken? Did he come to think that a psychic vortex pulls in a higher incidence of coincidence itself?

---

[31] For that matter, Dwight Chapin, appointments secretary to Nixon, moved over two months later to an executive position at United.

"A man may defend himself against all enemies save those who are resolved that such a man as he should not exist."
— Tacitus, epigraph to *Undercover*

Reflect on the phenomenon: A higher incidence of coincidence itself. The more central the dreadful act, then the greater is the number of accidents, disasters, and astonishing connections which surround it. By such a cosmic thesis, more than one assassination plot would come to collision on those murderous days of our history (when Americans began to live in fear of more than the atom bomb) and so, too, more than one agency, more than one enclave, more than one motive, yes, more than one plot have been set up, or unhinged, at Watergate. We have to free our minds of a hundred certainties we have been provided (and have provided ourselves) on that third-rate burglary. We have preferred to rely on the testimony of a hundred skilled and professional liars rather than face into a vision of reality which would recognize that Franz Kafka is the true if abstract historian of the modern age, and the Möbius strip is the nearest surface we can find to a plane.[32]

To free our minds! We live in one existence, but have the overlay of another upon us. We strive to make our history, and sense, with the uneasiness of confrontations never faced, that we may dwell under the overall domination of an invisible second government (at odds with itself?) whose touch is subtle, but whose scenarios sit like an incubus upon Intelligence itself.

Of course we also live in a world more dazzling with the montage of startling connections than a Kenneth Anger film. Maybe, it is our reward. During that season when Bobby Kennedy, weary from stalking Jimmy Hoffa, would relax with Marilyn Monroe, we find out Hoffa, in his turn, hired a wiretapper, Bernard Spindel, to listen in on Bobby.[33] Spindel, who must have been as proficient as Gene Hackman in *The Conversation*, was going to be arrested eventually and would die in jail. There is reason to think the Kennedys never forgave him, for Spindel seems to have gotten some tapes on Bobby, and the wiretapper's widow appears to have kept and concealed them. She rose up to the polluted surface of the news a year or two ago, Mrs. Barbara Fox Spindel. A small munitions company she

---

[32] A Möbius strip is like a paper band curved into a circle, but twisted a half turn before it is glued. If you start drawing a line down the middle of the band your pencil will end up on the opposite side of the paper once you have circled the ring. Stated by it s paradox, the top surface of the plane is now the bottom surface.

[33] Robert F. Slatzer, *The Life and Curious Death of Marilyn Monroe*.

owned had been offering (by the claim of its promotion material) to be able to produce fatal exploding cigarette packs and other small works of surprise for the use of the CIA and other espionage. Her company and her name became connected by way of the newspaper story to Lucien "Gus" Conein, an old CIA hand who had long worked for General Lansdale, the CIA station chief in Saigon. Conein denied the connection vehemently, of course, but then we can imagine how quickly somebody in his line of work is going to admit a professional association with Mrs. Spindel.

Now, it happens to be Conein, an old Company associate, whom Hunt interviewed when Chuck Colson was looking for a way to cook up a few false Kennedy cables on the assassination of Diem. It is a long trail which leads from the tragedy of Marilyn Monroe to E. Howard Hunt and his thunderstruck fun and games, and there is not much voltage in these connections. No shock comes across the gap. It is just that like Agatha Christie's characters we all seem to end up knowing one another. Before too long, if irony does not paralyze, we may be singing, "No man is an Iland, intire of it selfe" in the godawful music of Ernest Hemingway's final whiskey-cracked voice. Listen to his record.[34] What a crazy country we inhabit. What a harlot. What a brute. She squashes sausage out of the minds of novelists on their hotfooted way to a real good plot.

Bibliography

Anderson, Jack. "My Journal on Watergate." *Parade*, July 22, 1973.

Anderson, Jack. The Washington *Post*, September 18, 1973; May 23, June 6, July 15, 16, 22, 1974.

Chester, Lewis, et al. *Watergate*. New York: Ballantine, 1973.

Copeland, Miles. "The Unmentionable Uses of the CIA." *National Review*, September 14, 1973.

Fay, Stephen, et al. *Hoax*. New York: Viking, 1972.

Hunt, E. Howard. *The Berlin Ending*. New York: Putnam's, 1973.

Hunt, E. Howard. *Undercover*. New York: Berkley, 1974.

Kohn, Howard. "Strange Bedfellows—The Hughes-Nixon-Lansky Connection." *Rolling Stone*, May 20, 1976.

Lukas, J. Anthony. *Nightmare*. New York: Viking, 1976.

Magruder, Jeb Stuart. *An American Life*. New York: Atheneum, 1974.

Marchetti, Victor, and Marks, John D. *The CIA and the Cult of Intelligence*. New York: Knopf, 1974.

[34] Ernest Hemingway Reading, *Caedmon Records TC 1185*.

McCoy, Alfred W., et al. *The Politics of Heroin in Southeast Asia*. New York: Harper & Row, 1972.

O'Brien, Lawrence F. *No Final Victories*. Garden City, N.Y.: Doubleday, 1974.

Prouty, L. Fletcher. *The Secret Team*. Englewood Cliffs, N.J.: Prentice-Hall, 1973.

Skolnick, Sherman H. *The Midway Crash and Watergate*. Chicago: Citizens' Committee to Clean Up the Courts, 1974.

Slatzer, Robert F. *The Life and Curious Death of Marilyn Monroe*. New York: Pinnacle, 1974.

Szulc, Tad. *Compulsive Spy*. New York: Viking, 1974.

Thompson, Fred D. *At That Point in Time*. New York: Quadrangle, 1975.

Tinnin, David B. *Just About Everybody vs. Howard Hughes*. Garden City, N.Y.: Doubleday, 1973.

Acknowledgments

❧

"Our Man at Harvard" originally appeared in *Esquire*, March 22, 1977.

"An Advertisement Advertised" was written for the reissue of *Advertisements for Myself* by Norman Mailer. Reprinted by permission of G.P. Putnam's Sons. Copyright © 1976 by Norman Mailer.

"Are We in Vietnam?" was written for the reissue of *Why Are We in Vietnam?* Reprinted by permission of Holt, Rinehart & Winston. Copyright © 1977 by Norman Mailer.

"Of a Small and Modest Malignancy, Wicked and Bristling with Dots" originally appeared in *Esquire*, October 20, 1977.

"Two Letters From Frank Crowther" originally appeared in *The Paris Review*, Volume 17, No. 67.

"Miller and Hemingway" has been adapted from *Genius and Lust*, copyright © 1976 by Norman Mailer. Reprinted by permission of Grove Press, Inc.

"Papa & Son" originally appeared as the preface to *Papa: A Personal Memoir* by Gregory Hemingway. Preface © 1976 by Norman Mailer. *Papa: A Personal Memoir* © 1976 by Gregory Hemingway. Reprinted by agreement with Houghton Mifflin Company.

"My Friend, Jean Malaquais" is reprinted by permission of Warner Books/New York from the introduction by Norman Mailer to *The Joker* by Jean Malaquais. Copyright © 1974 by Warner Books, Inc.

"Narcissim" originally appeared in *American Review*, No. 24, April 1976, published by Bantam Books, Inc. Copyright © 1973 by Norman Mailer.

"Tango, Last Tango" originally appeared in *New York Review of Books*, May 17, 1973 as "A Transit to Narcissus." Copyright © 1973 by Norman Mailer.

"The Faith of Graffiti" originally appeared in *The Faith of Graffiti*, an Alskog Book. Copyright © 1974 by Norman Mailer.

"A Harlot High and Low" originally appeared in *New York* Magazine, August 16, 1976. Included in that piece were a number of quotations from other works, a bibliography of which appears in the piece itself. The only sources requesting permission were:

The Rolling Stone for excerpts from "Strange Bedfellows — The Hughes-Nixon-Lansky Connection: The Secret Alliances of the CIA From World War

II to Watergate" by Howard Kohn from Rolling Stone #213, May 20, 1976. By Straight Arrow Publishers, Inc. © 1976. All rights reserved. Reprinted by permission.

The Washington Post, 6/21/72 issue.

At That Point in Time, the Inside Story of the Senate Watergate Committee. Copyright © 1975 by Fred D. Thompson. Reprinted by permission of Times Books, a division of Quadrangle/The New York Times Book Co., Inc.

Pontifications

INTERVIEWS
Edited by Michael Lennon

Preface

❧

These interviews were put together through the labor of my friend, Michael Lennon, who searched them out and did much of the work of selecting them since there were something like one hundred interviews from which to choose. It is appropriate that he should write the introduction. By now, he knows more about these dialogues than I do. I wish only to say that we have one friendly but real disagreement. He ascribes value to my conversations and that is his right, but it is mine to shift my feet at the generosity of his praise.

I would add that "Pontifications" is a good description of what follows. In an interview, one answers the questions out of one's experience, out of the church — if the word may be allowed — of one's acquired knowledge. Logic may come in to serve your argument, and a fact can make its appearance now and then to bolster your reasoning, but the remarks are underwritten by experience. One's thought comes out as pronouncement — pontifications, indeed. And at their worst, these interviews can be pompous. But then pomposity clings as closely to pronouncement as a beer belly to a beer drinker.

It is obvious by these remarks that I am not fond of the form. I think an interview is truly an unhappy way to get it said, particularly for someone who speaks as poorly as I do. After years of hammering out consecutive sentences of reasonably good prose by dint of much repetition and reshaping of each phrase in my throat, before moving on to the next, I think the salt of good speech is leached out of one's mouth. When I write, I am forever going over the words. "Now, the best road, that is, the most agreeable, no, the most indigenous, say rather, the most comfortable to travel of all the roads to Burlington is, uh, that is, the road you are likely to find most agreeable, yes, the agreeable road . . ." Authors in raw transcript can seem as bad on occasion as politicians.

So I wince when I read over my remarks, I even improve them to a degree. There is hardly one of these interviews that was not edited by me years ago to get out the worst of the repetitions, and again for this book, and here and there — not too often — I have bolstered a few thoughts by a few after-the-fact phrases. You try to obtain a fair balance between the original tone, and the rights of the reader to respectable syntax, and you wince, as I say, you wince as you read your remarks, and true to your responsibility you keep most of the flat phrasing you would improve if committing such thoughts to writing.

Still, if you hold as I do to the notion that artists are not fond darlings of the universe who have been touched with talent the way certain women are blessed with beauty, but that, to the contrary, artists and beauties alike bear more resemblance to pack-horses carrying divine (or satanic) messages from one corner of our world to another, their talent or beauty only leased to them in order to do something interesting with it, then woe to those who don't. You can be certain there is a cry of failed endeavor behind every writer's interview, his mute apology for the book or the essay or the philosophy he did not achieve in the way he was meant to. Often, the particular answer is his last lunge as a relay runner. "Here," he gasps to the interlocutor, "is the message. Carry it to the reader. I am too pooped."

These interviews, from 1970 to 1981 (with excerpts from five earlier ones) take up, ergo, a number of questions I never developed to real satisfaction in my writing. They are part of the philosophy I promised myself to fashion and never did, never by formal means, and as the decades go by, and I come to recognize that I, too, can grow old, and never write all of what I thought I would, so, in resignation, I consign large parts of what I know to conversation.

One guide to the reader: Of the twenty interviews reprinted here, five — the first five — were given in the years from 1958 to 1967. Since four of them can be found in my other collections, they have been cut approximately by half for inclusion in this book, and would have been passed over if not for the foundation they provide. Just about all the matters that are discussed in later interviews have their origins here. Besides — as Lennon points out, interviewers can be like chess players "aware of the games of their predecessors" — and so these early exchanges while overdramatic, and excessive in language, are probably worth including for their undeniable relevance.

Contents

Pontifications

✣

Preface by Norman Mailer   iii
Introduction by Michael Lennon   ix

An interview with

Richard G. Stern and Robert Lucid:
   Hip, Hell and the Navigator   1
Paul Krassner: An Impolite Interview   6
Steven Marcus: Craft and Consciousness   17
W. J. Weatherby: Talking of Violence   28
Paul Carroll: Vices   32
David Young: On Science and Art   46
Richard Stratton: In Search of the Devil   58
Laura Adams: Existential Aesthetics   78
Buzz Farbar: Marriage   90
Cathleen Medwick: One-Night Stands   103
Jeffrey Michelson and Sarah Stone: Ethics
   and Pornography   108
Paul Attanasio: Prisoner of Success   129
Anita Eichholz: A Brief Exchange   137
Michael Lennon: Waste   140
Hilary Mills: The Mad Butler   145

vii

Michael Lennon: An Author's Identity 151
Writers and Boxers 158
Literary Ambitions 163
Joseph McElroy: A Little on Novel-Writing 172
Barbara Probst Solomon: To Pontificate on
America and Europe 183

Introduction

by Michael Lennon

❧

I think Gertrude Stein may have been too sweeping when she said to Hemingway, "Remarks are not literature." It depends. Hemingway's remarks in his 1958 interview in *The Paris Review* certainly qualify, and several of the interviews with Norman Mailer collected here are of comparable stature. Collectively, these twenty interviews express his views on every subject close to his concern for the past quarter of a century. If these selected conversations with friends, journalists, academics and students are not literature, not certifiably a formal part of Mailer's literary work, they are at the least, an indispensable adjunct to it.

On some subjects — pornography, drugs, marriage, his books, his career, his theology and the psychological stances involved in writing a novel — the interviews may even be accorded the status of the major biographical sources. But they are to be recommended for more than the exportable information that they provide. As a literary form, the interview has much to offer someone of Mailer's temperament. As sensitive to mood as Hemingway, he has been more willing than his old mentor to exercise that portion of himself most serviceable for the occasion. The chemistry between Mailer and his different interlocutors stimulates him to a variety of conversational gambits: elucidative, admonitory, quasi-confessional, speculative and, of course, forensic. Since Hemingway's death Mailer has been the literary world's finest counterpuncher, although he displays none of Hemingway's archness (or Faulkner's sullenness). He does unload a few good, solid antipathies though: corporate America, plastics, the FBI and modern architecture. His method is more dialectical than peremptory, however. Indeed, the interviews bear some resemblance to a twenty-five-year chess match, new players (most of whom are aware of the games of their predecessors) succeeding old, and Mailer adapting his tactics for each. A great part of the pleasure the interviews provide lies in the opportunity to savor the various gambits Mailer employs, and to watch for the signs of change in his ideas. Even when an interviewer appears to have summed up some aspect of Mailer's thought or art, he resists in favor of a more subtle formulation. Occasionally he asks the questions; at other times he plays devil's advocate and notes the weakness of his own position, stating it earlier or more firmly than his interviewer, a tactic he mastered in *The Armies of the Night*. He enjoys a fast, tough exchange (the one with Anita Eichholz in "A Brief Exchange," on the question of the Women's Liberation movement, for example, which is the perfect pendant to *The Prisoner of Sex*); it seems to notch his own thinking higher. His ego, which he once compared to an egg, is more like a golf ball — the harder it is hit, the more lively it becomes. He finds artful ways to answer uninformed questions and can usually find a decent peg on which to hang an answer to imprecise ones. An excellent listener, he seems to deploy just enough acumen to raise the discussion one rung higher and he never tries to embarrass. So he will answer dull questions with a modicum of wit, turn intellectual batteries on academics who know his work well and use his knowledge of old-friend interviewers where it will be helpful. In sum, he is a great talker.

Paradoxically, the final worth of these interviews may reside in the fact that Mailer is suspicious of the form. Because he believes that there is an umbilical relation between good thinking, good writing and mild depression, his first instinct is to be skeptical of any idea that comes too easily, or too enthusiastically. The insight has been well endowed by experience. Imagine then his mistrust of ideas that arise in casual conversation. Consequently, he works to maintain the life of the discussion at its highest possible level. Advancing the argument is more important than making points.

Mailer is, among many other things, an unfrocked prophet, full of foreboding about contemporary American culture, and this collection shows how he has gone about this business. In the earlier interviews, especially, he barnstorms through familiar territory: the sexual revolution, drugs, technology, violence, the media, God and the

Devil, the death of the romantic spirit, American politics, existentialism and the various forms of totalitarianism, "displaying," as Robert F. Lucid once noted, "a hundred different moods and attitudes when he is in them, above all trying always to evoke the essence of the moment through his endless conjuring of metaphor."

In the later interviews Mailer's range is even greater, and he is just as concerned to refine his metaphors, but he is more conjectural. His ideas have changed over the years, of course, significantly in some cases, but then so has the country. Yet the changes in his emphases have never been purely reflexive. Mailer chooses his targets, and his arrows, with care. If he has no idiosyncratic insight or perspective on a matter, he passes, which partly explains why his most controversial remarks are often his most serious. If he cannot inform he won't provoke. His goal is to tell us how the world works. In this sense, he is still a realist in the tradition of Zola and Dos Passos.

In the late Eisenhower period Mailer billed himself as a "psychic outlaw." Thirteen years later during the Nixon–McGovern campaign, a "modest and half-invisible Aquarius" vibrated in the winds of the *Zeitgeist*. These are the extremes that are represented in these interviews. Compare for example the all-out slugging exchanges with Krassner in 1962 with the reflective conversation he has with McElroy and a group of writing students at Columbia University in 1981. In the earlier interview "the subjects grind by like boxcars on a two-mile freight," as Mailer later put it. In the Columbia interview, he proceeds with Jamesian deliberation, lingers actually, in his discussion of the lore and craft of novel-writing, admitting uncertainties, offering suggestions and making subtle forays into an area at the edge of the word system: the mysterious powers of ego and identity that have sustained him in his life as a writer. Mailer is considerably more intrigued with questions of craft and style in the recent interviews than he was, for example, in the 1963 interview with Marcus, perhaps for no better reason than he has now lived the writer's life for twice as long, over forty years.

Each interview illumines some moment of his career and most cover a multitude of topics (the 1967 interview with Carroll and the Munich conversations he conducted with me in 1980 come closest to being synopticons of his views). Even those with similar subjects (with Farbar, for example, in 1973, Medwick in 1980 and Michelson/Stone in 1981 on sex, love and marriage; and with Stern in 1958, Stratton in 1974 and Adams in 1975 on God and the Devil) are markedly different. Some of the interviews, moreover, offer

Mailer's most important or only substantial utterance on a major topic and so have their claim to interest. His long discussion of pornography in the Michelson/Stone interview is one; the portions of the 1970 Young interview in which he explores the primitive sensibility is another. A third is his conversation with Stratton on Charles Manson and rock music. Several of the interviews contain unrehearsed and incisive comment on writers, or "fellow racketeers," as he calls them, that he has discussed little or not at all before: Borges, Márquez, Hannah Arendt, Doctorow, Tom Wolfe and Ann Beattie. There are also some surprising remarks on writers he has had on his mind for decades: Marx, Freud, Hemingway, Faulkner, Fitzgerald and Sartre. Speckled throughout are asides and quick references to many more: Kafka, Forster, Burroughs, Penn Warren, Steinbeck, Graham Greene, Heller, Nin, Tolstoy and Dostoyevsky, Porter, Capote, Durrell, Fowles and Raymond Chandler. The 1980 interview with Attanasio is notable for its capsule discussions of writers. (Note: Dates given here and at the end of each interview refer to the years the interviews were conducted, not the years of first publication.)

In the earliest interview presented here, his 1958 dialogue with Stern on his unique theology, Mailer begins by saying, "I started as one kind of writer and I've been evolving into another kind." Over the twenty-four-year period (1958–1981) from which these interviews are drawn, Mailer has become another kind of writer at least three times. The first metamorphosis came a year after the Stern interview with the publication of *Advertisements for Myself.* There, he dropped all pretense of separating his personal and creative lives and candidly dissected his achievements, failures and ambitions. The second was revealed nine years later in *The Armies of the Night,* in which he describes his former self in the third person, thus casting his outspoken public persona into sharp relief. Mailer used this unusual point of view in the four nonfiction narratives he published after *Armies,* all of which are personal testaments of the public life of the nation during the period from 1967–72. If the Sixties could be considered Mailer's autobiographical decade, the Seventies may fairly be called his biographical period. After the 1972 elections he all but lost interest in himself as a protagonist and devoted the rest of the decade to a series of works on famous-infamous Americans: Marilyn Monroe (*Marilyn: A Novel Biography,* 1973); Muhammad Ali (*The Fight,* 1975); Henry Miller (*Genius and Lust,* 1977); Gary Gilmore (*The Executioner's Song,* 1979); and Marilyn again in *Of Women and Their Elegance*, published in 1980. These four figures, and their narcissistic obsessions, are discussed in several of the interviews from 1974 on.

Mailer is now poised for another change, by his own estimate perhaps the largest. From reports of his public readings from the huge novel set in ancient Egypt that he has been working on since 1971, it seems likely that its publication in a year or two will reveal still another kind of writer. For the first time, it looks as if we will encounter the author trying to get outside of both history and personality — to get so far back in time as to stop it, to imagine human society in a time and place where historical memory cannot reach. He makes a number of tantalizing comments on this long-awaited novel in several of the later interviews, and also explains why he is usually unwilling to discuss his fictional, as opposed to his nonfictional, work-in-progress.

Novelists, Mailer says, must believe that words can change lives — if they are good enough. So words are best devoted to novels. Agreed; and there is where our chief interest will be. But if we wish to glimpse the process as well as read the product, these conversations may be the best place to look.

Pontifications

Hip, Hell
and the Navigator

An Interview
with Richard G. Stern and Robert Lucid

❧

RICHARD STERN: I've been reading "The White Negro" and a fair amount of other material on the hipster, and I must say that intellectually I resent Hip as much as I can resent anything. Now I wonder about the extent of your allegiance to Hip. Are you using this material for fiction, or are you committed to it as a style of life, one which you want to practice yourself and recommend to others?

NORMAN MAILER: All right, good, I think the difficulty for most people who are at all interested in my work is that I started as one kind of writer, and I've been evolving into another. Most serious readers like a writer to be a particular thing. It's important; it's reassuring, somehow. So, I think if I'm going in this direction, it has to be assumed at least from the outside that I'm serious.

STERN: The interesting thing about Hip is that Hip shouldn't belong to writers. If you're a genuine hipster you're committed, it seems to me, to a kind of anti-expressionism. If you're a sincere hipster you shouldn't be a writer. Then there's another thing as far as writing goes. Isn't a novel controlled by some overriding notion, by a kind of fanaticism which organizes a great deal of disparate material? In a sense, a novel is like the mind of a madman: everything — casual looks, street signs, world news reports — is charged with meaning. That's why novelists write about ruling passions like love and ambition, passions which put their mark on

1

all they touch, trivial or major. Now I can't believe that Hip allows for such overriding notions and passions. For the hipster, the cool one, detail is illumined, livid, but for its own sake, unqualified by the sort of organization which novels demand. I wonder if such material can be put into fiction.

MAILER: I think it can; and not only that, but I think Hip is particularly illumined by one notion so central and so shattering that its religious resonances and reverberations are going to dominate this coming century. And I think there is one single burning pinpoint of the vision in Hip: it's that God is in danger of dying. In my very limited knowledge of theology, this never really has been expressed before. I believe Hip conceives of Man's fate being tied up with God's fate. God is no longer all-powerful.

STERN: Now that's a fantastic assertion. That really makes me sit up. What is the notion of God behind all this? Do you mean that some kind of personal god is dying with us?

MAILER: Now I only talk about my own vision of it, really. I think that the particular God we can conceive of is a god whose relationship to the universe we cannot divine; that is, how enormous He is in the scheme of the universe we can't begin to say. But almost certainly, He is not all-powerful; He exists as a warring element in a divided universe, and we are a part of — perhaps the most important part of — His great expression, His enormous destiny; perhaps He is trying to impose upon the universe His conception of being against other conceptions of being very much opposed to His. Maybe we are in a sense the seed, the seed-carriers, the voyagers, the explorers, the embodiment of that embattled vision; maybe we are engaged in a heroic activity, and not a mean one.

STERN: This is really something.

MAILER: Well, I would say it is far more noble in its conception, far more arduous as a religious conception than the notion of the all-powerful God who takes care of us.

STERN: And do you take to this conception for its perilous nobility, or do you take to it because you believe in it?

MAILER: I believe in it.

STERN: You believe in it.

MAILER: It's the only thing that makes any sense to me. It's the only thing that explains to me the problem of evil. You see, the answer may well be — how to put it? — that God Himself is engaged in a destiny so extraordinary, so demanding, that He too can suffer from a moral corruption, that He can make demands upon us which are unfair, that He can abuse our beings in order to achieve His means, even as we abuse the very cells of our own body.

STERN: Is it a person's duty to find out whether he's of God's party, whether he's working with God-beneficent or God-maleficent?

MAILER: Well, look, let's go back; let's go back to something much more modest for the moment which I think may tie this up, to a small extent, anyway. You asked me before why Hip is interesting for the novel. Well, up to now, when a novelist treats someone like a drug addict, the Square way is to treat the addict as a poor sociological cripple who is doomed and damned and goes down to his inevitable defeat. In Hip, which has after all to a certain extent come out of drug-taking (it's one of the elements in the growth of Hip) the attitude would be more that if taking drugs gives one extraordinary sensations, then the drug-taker is probably receiving something from God. Love perhaps. And perhaps he is. Let's just entertain the notion as a rational hypothesis which may or may not be true and let's see how far we go with it. If the hipster is receiving love from God he may well be draining some of the substance of God by calling upon this love, you see, which the drug releases. And in draining the substance of God he's exhausting Him, so that the drug-taker may be indulging an extraordinarily evil act at the instant he is filled with the feeling that he is full of God and good and a beautiful mystic. This involves new moral complexities which I feel are far more interesting than anything the novel has gotten into yet. It opens the possibility that the novel, along with many other art forms, may be growing into something larger rather than something smaller, and the sickness of our times for me has been just this damn thing that everything has been getting smaller and smaller and less and less important, that the romantic spirit has dried up, that there is almost no shame today like the terror before the romantic. We're all getting so mean and small and petty and ridiculous, and we all live under the threat of extermination. In contrast, the notions of Hip enlarge us, they make our small actions not necessarily large, but more meaningful. If we pick up a bottle while listening to some jazz and we feel each of our five fingertips in relation to the bottle, the bottle begins to have a kind of form for us and we begin to feel each of our fingertips is receiving a different thing from the shape and the structure of the glass, and we then begin to think that maybe the very structure of this glass could conceivably contain some kind of hell within its constitution, some inorganic frozen state of imprisoned being less being than us. I think it's a more interesting notion that just picking up a bottle and pouring out some whisky.

STERN: It's a very pretty notion.

MAILER: Hip is pretty.

STERN: But it's all action, it's all erectile, isn't it? It's all feeling and taste and touch and smell. Isn't that the trouble with it?

MAILER: The trouble is that it's enormously difficult to return to the senses. We're all civilized, and to return to the senses and keep the best parts of our civilized being, to keep our capacity for mental organization, for mental construction, for logic, is doubly difficult, and there's a great danger that the nihilism of Hip will destroy civilization. But it seems to me that the danger which is even more paramount — the danger which has brought on Hip — is that civilization is so strong itself, so divorced from the senses, that we have come to the point where we can liquidate millions of people in concentration camps by orderly process.

STERN: Every powerful and refining force involves danger and waste. Does this divorce from the senses you talk about justify cashing in two or three thousand years of continuous culture?

MAILER: Well, your argument is moot. It's too vast for this — for me. But let me try to put it this way. If the divorce from the senses I talk about is becoming a human condition, then by all means, yes, civilization must be cashed in or we will destroy ourselves in the cold insensate expressions of due process of law and atomic radiation.

STERN: All right, let's concentrate on what all this has to do with you as a practicing novelist. How are these notions going to work for you? The idea of art seems to me to be to generate emotion from the treated material, not to point out some material and some feeling and say, "Put them together, reader."

MAILER: Well, let me avoid answering you directly. I feel that the final purpose of art is to intensify, even, if necessary, to exacerbate, the moral consciousness of people. In particular, I think the novel is at its best the most moral of the art forms because it's the most immediate, the most overbearing, if you will. It is the most inescapable. Ideally, what I would hope to do with my work is intensify a consciousness that the core of life cannot be cheated. Every moment of one's existence one is growing into more or retreating into less. One is always living a little more or dying a little bit. That the choice is not to live a little more or to not live a little more; it is to live a little more or to die a little more. And as one dies a little more, one enters a most dangerous moral condition for oneself because one starts making other people die a little more in order to stay alive oneself. I think this is exactly the murderous network in which we all live by now.

STERN: And this is what the hipster does; he strikes out at others; he's constantly craving for more. He faces the risk of the extinction of his senses, extinction of his being, extinction of his capacity for making distinctions.

MAILER: He does certain things that are very brave in their way; he gambles for one thing with his soul — he gambles that he can be terribly, tragically wrong, and therefore be doomed, you see, doomed to Hell. Which the churchy people don't do at all. They're thinking of nothing but maintaining their souls for some careful preservation afterward. The hipster is gambling with death and he is gambling with the Hereafter; and he may be wrong.

STERN: And the novelist is gambling with his talent as a novelist.

MAILER: Oh, yeah. Yeah.

STERN: The one talent he's got.

ROBERT LUCID: This is what kills me. You presume consciousness, you presume purpose, you presume direction on the part of this class — if that's the word — analogous to the novelist. And it seems to me that the whole notion of Hip is, in fact, unconscious, it is mere action. It seems to me the kind of guy we're talking about as hipster *qua* hipster is a guy who is, in fact, unconscious of risks of this kind, of the profundity . . .

MAILER: Consciously, he may think it's cutting quite a few corners as far as that goes. What I'm postulating in all this — the notion I've been working with all along that's been tacit to my remarks, implicit in my remarks, is that the unconscious, you see, has an enormous teleological sense, that it moves towards a goal, that it has a real sense of what is happening to one's being at each given moment — you see — that the messages of one's experience are continually saying, "Things are getting better," or "Things are getting worse." For me. For that one. For my future, for my past, mmm? It is with this thing that they move, that they grope forward — this navigator at the seat of their being.

1958

An Impolite Interview

An Interview with Paul Krassner

⸙

PAUL KRASSNER: When you and I first talked about the possibility of doing an impolite interview, we kind of put it off because you said: "I find that when I discuss ideas, it spills the tension I need to write." Which seems like a very Freudian explanation. Does it still apply?

NORMAN MAILER: It does. Sure it does. I think putting out half-worked ideas in an interview is like premature ejaculation.

KRASSNER: Then why bother?

MAILER: I'm beginning to get a little pessimistic about the number of ideas I never write up. Perhaps the public is better off with premature ejaculation than no intellectual sex at all. I'm just thinking of the public, not myself.

KRASSNER: All right, you once referred in passing to the FBI as a religious movement: would you elaborate on that?

MAILER: I think a lot of people need the FBI for their sanity. That is to say, in order to be profoundly religious, to become a saint, for example, one must dare insanity, but if one wishes instead to flee from insanity, then one method is to join an organized religion. The FBI is an organized religion.

The FBI blots out everything which could bring dread into the average mediocrity's life. At bottom, I mean profoundly at bottom, the FBI has nothing to do with Communism, it has nothing to do with catching criminals, it has nothing to do with the Mafia, the Syndicate, it has nothing to do with trustbusting, it has nothing to do with interstate commerce, it has nothing to do with anything but serving as a church for the mediocre. A high church for the true mediocre.

KRASSNER: In terms of the mass media being a force to which one subjects oneself more voluntarily than to the FBI, isn't it possible that the mass media which you call totalitarian are a reflection rather than a cause of this condition in society?

MAILER: A reflection of what people want? No, I don't think so. That's like saying that the United States Army was a reflection of what the soldiers wanted.

KRASSNER: But they were drafted —

MAILER: And you're not drafted — your eye is not *drafted* when you turn on that TV set? To assume that people are getting what they want through the mass media also assumes that the men and women who direct the mass media know something about the people. But they don't know anything about the people. That's why I gave you the example of the Army. The private exists in a world which is hermetically alienated from the larger aims of the generals who are planning the higher strategy of the war.

The mass media is made up of a group of people who are looking for power. The reason is not because they have any moral sense, any inner sense of a goal, of an ideal that's worth fighting for, dying for, if one is brave enough. No, the reason they want power is because power is the only thing that will relieve the profound illness which has seized them. Which has seized all of us. The illness of the twentieth century. There isn't psychic room for all of us. Malthus's law has moved from the excessive procreation of bodies to the excessive mediocritization of psyches. The deaths don't occur on the battlefield any longer, or through malnutrition: they occur within the brain, within the psyche itself.

KRASSNER: To change the subject: Several months ago I mentioned, in order to make a very definite point, a Cuban prostitute — this was the first prostitute I'd ever gone to, and I had been asking her all these questions about the Revolution — and she stopped later in the middle of fellatio to ask me if I was a Communist.

MAILER: You were in Cuba at the time?

KRASSNER: Yes. And she was anti-Castro.

MAILER: Because he was cleaning them out of the whorehouses?

KRASSNER: Well, there were no more tourists coming to Cuba, and it was ruining their business. Anyway, I described this incident in the *Realist,* and was accused of exhibitionism by some friends of mine. And I'm secure enough in my life that I had no need to boast about this; but it was a funny, significant thing which I wanted to share with the readers.

MAILER: Oh, I remember that, I remember reading your piece now. I was a little shocked by it.

KRASSNER: You're kidding.

MAILER: No, I was shocked. I wasn't profoundly shocked. It threw me slightly. I had a feeling, "That's not good writing." And the next thought was, "Mailer, you're getting old." And the next thought was, "If you're not really getting old, but there is something indeed bad about this writing, what is it that's bad about it?"

KRASSNER: And?

MAILER: A whore practicing fellatio looks up and says, "Are you a Communist?" — that's what the modern world is all about in a way. Saying it head-on like that probably gave the atmosphere honesty. But, in some funny way, it didn't belong.

If the reader had been able to guess that this was what was going on with the whore — I don't know how you could have done it; that would have been the art of it — to phrase the language in such a way that the reader thinks, "Oh, Jesus, she's sucking his cock, and she asks him if he's a Communist." If it had happened that way, it might have been overpowering. What a montage.

Maybe it was the use of "fellatio," maybe you just should have said, "I was having my cock sucked and she said, 'Are you a Communist?'" If you're getting into the brutality of it, get into the brutality of it. Throw a beanball. Don't use the Latinism. Maybe it was the Latinism that threw me. All I know is that there was something bad about it, the effect was *shock.*

KRASSNER: So you were shocked by a euphemism . . .

MAILER: Shock is like banging your head or taking a dull fall; your wits are deadened.

KRASSNER: That's what I wanted to do in the writing, because that's what happened to me in the act.

MAILER: Then you're not interested in art, you're interested in therapy. That's the trouble — there are too many people writing nowadays who give no art to the world, but draw in therapy to themselves.

KRASSNER: No, not in my case. It didn't change me one way or the other, writing it. I just wanted to put it into the consciousness of the reader. That's not therapy for me.

MAILER: Well, then you should've said, "She was sucking my cock." I mean that's my professional opinion.

KRASSNER: If you were a future historian of sex, how would you look upon the Kennedy administration?

MAILER: I'd say there's more acceptance of sexuality in America today than there was before he came in. Whether that's good or bad, I don't know. It may be a promiscuous acceptance of sexuality.

KRASSNER: Are you saying it's because of. . . ?

MAILER: Because of Kennedy — *absolutely*. I mean, just think of going to a party given by Eisenhower as opposed to a party thrown by Kennedy. Do you have to wonder at which party you'd have a better time?

The average man daydreams about his leader. He thinks of being invited to his leader's home. If he thinks of being invited to Eisenhower's home, he thinks of how proper he's going to be. If he thinks of going to the Kennedys for a party, he thinks of having a dance with Jackie. Things liven up.

Why do you think people loved Hitler in Germany? Because they all secretly wished to get hysterical and *stomp* on things and scream and shout and rip things up and *kill* — tear people apart. Hitler pretended to offer them that. In some subtle way, he communicated it. That's why they wanted him. That's why he was good for Germany — they wanted such horror. Of course, by the end he didn't tear people apart, he gassed them.

If America gets as sick as Germany was before Hitler came in, we'll have our Hitler. One way or another, we'll have our Hitler. After all, one can have Fascism come in any form at all, through the Church, through sex, through social welfare, through state conservatism, through organized medicine, the FBI, the Pentagon. Fascism is not a philosophy but a murderous mode of deadening reality by smothering it with lies.

Every time one sees a bad television show, one is watching the nation get ready for the day when a Hitler will come. Not because the ideology of the show is Fascistic; on the contrary its manifest ideology is invariably liberal, but the show still prepares Fascism because it is meretricious art and so sickens people a little further. Whenever people get collectively sick, the remedy becomes progressively more violent and hideous. An insidious, insipid sickness demands a violent far-reaching purgative.

KRASSNER: Then you're saying it's bad times which result in bad leaders.

MAILER: Well, if a time is bad enough, a good man can't possibly succeed. In a bad time, the desires of the multitude are bad, they're low, they're ugly, they're greedy, they're cowardly, they're piggish, shitty.

KRASSNER: In *The Naked and the Dead*, there was a theme about the futility of violence on a grand scale; and yet, in "The White Negro," there's almost a justification of violence, at least on a personal level. How do you reconcile this apparent inconsistency?

MAILER: What I still disapprove of is *inhuman* violence — violence which is on a large scale and abstract. I disapprove of bombing a city. I disapprove of the kind of man who will derive aesthetic satisfaction from the fact that an Ethiopian village looks like a red rose at the moment the bombs are exploding. I won't disapprove of the act of perception which witnesses that; I think that act of perception is — I'm going to use the word again — noble.

What I'm getting at is: a native village is bombed, and the bombs happen to be beautiful when they land; in fact it would be odd if all that sudden destruction did not liberate some beauty. The form a bomb takes in its explosion may be in part a picture of the potentialities it destroyed. So let us accept the idea that the bomb is beautiful.

If so, any liberal who decries the act of bombing is totalitarian if he doesn't admit as well that the bombs were indeed beautiful.

Because the moment we tell something that's untrue, it does not matter how pure our motives may be — the moment we start mothering mankind and decide that one truth is good for them to hear and another is not so good, because while *we* can understand, those poor ignorant unfortunates cannot — then what are we doing, we're depriving the minds of others of knowledge which may be essential.

Think of a young pilot who comes along later, some young pilot who goes out on a mission and isn't prepared for the fact that a bombing might be beautiful; he could conceivably be an idealist, there were some in the war against Fascism. If the pilot is totally unprepared he might never get over the fact that he was particularly thrilled by the beauty of that bomb.

But if our culture had been large enough to say that Ciano's son-in-law not only found that bomb beautiful, but that indeed this act of perception was *not* what was wrong; the evil was to think that this beauty was worth the lot of living helpless people who were wiped out broadside. Obviously, whenever there's destruction, there's going to be beauty implicit in it.

KRASSNER: Do you think you're something of a puritan when it comes to masturbation?

MAILER: I think masturbation is bad.

KRASSNER: In relation to heterosexual fulfillment?

MAILER: In relation to everything — orgasm, heterosexuality, to style, to stance, to be able to fight the good fight. I think masturbation cripples people. It doesn't cripple them altogether, but it turns them askew, it sets up a bad and often enduring tension. I mean has anyone ever studied the correlation between cigarette smoking and masturbation? Anybody who spends his adolescence masturbating, generally enters his young manhood with no sense of being a man. The answer — I don't know what the answer is — sex for adolescents may be the answer, it may not. I really don't know.

KRASSNER: Is it possible that you have a totalitarian attitude against masturbation?

MAILER: I wouldn't say all people who masturbate are evil, probably I would even say that some of the best people in the world masturbate. But I am saying it's a miserable activity.

KRASSNER: Well, we're getting right back now to this notion of absolutes. You know — to somebody, masturbation can be a thing of beauty —

MAILER: To what end? To what end? Who is going to benefit from it?

KRASSNER: It's a better end than the beauty of a bombing.

MAILER: Masturbation is bombing. It's bombing oneself.

KRASSNER: I think there's a basic flaw in your argument. Why are you assuming that masturbation is violence unto oneself? Why is it not pleasure unto oneself? And I'm not defending masturbation — well, I'm defending masturbation, yes, as a substitute if and when —

MAILER: All right, look. When you make love, whatever is good in you or bad in you, goes out into someone else. I mean this literally. I'm not interested in the biochemistry of it, the electromagnetism of it, nor in how the psychic waves are passed back and forth, and what psychic waves are. All I know is that when one makes love, one changes a woman slightly and a woman changes you slightly.

KRASSNER: Certain circumstances can change one for the worse.

MAILER: But at least you have gone through a process which is part of life. One can be better for the experience, or worse. But one has experience to absorb, to think about, one has literally to digest the new spirit which has entered the flesh. The body has been galvanized for an experience of flesh, a declaration of the flesh.

If one has the courage to think about every aspect of the act — I don't mean think mechanically about it, but if one is able to brood over the act, to dwell on it — then one is *changed* by the act. Even if one has been *jangled* by the act. Because in the act of restoring one's harmony, one has to encounter all the reasons one was jangled.

So finally one has had an experience which is nourishing. Nourishing because one's able to *feel* one's way into more difficult or more precious insights as a result of it. One's able to live a tougher, more heroic life if one can digest and absorb the experience.

But, if one masturbates, all that happens is, everything that's beautiful and good in one, goes up the hand, goes into the air, is *lost*. Now what the hell is there to *absorb?* One hasn't tested himself. You see, in a way, the heterosexual act lays questions to rest, and makes one able to build upon a few answers. Whereas if one masturbates, the ability to contemplate one's experience is disturbed. Instead, fantasies of power take over and disturb all sleep.

If one has, for example, the image of a beautiful sexy babe in masturbation, one still doesn't know whether one can make love to her in the flesh. All you know is that you can violate her in your *brain*. Well, a lot of good that is.

But if one has fought the good fight or the evil fight and ended with the beautiful sexy dame, then if the experience is good, your life is changed by it, in a less happy way. But at least one knows something of what happened. One has something real to build on.

The ultimate direction of masturbation always has to be insanity.

KRASSNER: But you're not man enough to take the other position, which is sex for the young. Except for petting, what else is there between those two alternatives?

MAILER: I'd say, between masturbation and sex for the young, I prefer sex for the young. Of course. But I think there may be still a third alternative: At the time I grew up, sex had enormous fascination for everyone, but it had no dignity, it had no place. It was not a value. It had nothing to do with procreation, it had to do with the bathroom — it was burning, it was feverish, it was dirty, cute, giggly.

The thought of waiting for sex never occurred — when I was young my parents did not speak about sex, and no one else I knew ever discussed the possibility of holding on to one's sex as the single most important thing one has. To keep one's sex until one got what one deserved for it — that was never suggested to me when I was young.

The possibilities were to go out and have sex with a girl, have homosexual sex, or masturbate. Those were the choices. The fourth alternative — chastity, if you will — was ridiculous and absurd. It's probably more absurd today. If you talked to kids of chastity today, they would not stop laughing, I'm certain.

But the fact of the matter is, if you get marvelous sex when you're young, all right; but if you're not ready to make a baby with that marvelous sex, then you may also be putting something down the drain forever, which is the ability that you had to make a baby; the most marvelous thing that was in you may have been shot into a diaphragm, or wasted on a pill. One might be losing one's future.

The point is that, so long as one has a determinedly atheistic and rational approach to life, then the only thing that makes sense is the most comprehensive promiscuous sex you can find.

KRASSNER: Well, since I do have an essentially atheistic and more-or-less rational approach to life, I think I can speak with at least my individual authority. As a matter of fact, the more rational I become, the more selective —

MAILER: You know, "selective" is a word that sounds like a refugee from a group therapy session.

KRASSNER: I've never been in any kind of therapy —

MAILER: No, I know, but there's a *plague* coming out of all these centers — they go around *infecting* all of us. The words sit in one's vocabulary like bedbugs under glass.

KRASSNER: But I can't think of a better word. "Selective" is a word that means what I want to communicate to you.

MAILER: Selective. It's arrogant — how do you know who's doing the selecting? I mean you're a modest man with a good sense of yourself, but suddenly it comes to sex and you're selective. Like you won't pick *this* girl; you'll pick *that* one.

KRASSNER: Exactly. It's arrogant, but —

MAILER: Yeah, yeah, yeah — but the fact that one girl wants you and the other girl *doesn't* — I mean, that has nothing to do with it?

KRASSNER: Well, they have a right to be selective, too.

MAILER: Then it's mutually selective.

KRASSNER: Well, what I'm saying is you make a choice. A human choice. It has nothing to do with a machine . . . I'll tell you what's bugging me — it's your mystical approach. You'll use an expression like "You may be sending the best baby that's in you out into you hand" — but even when you're having intercourse, how many unused spermatozoa will there be in one ejaculation of semen?

MAILER: Look, America is dominated by a bunch of half-maniacal scientists, men who don't know anything about the act of creation. If science comes along and says there are one million spermatozoa in a discharge, you reason on that basis. That may not be a real basis.

We just don't know what the *real* is. We just don't know. Of the million spermatozoa, there may be only two or three with any real chance of reaching the ovum; the others are there like a supporting army, or if we're talking of planned parenthood, as a body of the electorate. These sperm go out with no sense at all of being real spermatozoa. They may appear to be real spermatozoa under the microscope, but after all, a man from Mars who's looking at us through a telescope might think that Communist bureaucrats and FBI men look exactly the same.

KRASSNER: Well, they are.

MAILER: Krassner's jab piles up more points. The point is that the scientists don't know what's going on. That meeting of the ovum and the sperm is too mysterious for the laboratory. Even the electron microscope can't measure the striations of passion in a spermatozoon. Or the force of its will.

But we can trust our emotion. Our emotions are a better guide to what goes on in these matters than scientists.

Sooner or later, every man comes close to his being and realizes that even though he's using the act, the act is using him too. He becomes, as you say, more selective. The reason he becomes more selective is that you can get killed, you literally *can* fuck your head off, you can lose your brains, you can wreck your body, you can use yourself up badly, eternally — I know a little bit of what I'm talking about.

KRASSNER: In his book *Nobody Knows My Name*, James Baldwin — referring to your essay "The White Negro" — complained about "the myth of the sexuality of Negroes which Norman Mailer, like so many others, refuses to give up." Are you still denying it's a myth?

MAILER: I don't believe it's a myth at all, for any numbers of reasons. I think that *any* submerged class is going to be more accustomed to sexuality than a leisure class. A leisure class may be more *preoccupied* with sexuality; but a submerged class is going to be more drenched in it.

You see, the upper classes are obsessed with sex, but they contain very little of it themselves. They use up much too much sex in their manipulations of power. In effect, they exchange sex for power. They restrict themselves in their sexuality — whereas the submerged classes have to take their desires for power and plow them back into sex.

So, to begin with, there's just that much more sexual vitality at the bottom than there is at the top. Second of all, the Negroes come from Africa, which is more or less a tropical land. It's easier to cohabit, it's easier to stay alive. If there's more time, more leisure, more warmth, more — we'll use one of those machine words — more support-from-the-environment than there is in a Northern country, then sex will tend to be more luxuriant.

Northern countries try to build civilizations and tropical countries seek to proliferate *being*.

Besides, the Negro has been all but forbidden any sort of intellectual occupation here for a couple of centuries. So he has had to learn other ways of comprehending modern life. There are two ways one can get along in the world. One can get along by studying books, or one can get along by knowing a great deal about one's fellow man, and one's fellow man's woman.

Sexuality is the armature of Negro life. Without sexuality they would've perished. The Jews stayed alive by having a culture to which they could refer, in which, more or less, they could believe. The Negroes stayed alive by having sexuality which could nourish them, keep them warm.

KRASSNER: Would you say that your conception of life is mystical as opposed to rationalistic?

MAILER: I don't like to call myself a mystic. On the other hand, I certainly wouldn't classify myself as a rationalist. I'm not altogether unhappy living in some no-man's-land between the two.

KRASSNER: OK, final question: You beat me two out of three times in thumb-wrestling matches; would you care to expound briefly on Zen in the art of thumb-wrestling?

MAILER: They are the same.

1962

Craft and Consciousness

An Interview with Steven Marcus

୬

STEVEN MARCUS: Would you say something about style, prose style, in relation to the novel?

NORMAN MAILER: A really good style comes only when a man has become as good as he can be. Style is character. A good style cannot come from a bad undisciplined character. Now a man may be evil, but I believe that people can be evil in their essential natures and still have good characters. Good in the sense of being well-tuned. They can have characters which are flexible, supple, adaptable, principled in relation to their own good or their own evil — even an evil man can have principles — he can be true to his own evil, which is not always so easy, either. I think good style is a matter of rendering out of oneself all the cupidities, all the cripplings, all the velleities. And then I think one has to develop one's physical grace. Writers who are possessed of some physical grace may tend to write better than writers who are physically clumsy. It's my impression this is so. I don't know that I'd care to attempt to prove it.

MARCUS: Well, how would you describe your own style? I ask this question because certain critics have pointed to deficiencies in it, or what they think of as deficiencies. Didn't Diana Trilling, for instance, criticize certain flatnesses in your style?

MAILER: I think that flatness comes out of certain flatnesses in me. And in trying to overcome that flatness I may push too hard in the other direction. Alfred Kazin once said something very funny

17

about the way I write: "Mailer is as fond of his style as an Italian
tenor is of his vocal cords."

MARCUS: Have you ever written to merely improve your writing,
practiced your writing as an athlete would work out?

MAILER: No. I don't think it's a proper activity. That's too much
like doing a setting-up exercise; any workout which does not in-
volve a certain minimum of danger or responsibility does not improve the body — it just wears it out.

MARCUS: In writing your novels, has any particular formal problem
given you trouble — let's say a problem of joining two parts of a
narrative together, getting people from point A to point B.

MAILER: You mean like getting them out of a room? I think formal
problems exist in inverse proportion to one's honesty. You get to
the problem of getting someone out of the room when there's
something false about the scene.

MARCUS: Do you do any research or special reading to prepare for
writing a novel, or while you're writing a novel?

MAILER: Occasionally I have to look something up. But I'm always
unhappy about that and mistrust the writing which comes out of
it. I feel in a way that one's ignorance is part of one's creation, too.
I don't know quite how to put it, but for instance if I, as a Jew, am
writing about other Jews, and if my knowledge of Jewish culture
is exceptionally spotty, as indeed it is, I am not so sure that that
isn't an advantage in creating a modern American Jew. Because
his knowledge of Jewish culture is also extremely spotty, and the
way in which his personality is composed may be more in accordance with my ignorance than with a cultivated Jew's immersion
in the culture. So in certain limited ways one's ignorance can help
to buttress the validity of a novel.

MARCUS: Have you ever written about a situation of which you
have had no personal experience or knowledge?

MAILER: I don't know. Let's see . . . *Barbary Shore*, for example, is
the most imaginative of my novels. But I did live in a rooming
house for a short period while I was writing *The Naked and the
Dead*. I certainly didn't live in it the way Lovett lived in it. I
never met an FBI agent, at least I had no sense of having met one
at the time I was writing *Barbary Shore*. I am sure I have met a
great many since. They didn't necessarily introduce themselves
to me. I had never met an Old Bolshevik, either, although ironically, writing about FBI agents and Old Bolsheviks in *Barbary
Shore*, the greatest single difficulty with the book was that my

common sense thought it was impossible to have all these agents and impossible heroes congregating in a rooming house in Brooklyn Heights. Yet a couple of years later I was working in a studio on Fulton Street at the end of Brooklyn Heights, a studio I have had for some years. It was a fine old studio building and they're tearing it down now to make room for a twenty-story building which will look like a Kleenex box. At any rate, on the floor below me, worked one Colonel Rudolph Abel who was the most important spy for the Russians in this country for a period of about eight or ten years, and I am sure we used to be in the elevator together many times. I think he literally had the room beneath me. I have always been overcome with that. It made me decide there's no clear boundary between experience and imagination. Who knows what glimpses of reality we pick up unconsciously, telepathically.

MARCUS: To what extent are your characters modeled on real people?

MAILER: I think half of them might have a point of departure from somebody real. Up to now I've not liked writing about people who are close to me, because they're too difficult to do. Their private reality obviously interferes with the reality one is trying to create. They become alive not as creatures in your imagination but as actors in your life. And so they seem real while you work but you're not working *their* reality into your book. For example it's not a good idea to try to put your wife into a novel. Not your latest wife, anyway. In practice I prefer to draw a character from someone I hardly know.

MARCUS: Can you describe how you turn a real person into a fictional one?

MAILER: I try to put the model in situations which have very little to do with his real situations in life. Very quickly the model disappears. His private reality can't hold up. For instance, I might take somebody who is a professional football player, a man let's say whom I know slightly, and make him a movie star. In a transposition of this sort, everything which relates particularly to the professional football player quickly disappears, and what is left, curiously, is what is *exportable* in his character. But this process while interesting in the early stages is not as exciting as the more creative act of allowing your characters to grow once they're separated from the model. It's when they become almost as complex as one's own personality that the fine excitement begins. Because then they are not really characters any longer — they're beings, which is a distinction I like to make. A character is someone you can grasp as a whole, you can have a clear idea of him, but a being is someone whose nature keeps shifting. Like a character of Forster's. In *The Deer Park* Lulu Myers is a being rather than a character. If you study her closely you will see that she is a different person in every scene. Just a little different. I don't know whether initially I did this by accident or purposefully, but at a certain point I made the conscious decision *not* to try to straighten her out, she seemed right in her changeableness.

MARCUS: Is Marion Faye a character or a . . .

MAILER: No, he's a being. Everybody in *The Deer Park* is a being except the minor characters like Herman Teppis.

MARCUS: How did Marion Faye emerge?

MAILER: The book needed something which wasn't in the first draft, some sort of evil genius. One felt a dark pressure there in the inner horizon of the book. But even as I say this I know it's not true to the grain of my writing experience. I violate that experience by talking in these terms. I am not sure it's possible to describe the experience of novel-writing authentically. It may be that it is not an experience.

MARCUS: What is it, then?

MAILER: It may be more like a relation, if you will — a continuing relation between a man and his wife. You can't necessarily speak of that as an experience because it may consist of several experiences which are braided together; or it may consist of many experiences which are all more or less similar, or indeed it may consist of two kinds of experiences which are antagonistic to one another. Throughout all of this I've spoken of characters *emerging*. Quite often they don't emerge; they fail to emerge. And what one's left with is the dull compromise which derives from two kinds of experiences warring with one another within oneself. A character who should have been brilliant is dull. Or even if a character does prove to be first-rate, it's possible you should have done twice as much with him, three times as much.

MARCUS: You speak of characters as emerging, and I gather by that that you mean emerging from yourself and emerging from your idea?

MAILER: They are also emerging from the book. A book takes on its own life in the writing. It has its laws, it becomes a creature to you after a while. One feels a bit like a master who's got a fine animal. Very often I'll feel a certain shame for what I've done with a novel. I won't say it's the novel that's bad; I'll say it's I who was bad. Almost as if the novel did not really belong to me, as if it was something raised by me like a child. I know what's potentially beautiful in my novel, you see. Very often after I've done the novel I realize that that beauty which I recognize in it is not going to be recognized by the reader. I didn't succeed in bringing it out. It's very odd — it's as though I had let the novel down, owed it a duty which I didn't fulfill.

MARCUS: Would you say that there was any secret or hidden pattern being worked out in your novels?

MAILER: I will say one thing, which is that I have some obsession with how God exists. Is He an essential god or an existential god; is He all-powerful or is He, too, an embattled existential creature who may succeed or fail in His vision? I think this theme may become more apparent as the novels go on.

MARCUS: When did this obsession begin?

MAILER: I think it began to show itself while I was doing the last draft of *The Deer Park*. Then it continued to grow as a private theme during all the years I was smoking marijuana.

MARCUS: You have spoken so often of the existential view. What reading or individuals brought you to this?

MAILER: The experience came first. One's condition on marijuana is always existential. One can feel the importance of each moment and how it is changing one. One feels one's being, one becomes aware of the enormous apparatus of nothingness — the hum of a hi-fi set, the emptiness of a pointless interruption, one becomes aware of the war between each of us, how the nothingness in each of us seeks to attack the being of others, how our being in turn is attacked by the nothingness in others. I'm not speaking now of violence or the active conflict between one being and another. That still belongs to drama. But the war between being and nothingness is the underlying illness of the twentieth century. Boredom slays more of existence than war.

MARCUS: Then you didn't come to existentialism as a result of some literary influence?

MAILER: No. I'd hardly read anything by Sartre at this time, and nothing by Heidegger. I've read a bit since, and have to admire their formidable powers, but I suspect they are no closer to the buried continent of existentialism than were medieval cartographers near to a useful map of the world. The new continent which shows on our psychic maps as intimations of eternity is still to be discovered.

MARCUS: What do you feel about the other kinds of writing you have done and are doing. How do they stand in relation to your work as a novelist?

MAILER: The essays?

MARCUS: Yes: journalism, essays.

MAILER: Well, you know, there was a time when I wanted very much to belong to the literary world. I wanted to be respected the way someone like Katherine Anne Porter used to be respected.

MARCUS: How do you think she was respected?

MAILER: The way a cardinal is respected — weak people get to their knees when the cardinal goes by.

MARCUS: As a master of the craft, do you mean?

MAILER: As a master of the craft, yes. Her name is invoked in an argument. "Well, Katherine Anne Porter would not do it *that* way." But by now I'm a bit cynical about craft. I think there's a natural mystique in the novel which is more important than craft. One is trying, after all, to capture reality, and that is extraordinarily and exceptionally difficult. Craft is merely a series of way-stations. I think of craft as being like a St. Bernard dog with that little bottle of brandy under his neck. Whenever you get into *real* trouble the thing that can save you as a novelist is to have enough craft to be able to keep warm long enough to be rescued. Of course this is exactly what keeps good novelists from becoming great novelists. Robert Penn Warren might have written a major novel if he hadn't had just that little extra bit of craft to get him out of all the trouble in *All The King's Men*. If Penn Warren hadn't known anything about Elizabethan literature, the true Elizabethan in him might have emerged. I mean, he might have written a fantastic novel. As it was, he knew enough about craft to . . .

MARCUS: To use it as an escape hatch?

MAILER: Yes. And his plot degenerated into a slambang of exits and entrances, confrontations, tragedies, quick wails and woe. But he was really forcing an escape from the problem.

MARCUS: Which was?

MAILER: Oh, the terror of confronting a reality which might open into more and more anxiety and so present a deeper and deeper view of the abyss. Craft protects one from facing those endless expanding realities of deterioration and responsibility.

MARCUS: Deterioration in what sense?

MAILER: The terror, let's say, of being reborn as something much less noble or something much more ignoble. I think this sort of terror depresses us profoundly. Which may be why we throw up our enormous evasions — such as craft. Indeed, I think this adoration of craft, this specific respect for craft makes a church of literature for that vast number of writers who are somewhere on the spectrum between mediocrity and talent. But I think it's fatal for somebody who has a large ambition and a chance of becoming a great writer. I know for myself, if I am going to make this attempt — that the only way to do it is to keep in shape in a peculiar way.

MARCUS: Can you explain what you mean by that?

MAILER: It's hard to talk about. Harry Greb, for example, was a fighter who used to keep in shape. He was completely a fighter, the way one might wish to be completely a writer. He always did the things which were necessary to him as a fighter. Now, some of these things were extremely irrational, that is, extremely irrational from a prize-fight manager's point of view. That is, before he had a fight he would go to a brothel, and he would have two prostitutes, not one, taking the two of them into the same bed. And this apparently left him feeling like a wild animal. Don't ask me why. Perhaps he picked the two meanest whores in the joint and so absorbed into his system all the small, nasty, concentrated evils which had accumulated from carloads of men. Greb was known as the dirtiest fighter of his time. He didn't have much of a punch but he could spoil other fighters and punish them, he knew more dirty tricks than anyone around. This was one of his training methods and he did it over and over again until he died at a relatively early age of a heart attack on an operating table. I think he died before he was thirty-eight, or so. They operated on him, and bang, he went. Nothing could be done. But the point I make is that he stayed in training by the way he lived his life. The element which was paramount in it was to keep in shape. If he were drinking, you see, the point was to keep in shape *while* drinking. I'm being a touch imprecise about this . . .

MARCUS: Well . . . what?

MAILER: He would not drink just to release his tension. Rather, what went on was that there was tension in him which was insupportable, so he had to drink. But reasoning as a professional he felt that if he had to drink, he might as well use that too. In the sense that the actor uses everything which happens to him, so Greb as a fighter used everything which happened to him. As he drank he would notice the way his body moved. One of the best reasons one drinks is to become aware of the way your mind and body move.

MARCUS: Well, how do you keep in shape?

MAILER: Look, before we go on, I want to say a little more about craft. It is a grab-bag of procedures, tricks, lore, formal gymnastics, symbolic superstructures, methodology — in short. It's the compendium of what you've acquired from others. And since great writers communicate a vision of existence, one can't usually borrow their methods. The method is married to the vision. No, one acquires craft more from good writers and mediocre writers with a flair. Craft after all is what you can take out whole from their work. But keeping in shape is something else. For example, you can do journalism, and it can be terrible for your style. Or it can temper your style . . . in other words you can become a *better* writer by doing a lot of different kinds of writing. Or you can deteriorate. Craft is very little finally. But if you're continually worrying about whether you're growing or deteriorating as a man, whether your integrity is turning soft or firming itself, why then it's in that slow war, that slow rearguard battle you fight against diminishing talent that you stay in shape as a writer and have a consciousness. You develop a consciousness as you grow older which enables you to write about anything, in effect, and write about it well. That is, provided you keep your consciousness in shape and don't relax into the flabby styles of thought which surround one everywhere. The moment you borrow other writers' styles of thought, you need craft to shore up the walls. But if what you write is a reflection of your own consciousness, then even journalism can become interesting. One wouldn't want to spend one's life at it and I wouldn't want ever to be caught justifying journalism as a major activity (it's obviously less interesting than to write a novel), but it's better, I think, to see journalism as a venture of one's ability to keep in shape than to see it as an essential betrayal of the chalice of your literary art. Temples are for women.

MARCUS: Temples are for women?

MAILER: Temples are for women.

MARCUS: Well, Faulkner once said that nothing can injure a man's writing if he's a first-rate writer.

MAILER: Faulkner said more asinine things than any other major American writer. I can't remember a single interesting remark Faulkner ever made.

MARCUS: He once called Henry James a "nice old lady."

MAILER: Faulkner had a mean small Southern streak in him, and most of his pronunciamentos reflect that meanness. He's a great writer, but he's not at all interesting in most of his passing remarks.

MARCUS: Well, then, what can ruin a first-rate writer?

MAILER: Booze, pot, too much sex, too much failure in one's private life, too much attrition, too much recognition, too little recognition, frustration. Nearly everything in the scheme of things works to dull a first-rate talent. But the worst probably is cowardice — as one gets older, one becomes aware of one's cowardice, the desire to be bold which once was a joy gets heavy with caution and duty. And finally there's apathy. About the time it doesn't seem too important any more to be a great writer, you know you've slipped far enough to be doing your work now on the comeback trail.

MARCUS: Would you say that is where you are now?

MAILER: Let others say it. I don't know that I choose to. The hardest thing for a writer to decide is whether he's burned out or merely lying fallow. I was ready to think I was burned out before I even started *The Naked and the Dead*.

MARCUS: What kind of an audience do you keep in mind when you write?

MAILER: I suppose it's that audience which has no tradition by which to measure their experience but the intensity and clarity of their inner lives. That's the audience I'd like to be good enough to write for.

MARCUS: Do you feel under any obligation to them?

MAILER: Yes. I have a consciousness now which I think is of use to them. I've got to be able to get it out and do it well, to transmit it in such a way that their experience can rise to a higher level. It's exactly . . . I mean, one doesn't want one's children to make one's own mistakes. Let them make better mistakes, more exceptional mistakes.

MARCUS: What projects do you have for the future?

MAILER: I've got a very long novel I want to do. And beyond that I haven't looked. Some time ahead I'd like to be free of responsibilities so I could spend a year just taking on interesting assignments — cover the World Series, go to report a war. I can't do that now. I have a feeling I've got to come to grips with myself, with my talent, with what I've made of it and what I've spoiled of it. I've got to find out whether I really can write a large novel or not.

MARCUS: You once said that you wished to become consecutively more disruptive, more dangerous, and more powerful, and you felt this sentence was a description of your function as a novelist. I wonder if you still think that?

MAILER: I might take out "disruptive." It's an unhappy word to use. It implies a love of disruption for the sake of disruption. Actually, I have a fondness for order.

MARCUS: Do you enjoy writing, or is such a term irrelevant to your experience?

MAILER: Oh no. No, no. You set me thinking of something Jean Malaquais once said. He always had a terrible time writing. He once complained with great anguish about the unspeakable difficulties he was having with a novel. And I asked him, "Why do you do it? You can do many others things well. Why do you bother with it?" I really meant this. Because he suffered when writing like no one I know. He looked up in surprise and said, "Oh, but this is the only way one can ever find the truth. The only time I know that something is true is at the moment I discover it in the act of writing." I think it's that. I think it's this moment when one knows it's true. One may not have written it well enough for others to know, but you're in love with the truth when you discover it at the point of a pencil. That in and by itself is one of the few rare pleasures in life.

MARCUS: How do you feel when you aren't working?

MAILER: Edgy. I get into trouble. I would say I'm wasting my substance completely when I'm not writing.

MARCUS: And to be writing . . . to be a writer?

MAILER: Well, at best you affect the consciousness of your time, and so indirectly you affect the history of the time which succeeds you. Of course, you need patience. It takes a long time for sentiments to collect into an action and often they never do. Still it's no little matter to be a writer. There's that godawful *Time*-magazine world out there, and one can make raids on it. There are palaces and prisons to attack. One can even succeed now and again in blowing holes in the line of the world's communications. Sometimes I feel as if there's a vast guerrilla war going on for the mind of man, communist against communist, capitalist against capitalist, artist against artist. And the stakes are huge. Will we spoil the best secrets of life or help to free a new kind of man? It's intoxicating to think of that. There's something rich waiting if one of us is brave enough and good enough to get there.

1963

Talking of Violence

An Interview with W. J. Weatherby

❧

W. J. WEATHERBY: People use "violence" — like "love" — in so many, often conflicting ways. Would you like to start by giving your own definition?

NORMAN MAILER: Well, it seems to me there are two kinds of violence and they are altogether different. One is personal violence — an act of violence by man or woman against other men or women. The second kind is social violence — concentration camps, nuclear warfare. If one wants to carry the notion far enough, there are subtler forms such as censorship, or excessively organized piety, or charity drives. Social violence creates personal violence as its antithesis. A juvenile delinquent is violent not because his parents were necessarily violent to him nor even because society is directly violent to him — he's not, let's say, beaten in school — but because his spontaneous expressions are cut off by institutional deadenings of his nature. The boy who lives in a housing project is more likely to be violent than the same boy living in a slum tenement because the housing project puts him in direct contact with a deadening environment. The housing project is not a neighborhood but a massive barracks.

Violence is directly proportional to the power to deaden one's mood which is possessed by the environment. Threatened with the extinction of our possibilities, we react with chronic rage. Violence begins, you see, as the desire to fight one's way out of a trap. Moral questions over the nature of one's violence come only as a secondary matter. The first reaction, the heart of the violence, is the protection of the self. The second question, the moral question, is whether the self deserves to be protected, that is to say — was it honorable to fight? was the danger true? For example, if a boy beats up an old woman, he may be protecting himself by discharging a rage which would destroy his body if it were left to work on the cells, so he takes it out on the old woman. The boy may be anything from a brute to Raskolnikov. It requires an exquisite sense of context and a subtle gift as a moralist to decide these matters at times. Mexicans have a saying that when you commit murder, you carry the dead man's soul on your back, and you have to work not only for one soul then, but for two.

It does seem more or less self-evident that men who have lived a great deal with violence are usually gentler and more tolerant than men who abhor it. Boxers, bullfighters, a lot of combat soldiers, Hemingway heroes, in short, are almost always gentle men. It is not because they have read Hemingway. They were gentle long before Hemingway was born. It is just that Hemingway was the first writer who observed the repetition of this fact and paid his profound respects to it.

I think the reason is that men who are otherwise serious but ready for personal violence, are almost always religious. They have a deep sense of dread, responsibility, of woe, of reluctance to make an error in violence and a grim, almost tragic sense of how far violence can carry them. If I think of the athletes, criminals, prizefighters I have known, and the Negroes living in Harlem (their lives have much in common with precisely athletes, criminals, and prizefighters), they all have an understanding of life which is comprehensive and often tragic. It is of course deadeningly void of any kind of culture that could sustain them in their more boring times, but they do have a specific gravity and a depth of compassion which one doesn't find in their social opposite, the university-trained intellectual.

WEATHERBY: Is he protected too much from this kind of experience?

MAILER: It's not that he is protected from violence — although of course he is — so much as he is not in contact with existential experience, which is to say experience sufficiently unusual so that you don't know how it is going to turn out. You don't know whether you're going to be dead or alive at the end of it, wanted or rejected, cheered or derided. Now obviously there are few experiences which can by these rigorous terms be called existential.

But the hoodlum is more likely to encounter existential experience than the university man.

Something happens in an act of violence which is beyond one's measure. If a bully is beating up a friend who is smaller than himself and knows precisely the point at which he is going to quit, that's not really an act of violence. That's simply excretion. That's why we despise the bully. But when violence is larger than one's ability to dominate, it is existential and one is living in an instantaneous world of revelations. The saint and the psychopath share the same kind of experience. It is just that the saint has the mysterious virtue of being able to transcend this experience and the psychopath is broken or made murderous.

WEATHERBY: How does this view of violence relate to our own time?

MAILER: I wouldn't call the twentieth century a violent period so far as personal violence goes. It is a time of plague. When people sense pestilence is upon them, however, they *tend* to be violent. The powerful impulse of the twentieth century has been to defeat this tendency by elaborate social institutions which destroy the possibility of personal violence before it can have a free expression. If individual feelings are discouraged at every turn and social irritations are blanketed by benefits and welfare programs, then the desire to reach towards one's own individual feelings as a solution becomes stupefied.

The impulse of the twentieth century seems to be a desire to make society run on rails. Anything may be tolerated, even Communism, provided that the dialectic is squeezed out of our nature. The very materials of our world suffocate us everywhere. A perfect material example — the technological signature of the twentieth century — is plastics: materials without any grain, any organic substance, any natural color or predictability. Yet reasonable predictability, after all, is the armature on which great societies in the past have been built. Plastic, however, cracks in two for no reason whatsoever. It bears up under killing punishments and then suddenly explodes in the night. A fiberglass hull can go through storms which would spring a leak in a wooden hull. Then, one day, in a modest squall, the fiberglass splits completely. Or abruptly capsizes. That is because it is a material which is not even divorced from nature but indeed has not ever been a part of nature. Plastic is the perfect metaphor for twentieth-century man and for the curious stupefying bewildering nature of much modern violence.

Our obsession with violence comes, I think, not because its daily incidence is so high but because we are suffocated and so think constantly of violence. Can one argue seriously that our streets are less safe to walk on than the streets of Paris in 1300? Or Naples in 1644? But the twentieth century, in destroying a romantic view of existence, has created an awareness of violence as electric as paranoia.

WEATHERBY: Does this apply in the arts, too?

MAILER: There was a time when an artist could feel respectable about being a naturalist. Zola, Ibsen, Shaw were heroes. So were De Maupassant, Dreiser, Farrell. The natural work of a good artist is to try to write or discover what it is all about. Realism was a way of moving into this mystery just as manners was a way. Now, violence appeals to the artist because it is the least tangible, the least explored frontier. It's exceptionally difficult to write about.

WEATHERBY: Because it so easily becomes melodrama?

MAILER: It is difficult to write about violence because — like love — while you are experiencing it, you can't observe it. You lose your professional consciousness. Heisenberg's principle of uncertainty is in the wings: If you observe an action, the action is affected by the observation. Now, perhaps such emotions as love can be recorded truly — one's memory returns the truth. One can remember in entirety meeting a woman whom one was once in love with, and so be able to write about it. A number of sentimental memories can be recorded truly. An act of violence, however, cannot be recorded truly because the action did not create a mood but shattered a series of moods. So to write about violence is always an act of creation. One must make up an act of violence in order to write about it.

The marvelous thing Hemingway did at his best was to show that the only way to begin to write about half the important matters on earth was to create the mood or the destruction of mood in which they occurred rather than try to establish the truth of the event. It is possible that his years as a reporter inspired him with a passion for such emotional accuracy since he knew that the onerous duty of a journalist is to replace the mood by the fact and so create one kind of history, a fictional history, in opposition to the violent — that is, palpable — actuality of the event.

1964

Vices

An Interview with Paul Carroll, from Playboy

⤲

PLAYBOY: We're reminded of your sentence in *The Deer Park* about growth: "There was that law of life, so cruel and so just, that one must grow or else pay more for remaining the same." Yet you've been charged by many critics with dissipating the potential growth of a major talent in American fiction by wearing so many hats. They point out that there's Mailer the politician; there's Mailer the journalist, who writes about the maladies in American life and about the political brutalities; there's Mailer the celebrity, who grabs headlines by booze brawls and other acts of public violence. How do you answer that criticism?

NORMAN MAILER: Moving from one activity to another makes sense if you do it with a hint of wit or a touch of grace — which I don't say I've always done; far from it — but I think moving from one activity to another can give momentum. If you do it well, you can increase the energy you bring to the next piece of work.

I've been accused of having frittered many talents away, of having taken on too many activities, of having worked too self-consciously at being a celebrity, of having performed at the edges and, indeed, at the center of my own public legend. And, of course, like any criminal. I'm my own best lawyer; the day I'm not will be a sad day. The defense I'll enter today depends on my favorite notion: that an expert, by definition, is opposed to growth. Why? Because an expert is a man who works forward in one direction until he reaches that point where he has to use all

32

his energy to maintain his advance; he cannot allow himself to look in other directions. In other words, he's become nearsighted. Now, I, as a man who's been nearsighted almost all of his life, know that anyone who's born nearsighted or becomes nearsighted early is a man become an expert prematurely. That's why kids with glasses are usually disliked by kids who don't wear glasses. The kids with good eyesight sense that the boy with glasses is an expert who's going to run the world. The first chronic personal shame I suppose I ever felt was having to wear glasses. And I don't wear them today, even though I'm so nearsighted I don't recognize old friends from ten feet away. Having been a premature expert myself, I think I may have reacted against it with a sense that expertise was the trap for me, that to get particularly good at any one thing would leave me top-heavy.

PLAYBOY: One of your celebrated experiments with growth was your experience with drugs. You were on marijuana, Benzedrine, and sleeping pills for a few years and were addicted to Seconal. Later, you said that a man on drugs will pay for it by "a gutted and burned-out nervous system." How do you feel about that topic today?

MAILER: Drugs are a spiritual form of gambling. This is a poetic equation that can be carried right down to the end of its metaphor, because on drugs you're even bucking the house percentage — which for a drug like marijuana is probably something like 30 or 40 percent.

PLAYBOY: Would you expand this?

MAILER: Marijuana does something with the sense of time: it accelerates you; it opens you to your unconscious. But it's as if you're calling on the reserves of the next three days. All the sweets, all the crystals, all the little decisions, all the unconscious work of the next three days — or, if the experience is deep, part of the next thirty days, or the next thirty years — is called forward. For a half hour or two hours — whatever is the high of the pot —you're *better* than you are normally and you get into situations you wouldn't get into normally, and generally more happens to you. You make love better, you talk better, you think better, you dig people better. The point is, you've got to get in pretty far, because you're using up three days in an hour — or whatever the particular ratio is for any particular person. So unless you come back with — let us say — seventy-two hours in one hour, you lose. Because you have to spend the next three or four days recovering. You might ask: What happens to the guy who smokes all the time? I don't know. But I do know something is being mortgaged; something is being drawn out of the future. If his own future has already been used up in one or another mysterious or sinister sense, then maybe the pot is drawing it out of the very substance of what I may as well confess I call God. I suspect God feeds drug addicts the way a healthy body feeds parasites.

PLAYBOY: How do you mean?

MAILER: Well, if God has great compassion, He may not be willing to cut the drug addict off from Him. During the time the addict has some of his most intense and divine experiences, it is because he is literally imbibing the very marrow and nutrient of existence. But since I do not believe that God is necessarily inexhaustible, the drug addict may end up by bleeding Him.

PLAYBOY: Do you think this happens on LSD?

MAILER: I don't think you have a mystical experience on chemicals without taking the risk of exploiting something in the creation. If you haven't paid the real wages of love or courage or abstention or discipline or sacrifice or wit in the eye of danger, then taking a psychedelic drug is living the life of a parasite; it's drawing on sweets you have not earned.

PLAYBOY: What is the danger of this parasitical self-exploitation on LSD?

MAILER: I'm not going to say that LSD is bad in every way for everyone, but I'm convinced it's bad if you keep taking it. Any drug is bad finally in the same way that being a confirmed gambler is bad. A confirmed gambler ends up losing all his friends because he blows their money and blows their trust. A gambler will tell any lie to get back into the action. By the same token, if you stay on any drug for too long, then you have a habit; you're a victim; to anticipate something, you're a totalitarian.

Let me put it this way: LSD is marvelous for experts to take when they get too frozen in their expertise. Let's suppose they've driven deep into something impenetrable, some obstacle that was bound to trap them because of the shortsighted nature of their expertise. Although they work and work manfully as experts, at this point they're similar to soldiers who have pushed far into enemy territory but are now up against a resistance they cannot get through. Their only action is to retreat, but they don't know how to, because they have no habits of retreat. They're experts; they know only how to move forward to amass more knowledge and put more concentration upon a point. When this concentration does not succeed in poking through the resistance of the problem, the expert is psychically in great trouble. He begins to live in increasing depression; he has to retreat and doesn't know how: he wasn't built to retreat.

My guess is: On LSD, you begin to die a little. That's why you get this extraordinary, even divine sense of revelation. Perhaps you taste the essence of your own death in the trip; in excess, it's a deadly poison, after all. Therefore, what's given to the expert is a broader vision: dying a little, he begins to retreat from his expertise and begins to rejoin his backward brothers. So that LSD taken a few times could be very good, I would imagine. But before very long, if the expert keeps taking LSD, he can become nothing but an expert on LSD.

PLAYBOY: What do you think of Timothy Leary?

MAILER: Well, I wonder who we were just talking about.

PLAYBOY: More of an answer, please.

MAILER: I never met him. Perhaps I'd like him if I did. Many of my friends like him. But I have heard him speak, and he is then naught but simple shit.

PLAYBOY: Alcohol seems to be another way by which you've tried to grow or "move forward." One of the characters in your stage version of *The Deer Park* declares: "A man must drink until he locates the truth." How does alcohol help a man do that?

MAILER: A man who drinks is attempting to dissolve an obsession.

PLAYBOY: What's the obsession?

MAILER: Talk first about what *an* obsession is. I've thought about obsession a great deal, but I'm not sure I know the answer. Everybody speaks of obsessions; nobody's ever really explained them. We can define them, but we don't really know what we're talking about. An obsession, I'd like to suggest, is not unlike a pole of magnetism, a psychic field of force. An obsession is created, I think, in the wake of some event that has altered our life profoundly, or perhaps we have passed through some relation with someone else that has altered our life drastically, yet we don't know whether we were changed for good or for bad; it's the most fundamental sort of event or relation. It has marked us, yet it's morally ambiguous.

PLAYBOY: What kind of event?

MAILER: Suppose a marriage breaks up. You don't know if it was finally your fault or your wife's fault. People move forward into the future out of the way they comprehend the past. When we don't understand our past, we are therefore crippled. Use the metaphor of the Army here: If you move forward to attack a town and the center of this attack depends upon a road that will feed your attack, and this road passes through a town, yet you don't know if your people hold it or someone else does, then obviously, if you were a general, you'd be pretty obsessive about that town. You'd keep asking, "Will you please find out who is there?" You'd send out reconnaissance parties to locate the town, enter it, patrol it. If all sorts of mysterious things occurred — if, for example, your reconnaissance platoon didn't return — you'd feel so uncertain you might not move forward to attack. The obsession is a search for a useful reality. What finally did occur? What is real?

PLAYBOY: You haven't told us yet how drink helps dissolve an obsession.

MAILER: Well, if a man's drink takes him back to an earlier, younger state of sensitivity, it is then taking him to a place back of the place where he originally got into the impasse that created the obsession. If you can return to a state just preceding the one you were in when these various ambiguous events occurred, you can say to yourself, "Now, I'm approaching the event again. What really did happen? Who was right? Who was wrong? Let me not miss it this time." A man must drink until he locates the truth. I think that's why it's so hard for people to give up booze. There's an artwork going on with most serious drinkers. Usually, it's a failed artwork. Once again, one's playing against the house percentage: one drinks, one wrecks one's liver, dims one's vision, burns out one's memory. Drinking is a serious activity — a serious moral and spiritual activity. We consume ourselves in order to search for a truth.

PLAYBOY: Do you feel that you've experienced moments of truth through drink?

MAILER: Extraordinary moments.

PLAYBOY: What sort of thing did you discover?

MAILER: Whatever the truth was. The kind of truths you find in moments like that. Discovering that somebody you thought loved you, hated you, or vice versa. All I'm underlining is that sense of certainty we all know when past moments of ambiguity are resolved. A relationship alters in one's memory from a morass to a crystal of recollection.

PLAYBOY: You've made in *An American Dream* and other writings a brilliant, dazzling, and rather puzzling remark concerning the possibility that God Himself may be involved in a process of growth. You've said that you have an "obsession with how God exists," and you've argued for the possibility that He may be a God whose final nature is not yet comprehended, even by Himself. Could you comment on this?

MAILER: I think I decided some time ago that if there is a God and He's all-powerful, then His relation to us is absurd. All we can see in our human condition are thundering, monumental disproportions, injustices of such dimension that even the conservative notion of existence — which might postulate that man is here on earth not to complain but to receive his just deserts and that the man who acts piggishly on earth will be repaid in hell, regardless of whether he was rich or poor — yes, even this conservative vision depends on a God who is able to run a world of reasonable proportions. If the only world we have is one of abysmal, idiotic disproportions, then it becomes too difficult to conceive of an all-powerful God who is all good. It is far easier to conceive of a God who died, or who is dying, or who is an imperfect God. But once I begin to think of an imperfect God, I can imagine a Being greater than ourselves, who nonetheless shares His instinctive logic with us. We as men seek to grow, so He seeks to grow. Even as we each have a conception of being — my idea of how we should live may triumph over yours, or yours over mine — so, in parallel, this God may be engaged in a similar war in the universe with other gods. We may even be the embodiment, the expression of His vision. If we fail, He fails, too. He is imperfect in the way we are imperfect. He is not always as brave or extraordinary or as graceful as He might care to be. This is my notion of God and growth. What gives me sustenance is that it enables me to love God, if you will bear these words, rather than hate Him, because I can see Him as someone who is like other men and myself, except more noble, more tortured, more desirous of a good that He wishes to receive and give to others — a torturous ethical activity at which He may fail. Man's condition is, then, by this logic, epic or tragic — for the outcome is unknown. It is not written.

PLAYBOY: Could you talk a bit more about the relationship between a man and this God who is still involved in discovering His own nature?

MAILER: In capsule: There are times when He has to exploit us; there are times when we have to exploit Him; there are times when He has to drive us beyond our own natural depth because He needs us — those of us, at least, who are working for Him: We have yet to talk of the Devil.

PLAYBOY: You said recently that maybe the Devil is God in exile. What did you mean?

MAILER: I don't know if the Devil is finally an evil principle of God — a fallen angel, a prince of darkness, Lucifer — a creature of the first dimension engaged in a tragic, monumental war with God, or whether the Devil is a species of nonexistence, like plastic. By which I mean every single pervasive substance in the technological world that comes from artificial synthesis rather than from nature. Plastic surfaces have no resonance — no echo of nature. I don't know if plastic is a second principle of evil just as much opposed to the Devil as it is opposed to God — a visitor from a small planet, if you will. So when I talk about the Devil these days, I don't really know whether I'm talking about a corrupter of the soul or a deadening influence. I don't know who or where the enemy is. In fact, I don't have the remotest notion of who or what I'm working for. That's despair.

PLAYBOY: Existential is a term that crops up frequently in your writing: existential God, existential politician. In what way was Kennedy an existential politician?

MAILER: Kennedy was a man who could define himself — or, in other words, comprehend himself — only by his actions. He had such extraordinary ambition that if he had not succeeded in being President, he might have ended up a bad piece of work. There is such a thing as a man starting as a bad piece of work because he has a nature that is extraordinarily disharmonious; he lives with unendurable ambitions. If he succeeds in what the psychoanalysts call "acting it out" — with some scorn they say "acting out" — the fact remains that he also has to have huge courage, high wit, and vast imagination. Kennedy succeeded in getting to play the one role that could allow him to realize himself: the President of the United States. When I call him an existential politician, I mean that Kennedy had no nature other than the particular nature he discovered in himself by the act of living. If he had tried to live a more conventional life, he would have sealed his psyche in a vault and probably have died young and schizophrenic.

PLAYBOY: How do you feel about Johnson's Great Society?

MAILER: It's a comedy. The Great Society is not only not going to come into being but it shouldn't. It's artificial. Any time you find a great society developed from the top, what you've got, in effect, is a test-tube baby — artificial insemination of the worst sort. Let's say the Great Society is drug addiction on a huge political scale. It's similar to shooting B_{12} complex into your butt. The patient may feel healthier for a while, but the fact of the matter is that his ass has been violated. The flesh has been visited abruptly by a tubular needle that punctures skin, rips delicate strands of muscle, and cuts holes in a vein wall. To what end? The body doesn't understand. If you're in a fight and get hit, your body can usually understand that: it was probably mobilized for action. But what action are you mobilized for when a needle goes into your flesh? The same thing happens, I think, with economic growth.

Take housing projects. I see no reason to come in with these tremendous urban-renewal jobs that are unspeakably ugly and tear up neighborhoods; they are like metal plates put in your head or plastic tubes stuck in your gut. These projects disrupt a neighborhood. Instead, some of these tenements could be saved. You might have a scheme where a man could start by being given one hundred dollars' worth of materials — I use the figure arbitrarily — and a little professional labor, and he could set out to improve his apartment: plaster a wall, this or that; say his wife will be in on it. He's working for his own apartment. If he goes out and drinks up the money, all right, he drank it up and presumably he won't get anymore. His neighbors might lean on him. Not lean on him hard, probably, because if he's the guy who drank it up he's possibly the meanest guy in the house. Still, what you get this way is a house interested in itself; whereas the other way, housing projects, poverty programs, Great Society — any Negro who doesn't set out to exploit the white man who is giving him money is nothing but a fool. With such handouts, honor for the Negro becomes his ability to lie, cheat, and exploit the white man. Whereas a few thousand dollars given bit by bit to a man working very hard on his own apartment over a few years would obviously do much more for that apartment than twenty thousand dollars spent to renovate it by outside methods.

PLAYBOY: Prior to the riots in Newark and Detroit, you said that civil war would erupt soon in this country. Did you see it as happening between Negroes and whites?

MAILER: I think there's a tendency toward civil war — not a war in the sense of people shooting it out over the hills and on battle lines; but certain kinds of functions might cease to exist in this society — technological functions. It may be that people will lose the habit of depending on the subway to get to work, or people might lose the real possibility of driving into certain cities at certain hours of the day or night. What might happen would be scattered outbreaks of violence: people, for example, overturning cars in traffic jams. All sorts of things — products getting worse and worse, shoddiness at the center of production, breakdowns, fissures.

PLAYBOY: How much of this will be the result of what you've often and passionately condemned as our technological society?

MAILER: Oh, much of it. Most of it, perhaps. Another great part of the tendency toward violence might derive from our guilt of the past: we've never paid for the crimes of the past; now we're trying to bury them. That's one reason the technological society advances at such a great rate: it frees people from having to look back into the horrors of the past. Western man has never faced up to the slave trade, the colonization of the world, the imperialization of the world, the concentration camps — the list could go on as long as one's knowledge of history.

PLAYBOY: In *Cannibals and Christians*, you described the cold war as useless, brutal, and enervating. You said we should stop it and get on with the destiny of Western man. What is that destiny?

MAILER: A huge phrase — I suppose I meant that the West is built ultimately on one final assumption — that life is heroic. It's a Faustian notion. Of course, the West is also Christian, but there's always been a contradiction at the heart. Christianity, the gentlest of religious professions, is the most militant and warlike of religions, the most successful and Faustian of religions. Indeed, it conquered the world. In that limited sense, Christianity is the most heroic. The alternative to this heroic notion of man is the passive acceptance of the universe that characterizes Hindu or Oriental philosophy and religion.

One of the ironies of our century is that the technological society creates an atmosphere of such passivity in people that they are now prepared to entertain Oriental notions precisely because they have lost much of the real power to shape their own lives. The citizens of a technological society are as powerless as an Oriental peasant. Their living standard may be vastly superior, but their social impotence is similar: they command less and less; they are manipulated more and more. They may think they are picking their channel, but TV channels them.

The more we wage a religious war against Communism, the more we create the real social equivalent of Communism in America — which will be the total technological society. You can look forward into a future where Communism's technological society grows nearly identical with ours; the differences will be of the mildest local color. For the natural tendency of the technological society is to try to clean up all sorts of social excesses and to root out random oppression because these activities are illogical. They interfere with the smooth working of the machine. You never want a piston to drive with more force than is necessary to direct the action of the machine; you never put a part in the machine that is heavier than it needs to be. So the natural desire of the technological society is to create a smooth totalitarian society free from the ranker forms of injustice. Its long-term tendency in Russia is to make a totalitarian environment that is relatively civilized and pleasant. Both countries may well end by serving up a life to their citizens about as anonymous and vitiated and pill-ridden and dull as some of our new office buildings.

PLAYBOY: Then why does America fight Communism?

MAILER: Because we're Faustian. We believe we have to grapple with the universe; we have the secret faith that we are inspired by a national genius that enables us to take on anything and do anything. The tragic irony is that in fighting Communism, we are creating the absolute equivalent of Communism in this country. And we will destroy our own Faustian dream in the act of fighting Communism, for the technological society looks to destroy any idea of the heroic. Such ideas seem irrational and unscientific to the technician.

On the other hand, each time Communism has captured some small part of the West, it has been shaken by Western complexities that open huge rents in the Russian Communist ideology. A backward country like Yugoslavia did more to halt Stalinism than fifty military adventures dreamed up by John Foster Dulles. Yugoslavia introduced a complex notion into the center of Communism: the idea that there could be two kinds of Communism, each equally devout and heroic in itself, each more or less oppressive. This made the Communist bureaucrat begin to contemplate the nature of his own system and therefore to doubt his faith and so look for ways to ameliorate the oppressiveness of it.

Communism is cannibalistic, as I said earlier. Any ideology that attempts to dominate all of existence has to split into sects and segments, because the moment disagreement exists between members, it cannot be adjudicated or compromised without losing the primitive force of the ideology. Compromise impossible, splits occur. What you get then is two ideologies equally monotonous, equally total, soon equally at war with each other.

PLAYBOY: Opposed to this, then, is what you call the heroic destiny of the West?

MAILER: Let's say, an *exploration* into the heroic.

PLAYBOY: Is existential politics an exploration into the heroic?

MAILER: To a degree. Existential politics can be understood only by talking practically, specifically, about what you are going to do here in this particular place and time. After you talk about, say, twenty such situations, you get some notion of existential politics. Existential politics depends on a certain intimacy between the law and the people upon whom the law is enacted. For example, not that there should be no capital punishment, but that if someone is going to get killed by the state, then make a spectacle of the event. Let people watch while a professional executioner and the condemned man fight hand to hand in an arena. Since the executioner is professional, he wins practically every time; but he doesn't win to a certainty; that gives the prisoner some last chance to fight for his own existence. It gives him the right of any man to fight for existence under extraordinary circumstances. Such a spectacle also opens the public to the real nature of execution. Let them see that blood on the sand. They may then decide if they still want capital punishment. If they do, more power to them. They like blood. But at least one profound hypocrisy — our quarantine of the execution from the eyes of the public that decrees the act — won't be able to exist anymore.

PLAYBOY: You have any prognostications about the American political and social scene in general?

MAILER: I'm gloomy. The technological society sits upon us like an incubus. It's impossible, for instance, to have any contact with anything in your existence that is not incapsulated by this technological society. I can't take a pat of butter at breakfast that doesn't have some chemical additive to deaden the taste of the butter just a bit, and therefore my taste buds, and therefore deaden me, as well as line my stomach cells with a new if minuscule addition of the chemical. If you could eat a fresh piece of butter for breakfast, certain sensory messages might be able to reach down deep into the secret needs of your nerves — enough to enrich you. You might live a hint better. The technological society gets between us and existence in everything we do, the air we breathe, the buildings we live in with their abstract monotonous forms, the synthetic fibers we wear; ever notice how a rash from a synthetic fiber is more disagreeable than one from cotton or wool? The list is endless. I've written about little else for years.

PLAYBOY: What can be done about it?

MAILER: I don't know. My feeling is that there is going to be some extraordinary holocaust. Who knows? We may all die off in mysterious fashion. For instance, about the time we discover some cure for cancer, a new disease even worse will probably be spawned by the cure — just as new viruses were spawned in relation to penicillin. Modern disease and modern technology are inseparably connected.

PLAYBOY: You've often connected this, which you call "the plague," with the modern technological society. How did the plague begin?

MAILER: Jacques Ellul, in his book *The Technological Society*, suggests that the beginning of all scientific technique came from a perversion of primitive magic.

PLAYBOY: You've written that one aspect of totalitarianism is fear of orgasm, particularly by the liberal mentality, because the orgasm, you claim, is "the existential moment. Every lie we have told, every fear we have indulged, every aggression we have tamed," you say, "arises again at that instant to constrict the turns and possibilities of our becoming." Could you tell us more about that?

MAILER: Orgasm is the moment when you can't cheat life. If the orgasm was no good, something in you — or in your mate — was no good.

PLAYBOY: Do you still believe, as you wrote several years ago, that birth control is evil — that it's a kind of murder of what may have been a man's best son?

MAILER: Yes. In fact, not too long ago, I was reading a very generous review of *Cannibals and Christians* in a Catholic magazine called *The Critic;* and at one point the writer said, Of course, Mailer's ideas are almost absurdly sentimental about birth control. I am now to the right of the Catholic Church.

PLAYBOY: Indeed, the Catholic Church is presently struggling with its birth control position, in order to square it with the problems of the world population explosion and the individual moral problems raised by families that are too large.

MAILER: Regardless of what the Church finally decides, the problem of birth control is the same as all of the other problems in our technological society. They're all part of the same damn problem; something is insulating us away from our existence. My guess is that in primitive times it was more difficult to conceive and — as a result — more natural. In a just existence, the best things are always the most difficult. We notice that many animals don't conceive unless they really want it to take.

In our modern life, on the other hand, the body is so deadened at its sexual center by contraceptives and pills that we no longer can afford to be as selective as we used to be. This adds desperation. People now conceive too easily because they're afraid if they don't, they won't conceive at all.

PLAYBOY: What would happen if there were no birth control?

MAILER: It's possible that it might then become much more difficult to conceive, because there would be more real terror of conceiving for too little.

PLAYBOY: Isn't it also possible that the social consequences would be calamitous — if your theory didn't work?

MAILER: Perhaps — but one thing you can be sure of: People would start making love a lot less; they'd make it only when they really wanted to make it; they'd have to be carried away more. One thing I've learned in all these years is not to make love when you really don't feel it; there's probably nothing worse you can do to yourself than that.

PLAYBOY: The "technological society" more directly affects — and you would say, oppresses — the middle and upper classes. Is that the reason you've written that the lower classes enjoy a more satisfactory sex life?

MAILER: I think the lower classes probably have more sexual vitality than the upper classes. They tend to work more with their bodies than with their minds.

PLAYBOY: But according to Kinsey, the lower economic groups suffer from more sexual rigidity and engage in less sexual experimentation than the upper and middle classes.

MAILER: All such statistics show is the attitude to which people are ready to confess. I don't know how valid such findings are. What we're talking about here is old-fashioned sexual perversion. Members of the upper classes and the more prosperous middle classes tend to be fond of their own pet perversion; they look upon it as an entertainment, an adornment, an enrichment; the lower class, on the other hand, looks upon sexual perversion as weakness; they see it in its other aspect. Perversion has two aspects: it is an adornment; it is also a need, and so they see it as a weakness and they despise it. To the lower classes, need is weakness.

PLAYBOY: What do you mean by "perversion"?

MAILER: Whatever it might be — fellatio, cunnilingus, name it.

Lower-class people see it as a weakness in themselves if they desire it. Envision a strong guy who wants to go down on his girl. He thinks he's weak. Of course he's weak. Giving head to your woman is weakness; it's also a good way to get rid of some of your weakness. It's also dangerous because it gives the Devil introduction into the vagina.

PLAYBOY: The Devil? How so?

MAILER: Oh, the mind's a devil. Didn't you know? And connected to the tongue.

PLAYBOY: You've said that D. H. Lawrence was the first novelist who gave you the idea "that sex could have beauty." Do you continue to admire Lawrence?

MAILER: Lawrence is sentimental about sex. Sex is not only a divine and beautiful activity; it's also a murderous activity. People kill each other in bed. Some of the greatest crimes ever committed have been committed in bed. And no weapons were used.

PLAYBOY: About the art of fiction in general, do you agree with critics such as Norman Podhoretz who claim that the novel as an imaginative art is dead because of the recent incorporation of reportage techniques into fiction?

MAILER: Obviously, I don't. The novel has its own particular resource, which is magical. You can establish a communion between yourself and the reader that can be found in no other art. And this communion can continue for hours, weeks, years. When the novel is dead, then the technological society will be totally upon us. You'll need a score card to tell the Communists from the Texans.

PLAYBOY: Do you think you'll continue to write political and cultural essays?

MAILER: In a way, I've been working on one book most of my writing life. Certainly since *The Deer Park*, I've been working on one book.

PLAYBOY: What's the book about?

MAILER: Existentialism. That is to say, the feel of our human condition, which, by the logic of existentialism, is the truth of the human condition.

PLAYBOY: At the beginning of our talk, you said interviews sometimes serve as a psychic housecleaning for your current ideas. Do you feel you've accomplished that here?

MAILER: I hope we haven't had a curettage.

1967

On Science and Art

An Interview with David Young

❧

DAVID YOUNG: I am interested in your definition of what an artist is.

NORMAN MAILER: I'm not sure I know.

YOUNG: Let me give you a statement that stuck with me. Just one sentence. An artist is someone who perceives relations that are not noticed by other people.

MAILER: By such logic an inventor's an artist; a mathematician is an artist; a physicist is certainly an artist. Besides, there are great artists who don't see many new relations but have an exceptional sense of how various styles and manners work.... There are playwrights who don't have original plots.

YOUNG: Shakespeare.

MAILER: I think in one sense he's actually quite an inventor — the relations he discovered in language. His metaphors are extraordinary. You could work up a thesis that Moore and Wittgenstein are a reaction against the metaphorical concepts Shakespeare left in the language.

YOUNG: Let's go back to our first question.

MAILER: It's a riddle, talking about an artist. I feel as if I'm sliding around.

YOUNG: Maybe a definition of art might help. Have you ever read Martin Johnson's *Art and Scientific Thought*? He defined art as the communication of feeling. And science as the communication of measure. But how do you measure feeling? I don't think it's possible. Now you can measure an orgasm, I guess, by some means, cardiograph and encephalograph and all that kind of stuff, but I don't think that is giving you any truth of that particular experience. I have a feeling that art and science and myth and magic are tending to grow together as our thinking progresses in a general sense. I was particularly struck by this when I was discussing anti-matter with a scientist. He said the top twenty scientists who can really deal with this subject have had to invent their own language form in order to be able to discuss it, it's so far out. And it has been discovered that five thousand years ago in Tibet a very similar language form was developed by certain monks who were discussing the sciences. It seems like the magic has come full circle. To me art has always been — well, indigenous to magic in one sense or another.

MAILER: Yet we have so many artists who literally invade technology. It's getting to the point where if you go to the Guggenheim, three out of four new artists are in technology as much as art. Some of it looks as if an engineer took pages out of his workbook and stuck them on a wall. Of course, we can also say that the physicist invokes magic when he works. Oppenheimer has his famous remark about how he always knew he was on the trail of something good when the hair stood up on the back of his neck.

YOUNG: Robert Graves used that as a test for a poem.

MAILER: Yes. They're related. If you stop to analyze it, the equation sign is nothing but a statement of metaphor. When you say: "y equals x^2" you are in effect establishing a metaphor. Or, the obverse: Some kid in a gallery, looking at a painting, says "I see God in the yellow." All right, that's a metaphor which can be stated mathematically: The yellow in this painting is a function of God. A simple mathematical statement. Either way, artist or physicist has penetrated an equation into the substance of things. In that sense I'd say the physicist and the artist are closer to one another than the artist and the gallery owner, or the physicist and the engineer.

YOUNG: Right. They might be married in the older sense of alchemy.

MAILER: You could say that art and science only separated at that point where alchemy turned into science, and those who refused to go along with the controlled experiment were left with magic. And witchcraft.

YOUNG: That was when men dealing with the heavens split into separate camps of astrology and astronomy.

MAILER: Maybe the essential intent which separates the artist from the physicist is in their relation to theology. But I'd rather not use the word theology. Let's say, brutally speaking, it is in their relation to God.

YOUNG: You mean to their own notion of God?

MAILER: Obviously, they all have their own notion. If many of them can easily — physicists and artists alike — think of themselves as atheists, and I come along and say it hardly matters how they think of themselves, I still say the difference is in their relation to God; it is obviously a way of saying *I* believe in God. Obviously. Then, everything I try to comprehend in others is going to come out of this fundamental belief in me. That is, of course, an arrogance. But the only way I ever begin to comprehend anything is by indulging such a stance. I don't believe it's possible to approach a tricky or mysterious question without assuming that you're right, or at least have an hypothesis to carry you every step of the way — at least until you find out your're not right. Then you can begin to search for the error in your intuition. Other kinds of inquiry can only lead to the computer. There you put in your collected experience plus the reported experience of others and wait for a statistic.

YOUNG: No room for the intuitive leap.

MAILER: I would assume that while the physicist is titillated, even thrilled, by the experience of magic in his work, and while the artist is often drenched in statistical detail (since he has to deal with a world that grows more and more technical and difficult to comprehend), at bottom their interests are opposed and they're enemies. Because the physicist is finally trying to destroy the fundament of magic, and the artist is trying to blow up the base of technology. The artist believes (and this is the greatest generalization I can make) that all cosmic achievement is attainable within the human frame, that is, if we lead lives witty enough and skillful enough, bold enough and, finally, illumined enough, we can accomplish every communication, and make every vault within the cosmos that technology would attempt to make. In fact, we're not coming face to face with the fact that technology has probably come to the end of one of its limits. As we go off into space, we're up against the knowledge that even if technology keeps expanding at the same extraordinary rate, nothing seems to offer any possibility of getting out of the solar system for thousands of years. Which means we may have taken the wrong road. Somewhere five, ten, and twenty thousand years ago, man took the wrong road. He separated himself from those dire disciplines of magic which might have enabled him to communicate with the cosmos. In fact, this language of the Lamas that you were talking about might have been precisely that same language. They were dealing with matter and anti-matter; they were communicating.

YOUNG: I have a feeling that an artist pursuing that notion now may be what will save us.

MAILER: Well, I don't know if we can pursue it. I'm talking about savage sensibility. The sensibility of the primitive who requires it to exist. You see, the primitive obviously had senses which were closer to the animal. He also had fears closer to the animal. Those fears are intense. Anyone who has ever felt dread in any real way knows it's so unendurable an experience that one'll do almost anything to avoid it. So I would come near to arguing that civilization came out of man's terror at having to face dread as a daily condition. Therefore we created a civilization which would insulate us from the exorbitant demands of existence. I'm not speaking now of those smaller or unbelievably pressing demands in that time of growing or killing enough food to be able to live simply. I'm talking of that greater terror when the trees spoke to one, and the message of the trees was not agreeable, and worst of all the trees were right. The message one got from the trees was true. The storm they told you about — that terrible storm which was going to make the river wash over its banks and destroy your hamlet in three weeks was true. What a terror. What a terror. I'm saying that man did everything he could, you see, to get away from that kind of intimacy with nature, that foresight, that dread.

YOUNG: Do you think that the invention of the devil might have come about from that phenomenon?

MAILER: Well, I'm not so convinced the devil is an invention.

YOUNG: Which brings me to one of my favorite quotes of Carl Jung: "The moment you remove the devil from society, you only allow him to re-appear in an infinite variety of anonymous forms."

MAILER: I would make an obeisance to that remark. A doctor inoculated my two-month-old daughter for diphtheria yesterday. He caught me at a weak moment. I argued with him feebly. They've found through experience that it's easier to inoculate kids at the age of two months than it is to inoculate them when they're four years old or five years old because the kids pass through the discomfort of the inoculation in a few hours when they're infants, and they're sick for a day or two later on. The larger argument that maybe people who get diphtheria should die of diphtheria can't begin to be ventured into. The doctor would have looked at my daughter and me through slant eyes. But what ate at me was that I had slipped my daughter into the technological chain of being. Chemicals stuck into her body at the age of two months. She was now going to be part of the chemical balance, imbalance, balance, imbalance, that all modern medicine consists of. She had gotten into that synthetic chain where chemicals which never grew out of the earth are installed into our bodies and we react to that in ways nobody understands. I think they keep giving us more chemicals to keep finding that balance that they've lost. As I was talking about it, I suddenly said, you know, they do to human beings what they wouldn't do to machines. And it's absolutely true that technology has more regard for the machine and fucks with it less than modern medicine plays with the human body. That's what I expect is the ubiquity of the devil. At the least, looking at it phenomenologically, there are powerful forces working to separate man's mind from his body. The intent of technology is to allow man to be a mind independent of all needs which keep the body within physical limitations. The fundamental notion of technology probably is that there is no wisdom of the body which the brain cannot relocate within itself. In other words, the disembodied brain is a superior piece of intelligence to the corporeal flesh-enclosed brain. As an expression of that, a lot of the functions of the brain having to do with habit are being taken over by the computer, with the terrible danger that about the time we lose the mental ability to do the intellectual tasks we are passing into the computer, we will be unable to spot errors in the computer. That is, we will be able to spot the errors but we won't be able to locate where they are and how they got there. Nobody will have the will, or the simple stamina, to trace out the circuits to see where the error got in. It'll be too boring, since we will have lost the habit of undertaking drudgery in mental work. Boredom will be as insupportable to the mind in such a future time as fire now is to the flesh.

YOUNG: I'd like to give you a quote. A friend of mine says, "Art is inarticulately certain, and science is articulately uncertain."

MAILER: I think that's true. But it doesn't help much, because next you have to get into fundamental philosophical questions like the relation of the articulate to existence. An existentialist could argue that because something is articulate, it does not by itself offer proof that it has any relation to being true. It may have a relationship to being — we usually assume it has a relation to being — but it may not. For example: The yellow matrix of the pyramidal doughnut probably has no relation to being.

YOUNG: Are you speaking of articulate in the sense of the word?

MAILER: The word as opposed to the feeling, to the unvoiced apprehension of things. Language may bear the same relation to man that technology bears to husbandry, or at least to any of the activities by which primitive man hewed out his existence. For instance, if I am a primitive, and alone in a forest, and live with all the terrors and agreeable forces of that forest, and walk with the principalities of the gods of that forest, terribly aware of the huge and ominous sense of pride in that giant oak which I believe is the center of the forest, well, then as I pass by its periphery I may have an exceptional sense of over how far a distance extends the hegemony of the oak. Think of that as equivalent to talking about the aura which surrounds a human. When we speak of charisma, we suggest that as you approach someone who possesses it, you can't get too near before you feel that you're entering some envelope of their presence. You can be three feet away from them, but something has changed in your own psyche. It's what people speak of usually as vibrations. At least one form of vibrations. Like entering a field of resonance which surrounds certain people who are highly charged.

YOUNG: Like an induction coil?

MAILER: Like a magnetic field. I think the primitive lived in a world in which all natural objects around him had these fields. Wherever one powerful psychic field met another, there was a mood. Where the presence of the oak met the presence of the field of tall grass, so there was a mood, and in that mood the savage walking through was aware that he was a third presence who was picking up some sense of events to come. Or picked up some sense of the past. One of the characteristics of most primitive languages, I suspect, is that their sense of past and future is different from ours. For instance, in classic Hebrew, there is no firm difference between past and future. In fact, there are merely two tenses, the present, and another tense which has to do with actions which occurred *either* in the past or in the future. Only a very simple shift is made in that verb form. If you want to talk about the past, you remark, "I left." If you wish to indicate "I will leave," you simply say, "And I left." My God, I spent years thinking about this. What a different sense of existence! Since primitive man keeps no records, the ability to distinguish between his memory of the past, and a dream, becomes next to impossible. Of course, primitive people also employ last night's dream as something which will give them intimations of the future. And, of course, it's possible the dream, far from being a wish fulfillment, is actually that instrument which enables us to anticipate those psychic problems we can or cannot afford to take on in the future. In other words, the anxiety system of the dream gives us clues as to how much intensity our nervous system can bear in different directions. That is why we re-play the experiences of the day before through the complications of the dream. We dramatize them in our imagination. We put ourselves in tense situations to see how much dread we can bear. Therefore the dream deals with the future as it is based on the experience of the past. Which means both past and future are part of the same psychic river. So it's as if the primitive Hebrew saw his experiences forming into two halves: two tenses, two modes of being — the sensuous-at-hand which was the present tense, and the sense of that other time which was not at hand.

YOUNG: That would tend to make the present of less importance, I would think. . . .

MAILER: I don't know. Particularly since primitive man was not abstracted in the way we are. His present, whatever it was, had to have an extraordinary difference from ours. He had to be immersed in it much more as he walked through the forest. Of course, I'm going along now on the not necessarily mystical notion that nature is an exquisite receiving and transmitting set. It's possible that one of the ways God would communicate with the earth and the earth communicated back with God, if you will, is that every tree and blade of grass is capable of sending transmissions. Because parenthetically we know nothing about radio. If you scratch a crystal, and lead the vibration out to any wire of a certain length, called an antenna, why then another wire of an appropriate length attached only to a crystal somewhere else can pick up your signal. That is the basic transaction of radio. We've put it through a million improvements. Amplified it unbelievably. Yet what more do we know about the inner nature of such communication? The assumption may not be unreasonable that other ways of communicating are equally good. One petal of a flower communicating to a bee, literally. Some of the messages we don't begin to perceive. And so, as I say, primitive man, moving through these fields, still able to communicate with these oaks, would have intimations beneath the level of language. At a certain point he knew in the way a plant knows or a tree knows that a storm was coming, or disaster was on the way, or the sun would be beneficent on the morrow.

YOUNG: Yes. And we've lost that. Almost completely.

MAILER: Well, let me say, we may have lost it at the moment language began. Here is the point: Once there is verbal language, then man has feedback. He no longer communicates to other men the way he once had a dialogue with the tree and the field. So long as he was communicating beneath the level of formal language, he had only to come back from the field and other men would see something in his presence which communicated his message. We just assume that primitives grunted at one another. We don't know. Primitive man may have had to do no more than move into the clearing or into the caves where others lived, and others knew his message. Since he was transmitting mood, others could decide whether he was true or false. But language, while it will often create mood, must as its first function interrupt mood, interpose itself against mood. Mood may be able to survive this insertion, but it is a different mood. The moment primitive man began to speak words to other primitive men — in other words, the moment the articulate was commenced — so the nature of man's reception of an experience larger than himself began to be altered profoundly. And something was lost. For in the grunt had been sounds from every corner of existence, while now, in the words, were oncoming abstractions of existence.

YOUNG: Which brings me, if I may interject, to the idea of art being inarticulately certain. I think what you've just said . . .

MAILER: . . . is an expansion of that remark. Yes. Art bears a relation to those intimations of the primitive. I know it's similar to the experience of every artist if I say that when I get an idea for a piece of work, I get it. There's an illumination in my head at that moment with which I don't have to argue. Trouble starts because you can't keep that incandescence, that illumination. And in fact, the reason it usually requires twenty or thirty years to make a good artist who's dependable as well as good is that it takes all those years to learn how to lose the moment and recover it, lose it and recover it, and learn how finally to be able to get it back each day in some tremendously diluted and warped and tortured form, but nonetheless, get it back. Enough so you can continue with your work. If you will, it's a function of the artist's relation to magic. It's his ceremony. For instance, you said a while ago that the artist now tries to return to magic. But I think the horror of it is that there's no one alive who can return us to anything. Our senses are so destroyed that we may be a light-year away from that primitive man. There may be no road back to him. None ever. We may not be able to begin to do — to comprehend where we lost the way, or where or how we can restore it. The artist may finally be merely some sort of extraordinary recorder of the failure.

YOUNG: I think the big problem for art today is to try to get back to the sense of creating a spell.

MAILER: Maybe you have brought us to the real separation between the artist and the physicist. Because the artist always seeks to create a spell. Today, of course, the artist is no primitive man, he's all but completely insulated from the senses primitive man had; and he usually acts as a mediator between magic and technology, between the world as instinct and scientific fact. But no matter how technologized the artist is in society, his central impulse is to create a spell equivalent to the spell the primitive felt when he passed the great oak and knew a message deeper than his comprehension of things was reaching him. It's possible the primitive felt something analogous to what we feel when we encounter a great work of art which tunes us in to some comprehension of something we can't even quite call any longer our knowledge. It's larger and less definable; to employ the word again, it's more resonant. It's as if art seeks to restore men and women by reproducing in them that sense of a lost spell, as if the artist is some sort of magician or midwife between the lost life of the primitive and the modern world of technology. And, if you will, the ultimate intent of the technologist, or any physicist who is drowned in technology one way and another, is to try to find ways of coping with existence which are independent of the spell. For the spell cannot be measured.

YOUNG: Do you think that art has much chance to flourish in this regard?

MAILER: Well, I think we've begun to come around some extraordinary corner. There is a recognition among technicians themselves that something desperately bad is happening in the very foundations of technology. That the whole machine of technology may finally have been bolted to a base which will not remain permanent, which is in fact rotting beneath. Sometimes, it's only when man enters a series of failures which destroy belief in a huge endeavor that a huge endeavor in an opposite direction can begin. The failure of the Crusades opened the Renaissance. I think this is happening now. I think one note of hope we can feel in these times is that faith in technology is beginning to waver, and in fact, it's possible technology is going to go through a period as destructive to its ambitions as was technology to theology. We could advance the argument that theology was a species of spiritual technology designed to insulate man from existential existence, from the lost senses of the primitive. Failing to work, theology was replaced by technology, but technology, in turn, if it fails to work — well, at that point, it seems to me there is nothing left but a return — if there's *anything* left — to the old notions of magic which orbit around the fundamental notion that we are capable of extraordinary psychic communication, not only with each other, but with elements of the universe we haven't begun to conceive. That may be the great turn of the wheel of history — that is, if we can clear the ecological system of the world. We may not be able to. We may be in the position of an invalid who's going to linger, even for centuries, in some sort of half existence. That could also happen. There's no reason to assume man was not capable of permanently injuring the world he inhabited. We may live on as some sort of crippled social existence.

YOUNG: Waiting for the freeze bags.

MAILER: I wouldn't doubt it. It's the apathetic people, I'd guess, who generate huge passions on the idea of a freeze bag. Technology sells people the notion they're going to give them something for nothing. Which is the essence of the message of the Devil. The reason the Devil is associated with magic in people's minds is that magic implies it will give something for nothing. But the word *magic* rather might suggest that there are subterranean relations between things which are deeper than we recognize. But never will you get something for nothing. Precisely, it's technology which promises that something for nothing by sidestepping all the disciplines of magic.

YOUNG: Perhaps it's this awareness of subterranean relations between things that does constitute a good part of what an artist is today.

MAILER: Well, I expect an artist secretly assumes he has some fine and subtle and possibly quite private relation to magic. In some

way, some little part of magic is his. He often pays for it by finding himself ineffectual and even tortured by the world. So it isn't
as if he's getting something for nothing with his magic. But it's as
if, if you will, that people who opt for magic are deciding that
they want a life which will have huge advantages and tremendous
disadvantages. They're stepping out of the sort of ordinary expectations other people have. Stepping into more and into less.

YOUNG: Choosing perhaps to be more alive.

MAILER: More alive and more bugged. More reduced. I mean, think
of people you've known who lived in depression for ten years at a
time — you think quickly of artists . . . Because of their sensitivity, their paranoia, because of their relation to magic . . . their
exquisite sensitivity to the possibilities of magic, to that communication between subterranean events which everything paranoid in one (for paranoia has to be a disturbed function of the
magical sense) would believe is having a powerful effect upon superficial everyday events. So when things are not breaking well,
such an artist will never get free of anxiety. His sense of magic
will keep producing more exotic conclusions. I mean, there's a
reason why man deserted magic and went into technology. Men
led lives of exacerbated uneasiness when they lived in the time of
primitive man and his magic. They sought, after all, to escape
primitive existence and existential life, in order to gain technological life. For precisely the reason that they thought it would be
easier. Now we've found that it isn't easier. It may even be
deadly. So now we've got to go back.

YOUNG: Would you see any relation to such going back in the way
hippies will wear their grandmother's clothes out of the attic or
just any kind of thing they feel like putting on? Is that sort of
stepping outside of fashion and in a sense stepping outside of
time?

MAILER: Oh, I think that's no mean nor small phenomenon. Maybe
it isn't so much stepping outside of time, as some profound desire
to reverse time. You see, hippies taking all those exceptional LSD
trips saw futures in man's continuation that were so terrifying
that they recoiled. That recoil has projected them back to the
nineteenth century. It's interesting that most of them do go for
nineteenth-century styles. You could say it's for practical reasons.
Nineteenth-century styles are easier to find, to copy, imitate and
wear, than eighteenth-century styles — But it's possible if this
continues that we will see all the centuries repeated, possible that

people in one era will yet be wearing all the clothes ever worn on earth. Yes, suppose we have got to go back to that universal dread we tried to escape five, ten, fifteen, twenty-five thousand years ago. Suppose it's now become the underlying trip of the world.

1970

In Search
of the Devil

An Interview with Richard Stratton

RICHARD STRATTON: Let's talk about psychopathy and murder. To what degree do you think Charles Manson might be an embodiment of some of the ideas you brought up originally in "The White Negro"? For some time I've been living with the unpopular thought that Manson was probably a very brave man in certain ways.

NORMAN MAILER: I think there's no question he was brave. One of the more depressing manifestations of public morality is that whenever someone commits a horror or monstrosity, they have to call the criminal a coward. It's automatic. Hitler's a coward. We used to call Tito a coward. Now they call Manson a coward. Part of the pain of maturity is that you come to recognize bravery is not enough. First you break out of the barbed-wire cocoon of a middle-class life with the idea that bravery is crucial to your existence. Maybe it's because the need for bravery is the one thing the middle class has refused to teach. So there's a period in one's life where you believe that anyone who does something brave is good.

Hemingway never got over that discovery. He had a cushioned life until he broke out of it, and like all of us he never broke out of it altogether. Then, years later, you come face to face with the

"In Search of the Devil" excerpted from "The Rolling Stone Interview with Norman Mailer" by Richard Stratton from *Rolling Stone* No. 177, January 2, 1975 and No. 178, January 16, 1975. By Straight Arrow Publishers, Inc. © 1975. All rights reserved. Reprinted by permission.

second recognition that people can be brave and still be no fucking good. That some brave people can be worse than cowards, and you can rue the day they discovered the grace of their own bravery, because finally they destroy even more than cowards do. Then you're face to face with the complexity of things and the difficulty of finding your way to any coherent ethics.

Manson is one of the most perfect examples of this. Because whatever else he is, you can't take away from him the fact that he's a brave man. Now, he wasn't altogether a brave man. And he wasn't a warrior. I mean, finally he was a general who sent his troops out to wreak the carnage, and he stayed behind.

STRATTON: But there were apparently certain aspects of his own personality which were very brave.

MAILER: Well, as an intellectual he was brave.

STRATTON: Yes. Then there was his method of dealing with men who tried to give him trouble. He was known to offer the weapon to the person he was fighting with and say, "Go ahead and kill me." And if that person didn't have the nerve to kill him, which ... they didn't ...

MAILER: Who ever has the nerve then? It's very hard to kill someone who stands before you, looks into your eyes and says, kill me.

STRATTON: That's bravery, and an instinctual sense of your opponent's strength, because no one ever took him up on the challenge.

MAILER: Well, that's not bravery, I'd say. That's a knowledge of the con, which is something else. Manson did grow up in prisons. He certainly understood that when you get into trouble you can't handle, then you still have the option to stand there and let the other person get their executioner's desire up to the point where they're going to kill you. It's not automatic.

It's reputed that Jimmy Hoffa once said: Flee a knife, and charge a gun. I have no idea if he ever said it, but I think, if he didn't, somebody who knew an awful lot about the subject had to be the author. Because there is something intimate about a knife, whereas there's something closer to moral decision about a gun. If you charge the gun, the man who holds it finally has to say to himself (since it's not a physical act, but a mental act), has to say to himself that he has the right to shoot you. At that point his moral sense of himself has to be invoked. He may not feel the sanction to shoot. Whereas if you charge a man who has a knife, his physical sense of himself is invoked, it's competitive. Am I going to hold this knife while he gets it away from me and humiliates me? But if you take your own knife and hand it over to the other man, that's different from charging a man with a knife.

We go back to the original advice: Flee a knife, charge a gun. If you hand it over and say, "Stab me," you make the knife a gun. And Manson may have had a particularly shrewd sense that the guy he was handing the knife to was a gun man. Weapons are metaphors which fit or do not fit our lifestyle. We do not mix metaphors when it comes to execution. So what we know about Manson is that he wasn't necessarily so brave about these matters as extraordinarily intelligent.

STRATTON: And he had an uncanny sense of where each personality he came in contact with was coming from.

MAILER: Oh, by every report he had an incredible sense of the people he was among. Obviously he had one of the more incandescent sensibilities of our time. The horror of it — not the horror so much as the pathetic aspect of it — is that once again we have a prisoner who's filled with talent, you know, the criminal who leads a prison life from beginning to end. Like Genet. Extraordinary talents. If Manson had become an intellectual, he would have been most interesting. He had bold ideas, and he carried them out — he worked for his ideas. The thing that characterizes Manson's life, whenever you look at it, is how hard that man worked for his ideas.

I like his sense of all these junior debutantes that would get into his gang. He'd have them out there, rolling in what? — not human shit, not cow shit — horse shit. Because if there's any single point of focus of social life in the upper middle class of America, it's that a young lady learns to ride a horse well and live comfortably with horse shit. Which of course is, you know, vastly more compatible than human shit or cow shit or dog shit or, perish the mark, wipe us out, cat shit. So, you know, there he has them rolling in horse shit. He knows how to get an orgy going.

STRATTON: Remember the day you and I went out to see the Spahn Ranch and found it had been bulldozed into nonexistence, which seems to me strikingly American. Like our attitude toward death, cover it up, make believe it doesn't really exist.

MAILER: Well, it's the American way. You know, we must destroy the past. When I was down in Dallas many years ago, a couple of years after Jack Kennedy was assassinated, naturally what's the first thing I do, I went over to see the plaza — the second thing: I went to see what happened to Jack Ruby's burlesque club. And you know, it had become a police gymnasium. They know how to do things in Dallas.

STRATTON: They know how to cut a connection or two.

MAILER: Right on.

STRATTON: To what degree do you think Manson was psycho-pathic? He had that other side to his personality, that hus-tler/pimp workingman's aspect. All the time he was doing his supposedly messianic trip with these young people, he was also hustling.

MAILER: Well, let's start playing with these words, set them up against each other. Not every psychopath is a hustler, not every hustler is a psychopath. Still, it's very hard to be a hustler with-out having some psychopath in you. It's hard to stay alive as a psychopath if you can't hustle a little. But we have to consider that at bottom the two are qualities opposed. Being a psychopath is existential. You don't know how a situation is going to turn out because you can't control it. Something inside you will not let you cut off the experience. You may be getting every warning that this experience is taking you into more and more bad places, and you can even get killed before the night's out.

STRATTON: Whereas the hustler tries to control the flow of the ex-perience.

MAILER: The hustler's dignity is that he controls the flow of the ex-perience. He considers it obscene if he doesn't.

Of course there's no such thing as a true or pure psychopath. Nor a total hustler. The hustler has elements in himself which are unmanageable, the psychopath has veins of shrewdness, calm judgment and a great ability to hustle. Part of the comedy in criminal affairs is to see how practical, sane, genteel, reasonable, clever and full of the final trick the hustler is. I mean, a good hus-tler always has a smooth hustle. Smooth's a word that fits with hustle. A player hates it if his cool is pricked. Manson is an in-tense mixture of the two. He's more psychopathic than just about any psychopath and more of a hustler than any average hustler that's come along. The vulgarity is to seize a personality as Dos-toyevskian as Manson's and assume immediately that he has to be uniquely a hustler and everything he did was as a hustler, so don't take him seriously. Or else see him as an example of pure evil, un-restrained psychopathy.

STRATTON: That's always seemed to me the problem with Truman Capote's work. I mean, even in *In Cold Blood*, where he looks for those easy, quick psychological containers he can pour his characters into. I don't think he got any real insight into those two characters, the murderers in *In Cold Blood*.

MAILER: Well, Truman's abilities, I think, lie in another direction. Truman's always had an exquisite sense of his readership. Which I must say has changed greatly during his career. He started with a special readership. And moved out to an enormously large one. But he's always had this exceptional sense of how much they can bear. And he has always had the accompanying sense of how to vibrate their prejudices without shaking them apart.

STRATTON: And he knows how to end a book just beautifully, the way he ended *In Cold Blood* with that young lady visiting the grave of her murdered friend.

MAILER: Truman's never without his tone. And it would be part of his virtuosity that the elegiac tone would belong naturally to him. Yes. It would be hard to think of Truman ending a book badly. The first time Truman does, I will have to sit down and read that book all over again because it's possible that Truman will have just written far and away his most adventurous book.

STRATTON: Because he's on to something?

MAILER: The only reason Truman couldn't end a book fantastically well is because he would be on to something large. So, I agree with you about *In Cold Blood* in the sense that I don't think he got near his characters. I think that what he did do, which makes it an important book to me, is end up telling us more about the prejudices and the limited ability of the middle-class reader to encounter criminality than any book I ever read. It tells you almost nothing about the criminals, but how much it does say about that sense of everything-in-its-place that *The New Yorker* has stood for for over forty embattled years.

STRATTON: Perhaps Manson and people who can live with these extremities in their personalities may in fact be the survivors. And all the highly civilized people may be ending up in the worst kind of deaths to themselves. And technological destruction. If it's only in extremes that the society will save itself, then the secret fear of most people is that they're dead ... moribund ... and these Manson people are more alive than they are.

MAILER: Yes, I think that's what they do fear. And I think the reason is we have all grown up in a society that's relatively new in its fundamental premise, a society that claims to believe in life. To coin a piece of jargon, of the worst sort, we could say that we exist in a keep-everybody-alive society. Ironically, most of the cultures to exhibit great energy in history, the societies which produced our society, were, on the contrary, built on killing.

The idea common to all animals, and prehistoric and primitive man, even among civilized societies like the Greeks, the Romans, during the Middle Ages, and the Renaissance, the idea was still that if you didn't have enough right to live — in other words, if you were a drag upon the mood and the energy and the sustenance of other people — you were better off — Christ to the contrary — dead. These societies were kill societies. They got their neatness, their elegance, they got their style — out of killing.

But we are a society which says in effect, "Be sure you live. Life is our only gift. We're not going to get anything after this." The kill societies, to the contrary, were religious. They believed in the immanence of God, or a devil, or in demons. Primitive man spent his time placating demons in every tree. If a wind blew a sudden leaf past his face, he began to propitiate some spirit. They believed nothing was accidental. They were, in fact, more scientific than we are, for they believed that anything you can't explain is tremendously disturbing, whereas we prefer to ignore whatever we cannot dominate with our minds. We wipe out the artifacts of the past as if they have no curse.

Well, this notion, this keep-everybody-alive society — is a vulgar notion. There's nothing more livid, more cancer-provoking, than the face of a distorted liberal who shrieks at you, "You're talking about a human being!" They always italicize — *hu-min*. You're talking about a *life* that can be *lost,* they say. They're the same people who will turn around and absolutely insist upon destroying life, the same people who will soon leap with glee to forbid people to procreate, that is, about the time we decide there are definitely too many people on earth and we have to cut down the population or we won't survive, they will end by insisting that people be electrocuted for daring to conceive without a license.

Of course, today, they're still on the side of keep-everybody-alive. So the thought that someone might be so profoundly repulsive that everybody in their immediate neighborhood wants to let them die, is something they cannot tolerate. Nor can we for that matter. We're not as tough as we sound. We too live in this enormous supermarket of suburban guilt. Because we know we are all destroying the landscape with our homes and our highways. There's such a gassy, dead dull air over everything. Which we create. When you traveled, it used to be the only bad air you ever

smelled was in a smoker on a train. Now that air is over everything.

Fresh air is the anomaly. We almost do not know what to do
with it. Given this guilt we live in, we opt for keeping everybody
alive because we know we're destroying everything. But that's
also why we're, on the other hand, nihilistic. That's why we
laugh every time a line or an idea or a disclosure cuts the feet off
somebody. We all sit in this guilt that we don't necessarily deserve to live, and that maybe we ought to get back to the old idea
of the kill society. So people like Manson just drive us up the tree.
This guy's going out and doing it.

STRATTON: Another aspect of Manson that upset everybody was
the sex orgies carried on by the "family." The real horror for the
American middle class was to know Manson and his family were
engaging in out-and-out sex orgies, exactly what so much of the
middle class were doing themselves.

MAILER: I don't think the horror was in the idea of orgy itself. After
all, one of the unspoken solutions to suburban life has been the
orgy. There have probably been more organized balls among respectable people in the seventh and eighth decades of American
life in this twentieth century than any other time, certainly in any
other mass democratic society. I don't think there's been anything
remotely approaching the incidence of systematized orgy we have
here. People putting aside Friday night or Saturday night for
their orgy, with their neighbors, their special neighbors.

But these orgies have always been, by every book report we
have of them, always highly civilized, indeed the most highly civilized expression of sexual endeavor you can find. I mean, nobody at an orgy ever throws a punch. Suddenly America learns
about this orgiastic life in Manson's gang that ends in mass murder. Anybody who's ever been in a civilized orgy knows that
what you're left with, besides a few interesting memories to feed
that part of your fantasy which still needs to be nourished, is a
kind of buried bleak sense not so far from murder. I mean, I don't
know that most people come out of an orgy full of love. No, a cold
icelike feeling is more usually awakened. Most people sense the
orgy has left them more murderous than when they started. Now,
suddenly, Manson comes along with *his* orgies, and Boom, the
murders do take place. Indeed, it's as if the murders were cooked
to the boiling point by those orgies. Measure the shock then in the
orgiastic suburbs.

STRATTON: Because Manson didn't come from their numbers. I

mean, he had been seventeen years out of thirty-five in prison. So he was a natural to take the orgy all the way to murder.

MAILER: Well, I don't think it was that automatic. He also had something inside him he couldn't control at all. His paranoid side, where he saw the blacks taking over the country. At a certain moment he was going to rise as some sort of gray eminence for the blacks and yet at the same time do his best to wipe them out. He had those huge plans to flee to the desert when the war was coming.

In the crudest psychoanalytical terms, his real connection was to his own timetable toward disaster. It was approaching very quickly. Because he was a man of Napoleonic ambition, he took this interior sense his body and his mind were providing him — the psyche secretly saying him, "Man, the climax is coming. You will not be able to keep your murderous impulses in hand more than another ten months, another ten days." That's why we shrink before any fanatic who comes up to us and says, "The end of the world is near."

STRATTON: Let's talk a bit more about the women's movement. I admit many of the women I find most exciting, most impressive, have tendencies toward women's liberation. But I don't think they understand what they call male chauvinism. I love women who have great character and spunk and are not content with being put in any simple category. But I fear the real thrust of this movement is to demean love and attraction between the sexes. A man who loves women is a pig. It's an antiromantic notion. It's sexual technology.

MAILER: Hey, Stratton, this isn't the way you were talking a year ago! I mean, the women are getting to you. They're getting to me and getting to you. Let's face it, they're winning their war.

STRATTON: You think so. They're winning their battle, perhaps. Meanwhile we're all losing our war. What women's liberation does is diminish sexuality.

MAILER: Well — I agree that the tendency is to diminish sexuality. I'm not pretending to know whether it's going to diminish sexuality for *all* time. But I think the immediate effect has been to take something out of it all. That's right in the need of the century. It's still a technological century and too much instinctive sex mucks up the machine.

There are two ways a technological society can weaken sex, through huge puritanism like the Russians, or you can do it through huge license — pornography, a sexual revolution, androgyny, gay lib, women's lib — huge license is even desirable to technology if it'll consume sexual energy and keep it at a low fucked-out level. I mean, what's the use of being able to make love to anyone, any man or any woman, if finally your incentive is taken away altogether? If the hunt is gone? The danger? The rebellion? The achievement? If you now ram it home to a woman and show her where she lives, what are you doing? Naught but revealing the secret boar in your asshole.

STRATTON: "My cunt is my chariot."

MAILER: Well, God bless them. You know, their cunt is their chariot. No one's ever going to be able to write about the way in which my generation grew up, you know, with this secret, profoundly sentimental adoration of the subtle superiority of women to ourselves. That marvelous sense of a woman's wit, that sly sense of the point which arrived so naturally into their thought. That sense of audience a woman provides. That notion we had of ourselves as audience to a woman. That tenderness. That respect for the immanence of a mystery so intimate, so nice, so near, so funny. We were so much stronger than women, and yet not at all. They were so much more powerful than we were, and yet never at all — never in any way. We lived as such romantic and sentimental equals.

Now we've come into another world where we recognize that they lied, they cheated, they worked overtime to give us this lovely sustaining notion, but all the while their egos were being rotted, their guts were filled with caustic, they were left with the dishes, they were left with the diapers. Left with the pale smell of water and grease and the slightly more unfortunate smell of formula milk and baby shit. And saw their careers going down into dull, somewhat incomprehensible dialogues with plumbers. While we came back and bayed at the moon, and said, you do not support me sufficiently, woman, to enable me to reach the moon. You know?

And then a couple of guys reach the moon, and some guys after them, and they all talk like women libertarians when they get there. In jargon. In a total, perfect, hermetic language. We'd looked upon these men in awe. These guys were cats, they were going out and doing things that really would stop up our stomach. And they had done it, they did it.

STRATTON: Yet they were sexless.

MAILER: They weren't sexless. They were women's libbies. What no one will ever understand is, the first guys to reach the moon — they were men, you know, in terms of bravery. More man than I for sure, maybe more than you, Stratton. They were men. But they had the minds of women's libbies. They were working for the team. They thought of only one thing, can't betray the team, cannot allow an alien idea to ever enter their eyeball, their nose, their mouth, their ear or their fingertips long enough to disrupt the ideological system.

STRATTON: A romantic idea is an alien idea to them.

MAILER: I don't mean a romantic idea. I mean any idea that's not in the system. You could have an antiromantic idea, they still wouldn't let it enter. They have nothing against romance.

STRATTON: Women's liberation is ultimately a team effort?

MAILER: Women's liberation is an astronaut system.

STRATTON: All right, let's talk about the music we just heard. Truman Capote was hired by *Rolling Stone* to cover the Rolling Stones concert when they were here the last time to tour the States. And he finally didn't do the article because he said the Stones had no mystery for him. But there's a lot of mystery in Jagger's personality and in the personality of the group as a whole.

MAILER: There's something unsatisfying about Jagger. We must have listened to two hours of music. Jagger's always promising so much more than he delivers. You know, finally he's in a sinister bag — he is certainly of all, if we take the three, four, five, six major rock groups in the last ten years, he has been the one who was the most sinister. Yet he's finally not terrifying. Maybe that's what Capote meant, I don't know.

STRATTON: Jagger himself, or his music?

MAILER: His music. I don't know anything about him. I think that the Beatles, you know, can hit eight bars in *Sgt. Pepper* that are more frightening, even though they're not sinister. The Beatles had more of a sense of powers they could summon by playing the wrong note at a given moment. It's as if they're more terrified by music than Jagger. Jagger's terribly spoiled. There's all that muttering in the background: "Oh, no God, you won't break this heart of stone."* What a threat. Beyond that constant dirge, beyond the throatiness which makes you think he's riding on the rims, through all that electric masturbation, you know, all that sound of distant musketry, every drumbeat, there's still a mountain of bullshit. It's not getting in and saying, I'm going to kill

---

* "Heart of Stone" by Mick Jagger and Keith Richard. © 1965, Abkco Music Co.

you, motherfucker. It's not saying, I'm here to call upon Satan. It pretends to. Some of his music I find, you know, marvelously promising. But it's irritating as hell to listen to for two hours because you keep waiting for the great payoff, and it never comes.

But again there's a kind of bullying that I've always distrusted in rock. Which is, it doesn't take big balls to have a big electric guitar and a huge amplifying system and fifty thousand American corporations that they're all sneering at, working overtime to amplify them. You know, it's a little bit like some politician that you despise saying, I represent the people. He only represents his power in his microphone and his media, his vested electronic office.

STRATTON: But let's look at the Stones in context. The Stones have stayed at the top, they're still the most interesting group playing together. They're all good musicians. Even the Beatles, as musicians, with the possible exception of George Harrison, weren't very exciting. Ringo Starr could never compare with Charlie Watts for drumming ability.

MAILER: Their drummer's incredibly good. In fact, I think their drummer's half of them. Because you've got all that caterwauling, you've got all those half-heard threats, that sense of sullen curses always riding in the background, you've got that sense of disarray, sense of mama with her nerves broken looking for her fix. You got all that. But what keeps it all together is you got this great big driving beat. That you can make anything you want. You can dream up a Third World coming through, Africa rising. There's a — the tension of the music is that one world's dissolving into a kind of marvelous — I mean, their comic gifts are superb. You really get this feeling of androgynous family, and androgynous family relations, like maybe it's never been done. All that's first-rate. I'm criticizing them at, you know, what I consider the highest level. But finally at the highest level, they are fucking disappointing. They depend on noise. You know, we listened to them not at top high. At middle high. And they don't make it.

STRATTON: Take a song like "Sympathy for the Devil." You have to go a long way — Bob Dylan's probably the only other one, plus some songs from the Beatles — you have to go a long way before you get lines as interesting in rock music as, "Just as every cop is a criminal and all the sinners saints."*

MAILER: What's splendid, what's new about that? Dostoyevsky used to go into an epileptic fit he grew so bored with that notion.

---

* © 1968 Abkco Music Inc.

STRATTON: Well, there's nothing new about it, but compared to most rock lyrics, the Stones have at least considered Dostoyevsky.

MAILER: I don't think these lyrics compare to Dylan's. I don't think they even try to — I think, in fact, I'd almost go the other way. I'd say that Jagger's lyric is interminably repetitive in order to allow for that captivating tension between the guttiness in his voice and the whine. To play that back and forth, you don't really want too good a lyric. Dylan's voice is thinner. At times I find it nasal to the point where I can do without it. There's something a little boring about a man who comes from a fine Jewish family in Minneapolis sounding like an Oklahoma Okie.

You know, Dylan is . . . not Johnny Cash. So I find that part of it a little boring. Dylan's voice is much less exciting to me than his lyrics, his lyrics are superb. Selden Rodman was the first to say this, but I think Dylan may prove to be our greatest lyric poet of this period. Like many another lyric poet, he can't necessarily read his own lyrics. With Dylan, what I think you feel is that it's the poetry that carries the song, not the singer.

With Jagger, it's the reverse. Jagger has got this marvelous sense of the day in which a family breaks up. The son throws acid in the mother's face, the mother stomps the son's nuts in, and then the fat cousin comes and says, What is everybody fighting for, let's have dinner. And they sit down, the son has no nuts left, the mother's face is scarred, but they go on and, you know, British family life continues. Jagger's got that like no one else's ever had it. If he'd been a writer he would have been one of the best. But that marvelous quality isn't caught in the lyrics so much as in the ensemble of everything, sound, instruments, everything.

STRATTON: And his voice.

MAILER: His voice first.

STRATTON: I don't know if you can find another rock group capable of coming up with a song like "Sympathy for the Devil."

MAILER: "Sympathy for the Devil," I felt, was arch, and much too self-conscious. I couldn't quite catch the words and that's one of the things about Jagger that's always suspect to me. When you play on the edge of the articulation of words it's because you're trying to do two things at once. I did hear him at one point wailing about the Russian Revolution — that the Devil was there at the planning of the Russian Revolution and, you know, that's news. No good Christian ever thought of that before. That, I thought, was finally on the edge of the revolting. You don't, you know, you don't infuse a bunch of dumb, spaced-out, highly sexed working-class kids with a little historical culture while you're singing. Come on! I decided Jagger must have picked up a magazine article about the Russian Revolution the day before he wrote the words. But, you know, there's more profundity in "Eleanor Rigby" than there is in "Sympathy for the Devil."

I mean, there are a lot of vulgar plays in "Sympathy for the Devil," gay-aim for game. A lot of dull choices were made. I expected to be knocked down by "Sympathy for the Devil," and I wasn't. I think maybe it's historically significant. It may be the first song that invokes the Devil in I don't know when. You might have to go back to black masses in the Middle Ages to find a lyric that invokes the Devil. But that doesn't mean it's good any more than *The Exorcist* is. Which is to say, it's phenomenal as an index of the time. What impresses us is not how good the artist is, but that he's right at the place where people are going to react. So Jagger anticipated, just as Blatty did, that there's subterranean belief in the Devil about ready to emerge. Given any kind of encouragement, it comes charging through.

Which brings us to Satanism. The Satanism of shit at the highest level, the standard of Satan. It's his escutcheon. It's his flag. He says, You've been rejected, you've been wasted by the system, passed over, yet you are more redolent, more interesting, more sexy, more incredible, more funky, more filled with undeliverables that should have been delivered than anything they got going out there. And, for years, the Devil has fought a desperate uphill battle.

But by now, when we got those superhighways, with that gas, and the whole world's getting to look more and more like the Jersey flats, given modern life up front, the suburbs, the smell of the gas, smell of plastic in every home, carpets smell of the plastic and the kids grow up licking plastic, play with Play-Doh which has that smell between cheap perfume and deodorant; when you think of the prevalence not of death in every one of our phenomena but of the void — of the presence of void — in every aspect of successful life today, you travel first class on a plane which is an envelope presenting its concept of the void, get off that airplane into an airport which in turn presents its concept of the void or you go through a smog-filled superhighway to that city which looks like every other city — Moscow, I hear, looks like Washington entering its terminal cancer . . . you then go out for your pleasures which are not as brilliant as they were in the depths of the boredom of the Victorian period; there's no such thing as a thrill for anyone alive any longer. You take all this, all this degradation of the void; because we all move around with a profound sense of degradation these days and under it there's the Devil calling, saying I'm shit, I'm everything that you've wasted, I'm all that rich, crazy passionate fuck guck funky possibility, I'm that other culture. And of course there's a profound desire to move over to that.

Now, in this twentieth century where our senses, our souls, are being leached out, where we're all entering a void, the horror of modern life is that there is no horror. So we begin to wonder whether selling the soul to the Devil may not be a life-giving transaction. That's the underlying terror of modern life.

STRATTON: The Devil has always been associated with materialism. There was always, you know, the idea of the temptation of Christ with riches and the wealth of the world.

MAILER: That doesn't deny what I was saying.

STRATTON: So isn't it conceivable that what we might have done is, collectively, sold our souls to the Devil a long time ago; say in the beginning of the nineteenth century, before the Industrial Revolution?

MAILER: If we sold our soul to the Devil centuries ago in order to prosper materially, in this twentieth century we're not happy materially. We're not gorging like Romans. We are prospering electronically. And suffering materially in all the voids and stinks of plastic and pollution.

STRATTON: And lost our karma too, sold our karma along with our soul. We've sold our opportunity for transcendence. That's why we're terminal. You see what I mean? I think that if anything the Devil is winning. I think he's winning and I think he's gloating because he has more control at this point. I think he is the prince of this world.

MAILER: That's one idea I hold. What I pose against it immediately is that the Devil is also miserable, because finally the air conditioner is not the Devil's paradise.

STRATTON: True. But there are those other alternatives we may get into in the next twenty, thirty years, you know. That when people get sick of technology and air conditioners and all the sterile dead aspects of plastic, they're going to revert more and more to Satanism and to orgies, to bloodletting and to shit, all those things —

MAILER: All right. But ask yourself: All those things you're talking about, that you just named, are they equal to technology?

STRATTON: Are they equal to technology?

MAILER: Or are they the opposite?

STRATTON: The opposite.

MAILER: It seems to me you ought to have your Devil, just for the sake of this little matter, one place or the other.

STRATTON: Yes, I said that I think technology may be a tool of the Devil, a means to an end, the end being the complete leaching out of our souls.

MAILER: To drive people toward shit and blood.

STRATTON: Right. Right. This is Satan's cunning. In a technological and spiritually starved society, he may gain complete control.

MAILER: Well, let me think about that. And have a drink.

STRATTON: Okay. Just to continue with this idea, it may be that technology is a transitional stage as far as the Devil is concerned. I've got to believe God is more opposed to the dead spirit of technology than the Devil would be. I think that the Devil may have said to himself, Well, it looks to me like the only way I'm ever going to win final control over mankind is to offer them all those things they seem to want most, material comforts, wealth, prosperity and lack of suffering, to eliminate suffering from the world. People don't want to suffer, they immediately reach for a pill, mother's little helper.

So, my notion, anyway, is that technology, science, pollution, whatever, is finally probably a tool of the Devil that is going to starve and deaden the soul to such a degree that man will reach out for the funkiness, then for horror — back to Charlie Manson.

MAILER: I think you're passing over too much. To begin with, there's no reason to equate science and technology any more than we put art and bestsellerdom together. After all, there's no reason to assume a bestseller is a work of art at a lower level. That may be a legitimate way to characterize a bestseller, or the opposite may be true, that a bestseller is the precise opposite of art, and to the degree the work is a bestseller, it is meretricious.

STRATTON: Technology may be the opposite of science, then?

MAILER: Well, I think there's much reason to believe that it is. Science, for most of its history, was essentially a poetic endeavor. Every metaphor, if you stop to think about it, is an equation. If you say, "The sparrow is on the wing," that's a scientific remark, it's a way of saying that the center of essence in the sparrow is within the wing, the sparrow is *on* the wing. It's a way of saying that the sparrow exists in two manifestations at once, body and flight, just as light consists of waves and particles. The sparrow is on the wing. As you start to bear down on the language, you begin to feel the very vibrancy of the wing. The condition of being in two states at once. The sparrow is *on* the wing. You can fix on that point endlessly because it's a metaphor, an equation, a moment of balance. Originally, science had that quality, that its fundamental recognitions were, dare I say it? — poetic.

STRATTON: It was an art at that point?

MAILER: Absolutely an art. Technology is finally, I would suggest, a tradition, and a dull one. A statistical tradition. Technology derives from General Ulysses S. Grant, who said that if I bring enough men and enough ammunition to bear at one point on this line, and if I don't care how many troops of mine get killed, and I just keep pursuing this, if my ego is finally larger than any question that's presented to me, then I am obliged to triumph because I do not care. And he won.

Grant changed the nature of war. Before that, war always consisted of the obligation to win with a certain minimum of skill and grace. There was a code of war. Robert E. Lee subscribed to that code, he believed that you did not win battles at any price, that you didn't lose half your army to win a battle. Because at that point something dreadful would happen. Grant, having to contend with a miserable drafted army, people who did not want to fight the war — the Civil War as far as the North was concerned was not too unlike the war in Vietnam, in the sense that the troops had absolutely no desire to fight — Grant just kept putting in more and more bodies to blast their way through the noise.

Now that's technology. Technology does not really care what happens in the aftermath, it wishes to succeed on this point. It does not even need to have theory in order to proceed, let alone art. It will push its way through. It is an ego manifestation, and — all right. There's nothing in this that says it's therefore opposed to the notion of the Devil. The Devil may indeed be ego. But we have to draw back just enough to ask ourselves one further question, and it comes up to me as follows. Where is God in all this?

STRATTON: Well, God may be the loss of ego.

MAILER: No, no, no. Face into technology. What's God's relation to technology? Do you believe in God?

STRATTON: Yes.

MAILER: Do you believe God is not dead at all? Is very much alive?

STRATTON: Yes.

MAILER: God, I would take it, knowing you fairly well, is a principle of some judicious mixture of courage and love?

STRATTON: Right. Absolutely. And harmony, a certain kind of
harmony, a physical harmony with life and one's place in life and
in the cosmos that is opposed to technology.

God, as far as I'm concerned, is mystery, and anything opposed
to mystery, that tries to answer out all the mystery of life, is anti-
God. Technology wants to eradicate mystery. I think at this point
if God exists, He exists as a revolutionary, He's got to be a violent
and passionate spiritual revolutionary, because He's out of grace
at this stage, very much out of grace.

MAILER: Not out of grace. Out of favor.

STRATTON: Out of favor.

MAILER: Out of favor of what? The universe . . .

STRATTON: No, with mankind, with technological man.

MAILER: We still separate here. Because I think we have to face the
possibility that technology is a third force, come to us from
the cosmos. That it may have very little to do with God
and the Devil.

STRATTON: May be separate altogether?

MAILER: Virtually separate. To go back to one of my oldest and
firmest ideas, what if the universe is finally a series of conceptions
which are at war with one another? And what we think of as God
is only one conception of this universe, out there, at war with
other conceptions? What if technology is an invasion of this earth
from without? Because technology gives us no evidence whatsoever of having any sympathy for the nature of our world, nothing
to do with our desires for an earth on which we can dwell.

STRATTON: No, certainly not. Its aim would seem to be to make
the planet uninhabitable in the name of making us all more comfortable. What is a higher standard of living if we are all dying?

MAILER: Well, if at that point — you see — at this point we're reduced to speculation. Either the Devil invited technology here or,
what I find more interesting, God entered into a dread compact.
At a certain point he decided that Satan had so invaded affairs on
earth that God could never begin to lead man up and outward to
the stars. So some compact had to be made with technology.
Technology, that spirit come to visit us from afar. If we dare to
personify our divinities, there's nothing extraordinary about such
speculation. Evil often triumphs, because good makes a mediocre

compact out of some dire necessity. Where we're far apart is, I don't believe in an omnipotent God. I believe in a God who's like us only more so. Who has a vision of existence of which we are very much a part. Because we will either fulfill that vision of existence, or we will fail God.

STRATTON: No, I can't agree. God is perfection. I don't actually believe in an omnipotent god as much as in a god whose nature is finally unknowable, as is perfection.

MAILER: The idea that the nature of God is unknowable, at this point, when the world's dying in the exudate of all its diseases, is a cop-out.

STRATTON: Not if you think of God in terms of a quality, a state of being toward which you're constantly trying to become closer, to get more in harmony with, as an ongoing struggle.

MAILER: You've been saying that you want to talk about drugs a little, and I think they're related to this question in a fashion. I think drugs bear the same relation to mysticism as technology to science.

We're coming to learn that most of the world's mystics, in one way or another, have or had their drug. The mystical societies most mystics have been revering for centuries did have, in one fashion or another, their drug ritual. So, it isn't so simple a matter as saying that if you take a drug then you're a technologist and not a scientist. It does mean that there is a use of drugs among mystics and mystical societies which was reverential, ceremonial, sacramental.

The use of drugs today, if we're going to employ an analogy, is again comparable to the war in Vietnam: If you have a great deal of money to spend and very few results to show, and if you can't find the enemy, well then, goddamnit, says Barry Goldwater, burn down the fucking foliage. Scorch those gooks, get them out of there. Denude the land and you will find what is there. That is what the allegedly best generation of our young are doing to their minds. They're saying, If I can't find the idea I was looking for yesterday, I am going to take twice as much tonight.

STRATTON: I'll take a thousand more mics of LSD and burn down the foliage of my mind.

MAILER: Burn down the foliage of my mind to find some of those ideas I can feel running around in there. It's a military operation, it's technological.

I don't think drugs are going to find God or the Devil. I think what they're going to create is the scorched earth of consumed karma. I believe, you know, that one has to be as reverential about drugs as about sex. The mark of an utter idiot, in my mind, is to find, let's say he's a man who falls passionately in love with a woman. He finds this divine cunt and he not only fucks the hell out of her but fucks the hell out of himself until his balls are as wet as gravel. You know, he is grinding his ass up over the stones to get in one more fuck for the ego. He's gone over. He is a gassed-out, farted-out goose. That is our drug addict. That's what the drug addict is doing to mysticism. If God is a rabbit, the drug addict is trying to kill that rabbit with a thousand flails.

In religious discussion, when we start to talk about this tripartite nature of the confusion, God, Devil and technology, and what is with whom, it may serve us to take one little look at cosmology today. One notion that the physicists presented to us about fifty years ago was the idea of the expanding universe. The galaxies were traveling outward. There's reason to decide that we live in a universe which expands and contracts. Curious, isn't it?

More than that, a universe in which stars expand and contract. Stars exhibit red light in their spectrum and blue — red lights as they expand, no surprise to any of us humans, and blue as they turn cold. As they contract more and more, they turn black. They become the essence of matter, become so compressed, so black, that a star which was once a million miles in diameter is now two miles in diameter, a mile in diameter. It becomes so compressed that finally it is the size of your thumbnail and weighs more than the sun. At least, that is what cosmological evidence and theory has brought certain physicists to thinking.

At that point, there's a gravitational mass so intense that it pulls in everything to it. It pulls in light. Einstein delivered the general theory of relativity, which was that light would be bent by gravity. Indeed it was, as the famous experiment in 1921 or 1922, was it 1919? showed — that light from Mercury in an eclipse was bent by the sun. Now, when we begin to consider these wholly concentrated implosions of matter which have more mass than the sun, they must pull everything into them. Everything disappears. You cannot ever see these particular stars, which are called black holes in space, because everything goes into it, and comes out where, somewhere else. Hm?

That is a more curious model of the universe than we're used to considering. Now physics deals with notions of matter and anti-matter. Is it so outrageous then to speak of death as having a life which has as many laws as life?

STRATTON: Existential states of death.

MAILER: Existential states of death. Exactly. We speak of the speed of light as being 186,000 miles a second and nothing can go faster than that. Except yesterday we were talking about, what if God is there to give a grace so speed can go faster? What if anti-matter lives on the other side of the speed of light? We live in a universe of such peculiar immensity and intimacy.

As we see more and more into these notions, the differences between the mightiest phenomena and the tiniest seem to have almost nothing to do with space. It's as if finally space becomes no more than our metaphorical incapacity to comprehend. Throw that out. It's rather as if space becomes no more than the measure of our inability to comprehend that every process, large and small, is without meaning as a process which is large or small in itself, because everything exists in its reverberation upon everything else. One atom, one most special atom, may have more significance than a star. So we inhabit a universe which is fell with purpose. And therefore must try to create, or at least try to exercise, our profoundest notion of champions and villains, of enemies and new gods within it. Theology will yet prove more amazing than science.

That's where I would like to let this rest. That any view we take of technology has to deal with the principle, that it is either a manifest of God or the Devil or else is some dissertation of purpose or malignity from that universe outside them which gives every suggestion of being a juggler's paradise. Because it can turn its pockets inside out.

1974

Existential Aesthetics

An Interview with Laura Adams

᠕

LAURA ADAMS: Since the late 1950s you've had a vision of God and the Devil at war for possession of the universe, a vision that has been the metaphysical and moral center of your work. Has that vision changed appreciably over the years?

NORMAN MAILER: I don't know the answer. When you deal with cosmology, the question becomes on the one hand enormous — do God and the Devil war in the galaxies? — yet is intimate on the other. Since we all have our own idea of God and the Devil, it's hard for the idea not to change, even fluctuate. I'd say that over the last ten or fifteen years I've kept going back and forth in my mind over a notion that's hard to formulate, and I don't know that I should try — it's the sort of thing that sounds silly unless you can write a book about it — but for the purpose of this answer, just let me say that if there is a war continuing between God and the Devil for humankind, for the *future* of humankind, then this war is much more complex than a simple confrontation. We have to ask ourselves what the role of technology is in all this, and I've had years when I've believed technology is an instrument of the Devil, other years in which I've seen God in a Faustian contract with technology. Technology is perhaps some third force, some element that's come into our universe from other universes. Now all this is too endlessly and chronically paranoid to try to get into it in the form of an interview. I think you can dramatize these notions in a major novel, but only a major novel. You would wreck a minor novel by introducing such ideas. Therefore to talk about it in an interview is hopeless. It leads to people saying you have a windmill for a brain. Still I can see by the look in your eye that you're hardly ready to give up.

ADAMS: Isn't it an obsession, a form of paranoia, or even atavistic to think that there are cosmic forces manipulating us for their own ends?

MAILER: Well, I've never felt we are the simple creatures of these forces. On the contrary, I think they are fighting for our allegiance or even our unwitting cooperation. It isn't only that man needs God, but recall us to the title of that old French movie, *God Needs Men*. (Of course you couldn't use such a title today. You'd have to say "God Needs *Persons*.") Here's what I'm trying to say: To the degree I have any intense religious notion it's that when we fail God we are not merely disappointing some mightily benign paterfamilias who'd hoped we might turn out well and didn't. We are literally bleeding God, we're leeching Him, depriving Him of *His* vision. You see, I start with the idea that the explanation for our situation on earth may be that we are part of a divine vision which is not, necessarily, all loving, but on the contrary is a vision which wishes to take us out across the stars — a vision of existence at war with other varieties of existence in the cosmos. By this light, flying saucers may be, or may represent, a certain unconscious human awareness that there is this possibility in the universe, that there are other forms of intelligence which have nothing to do with us. Nothing even to do with our divinities.

ADAMS: Do you know the Arthur C. Clarke novel, *Childhood's End*?

MAILER: No.

ADAMS: In it the human race mutates into an essence, a form of energy, that unites with a kind of benevolent Oversoul which, interestingly, has used another race of benevolent beings in the form of devils to prepare the way for the human mutants. It appears that our fear of devils was based on a premonition that they would have something to do with the dissolution of our race. The unconscious awareness you spoke of reminded me of this. But isn't this notion that, as D.J. expressed it in *Why Are We in Vietnam?*, "You never know what vision has been humping you through the night," contradictory to the perception of good and evil in *An American Dream*? There it seemed that good and evil were for the most part clearly demarcated, known to Rojack. Deborah and Barney Kelly were evil; Cherry was good.

MAILER: That was his view of it.

ADAMS: His view of it?

MAILER: That was all it was — Rojack's view of it. To the degree a reader sympathizes with Rojack, that would be the reader's view of it. To the degree a reader decides that Rojack is an absurd hero, he won't go along with that view. But even assuming that Rojack's view had something to do with *my* view of the characters, I was certainly attempting to make Deborah more complex on any spectrum of good and evil than Barney Kelly. Barney Kelly was supposed to be the focus of evil in the book.

ADAMS: The Devil personified.

MAILER: Well, the Devil approached, anyway. Whereas Deborah was someone who was, in quotes, "in thrall" to the Devil. But a woman of complexity, not altogether unacquainted with goodness.

ADAMS: And Cherry?

MAILER: I didn't mean Cherry to be all good by any means. To the degree that she's better than she ought to be, she's too sentimental a character. A gangster's moll is not the simplest kind of goodness we arrive at. But I wanted to indicate some characters had more purchase on good than others.

ADAMS: Cherry seemed to have a hard kernel of goodness even though she was surrounded by corruption.

MAILER: I think she's finally an enigmatic character. In my opinion, she's the weakest character in *An American Dream*. I think people who don't like the book have their strongest argument starting with Cherry. To a great degree, I'm afraid she's a sentimental conception. We don't really know much about her. We're asked to believe that this goodness exists in her but we don't have any idea of the real play of good and evil in her. She's a shadowy figure. Of course, my cop-out is that she's seen through Rojack's eyes. He's in an incandescent state of huge paranoia and enormous awareness. He's more heroic and more filled with dread than at any point in his life. So she seems like a lighthouse in the fog. What else does one do in such a state but fall madly in love for twenty-four hours and lose the love? It would have taken more wit than I possessed to have made her a character of dimension under these circumstances. Perhaps she did have to appear as a sentimental figure. Still I think there's no getting around it, she's the first weakness of the book.

ADAMS: But it's a highly metaphorical novel. One of the mistakes many critics made in first reviewing it was to take it too literally. Isn't Cherry seen metaphorically as love, the reward of courage?

MAILER: Well, no. I don't believe a metaphorical novel has any right to exist until it exists on its ground floor. You know I never start with my characters as symbols. I'm unhappy if I can't see my characters. I mean, I not only have to know what they look like, and how tall they are, whether they're good looking or plain, but I also like to have some idea of what they smell like. So I had a pretty good idea of Cherry *physically*, a very clear idea in fact, but I would have been happier if her character had emerged somewhat more. I think Deborah, for instance, is vastly more successful. Deborah is worthy of a book in herself. In fact, at one time I thought idly of doing a book on Deborah, and then chose not to. But how she drew coincidences to herself. One of the things about *An American Dream* that's not often realized is my little theory, if you will, that as events become more dramatic so does the play of coincidence become more intense. You can reverse it. You can say that coincidence may fail to occur unless events are dramatic. I think there's a reason for that. If you believe in Gods and Devils, and I choose the plural because not only is God on one side, Devil on the other but they certainly have armies, adjutants, aides, little demons, angels, well, when important events occur why wouldn't they be concerned? Why wouldn't they be present? Why not try to tip the scales? Why wouldn't God and the Devil have their department of dirty tricks? You know, see them as some sort of sublime extension of the CIA.

ADAMS: That is why I see the novel as so highly metaphorical. The kinds of experiences Rojack has, the vision of shooting arrows into Cherry's womb while she's singing in the night club, for example, seem to me to exist in a dream allegory but not at the literal level.

MAILER: I would disagree. I'd had the experience of being in night clubs and thinking evil thoughts and really barbing them like darts and sending them to people and seeing them react. At the time I didn't know whether I was profoundly drunk or, you know, was I all alone in the world? But I had to recognize that there was a psychic reality to it. It wasn't just a fantasy. Since then, there's been any amount, my god, there's so much material now to indicate that this is not at all unreasonable. For one thing, we do have telepathic powers, we talk about the human aura, about the ability to send hostile vibrations, everybody uses that phrase, but, you know, if you can send a hostile vibration, which is to say, a hostile wave, why not employ modern theories of light and say hate appears not only in the form of a wave but also as a particle? If you can do it with light, you can do it with hate. In other words, send a damn particle into someone. Why not assume you can sting someone with a thought so concentrated that they'll turn around and rub the back of their neck? I invite people who are reading this interview to try it from time to time. It helps if you're drunk, of course.

ADAMS: Is that what you've been doing to tape recorders all these years?

MAILER: Oh, I think there's a good reason why tape recorders bomb out on me. Why not assume we have electrical powers — we know there are pictures taken of the human aura in Russia. What is it called, the Kirlian process? Did you ever notice when you're in a real hurry to make a phone call, and you've got one of those button phones where you can dial quickly, that if you dial too quickly with too much desire, you never get your number?

ADAMS: Yes.

MAILER: Then you have to stop and say, "Okay, I don't really care if I get the number or not," and dial more slowly. Then the phone becomes your servant again. It's as if there's an electrical resistance to your electrical intensity.

ADAMS: I simply assumed the computer couldn't handle the digits as fast as I could push them.

MAILER: Well, I notice it with a dial phone, too. The phenomenon is not only in the speed with which you dial, but the intensity with which you want to get that call through. It's almost as if there is something in the center of electricity that mocks us. I've felt this with all sorts of electrical phenomena. It's possible I'm more charged, have more electricity about me. I don't mean that as any agreeable or attractive condition, it's bound to be disagreeable, but possibly I could have more effect upon electrical instruments than other people, a little more effect, ten percent more, whatever. At any rate, to go back to *An American Dream*, my point is that there wasn't a single phenomenon in that book that I considered dreamlike or fanciful or fantastical. To me, it was a realistic book, but a realistic book at that place where extraordinary things are happening. I believe the experience of extraordinary people in extraordinary situations is not like our ordinary realistic experience at all. For example, one of the reasons I've never written about great prizefighters in a novel is that the experience they have in the ring is, I think, considerably different from what we believe it is. More intense, more mystical, more "spooky" if you will, than anything we see on the outside. Who wants to write about a fight the way sportswriters do, or even as fighters discuss it after the fight: "I was waiting to set him up with a good right. He dropped his guard and I popped him." That's the way they talk. Only, it isn't their experience.

ADAMS: I grant you that the characters in *An American Dream* perceive and experience reality altogether differently from us ordinary folks. Still, it seems to me that their literal reality has a metaphorical level as well, just as your literal realities nearly always turn into metaphorical ones linked to the central set of metaphors regarding the existence of God or the Devil. I've come to see them as metaphors for our moral directions, which in the absence of absolutes become existential, unknowable as good or evil.

MAILER: My metaphors explain more phenomena to me than any theology I can adopt. I was an atheist for years because I couldn't stomach the notion of the all-good, all-powerful God who calmly watched all sorts of suffering which by any extension of our human imagination could not be productive of anything, not even productive of future karma. In other words that whole waste of human possibilities of the most grinding, grim, dull sort. It seems to me that the only explanation is God is not all-powerful: He's merely doing the best He can.

ADAMS: But how literally does God exist?

MAILER: I believe He exists literally.

ADAMS: How?

MAILER: It's not for me to know how or where He exists. It's reasonable to assume He exists in a great many ways, in places we can comprehend and a great many where we cannot. All I'm saying is that He does not have to be all-powerful. What is there that makes Him all-powerful? He was powerful enough to have created our solar system, perhaps. And if you ask what are His limits, that might be my guess. But this is babbling. It isn't important where God's limits are. What's significant is the idea that God is not all-powerful, nor is the Devil. Rather it is that we exist as some mediating level between them. You see, this notion does restore a certain dignity to moral choice.

ADAMS: Of course, it does.

MAILER: It becomes important whether you're good or bad.

ADAMS: In trying to know what is good or evil aren't you in effect trying to take existentialism to its logical end, that is, to end existentialism?

MAILER: Not end it, seat it. Of all the philosophies, existentialism approaches experience with the greatest awe: it says we can't categorize experience before we've experienced it. The only way we're going to be able to discover what the truth about anything might be is to submit ourselves to the reality of the experience. At the same time, given its roots in atheistic philosophers like Sartre, existentialism has always tended toward the absurd. By way of Sartre, we are to act as if there were a purpose to things even though we know there is not. And that has become the general concept of existentialism in America. But it's not mine. I'm an existialist who believes there is a God and a Devil at war with one another. Like Sartre in his atheism, I offer a statement of absolute certainty equally founded on the inability to verify it. Atheism is as removed from logical positivism as theology. Still, I don't give a goddamn if I can verify this or not. There has to be something out there beyond logical positivism. I want my brain to live. I want to adventure out on a few thoughts. The fact that I can never demonstrate them is not nearly so important to me as the fact that I may come up with an hypothesis so simple, so central, that I may be able to apply it in thousands of situations. If it begins to give me some inner coherence, if I begin to think that I know more as a result of this philosophy, why not?

ADAMS: But isn't what you've identified as existentialism, extended to its logical end, seeking to know what is finally unknowable?

MAILER: That's not my definition of existentialism. I'd say we find ourselves in an existential situation whenever we are in a situation where we cannot foretell the end. Some of these situations are grave. If you get into a skid on an icy road, at a speed that's uncomfortably high, you don't know if you're going to be able to pull your car out of it without a smack-up. That's an existential situation. When people talk about it afterward they think of that quality of time when it is slowing up. The first time people connect with marijuana — not the first or the twentieth time they smoke it, but the first time they *connect* with it — they're in an existential situation. It's not the universe they have been sitting on all the time. It's slower, more sensuous, more meaningful, more natural, but filled with awe. The light tends to have a little of the hour of the wolf, a light close to a lavender or purple, that light you get on certain kinds of evenings, or very early on certain kinds of dawns full of foreboding. But it's — there are all kinds of situations. A woman losing her virginity is in an existential situation. Of course, part of the comedy of twentieth-century technology is that it's gotten to the point where a woman can lose her virginity without being in an existential situation for a moment. It's all exactly the way she thought it was going to be, she's been so well oriented.

ADAMS: I think that assumes that her partner is not also a virgin. . . . All right. Your basic existential situation is a situation anyone enters at any moment in time when the end result of his actions is unknown. But isn't to a larger extent your aim in all the work that you've been doing to uncover what is essentially good or evil in our natures and God's nature when that kind of thing is actually unknowable? What I was going to suggest earlier in talking about the demarcations of good and evil in *An American Dream* is that you seem to have become increasingly obsessed since that time with your inability to know what is good and what is evil.

MAILER: You say I'm obsessed, but where would be the literary proof of that? What books would show that?

ADAMS: Start with the case of Richard Nixon in *Miami and the Siege of Chicago* and *St. George and the Godfather*: your inability to know or to intuit whether Nixon is basically good or basically evil; to know, in *Of a Fire on the Moon*, whether our space program will carry God's vision to the stars or the Devil's; to know in *Why Are We in Vietnam?* whether America has made a Faustian compact with the Devil or whether God is using us for evil ends; whether or not our national leaders and events win or lose us ground in this divine battle. It seems to me that you lead us to this question, with increasing desire to know the answer, in every work.

MAILER: Well, it could be said that all I'm doing is leading people back to Kierkegaard. I'd remind you I've written this several times: Kierkegaard taught us, or tried to teach us, that at that moment we're feeling most saintly, we may in fact be evil. And that moment when we think we're most evil and finally corrupt, we may, in fact, in the eyes of God, be saintly at that moment. The first value of this notion is that it strips us of that fundamental arrogance of assuming that at any given moment any of us have enough centrality, have a *seat* from which we can expound our dogma, or measure our moral value. So we don't have the right to say Richard Nixon is: A. good; B. evil. I might have my opinion of Richard Nixon, but I don't have the right to say that man is evil, any more than I have a right to say he is good.

ADAMS: Do you have a clear notion of the good?

MAILER: No. But I have, if you will, I have and I submit to the force of this word, I have a fairly well-formed *cloud* of intuitions about the nature of the good, and, like a cloud, it has to a certain degree a structure, and yet the structure is capable of altering quickly, depending on the celestial winds blowing and the less celestial winds. A cloud changes shape quickly but it remains a cloud. It's not just simply an unformed chaos.

ADAMS: You've said that an evil person is someone who has a clear notion of the good and operates in opposition to it.

MAILER: Therefore by my own definition I'm definitely not evil.

ADAMS: All right, but are you wicked?

MAILER: Unquestionably wicked, yes.

ADAMS: By your own terms, which is not knowing what is good or evil in any situation, but upping the ante each time.

MAILER: Upping the ante, yes. I'd say I may be one of the most wicked spirits in American life today. Maybe. America may be changing faster than I am.

ADAMS: Is it fair to say that your existentialism is leading us to know the nature of good and evil?

ADAMS: It's leading us to — well, let me take a detour. People who submit to logical positivism, and go on from there into philosophies as difficult as Wittgenstein's, will answer if you ask, "Why go through these incredible disciplines in order to verify the fact that you're able to verify the wing span of a gnat but not of an archangel?" They will answer, "Well, it isn't what we are able to verify that is interesting, so much as that we go through a discipline which enables us to think cogently. We're less likely to go in for sloppy thinking thereafter." That's the value of it. I'd say by going in for my variety of associational, metaphorical thinking (which is, of course, the exact opposite) I may be able eventually to think speculatively without feeling philosophical vertigo. You see, it doesn't take any more illogic to posit that there's a god or devil than it takes to say there is none. The latter statement is absolutely as potent an act of faith. There's a marvelous line in *Jumpers*, the play by Tom Stoppard, to that effect. I paraphrase:

"Well, maybe atheism is that crutch people need to protect themselves against having to face the enormity of the existence of God." You know, once you contemplate the notion that there is God and this God may be embattled, the terror you feel is enormous.

ADAMS: It's a terror, but isn't it also paranoia?

MAILER: No. The terror is not that some force is working on you to ruin you. It's another kind of terror: It's that nothing is nailed down. That we are out there — that our lives are truly existential. That we're not going to end up well. Not necessarily. You see, there's always been this sort of passive confidence implicit in Christianity, the confidence that things are going to work out all right. One does have to die, that's true, but if one keeps one's nose reasonably clean, one is going to heaven. That gave security to everybody. The ship of state was built on that security. The ship of state was nailed down. It didn't travel the stormy seas. Rather, it was carried by the strongest pallbearers of the nation. And what's happened now is we're entering an existential period in our history where nothing is nailed down. All the American faiths, one by one, are being exploded. We lived for too long in a paranoid dream world that believed communism was the secret of all evil on earth because it was the social embodiment of the Devil.

ADAMS: That's paranoid.

MAILER: That's paranoid. But I don't believe the Devil is the secret of all evil on earth. I believe something more complicated than that. I think God might be the source of a considerable amount of evil. Because if God is embattled, He could fail to take care, much to His great woe, of people who are devoted to Him, in the same way that a general might have to surrender soldiers on a hill. And those soldiers could give up with great bitterness in their hearts.

ADAMS: You've talked about evil in one sense as God's shit, God's excrement.

MAILER: Where did I say that?

ADAMS: It comes up in "The Metaphysics of the Belly." A colleague of mine once remarked that it's but a step from scatology to eschatology and I've often thought of this remark with regard to your work. Now I'm interested in the relationship between excrement and eternity. If God's shit is evil, but shit is associated with the Devil, doesn't this imply that God creates evil?

MAILER: There are references in my work to the idea that shit and the Devil have an umbilical relation, but it's not my idea after all. Luther had a few notions about it.

ADAMS: As did Jonathan Swift.

MAILER: It's an idea that goes — it starts with the most primitive peoples. It goes all the way. There's a reason for it. Shit is what we reject, at least to the degree that the shit felt it deserved a better end for itself. In other words, a lot of our shit has nutrients in it, worth in it. It's just that the body couldn't take it, and so passed it out. Some of the best of the food goes out with the shit as well as some of the worst. That's what I said in "The Metaphysics of the Belly." All right. To the degree that we can loosen our imagination to assume this stuff might have a soul, after all we're beginning to discover now that plants have feelings and souls, so it may be that food, even though in a peculiar relation to life, not as alive as a plant, let's say, or as an animal, but still alive to a degree, has a mood, has a spirit, has something. If food feels it has been violated, suppose it can die with a curse. Of course, the Devil loves to be around and pick up those who die with a curse. Malcolm Muggeridge once had Mother Theresa of Calcutta on a television show with him. Muggeridge, who is by any measure a devoutly religious man, had just written a book about Mother Theresa and obviously revered her. He told me what she used to do in Calcutta. Her order of nuns would take people who were dying on the street and move them into her convent where they'd die anyway a few days later — they didn't begin to have medicine to take care of them or anything like that — but her notion was, and Muggeridge was moved by this, and I agree that it is a moving idea, was that she didn't want them to die with absolutely nothing. She wanted them to be able to come in and get a little attention before they died so they wouldn't go out with a complete bitterness in their hearts. Now that is a religious woman. The recognition that one not die with a curse is fundamental to any inquiry into what could be the possible nature of God and the Devil. If God is embattled, and can't give fair justice to all, then what of those who do not achieve what they saw as their own fulfillment and thereby become spiritual material for the Devil, if not in this life then in another? We haven't said one word about karma, but my first idea these days is that any attempt to speak of these things makes no sense unless you take into account the peculiar calculus of karma. We may have to recognize that we're not only acting for this life but for other lives. Our past lives and our future lives. Paying dues, receiving awards. Reducing the cost of future dues, for example, by certain acts of abnegation that make no sense to us or our friends, yet ready to dare, on the other hand, sometimes desperate activities because we *are* desperate. The condition in which we live is hurting our karma.

ADAMS: Karma is a word you've used increasingly in the last few years. It's a term that you did not use in "The Metaphysics of the Belly" or "The Political Economy of Time," but which you could have in describing the nature of the soul. Is this something new in your metaphysics or is it a term for something that you've already described, like the way in which the soul exists, in "The Political Economy of Time"?

MAILER: I had come across the word in books but never paid any attention. In about 1953, I think it was in Robinson, Illinois, I went out to visit James Jones in his writers' colony and he and Lowney Handy were talking about karma and I said, "What's all that?" So he gave me the standard explanation which is that we are not only reincarnated, but the way in which we are is the re-flection, the judgment, the truth, of how we lived our previous life. If you exist in a simple form of karma with no interference by Gods or Devils, a natural flux of karma, then to the degree you lived a life that was artful, your reincarnation was artful. To the degree you lived a life that destroyed the time of others and dredged up all the swamp muds, so you are a creature of the swamp in your next life. The beauty of this may be that there is now good purpose to the swamp. (This isn't Jones's talk any longer, just a more general explanation of karma.) At any rate, Jones went on about it and I said, "You *believe* in that?" Because I was an atheist and a socialist in those days. He said, "Oh, sure. That's the only thing that makes sense." Well, the line rang in my head for years. "The only thing that makes sense." I thought about it over and over and in the last three or four years I began to think, "Yes, that does make sense. Jones was right."

1975

Marriage

An Interview with Buzz Farbar

⚘

BUZZ FARBAR: In your book on Marilyn Monroe, you say of her marriage to Arthur Miller, "It was only a few marriages (which is to say a few failures) later that he [Mailer] could recognize how he would have done no better than Miller, and probably have been damaged further in the process." Why do you feel a few marriages can be equated with a few failures?

NORMAN MAILER: People used to go into marriage without questioning the institution, never thought of a life where they might not be married. By now, weddings are beleaguered. When people go into it today, we have an existential adventure, for they don't know how it will turn out. In other words, marriage has become interesting again. It's a gamble they well may lose. Of course, I'm not referring to all of society — more to that educated leisure class which is the base of the establishment. Precisely in that part of our world, marriage is weakest.

So, in a sense, such men and women are gambling against a social tide. They're saying: We're going to make this marriage work, even though ten thousand obstacles in the scheme of things fight against us. Including almost everybody's greater desire for promiscuity. So it may be legitimate to speak of a marriage that's terminated, as a failure. Like a lost bet.

FARBAR: How about the termination of a bad marriage? Is being able to end it a failure or a success?

MAILER: Obviously there are all kinds of marriages. I suppose I was referring to people who are relatively independent, and sufficiently narcissistic to want to live their own kind of life. For them to be able to live with someone else is not an automatic venture. But then you can always find men and women who get married out of deep dependence on one another. Such marriages are usually a tyranny on one side, an enslavement on the other. Sometimes they are awful marriages where it may be a victory for the weak mate to split.

FARBAR: Do you feel you learned something from each marriage? Does each marriage get better, or worse, or is it all the same?

MAILER: Oh, each marriage is different. Being married to a woman is the equivalent, I think, of living in a major culture. Should you find yourself married to one woman and then to another, you have gone through the equivalent of spending five years in England after five years in France.

I don't look back on these marriages with bitterness. It seems to me you often get as much as you lost. I even discovered there may be four stages to knowing a woman. First, there's living together. It's often thought equal to marriage. Not by half. You can live with a woman and never begin to comprehend her at all, not until you get married to her. Once you do that, you're in the next stage. The third, obviously, is children. Once again your woman is different. Say it's analogous to a culture going through major transformations. The fourth stage is knowing a woman once you're divorced. Then, indeed, you come to know something at last. So if it weren't for the fact that there are children, there would be something almost agreeable about moving from marriage to marriage, just as there is something exciting about spending five years in England and five in France.

But there are children, and that's the vortex of all postmarital pain, which is always so surprisingly huge. Because finally the children come out of a vision in the marriage. It doesn't always even matter how casually they may have been conceived. Children can be created out of desperation, out of laziness, out of apathy, as a sporting proposition. But, usually, children come out of some covert union, some feeling that you have something together which should be embodied in a child. Otherwise, it's a little absurd to conceive. Therefore, once you have children, if the marriage breaks you can speak of it as failure. The vision that's embodied in that child is now broken. Not to count the damage to the child.

FARBAR: Knowing you as well as I do, I know that you are, to use your word "profoundly," a profoundly moral person —

MAILER: Can I interrupt you? I'm usually called a profoundly moral person by people who are trying to startle others who say I'm immoral or amoral, people who don't know much about my work and think of me as some sort of sexual ogre. Of course, my defenders then say, "On the contrary, he's a very moral man." I don't consider myself moral at all. I see myself as a man who lives in an embattled relation to morality. In other words, it isn't so much that I am moral, as that I have an advanced sensibility toward what may be moral and immoral in my actions. Which I find intolerable as a result, because I know when I'm being immoral, and I'm being immoral most of the time. By my own lights. In other words, I'm so rarely true to my own code that it's hard to maintain any self-respect. But I would never speak of myself as a moral man. Quite the contrary.

FARBAR: Can you love deeply more than one woman? If you're committed to one woman, how do you feel about a relationship with another one at the same time? Do you feel good or bad during an affair?

MAILER: I think it's impossible to be in love with two women at the same time. By now, in the middle of the twentieth century, so few of us get anywhere near that kind of love that it seems a sentimental fallacy. Just think of the people we know. Think of speaking to them of love. A titter runs through the table. What does it mean to most people when you talk about being in love with two people at once? It means you're fucking two women at once, that's all it means.

But if you're really in love with a woman, I think it's almost impossible to be in love with another. If you love a woman, you are engaged in a vision with her. That rarely happens. Maybe two, three, four times in our lives. But once you do, every time you give something to another woman, the beginning of a different vision is being sent to a different place. It can only work successfully when you have people whose souls are neatly separated. I believe we all have divided souls, but few of us have souls that are divided formally — in other words, Dr. Jekyll and Mr. Hyde. Those two psyches can have two great love affairs, yes. But most of us have double personalities that are more amorphous. The edges interreact. They're never clear-cut. And it's not simple for us to decide what our two personalities might be. The borders are not clear to us. As a result, being in love with two people usually muddies the distinction further.

FARBAR: Getting back to the Monroe book. You say, "It's no accident that studs are usually heartless about the aftermath. By their logic they've already treated the mother well and given the baby a good beginning."

MAILER: That's the stud's vanity. He's given a woman what she needs. We start with the natural assumption that studs are male chauvinists. Obviously, I was trying to explore one facet of that. Other people think, "God, he's a heartless man, he went in and knocked that woman up, walked away, never thought twice about it, he never bothered. How can anyone be that inhuman, that brutal?" I was trying to look for the stud's own self-justification. Wouldn't it come out as, "After all the pleasure I gave that woman, she has no cause for complaint"? To me, there's something a hint comic to it. Anybody who knows anything about women can recognize that the pleasure we assume we are giving to them can be a little less, in most cases, than we assumed.

FARBAR: There's always that little bit of doubt in a stud's mind, too.

MAILER: Oh, of course. You know studs, they're like professional athletes. They don't think of all the guys who can't make love. They think of other studs. They live in the terror that some other dude might be a little better than them. They're like street fighters.

FARBAR: You write about Monroe that "she can be tender, yet cold-blooded — her love tends to end when the role ends." Generally a woman is more cold-blooded than a man. Why is this so?

MAILER: A man is in a more existential position than a woman, he has to get an erection. The act doesn't take place in crackerjack fashion without that erection. So there is a limit to how much a man can simulate in sex. Unless a woman is suffering from a vagina so dry it's impossible for a man to enter her, she can simulate, and throw out a huge number of passions without feeling one. Much harder for a man to pretend to great sexual excitement if he's not feeling it. So it may not be that women are more cold-blooded than men so much as it's easier for women to get away with it.

FARBAR: You say of the marriage of Miller and Monroe, "Actually, they settle into good days and bad days. Which is the narrative line of marriage."

MAILER: Well, you could speak of certain human relations as being comparable to literary forms. For instance, the one-night stand was like a poem, good or bad. An affair of reasonable duration, a short story. By this logic, a marriage is a novel. In a short story we're interested in the point. In a novel we usually follow the way people move from drama to boredom back to drama again. And we often judge a novelist by his skill in moving people in and out of these high and low areas of existence. Of course, marriage is exactly like that. In a marriage, our interest is not that a given point is made in a given night, but the way that recognition is confirmed or eroded over the weeks or months to follow. The narrative line of all marriage, in that sense, is good days and bad days. And most people like to live in the form of a novel. Just as there are people who like to live in the form of the short story.

FARBAR: And psychopaths?

MAILER: They have lives that consist of poems, mostly bummers. But a majority of people seem to prefer endless, meaningless days. They don't want the ups to be so high they can't manage to come down to a life of lower pressure. They are the people who love marriage precisely because it offers an agreeable way to live in a slightly bored state. They seek out boredom, because it relieves them of dread. A mild boredom, not an intense boredom. An intense boredom, of course, is a form of torture.

FARBAR: Do you think that a man, when he is making love to a woman, is always measuring himself in some way, or is he being measured by the woman?

MAILER: Competitive men are obviously going to measure themselves against other men. Many women will have, perhaps, their own private scores for the man. But when a woman is in love, a man can be . . . well, in the sense of a sexual athlete, he can be unpromising, yet he can seem sublime to a woman, because she is open to him. The most tentative caress he offers arouses feeling that more skillful men won't. Obviously, sexual pleasure is not simply related to performance. Otherwise, we would have sexual Olympics. If people are not in love, but happen to like sex as a sport, the way other people like horses or skiing or motorboat racing, then performance comes to the fore. It was my assumption that when Marilyn fell in love, her man became sublime. For a time at least. In fact, it's usually necessary, in love, to believe that the man or woman you're with is better than anyone who has come before, so we find that way in which they are better than others. We have a need to believe our sex life is becoming more alive all the time. Otherwise, it's hard to continue. Especially as you get older.

FARBAR: Do you feel, as I do, that when a woman says to you, "So-and-so is a lousy lay," you then feel ill-will toward her? Is that purely a male ego thing, not wanting to hear that another man was a bad lay?

MAILER: I'd say we usually take pleasure in hearing another man is a bad lay. But if we have any sense, we recognize it's mostly meaningless. If you hear all over town that a certain man is a bad lay from just about every woman who has spoken about him, there's a reasonable assumption the guy is not too good. But would you like to be described by a woman on the worst night you ever had in bed? Or any of the hundred worst nights? I dread to think of certain descriptions of me. Speaking just of perform-ance, we have a spectrum. So when a woman says of a given man that he was a bad lay, I wince. Unless there's real cause, the woman is usually avenging herself. But then we know that women, maybe out of self-protection, lie a vast amount in sex, even lie to themselves about the past. We have all seen women who couldn't keep their hands off their man; then the years went by, and the man was out of her life. Slowly his sexual reputation sank, inch by inch. A part of the comedy of sexual affairs.

FARBAR: I wonder what your feelings are about promiscuity in women. And promiscuity in men.

MAILER: I suppose I believe you pay for every last thing you get out of life. Years ago, Calder Willingham told me a story about a situ-ation where he tried every trick to make a woman leave him. Fi-nally she began going with another man. Then he discovered he was jealous. He told this story on himself with great humor, and looked at me and said, "Norman, you can't cheat life." He said this in his inimitable Georgia accent. It's not a remark one hasn't heard before. But there's such a thing as hearing a maxim at just the right moment for oneself. Then it goes all the way in. So that remark stayed with me. Whenever I'm trying to work out some sort of moral balance for myself, I find the thought useful.

Of course, certain people get more out of being promiscuous than others, and pay less for it. But the idea that people can be promiscuous without exploiting their own sensitivity is impossi-ble. On the other hand, promiscuity is altogether necessary for some, especially if you have a personality that consists of frag-ments, as most of us do by now. We live in a time of interruption. The art of the absurd is built on the fact that we live in a continuum of interruption. Turn on the television and see a story slam into an advertisement, and so forth. As a result, there's a huge tendency to become fragmented. Then different relations give us different things in different places.

But as you get older, you begin to discover that promiscuity gets more and more difficult, because it makes you commit too much of yourself. I'm fifty now. I've reached the point where conceivably I could be making love to a woman and die in bed. That can happen. If it did, which woman would I be with? Does one want to die with a stranger? As you get older, making love becomes more apocalyptic exactly because you're closer to the end of your life each time. As a result there's less desire to be promiscuous. On the other hand, if people are rooted in the promiscuous, the attempt to keep themselves monogamous can induce all sorts of neuroses and diseases, no question.

What I distrust always, however, are professional swingers. Come on, join the gangfuck, it's good for you. Those people are as totalitarian as the ones who say chastity is the only good on earth. By now, they're more. Part of the totalitarian is to make an absolute out of the prevailing tendency of the time.

FARBAR: But if you pick up a girl in a bar at three in the morning and have a flying fuck at four and go home at five or six, that to me is not promiscuity. It's just something that happened. It's almost a physical act, like going to the bathroom. Don't you feel that?

MAILER: Yeah, but I hate it. Look, there are times when one has to depart from one's identity. As in *Last Tango in Paris* people making love without identity is exciting. Obviously, there is a need to treat sex as a species of evacuation. We've all had great fucks with people we hardly know. While that satisfies something, by now I hate it. Hate having too much sexual pleasure without feeling a great deal for the woman. I tend by now to stay away from fucking a girl I don't love but really enjoy fucking. I used to like that years ago, loved the power, but by now I kind of hate it. I hate the feeling afterward. I don't hate the fuck. I love the fuck, but I hate what comes afterward.

FARBAR: Because of the way you think she must feel when she knows it's a dead end?

MAILER: No. I'm not even thinking about her. Well, I'm thinking about her in the sense that I'm a guilty enough man so that I can't use people around me much anymore. We were speaking about morality earlier, and it isn't that I'm moral, it's almost rather that

I have enough respect for morality to feel I can't abuse the edges of it forever, can't abuse some of my central premises forever. I have this belief in karmic balance — that we come into life with a soul that carries an impost of guilt and reward from the past. And at the end of each life we may be reborn, which I think is a reward in itself. Which not everyone gets. Some people's souls die, literally die, just as the body dies; some people's souls die in a given life. As you know, I believe in two kinds of death. Final death as some species of oblivion, and transcendental death, where you're reborn in some other form of existence that gives fair measure for your previous lives. So I think as we get older there comes a time when we have to worry about this moral balance in ourselves. Maybe I've come to the point where I can't use people anymore. I do know it leaves me depressed to think I've had a woman for too little, offered no real feeling. I tend to stay away from such women. That wasn't true years ago.

FARBAR: That leads me to another question. How have you been able to maintain such extraordinarily good relationships with three of your four ex-wives? They truly seem to be your good friends. It's more than just being civilized, it's a special kind of talent, I think.

MAILER: I think we loved each other. I certainly loved each of them, and I believe they loved me. We have children together, and we love those children. When we broke up there was a recognition . . . well, we broke up for different reasons each time, but there was a recognition that there had to be something low about making the children suffer.

Of course, each time the marriage broke up, it was hardly agreeable or nice. Maybe over the years we've come together a little. When you're divorced from a woman, the friendship can then start. Because one's sexual vanity is not in it any longer. At least not in the same way. You can look back on it and say, "Yes, we were pretty good together, but not good enough." And let it go at that. Then, of course, everything in the woman you liked in the first place, her charm, the more attractive aspects of her character, now can come back into play, as well as everything that got lost in the harassments of marriage. A hint of tenderness returns.

When you're in love, the stakes are high. There's much more anger when there's love. Because if one's love is frustrated, it means a good deal more than if one's liking is balked. So there's a readiness in marriage to walk around in a state of resentment which starts to flatten all the smaller affections. Of course, there are marriages where the opposite occurs. When the sexual impulse quiets down or dies even, the people become great friends. Carnally speaking, they're divorced, but they don't separate legally. They live together as dear friends. Such marriages are often nice. I've never been in one, but I imagine it could be very nice.

FARBAR: Let's change the subject completely. I wondered how you felt about lesbianism. If you had any thought that you could —

MAILER: It's funny, you know, I've always had a puritanical attitude about homosexuality, almost as if I couldn't afford to begin to get homosexual, because God knows where it would all stop. You know about that old Talmudic notion, that if you want to restrain an impulse don't just build a fence around the impulse itself, build a fence around the fence. By analogy, I've never been tolerant of the idea of homosexuality for myself. But I've always had the feeling that if I were a woman, that I somehow would enjoy lesbianism. I think if I were a woman it would mean very little to me to be a lesbian part of the time.

FARBAR: Is that because lesbian women you've known or read about are always saying they know how to do whatever it is they're doing better than men do?

MAILER: Well, obviously there must be fine sensuality among lesbians. Listen, what am I edging around it for? I have seen women together and it's lovely. Or, let us say, it is lovely provided it isn't finally designed to exclude men from every relation with women.

FARBAR: Last spring, in a piece in *New York Review of Books* on *Last Tango* you wrote about Brando and Maria Schneider being nameless when they meet each other, and this made their sexual relationship intriguing. As soon as some sort of relationship begins, and they get to know one another's names, it ends. Why do women enjoy anonymous sex?

MAILER: I think once a woman becomes anonymous in a sexual relationship — it's as if she's weightless. She no longer has the gravity of old responsibility. She can cut loose.

But I think one thing's rarely understood about promiscuity. In *Last Tango* there's that line "Fuck God," with which the picture begins — you can hardly hear it. Brando screams it as the Metro goes overhead. One of the profoundest motives in promiscuity and in perversion is fuck God. God, I'm defying you. A most basic human emotion. Now, whether we actually defy God when we think we do, or are unwittingly dignifying Him, even expressing His will, which has been kept from us for two thousand years — in other words, it is the pagan who expresses the will of God rather than the Christian — that we don't know. But the impulse is there.

What we can count on is that when a woman throws off her social responsibility, her tendency is to be wilder than a man. Not only in anonymous relations but in orgies. Is there anything in the literature of orgy that doesn't suggest that women are always wilder? After men are used up, the women get together. They can make love to one another for hours until the men are restored. Or maybe it's that women sit upon an endless well of sexuality, whereas men have to keep rebuilding it.

FARBAR: The opposite of orgy is marriage, I suppose. Do you feel that you are still married, in some karmic sense, or some essence of you is still married to each of your wives, and you are never away from them?

MAILER: No, but it's possible certain relations continue from one life to another. Because of a great love or a great hatred, or perhaps because they're unfulfilled.

The logic of karma, it seems to me, is that God, whatever His other motivations, may as well be considered some kind of cosmic artist, engaged in a dialogue, at the least, about the nature of existence with other cosmic artists in other parts of the universe, other gods. So the point of karma may be to enable Him to go back to certain projects, just as an artist sometimes wishes to improve his first attempt. Sometimes what an artist does is perfect. Sometimes one wants to work it further, go to the point where you can do better or, if not, know you've failed and abandon the notion. Perhaps human souls represent some of the most poignant notions of God. You see, there's an extraordinary beauty in the potential of most human relations if we're willing to assume that under all the absurdities, all the spleen and waste and brutality, there's a blocked aesthetic conception. Maybe that's why I object to some of the more casual forms of promiscuity. I don't object across the board. There are times when you need a fuck the way you need a shit. Simple as that. Let's not pretend. One of the troubles with promiscuous fucking is that you not only get the wastes out, but take in waste from the other person's system. You shit on them, and they shit on you. I think one of the best lines in *Marilyn* is, "Less is known about the true transactions of fucking than any science on earth."

FARBAR: Well then, why do so many women look upon the sex act in a much more holy way than a man does?

MAILER: They do, they don't. Some have absolute contempt for sex. Probably just as many women think of sex as evacuation as men. They enjoy sex, but despise it. One of the drives in women's lib is to insist that women are absolutely as cynical about sex as men and have the right to be absolutely as cynical.

FARBAR: Remember when the Pill first came on the scene and made a lot of young people very happy? There was a lot of screwing, and then gradually, the way it is now, there seems to be less joy in sex. When I was eighteen or twenty, I'd be screwing my brains out if it were possible.

MAILER: You were screwing your brains out because it was a criminal activity in your day, and so offered more pleasure than law-abiding activity. Which has been my argument about permissiveness in sex from the beginning. It's why I'm opposed to legalization of marijuana. Reduce the penalties, but don't have marijuana legal. The corporation will take it over. Marijuana with filter-tip cigarettes. You'll have vitamins in the marijuana, and every pollution of advertising. You'll come to hate the very thought of smoking because they'll be working their scheme on you.

By the same token, the moment you get too much permissiveness in sex, you get pulled into somebody else's manipulation scheme. My idea these years is that total promiscuity is the unstated need of the technological society. Its impulse is to accept indiscriminate fucking. It wants humans to become units. About the time we no longer distinguish between a man and a woman, he-she has become an interchangeable sexual part. We put it into the hole of those weaker than us, and get it put into our own hole by those stronger; we become a link in a technological chain of sex.

I've always hated the Pill. It reduces the fuck to a species of upper masturbation. Part of the beauty of the fuck was that you were taking a terrible chance. You could knock the girl up, and if you did, then by God you found out what you really felt about her, how phony were you, how true. When a woman comes to you and says she's pregnant, you know more about what you feel for her than you did before.

All right, the women will counter and say, That's good for you, finding your identity, but we're losing ours. Because we have to get butchered by abortionists. I've never been able to answer this. I will agree that the absence of the Pill was better for the sanity of men than women. I think women, if they are willing to look at themselves in such fashion, are in the embattled position. Since they are closer to creation, they have to pay more for the privilege. They hate it now. They hate it because we live in a technological world, where to be pregnant means that you're removed for a time from the major scene, which is to say the whole technological process. The last power of the human heart as we approach apocalypse is ambition. Everybody gets more ambitious to be in on more. If we can't wield the power, then we want to be in on the shaping of the power.

FARBAR: What about legalized abortion?

MAILER: I think when a woman goes through an abortion, even legalized abortion, she goes through hell. There's no use hoping otherwise. For what is she doing? Sometimes she has to be saying to herself, "You're killing the memory of a beautiful fuck." I don't think abortion is a great strain when the act was some miserable little screech, or some squeak oozed up through the trapdoor, a little rat which got in, a worm who slithered under the threshold. That sort of abortion costs a woman little more than discomfort. Unless there are medical consequences years later.

But if a woman has a great fuck, and then has to abort, it embitters her. A profound and awful transaction. The Pill didn't come into existence for nothing.

FARBAR: Do you see any future in a formal structure of marriage? Many young people in various strata of society are no longer getting married.

MAILER: We return to our beginning. I think marriage has a future of a sort. I think it's going to become a classical demand on people. Of course, few people are interested in classical demands. Those who are will look upon marriage with more regard than they have in a century. Because it's not going to be easy to imagine a man and woman getting married when they're young and both virgins, say at the age of eighteen or twenty or twenty-two, and then proceeding to live in happiness and fidelity for fifty or sixty years in order to die together. That is soon going to be equal in difficulty to pitching a no-hitter. And will be respected in the same fashion. The virtuosity of the demand is finally going to keep marriage alive. Not necessarily as a fundamental social institution, but as a grand curiosity. Because there will always be that human wonder. Maybe that was the way it was supposed to be. Maybe there is nothing more beautiful than one man and one woman managing to be that much to each other. What courage it takes, what extraordinary leaps, what a transcendent vision one needs of the mate. What a transcendent vision one needs of existence in order to ride out the boredom, the entrenched monotonies, the temptations, the small betrayals, the social pressures, and finally the huge social weight of that oncoming future, which will hardly encourage anyone to remain faithful, for to stay in marriage will appear absurd.

The point is you can't cheat life. Go back to Willingham's notion. You pay for everything. The worst notion afoot among the young people I know is that you can get fucking for nothing. You don't get it that way. You pay for fucking with your life and you end with your death. Then something in the balance of things may decide whether you've earned your reincarnation. The new life we're given may be the closest we ever come to the truth.

1973

One-Night Stands

An Interview with Cathleen Medwick

ᕲ

CATHLEEN MEDWICK: What we're thinking about is an interview on love.

NORMAN MAILER: Love?

MEDWICK: Primarily.

MAILER: Oh — I don't know if I can talk about it.

MEDWICK: I know — I don't know if I can ask you.

MAILER: Let's say that I have enough respect for love so that I think if you start to talk about it, you can get into an awful lot of trouble. You're likely to let all the devils in the cosmos in on your little secret, whatever it is that enables you to trap a little of that substance that's rarer than gold. I mean, if a man had a small supply of gold, he wouldn't go around telling people where he mined it, would he? So I think that the only people who want to talk about love are those who don't have any and pretend to know something about it.

MEDWICK: The reason we're so curious is that people don't necessarily associate sex with love, and I think that you do, almost invariably.

MAILER: Well I think they have a fugue-like relationship, and keep going in and out of one another.

MEDWICK: Yes. You know, I should tell you, or maybe I shouldn't, that most of the time when I read your descriptions of very intimate sex, it reads — it reminds me of something, I couldn't figure

103

out until recently what it was. And I realized that it reminded me of medieval romances that I had read as a graduate student.

MAILER: Yeah, Marion Faye at the end of *The Deer Park* when he's thinking of his relation to Elena, and I guess Rojack in *The American Dream*. Sure. That's as close as I ever came really to writing about sex. I find that in a funny way I'm slightly embarrassed by explicit descriptions. You know, I did a book about Henry Miller a few years ago and he is such a marvelous pornographic writer, that is I don't know whether he'd call himself a pornographic writer or not, and I don't want to insult the old boy, especially now that he's gone, but let's say he wrote about rip-roaring sex like nobody else. I really felt like a maiden aunt next to him, I'm so nice-nelly compared to Miller. I'm not sure that I really know how to write about sex. I'm always making it too metaphorical.

MEDWICK: Did you ever by any chance read anything that Saint Teresa wrote about her mystical experience?

MAILER: No.

MEDWICK: Well, she described being invaded by the spirit of God in terms that were extremely sexual by modern standards. When the nineteenth-century critics read it they thought, "My God, she thought she was talking about something spiritual but she was really talking about a complete sexual experience." It was very hard to convince them that not only was she aware that she was translating it that way but that there was no reason not to talk about it that way. Do you consider your feelings about sex and love to be somewhat mystical; romantic?

MAILER: That's why I'm not happy talking about it. If you interview a mystic, you've got the single most difficult variety of interview on your hands. Mystics feel about interviews the way primitive people feel about being photographed. It goes back to Hemingway's notion: "If it feels good, don't talk about it." One can talk around it, but I'm not going to give you a definition of love and a definition of sex. I'm going to speak guardedly and circumferentially and let readers make of it what they will in relation to their own experience. That's the way most people talk about sex and love most of the time anyway. My mother once described the plot of *Romeo and Juliet* by saying, "Well, I think they kind of liked each other," my mother having been brought up in a school which believed you should never talk about personal relationships at all.

MEDWICK: Well, do you think that men love differently than women?

MAILER: Let's try to separate sex and love. For instance, it's possible sex inspires more mystical feelings than love. I'm talking about love in the immediate sense, A loves B. Terribly concrete and particular. You love the way someone walks, the way they talk, the way they do all those things in the songs, you love the way they smell and you love the way they wear clothing, you love the way they laugh, you love the way they tell a joke, you love the way they say no to somebody — it's all the things they do. Whereas sex very often makes you feel close to God. Now if you love someone, and if you also have good sex with her, then you can feel very close to God as you love. In fact, it's easier to feel close if you have good sex with someone you love, because having good sex with somebody you don't like can leave you with an angry, confused, lustful feeling that may inspire you to more and more sex until you burn it out, and it drives you further and further away from any tenderness. To that extent you offer nothing to God, you're only thinking of the Devil. Sex also inspires, very often, a feeling that you're awfully close to the Devil. But I think the paradox of sex is that you can have sex with someone you don't know, on the first night, and feel closer to God in that moment than you're likely to feel again for five or ten years, even if you're never going to see the person again. You may say goodbye in the morning and never see each other again, a romance in the airport or something. Although I must confess I've never had a romance in an airport — can you imagine finding God in all that plastic?

MEDWICK: I'm not sure where that leaves love. How much of that feeling remains, that close-to-God feeling remains in a long-term relationship?

MAILER: Well, if one loves one's wife and loves one's children, after a while you begin to feel very close to God — not that your wife is God or the child's God but you're married to still one more aspect of the creation, whatever it is. That is, you touch God. That is the way in which most people become quietly religious, and say at the end of a period of many years, "Yes, I believe in God, I believe in God very much." There's been a quiet growth of sentiment without them necessarily thinking about it. They go along for years with their children, and at a certain point they find themself praying. Let's say a child is ill, they're praying for the child's protection and they realize they've gotten very close to God because they've seen this extraordinary miracle of a child growing every day, and changing and having some life that's just not explicable by the wife's wit or the husband's. So the creation becomes beautiful, and manifest. But as I say, that's not the way of the mystic. If you would, that's finding Christ through works.

The first time that someone has a profound sexual act, when it's all over, there's this shocked, stunned, incredible recognition: "Why God, God exists." Which is what Saint Teresa felt perhaps. I say it usually happens in sex rather than in love because it's got to happen quickly, a sudden revelation. So there are certain advantages to one-night stands. One brings none of one's baggage to a one-night stand and that makes it possible to have, once in a while, extraordinary emotions. The average one-night stand is, after all, not necessarily a small disaster, but unless it's very, very good indeed it leaves a terrible aftertaste. They can be exceptional once in a while; when that happens one often has this religious sentiment. It doesn't come from the person — you don't know the person — it comes from something in sex itself. Sex may be something that's outside of people.

MEDWICK: I can't seem to think of a woman who has written about sex in this way, or love in this way. I can think of five or six men.

MAILER: I would argue that women have an immense horror of exposing themselves. Let me give an example. When I wrote *An American Dream*, many people were offended profoundly by the sexual act that takes place between the hero Rojack and the German maid Ruta. It would have been impossible — if Ruta, and not Rojack, had been telling the story — for her to write about that act without revealing herself completely, and in a disadvantageous way. The man could write about it, because one-night stands are altogether different from a continuing sexual relationship where the man dominates in one way, the woman dominates in another, they share here, they're apart there, and it changes over a period of time. In the one-night stand there was, at least until very recently, the notion that no matter what they did in bed, the man was dominant in that he had scored the breakthrough and the woman had been taken, at least in the eyes of society.

MEDWICK: Is that changing now, do you think?

MAILER: Oh, a great deal. It's almost getting to the point where women are saying, "*I* scored."

MEDWICK: What does that do to the mythology?

MAILER: Well, I don't think one generation can wipe out what may or may not be biological and is certainly historical. But a woman is not going to admit as readily as a man that she had an extraordinary experience on a one-night stand. Ten or twenty years ago you'd hear of a woman who slashed her wrists — often what happened was that she had an extraordinary experience with a man she met for a night and never heard from again, and that made her feel she was crazy or evil or didn't deserve to live. I'm not saying that one-night stands are better than living in considerable sexual intensity with someone for a long time. I'm not saying that at all. I'm saying that it can be hard for the long-term relationship to be mystical. One reaches heights from time to time, and in fact one may go higher and further with someone one knows very well than one could ever go on a one-night stand, but since a one-night stand is often transcendental to the degree that you really don't know the other person, that they are *strange* — like the cosmos — it suggests that when you're living with someone you love, sex can't be transcendental in that particular way at all. Of course it gets its richness in other ways, but we've talked of that.

1980

Ethics and Pornography

An Interview with Jeffrey Michelson and Sarah Stone

❧

JEFFREY MICHELSON: What do you think makes for great sex?

NORMAN MAILER: Great sex is apocalyptic. There's no such thing as great sex unless you have an apocalyptic moment. William Burroughs once changed the course of American literature with one sentence. He said, "I see God in my asshole in the flashbulb of orgasm."* Now that was one incredible sentence because it came at the end of the Eisenhower period, printed around 1959 in *Big Table* in Chicago. I remember reading it and thinking, "I can't believe I just read those words." I can't tell you the number of taboos it violated. First of all, you weren't supposed to connect God with sex. Second of all, you never spoke of the asshole, certainly not in relation to sex. If you did, you were the lowest form of pervert. Third of all, there was obvious homosexuality in the remark. In those days, nobody was accustomed to seeing that in print. And fourth, there was an ugly technological edge — why'd he have to bring in flashbulbs? Was that the nature of his orgasm? It was the first time anybody had ever spoken about the inner nature of the orgasm.

MICHELSON: Yeah.

MAILER: OK. Looking at it now, that marvelously innovative sentence, with all it did, one of the most explosive sentences ever written in the English language, we can take off from it and say that unless sex is apocalyptic, we can't speak of it as great. We can

---

* The first sentence in *Naked Lunch* as it was printed in *Big Table*.

speak of it as resonant. We can speak of it as heart-warming. We can speak of it as lovely. But we can't speak of it as great. Great is a word that should never be thrown around in relation to sex. My simple belief is that sex that makes you more religious is great sex. I'm going to live to pay for, to rue, this remark if it gets around.

MICHELSON: I'll never tell anyone. (*laughter*)

MAILER: Remember that awful priest who said, "There are no atheists in foxholes?" It was a remark to turn people into atheists for twenty-five years. I remember every time I got into a foxhole I said to myself, "This is one man who's an atheist in a foxhole!" (*laughter*) Well, what I do believe is that you can't have a great fuck and remain an atheist. Now that means the atheists of America are going to excoriate me. This is striking at them; this is a true blow at their sexual happiness.

MICHELSON: What is the relationship between God and sex, and the Devil and sex?

MAILER: You can't talk about it that way.

MICHELSON: Tell me about the orgies you went to when you were younger?

MAILER: I'm not going to tell you. Certain things belong to my novels. Look, let me make one thing clear: there are matters I won't talk about in an interview. Anything I would find tremendously difficult to write about in a novel, I'm not going to try to discuss in an interview. If it can't be done in a novel, it certainly can't be done here.

MICHELSON: Did you go to one orgy as a philosopher, or did you go to many as a pervert?

MAILER: You're referring to Voltaire's little remark, "Once a philosopher, twice a pervert." Voltaire went once to a male brothel and his friends asked him afterward did he like it, and he said, "Oh, yes, very much. It was better than I thought it would be." They said, "Are you going back?" and he said, "No. Once a philosopher, twice a pervert." Well, I'm not going to tell you.

MICHELSON: I would like to get on to your feelings about sexuality. Not to intrude on your own life, but just to discuss certain things. What do you think you know about sex that most other people do not?

MAILER: Jeffrey, I can't possibly answer that. I'd have to believe it's true . . . Really, all I believe is that I'm more aware of my limitations than most men. I have less vanity about sex than most men.

MICHELSON: You've grown to have less vanity?

MAILER: Yeah. I used to have an immense amount when I was younger. I needed it. I had an immense amount to learn. Sexual vanity probably has an inverse proportion to sexual sophistication. When we're young, we have to believe we're the greatest gift given to women because if we didn't, we would know how truly bad we are. When I was a kid, I remember I had an older cousin who was immensely successful with women. And I was always obsessed with performance. He used to say to me, "You're wrong on that; performance has nothing to do with it." I never knew what he meant. It took years — he was considerably older than me — to come to understand what he was talking about. Performance is empty in sex. Performance is pushups. I mean, we've all had the experience of making love for hours, and getting that airless, tight, exhausted feeling, you know, my God, will she ever come? For God's sakes, please, God, please, let her come! (*laughter*) I have a bad back today and one of the reasons is that I worked so hard when I was younger.

MICHELSON: At sex?

MAILER: I didn't work at lifting furniture, I promise you. If I'd been a furniture mover, at least I'd have some honor. (*laughter*) No, I have a bad back because I was stupid. Because I tried to . . . you see, the minute you try to dominate sex through will, sex escapes you. The connection of female sexuality with cats is not for too little. You cannot dominate a cat with your will. If you do, the cat goes right around you. Sexuality is the same way: can't dominate it. So over the years as you come to recognize this, you begin to approach it from the side, so to speak.

MICHELSON: Tell me about your first experience with pornography. Do you remember when you were a kid and the first magazines you had?

MAILER: I think it was *Spicy Detective*.

MICHELSON: *Spicy Detective?*

MAILER: There used to be magazines called *Spicy Detective* and *Spicy* — I can't remember the others, maybe *Spicy Romance*. The girls always had marvelous large breasts, with tremendously pointed nipples. I don't know how to describe these breasts, it almost fails me. You couldn't call them pear-shaped, nor melon-shaped, somewhere in between. They were projectile-shaped. Literally, they looked like the head of a 105 Howitzer shell, about 4 inches in diameter, and went out about 5½ inches, with those tremendously pointed nipples. The girl always used to be tied to some sort of hitching post with an evil man approaching. They always had one arm under their breasts. I remember that it made the breasts project out even more. They'd have a wisp of clothing. A torn panty would cover their loins. I've never seen anything I enjoyed as much. Now, I didn't learn much from it.

MICHELSON: Do you feel that there are any social benefits that result from a sexually free press, or do you feel that sexually explicit material must be tolerated simply to protect the wider benefits of the First Amendment?

MAILER: Well, the first benefit is sexual sophistication. Talk about pornography always revolves around: Does it excite more violent impulses, or doesn't it? The women's movement is absolutely up in arms about pornography. An encouragement to rape, et cetera. I just can't agree. I think they don't know quite what they're talking about. Of course, some kinds of pornography are on the cusp. I wouldn't have anything to say for pornography that uses children as models. I'm against anything that sets people's lives on certain tracks too early. Using a child to make money from sex is obviously offensive. If you were a magazine that had pictures of children performing sexual acts, I wouldn't be in it. That's where I draw the line.

But you asked what the social value might be. Pictures of men and women making love is not going to hurt people as much as it's going to help them. It gives them — and I would include pornographic movies — an education in that part of sex which is universal, as opposed to the part that's particular. Those tragedies of high school kids who get married too young, only to discover three, five, eight years later, with a couple of children between them, that they weren't meant for one another at all, and so split, come about because the sex is so compelling when they're young and they know so little about it. That's a profound error we've all made one way or another. We mistake the beauties of sex for the beauties of the particular person that we're with, that is, think the particular person is beautiful because of the sexual feelings they arouse in us. We don't understand those feelings are more or less universal, and could be felt with someone else. The faculty of choice is not present. Now when I was a kid, and I've never known a kid who wasn't absolutely riveted by pornography, I wanted more and more of it. I never saw enough of it to satisfy myself. That's because there's tremendous knowledge there, tremendous knowledge about human behavior. You cannot look at a pornographic picture without learning more about human nature. I can look at some girl who has, on the face of it, a stupid face, let's say — some of the girls who appear in pornographic magazines look stupid, some rather bright. But let's take one that looks stupid. Nevertheless, there's something in the very way she holds her hand (even if the photographer arranged her hand for her, she had finally to embody his order) there's something in the way her hand is holding a cigarette that'll tell you a great deal about her if you look carefully enough at these matters.

You also get a sense of the sexual behavior of a panorama of people that you couldn't possibly have in your own life unless you devoted your life to sex. One of the ironies of pornography is that it enables people to free themselves from chasing after sex. A lot of that knowledge can now be obtained in a secondary fashion, through pornography.

MICHELSON: Knowledge as opposed to pleasure?

MAILER: Yes. If we all had to go out and acquire every bit of understanding through our own experience, it would take us forever to learn anything. That's why, in fact, civilization moved so slowly for so many thousands of years. From Gutenberg on, there's been an incredible rate of acceleration. Now, people were able to acquire most of their knowledge by reading. They didn't have to go through the experience themselves. The worst thing you can say against pornography, I mean, the only argument I would use if I were determined to stamp pornography out is that it tends to accelerate the same things that are being speeded up by all other communications. Pornography, right at this present point, is a peculiar frontier of communications.

SARAH STONE: What exactly is accelerated?

MAILER: The consciousness of people. In the simplest literal sense, a kid of eighteen will now know what he wouldn't have known till he was twenty-eight.

STONE: Why is that against pornography?

MAILER: Well, if you say that everything is speeding up too quickly and we may end up destroying ourselves because we're advancing at too great a rate and don't really know what we're doing, then, in that sense, pornography is dangerous. But by the same measure, television is endlessly more dangerous. Conservatives who believe that human nature should be slowed up have a legitimate argument, I'd say, against pornography. But they're not consistent. Because if this is their argument against pornography, let them ban television first.

MICHELSON: Do you feel comfortable about appearing in *Puritan*?

MAILER: Not altogether. I've thought about it, and finally decided I probably ought to. I'm not opposed to pornography — in fact, I think it probably has a social benefit. On the other hand, in *Playboy* I've had the experience of seeing my work printed between beaver shots. Now, *Playboy* happens to treat its writers exceptionally well. No magazine is nicer in terms of courtesy, and you get fine pay for your stuff. They're a godawful magazine, however, in terms of layout, at least from the point of view of the writer, because the last thing you want for your prose, is to have a photo of a gorgeous model with her legs going from Valparaiso to Baltimore! Right in the middle of your prose! I'd rather you took an axe and drove it into the middle of the reader's head. Because the reader's not going to follow my stuff. His eye is on the bird. So there have been times when, despite the attractions of *Playboy*, I don't really want that piece there. It's not going to be read properly. In that sense, pornography is a tremendous distraction for a writer.

MICHELSON: I'll try to make sure the layout keeps all your words together.

MAILER: At least let me pick the pictures.

MICHELSON: When does a graphic representation of a sexual act become art, and when, smut? Can you suggest any criteria on which to base a judgment?

MAILER: Let me ask you: what would be *your* idea of smut?

MICHELSON: Things that are particularly degrading to either sex.

MAILER: Get specific.

MICHELSON: I guess it's stuff that turns me on in a way I think I shouldn't be turned on.

MAILER: Excellent.

STONE: I feel the difference is if it's commercially and sloppily done just to get another page in the book, then the insult is to the art. Where it's a true and honest representation of feeling, then no matter what it represents, it's got to be respected.

MAILER: Mmm, that's well put too. You would be saying in effect, then, Sarah, that smut is the equivalent of a sexual act that's casual, what we call sordid, no love, not any real pleasure in it, a cohabitation with a rancid smell to it. So a lack of respect for the seriousness of the occasion when a photographer takes a picture of a woman in a pornographic position makes for smut.

Jeffrey is saying, as I gather, that there are certain acts that tend toward the bestial, the fecal (I assume these are the sort of things you're thinking of) that may be arousing, but you find that your moral nature disapproves.

MICHELSON: I'm wondering: Is smut to pornography, to good pornography, as trashy romance novels are to good literature? Is it just the lower end of the genre?

MAILER: It's certainly complicated. Take Sarah's criteria, pictures that are transparently cynical. The model's worn out, the photographer's worn out, disgusting. Yet that can be arousing in a funny way. For instance, in *Hustler*, often I find that the most interesting section is those cheap Polaroid pictures that untalented photographers send in of women who are not professional models.

MICHELSON: The reality turns you on?

MAILER: The sordid reality. My sexuality, I expect, is aroused by knowledge. The moment I know more than I knew before, I'm excited. Those gritty Polaroid shots in *Hustler* are often more interesting. They communicate. You know, the picture of some waitress who lives in Sioux Falls. I know more at that moment about Sioux Falls, about waitresses — even if they're lying, even if she isn't a waitress, there's something about the very manifest of the lie that's presented that's fascinating. It arouses your curiosity. Whereas superb pictures of models can get boring. There tends to be a sameness to them. Aren't enough flaws present. The very question of the sordid is . . . tricky.

STONE: In Woody Allen's movie *Annie Hall*, he's on the street and he walks up to this little old lady and says to her something like "Why are relationships so difficult?" And she says, "Love fades . . ." As a man who's had six marriages, what is your reaction to this dialogue? Do you think that love fades and do you feel that sex fades?

MAILER: I don't think that sex fades in marriage necessarily. Without talking about my personal life, I'd say that compatibility is nearer to the problem than sex. What I mean is people can have marvelous sex and not be terribly compatible. That sets up a great edginess in marriage. Some people, in fact, can only have good sex with people who are essentially incompatible for them. I might have been in that category for years, I don't know. If you're terribly combative, then you're drawn toward mates who are not too compatible. Anyone who has a violent or ugly or combative edge is not going to be comfortable with someone who *is* really sweet and submissive. They want something more abrasive in their daily life. Otherwise they are likely to lose their good opinion of themselves. There's nothing worse than being brutal to somebody who's good to you. Whereas if you're living with someone whose ideas irritate the living shit out of you, and you fight with them every day and feel justified about it, that can be healthier than living with a soul whose ideas are compatible to yours. All the same, if you do choose this fundamental imcompatibility, there will come a point where it ceases to be fun and turns into its opposite. Faults in the mate that were half-charming suddenly become unendurable. Every one of us who has been in love knows how fragile — what's a good word for skin? — how fragile is the *membrane* of love. It has to be mended every day and nurtured. We have to anticipate all the places where it's getting a little weak and go there and breathe on it, shape it again. In a combative relationship, obviously, that's difficult. You have to have a great animal vigor between combative people or they just can't make it for long.

MICHELSON: What about love fading?

MAILER: Well, I don't think love fades; I don't think there's anything automatic about it. I think most of us aren't good enough for love. I think self-pity is probably the most rewarding single emotion in the world for masturbators, which is one of the reasons, I suppose, I'm opposed to masturbation, because it encourages other vices to collect around you. Self-pity is one of the first. You lie in bed, pull off, and say to yourself, I have such wonderful, beautiful, tender, sweet, deep, romantic, exciting and sensual emotions, why is it that no woman can appreciate how absolutely fabulous I am? Why can't I offer these emotions to someone else? Self-pity comes rolling in, and cuts us off from recognizing that love is a reward. Love is not something that is going to come up and solve your problems. Love is something you get after you've solved enough of your problems so that something in Providence itself takes pity on you. I always believed that whoever or whatever it is, some angel, some sour sort of angel, finally says, "Look at those poor motherfuckers. He and she have been working so hard for so many years. Let's throw him and her a bone." So they meet and find love. Then they have to know what to do with it.

MICHELSON: Love is a function of having paid your dues?

MAILER: Truman Capote has got this book he's writing, *Answered Prayers*. I gather from something he said once that its theme is that the worst thing that befalls people is that their prayers are answered. Which is not a cheap idea. Love is the perfect example. Everybody prays for love, but once they get love, they have to be worthy of it. Love is the most perishable of human emotions. It never fades. That's my answer to the question. There is absolutely no reason in the world why people can't love each other more every day of their lives for eighty years. I absolutely believe that. Without that, I have no faith in love whatsoever. I think it would be a diabolical universe if you're introduced to all these wonderful sentiments that illumine your existence but something is put into the very nature of it that will make it fade. That's the sentiment of a person who is full of self-pity: Love fades. That old woman was full of self-pity.

MICHELSON: Do you feel that there is a spiritual obligation to sexual relationships, and if so, what price do we pay if we don't live up to it?

MAILER: Well, it's always a spiritual obligation. But the trouble with the word spiritual is that we think of churches and priests and clergymen. I do think there's a spiritual demand in love, however, more a demand than an obligation. Love asks that we be a little braver than is comfortable for us, a little more generous, a little more flexible. It means living on the edge more than we care to. Love is always in danger of being the most painful single emotion we can ever feel, other than perhaps a sudden knowledge of our own death. La Rochefoucauld has that wonderful remark that half the people in the world would never have fallen in love if they had not heard of the word. I think that most people I know, maybe three-quarters of the people I know, have never been deeply in love.

MICHELSON: Talking about not being deeply in love, have you ever paid for sex, and what is your opinion about hookers and johns and the outright exchange of sex for money?

MAILER: Well, take it at its best. Because at its worst, there is nothing worse than paying for sex, and being thrown a bad, cynical, dull fuck by a whore who either has no talent, or no interest in you, or feels you don't deserve anything better than you are getting. That's one of the worst single experiences there is. On balance, counting the number of times I've had good sex in whorehouses and bad, I could almost do without it. But, you know, living fifty-eight years, you end up with a lot of experiences. I've had a few extraordinary times in whorehouses, which I'll have to write about some day, too. So I wouldn't put it down altogether. It's just that it's immensely more difficult, I think, to have good sex with a whore unless you're oriented that way.

There are a lot of guys who are not homosexual, but grow up in a male environment. They have four brothers, or they're jocks, or just live in a male environment as so many smalltown kids do. They're less comfortable with women, and so if all their buddies have been plowing the same broad — and I use these two words, "plowing" and "broad" because that's the way they're looking at it; they're really looking upon it as a field — the fact that they're going to be mixing their semen with the effluvia of their buddies is tremendously aphrodisiacal to them. So sex can be intense for men in whorehouses. It doesn't mean that they're homosexual; that's too quick a jump to make. What it does mean is that they have to cut that close to the edges of homosexual experience in order to get a real send-off.

MICHELSON: You said to Buzz Farbar in a *Viva* interview that you couldn't afford to begin — this is a quote, you "couldn't afford to begin to get homosexual because God knows where it'd stop." Do you feel that homosexual impulses should be repressed, and quite candidly, have you ever experienced such impulses?

MAILER: I've never experienced them dramatically. I've never ever said, "Oh, I got to have that boy," or "I've got to go to bed with that man." I feel it's been a buried theme in my life but a powerful one. It creates its presence by its absence. I don't think you can be an artist without having a . . . well, let's try to define the elements a little.

There are homosexuals who have essentially male experience and others who have female. In a funny way, the difference between male and female in homosexuality is more marked, probably, than it is between men and women. When a man and a woman make love, they can take turns: one more aggressive, then the other — there are many ways in which a woman can almost literally fuck a man. The woman can be active, the man passive, then they reverse it. Many good sexual relationships consist of that back and forth. Nothing like the dialectic when you get down to it. But, in male sexuality, there is a tendency to either be top or bottom, back or front. They have an expression: Did you do it or were you done to? There is much more identification with whether you're going to be the male or the female in the relationship.

Now, I think all humans are born with a man and a woman in us. I think that's self-evident: we have a mother and a father, and to the degree that the mother is female and male both, we have a female-male component in ourselves. In turn, through our fathers we have a male-female side to ourselves. At the least, two sexual systems within us, psychically, at any rate. I also suspect male artists have more of a female component to their nature than the average male. I think that's why I've always stayed away from homosexuality. I suppose I felt the female side of my nature would have been taken over by homosexuality to a degree that would have been repulsive to me. What you get down to is that it's a man who's doing it to you. And the man in me does not wish to be dominated by another man, not that way, not that way.

Now the homosexuals whose masculinity comes out through homosexuality are very proud of themselves. I mean, those homosexuals will say, "We're more men than the average heterosexual. The average heterosexual makes love to a woman who is physically weaker than himself. But we men, we go out and we stick it in the asses of men who can fight back, we're real men." In prison, there's great pride in who's doing it to who, because finally what you may be doing is putting it up the ass of a killer — which would give me pause, I'll tell you that. So, when I was younger, I used to cover all these feelings by feeling antipathy toward homosexuals. I don't feel that now. I just think all that is not for me. Any more than becoming a Hindu fakir would be a way of life for me, or going down at the age of fifty-eight to Texas to work in the oil wells, that wouldn't really be a reasonable life any longer.

MICHELSON: A friend of mine who grew up in Puerto Rico said that there the onus is only on the catcher, not the pitcher. Puerto Ricans, he said, didn't consider people who fucked people in the ass homosexuals. They only considered people who got fucked in the ass homosexuals. So that's just a cultural bias.

MAILER: Didn't I say earlier that the difference between the male and female sides of homosexuality is greater than the male and female aspects of heterosexuality?

MICHELSON: As long as the Puerto Rican was in the male role, he was still a male.

MAILER: Certainly criminals, and ghetto people, and tough ethnics do have that attitude, there's no question to it. To some men, active homosexuality doesn't hurt their masculinity; it reinforces it from their point of view.

One thing on which I have a bugaboo is that Women's Liberation keeps talking about rape, rape, rape. So far as I can make out, more men are probably raped every year than women, at least when you get into true cases of rape where it's absolutely against your will. I'll grant that there are many marginal cases of rape between men and women, where the woman rather likes the guy, but doesn't want to do it tonight, and the guy insists, and lo and behold, she ends up doing it tonight. But that's much nearer to lack of moral consent than rape. Women's Lib throws all those cases into rape. If you only count cases of true force, where there's absolutely no desire on the one hand, and absolute determination on the other hand, I'm willing to bet there are more cases of male rape every year than female rape. Because in the prisons, thousands of men are done to every year.

MICHELSON: I know you're now to the right of the Pope on masturbation. But in the past, have you ever masturbated to an erotic photograph?

MAILER: Of course. In adolescence.

MICHELSON: Why have you become so puritanical about masturbation?

MAILER: I'm not puritanical about it. Puritans put people in jail for their activities, or bring social censure against them. I don't go out with a flag and walk it up and down outside certain people's houses . . .

MICHELSON: Ban masturbation!

MAILER: . . . but, God, I happen to believe, just like the nineteenth-century preachers, that the ultimate tendency of masturbation is insanity.

MICHELSON: You think it does lead to insanity?

MAILER: Well, it doesn't lead to it instantly. People can jerk off all their lives and they're not going to go insane. I said the *ultimate tendency* of masturbation is insanity. Now the ultimate tendency of driving a car at 80 miles an hour in a 55-mile-an-hour zone is collision. But there are people who drive at 80 miles an hour until the cops stop them or indeed, never get caught, but neither do they collide. The ultimate tendency remains just that. My point, however, is that left to itself masturbation does not bring you back into the world, it drives you further out of the world. You don't have the objective correlative.

You see, one of the arguments I would bring against pornography, especially the pornography of my adolescence, is that it encourages fantasy and romance. If I had a fault to find with the pornography magazines in general, it would be that they tend to satisfy elements of fantasy and romance. In other words, they don't — let me see if I can find some analogy. If a kid dreams about football as a wonderful game where he is running for touchdowns, and that's all he ever visualizes, he'd have a rude shock, to say the least, the first time he got into an actual game, was dumped hard and had a headache afterward. There's nothing like the first tackle or block you throw to wake you up to one fact: If you're going to love football, you have to love it *with* its punishment. And at that point, loving it that way, you have a profound relation to football. To love with the full awareness of punishment is the nature of profundity. So, to the degree that pornography encourages people to believe that sex is easy, it's harmful. But I can't see this as a social harm, since everything in the scheme of things encourages us to believe that life is easier than it is.

One of the fundamental tenets of this business of selling America, selling modern life, is to present modern life as *nicer* than it is. As an example, you have these ads that show the happiness of dishwashing machines. Well, the nearest I came to have a major fight with my wife was the other night, she'd bought a new dishwasher and the thing smelled of plastic. It had the most hideous smell, that kind of antiseptic odor insane people douse themselves with. You know how certain insane people put sort of an antiseptic perfume on themselves. Ever smell that? That damn dishwasher smelled that way. I went into a rage. I said, "You've just bought part of the grand American scheme to drive us out of the kitchen. This thing stinks so bad that you'll never spend time cooking anything."

STONE: It smelled because it was new?

MAILER: That's what she claimed. But I'm telling you that smell's never going to go away. They're putting the odor in so people will go out and buy TV dinners. That's part of the scheme. That's what McDonald's, superhighways, and all general plastic crap is all about. Everything in the scheme of things drives us toward living in a way we don't want to live.

Pornography, to the degree it's sentimental and romantic, is fudging the issue too, not increasing knowledge, but muddying knowledge.

MICHELSON: Are you against fantasy?

MAILER: Against sentimental fantasy. That, I think, is our introduction to cancer. A ticket to the gulch.

STONE: What sexual fantasies get you hot?

MAILER: I won't get into it for a variety of reasons. Years ago a friend of mine agreed to fill out a sexual questionnaire. He had to go through every girl he'd laid, describe her in detail, what they did, their fantasies, their water sports. After he was finished, for the first time in his life (and this kid was a stud) he was impotent for three months. So one holds onto one's little fantasies.

Actually, I have very few left at this point. As you get older, you need fantasy less and less. Let me put it this way: Fantasy gives resonance to sex so long as it's on the threshold of reality. If two people are making love and play a little game, and pretend they're other people, well, that's perfectly all right. Finally they have to do the acting job. It's not just simple fantasy. But if a man and woman are making love, and the man secretly thinks that he is fucking the Countess Eloise of Bulgaria, and the woman is visualizing a stud from Harlem for herself, then they're in trouble whether they know it or not. Essentially they are masturbating. The ultimate tendency of such love-making is insanity.

MICHELSON: Upper masturbation.

STONE: Then what sexual realities get you hot?

MAILER: Nothing remarkable about it. The innermost parts of the female body exposed, that gets me hot. A fine pair of breasts, a beautiful ass. Hands can get me, not hot, but started. I mean, some women have beautiful hands. It's really not important. To find a woman attractive there has to be some one feature that truly keeps pulling you back. It could be her face, her hands, it could be her toes — you don't have to be a shrimper to love a woman's feet, because it isn't literally the hands or the feet that turn you on. A certain statement about the private nature of that woman's sexuality is in the part of the body that excites you. A breast could be adventurous. That would excite certain men. Others might like a breast that's very domesticated, I mean, men that want to dominate a household are not going to be turned on by a breast that's adventurous. It may turn them on, but it's not going to bring them back again and again 'cause such a breast means trouble to them. Brings out their violent impulses. On the contrary, if they find a woman who's got a gentle, domesticated breast, that'll turn them on because it means they can dominate that woman. And so forth. You can go through the various parts of the body. Every body, in effect, presents a possible lock to our key.

STONE: How can a breast look adventurous?

MAILER: It can suggest that it would be unfaithful to you unless you're very good indeed. (*laughter*)

STONE: Why do you think physical beauty plays such an important part in men's attraction to women, and why does it play such a lesser role in women's attraction toward men?

MAILER: Well, because beauty, finally, is a scalp, no getting around it. When a man goes out with a beautiful woman, he's more respected in the world. I can remember a few ugly women who were attractive to me. Ugliness can be sexually exciting . . . But I will say that I wasn't very happy to be seen in the world with those women. You could say that was demonstrably unfair to them.

Except I'm going to stick at this liberal point. I think there may be — and here we enter into waters that are much too deep for all of us — but it may be that beauty and ugliness are karmic. One reason people are so drawn to beauty is that it speaks of healthy karma, whereas ugliness suggests debts in previous lives that were too hideous to be paid in those lives. So the penalty is worn on the face in this life. Which is why ugly people have such a rage toward God at their ugliness.

MICHELSON: But still, it's much more important for a man to have a beautiful woman than it is for a woman to have a beautiful man.

MAILER: Yeah.

MICHELSON: Please explain the nature of the inequity.

MAILER: Well, I think if you believe, as the more radical Women's Liberationists believe, that the only difference between the sexes is an extra six to eight inches of male skin in a certain place, then it just seems vastly unfair and unnatural. But I happen to believe in the asymmetry of the sexes. The only equality of the sexes comes, I would say, out of the rough balance. Women are strong here, men there. That doesn't mean we can't agree on anything, or that women are not entitled to equality in a thousand ways they do not have it now. Women's Liberationists are not wrong when they say that women've been treated unfairly for centuries. They're right. But that doesn't mean that we're alike.

MICHELSON: Apples and oranges?

MAILER: Apples and oranges are entitled to the same treatment when they're presented to the consumer. But they are still apples and oranges, not one big oraple. Presumably, men and women are entitled to the same treatment before they enter eternity.

MICHELSON: How do you feel about your sexual generation, those people who came of age sexually when you did?

MAILER: We had kind of a nice generation if you're going to look at it from the point of view of sexuality. We were all pioneers. We saw ourselves as breaking ground, as sexually liberated. One of the things that appalls me about Women's Liberation is the way they feel they discovered it. I remember my first wife was tremendously taken with the ideas of Simone de Beauvoir back in 1950. She spent an unproductive year trying to write a book which in effect would have been a precursor of Women's Liberation. She was a Women's Liberationist; I lived with a premature Women's Liberationist.

MICHELSON: Your first marriage.

MAILER: Yes. And one reason our marriage finally broke up was on precisely that. She was a very strong woman. She profoundly resented the female role into which my success had thrust her. You see, when we married, she was, if anything, stronger than me. She was perfectly prepared to go out and work for years in order to make enough money for me to stay at home and write a good many books. And if that happened, we probably would have been a happy couple of that sort, she the strong one, I the gentle one. Then what happened? I become successful so suddenly I got much more macho. My God, nothing like success for increasing the size of your muscle! I literally went from 140 to 180 pounds in one year — it wasn't all fat, it was muscle. I suddenly felt like a strong man. That altered everything between us.

STONE: There is a certain anger I've encountered with friends of mine when I've said that I know you. You approached this anger in *Prisoner of Sex*. I was wondering if you've discovered whether some of their feelings are based on something real?

MAILER: More and more I think the reason they feel this antipathy toward me is not because I am a conventional sexist. Anyone who reads this interview can see this. I don't have simple notions of machismo or anything of that sort — I think the reason is that my ideas about sexuality are more complicated than theirs, and they hate that. They have a very simple idea of sexuality and they want to ram it through. As far as I'm concerned, when they get like that, they're worse than the Communists I used to know in the '40s and '50s. I mean they are totalitarian in this aspect. They do not want deviation from their view of life. Now the only way you can ever learn anything is by deviation from your own point of view of life. You encounter it, you argue with it, you grapple with it, you're convinced by it or you convince it, and you move on.

MICHELSON: You feel like you're dealing with people with blind prejudice?

MAILER: Well, worse. I'm dealing with people with militant prejudice.

MICHELSON: Norman, I'd like to discuss the nature of inhibition, something that interests me. To put it bluntly, why is it that some women like to get fucked in the ass and some women find it distasteful? Some women like to suck cocks, some women don't. It surely is not purely physical.

MAILER: You can't talk about it generally, you just can't. Everything we do sexually is as characteristic of us as our features. The question you ask is truly bottomless. You could say to me, why do some people have noses with an overhang, and why do some tilt up? Why do we respond to these noses in different ways? I could give an answer; I mean, a nose that tilts up often suggests optimism, confidence about the future, fearlessness, but a nose that turns over suggests a certain pessimism about the very shape of things, an attachment to sentiments of doom. You have to ask next: What is the nature of form? Why do curves do these things to us? But in sexuality, you also have to ask which period of one's life are we talking about? Anyone who's lived with a woman for a few years learns that a woman's tastes can change as much as a man's. There are women who detest being fucked in the ass, as you put it — you see, I refuse to use those words myself . . . The woman who wants nothing to do with a phallus in her crack one year is turned on immensely by it another year. I will make one general observation: It's very dangerous to stick it up a woman's ass. It tends to make them more promiscuous. I'll leave that with your readers. They can think about it from their own experience. They can test it out. Those who are scientifically inclined can immediately approach their mate and tool her, if they're able. Then they can observe what happens, watch her at parties, get a private detective, check up on her. So I guess I answered your question: A woman doesn't want it up the ass because she's doing her best to be faithful to that dull pup she's got for a man, and she knows if it blasts into the center of her stubbornness, that's the end of it. She won't be able to hold onto fidelity any longer. That's one explanation. It doesn't have to be true. But you might ponder it.

MICHELSON: Have you ever been surprised by a woman because she seemed very proper outside and then was very wild in bed? Or a wild woman on the outside and still wild in bed? Is there a relationship between inhibition and personality?

MAILER: No royal road to success. (*laughter*) I'm not sure that women have a sexual nature as such. I mean, think of the variation in sexual performance — to go back to that word — you've had over your life. I'm sure you haven't been the same with all women, better with some than others, obviously. With women, I think such changes are even greater. When I was a kid in Brooklyn, we'd walk around muttering, "Ah, she's a lousy lay." You know, sure, she was a lousy lay for A, B, C, and D, then E came along. And she was so good, he couldn't even talk about it.

MICHELSON: Let me ask you your thoughts about Plato's Retreat and other on-premise swing clubs. I don't know whether you've been or not, but you certainly know what it's about. This type of anonymous sexual expression was once exclusively the province of the gay community. Does it mean anything that it's filtered into the heterosexual community? That you can go, on any given night, with your wife and these places are full of friendly people from Queens, Long Island — you know, regular, human people are going there and having their —

MAILER: Regular human people as opposed to what?

MICHELSON: People with unconventional lifestyles.

MAILER: People with conventional lives very often are tremendously drawn to orgiastic sex. That's their artistic expression. That's the way in which they are fighting society.

See, I think if there's any guarantee to America, and I believe there is (I hate to say it because it's used so cheaply by all those people who keep shouting, "Our great America, our great democracy") but I think there may be a greatness to democracy. It rests in the profound wisdom that a society can't expand unless, implicit in it, is the acceptance that people are busy working overtime to destroy the society. By that logic, democracy is more dialectical than Soviet Communism. What we recognize is that if you have a society, then you need people who are working to destroy that society. Out of the war comes a metamorphosis, which ideally will be more adaptive to the nature of a changing historical reality than more totalitarian, monolithic states. So — as I say — one natural, normal, healthy function of people is to fight society. The way in which conventional people often do it is through orgiastic behavior. I mean, Saturday night they have a ball with their friends, who either live next door in the next ranch house, or they drive 300 miles to see some other swinging couple. On Sunday they all go to church together. And they're giggling a little. They're living two lives at once. They were having that ball last night, the four of them, now they're in church together. And nobody's going to know. Some people can only feel a sense of balance and satisfaction, happiness, I might say, if they're living two lives at once. Orgiastic life provides that. Orgiastic life provides a lot of solutions for people. But it is sheer hell for people who are deeply in love. It's almost impossible, I think, to have much orgiastic life if you're profoundly in love with a woman. You can do it, but it takes the edginess in love, and absolutely exacerbates it.

MICHELSON: You've spoken about something totalitarian in people who were proselytizing orgies.

MAILER: The moment there's an attempt to make anything a panacea, then it's totalitarian. Panacea suggests that there's one way to do it. So does totalitarianism suggest that there's only one way. But the cosmos was designed by some divine intelligence who foresaw that if there was only one way to do it, everybody would go there. The world would quickly tip out of balance.

STONE: Have you been sexually pursued by literary groupies? What's it like being fucked as an image rather than a person?

MAILER: Well, I've usually been drawn to women who aren't necessarily that interested in my work. My present wife had read one book of mine before we met. She hardly knew anything about me. It's probably analogous to the poor young rich girl, who wants to be loved for herself and not her money, remember all those movies?

MICHELSON: Sure.

MAILER: You definitely don't want to be loved for your literary fame because you know more about it than anyone else and you know that literary fame has very little to do with your daily habits. I mean, finally you're an animal who lives in a den and goes around, and finally, you know, has to be liked or disliked as an animal first.

STONE: Is jealousy a necessary part of an intense sexual relationship or do you feel that it's a disease?

MAILER: It's a very good question until you realize that you can't answer it. Because you end up with platitudes. It's my general experience that if you don't feel any jealousy at all, a woman will have profound doubt of your love. A little jealousy is marvelously aphrodisiacal, you know that, but real jealousy, when it takes over, is delusional, and has all the dirty pleasures of delusion. Delusion is one of the most profound forms of mental activity. If we have a delusion, we are, in effect, a detective on the scent of a case, picking up clues all over the place. We're trying to bring in the malefactor. So it enables us to go through life with an hypothesis. For some, it is unendurable to live without some hypothesis. So jealousy becomes one of the most satisfactory delusional schemes.

You have an hypothesis: She or he is not faithful to me. Then you study it. You listen to the voice. You check out alibis. It sharpens one's senses. Jealousy gives us a ride we would not have without it. People often come into love with their senses drugged by all their bad habits — I mean, one of my fundamental theses is that virtually everything in American life works to deaden our senses. The proliferation of plastics first. So, given the fact that we find ourselves in a state of love with senses dulled, we have to sharpen them up. Very often jealousy hones that point. Taking off on a delusional trip keens our instincts. We can feel more alive than we were before if we don't destroy too much en route. Of course, being on the receiving end of jealousy can be abominable. It mickey-mouses you. You're always saying, "No, honey, honest, honey, no, I didn't turn around, no, I didn't look!"

Then there's a lighter form of jealousy that is fascinating. It's jealousy as a way of keeping in touch. Once in a while I'll come home and Norris will say, "What were you doing at three o'clock today?" Not that she does this often, but once in a while. I'll say, "Nothing. I don't know what you're talking about." But then I'll remember, somewhere around three o'clock, *probably* it was three o'clock, I was crossing the street, and I noticed a truly attractive woman. Maybe I turned around and looked at her. It's as if this little act flew through the firmament and lodged in my beloved's head. And at three o'clock she turned around at home and said to herself, "What's that son of a bitch up to?" In that way, that kind of jealousy can be agreeable, can even give you a little glow, oh, God, that dear woman is sure tuned in to me. You see, so that was OK.

MICHELSON: Do you think being in love sharpens psychic connections?

MAILER: Sharpens certain connections at the expense of others. It isn't that love is blind. Love has intense, laser-like tunnel vision, you know, which probably would be a closer way of describing the nature of how love sees.

MICHELSON: One other question: Great artists take risks in their work. What's the greatest risk you've taken?

MAILER: I tend to do things that are chancy, but I wouldn't necessarily dignify them with the word risk. Maybe my novel about Egypt is the one that's —

MICHELSON: The one you're working on now?

MAILER: Yes — is the one most filled with risk. What do we mean by risk? Do you mean going wrong in a book? In other words, embarking on a book so ambitious that you can fall on your face?

MICHELSON: Yes.

MAILER: Maybe the book on Egypt qualifies for that.

MICHELSON: One final question. What have you told your daughters and sons about sex?

MAILER: One of my daughters was talking once about losing her virginity, and I said, "Oh, God, don't lose it because you come to that decision. Lose it because you can't help yourself. Because you are so attracted to the guy that it happens." That's the sum of my sexual wisdom. Ah, I don't think she took my advice. (*laughter*)

1981

Prisoner of Success

An Interview with Paul Attanasio

❧

PAUL ATTANASIO: I guess the obvious first question would be: Why another Marilyn book?*

NORMAN MAILER: Well, after the reception, I'm asking myself that question. (*laughs*) I did it because I wanted to, and I thought everybody would say, you know, "Hurrah for Norman Mailer, isn't he a virtuoso?" Instead, they said, "That outrageous slanderer!" I was intrigued with trying again. I never was satisfied with the first book, *Marilyn*. I felt that it had an awful lot to say *about* her but that she never necessarily emerged, she was never a presence. So I wanted to try and do her from the inside — see if I could.

I must say Marilyn fascinates me. She's an angelic witch. There are very few witches who arrive at immense celebrity, very few; the nature is to be secretive. And I've always been fascinated with angels, the idea that certain women have something angelic about them. It's a profoundly sentimental idea, in fact, it's so sentimental it goes beyond being sexist: It's probably — could you say, machoist?

ATTANASIO: I agree with you that it is fascinating. I think one of the problems with the Women's Liberation movement, which I think did a tremendous amount of good, mostly for men —

MAILER: I think that's a good point. I think it did more good for men than for women.

---

* *Of Women and Their Elegance.* Simon & Schuster, 1980.

ATTANASIO: I think a lot of it was harmful in that it tried to flatten the differences, and make things a whole lot less interesting.

MAILER: I think it succeeded in wrecking the Democratic Party. Ever since the Women's Movement came along, there hasn't been a Democratic politician who's dared to open his mouth and let anything more forceful than oatmeal come out.

ATTANASIO: One thing that struck me about the book, though, was that I didn't think it was progressive in the way almost every other one of your books was. I thought that probably no other writer in America could do it, but I didn't think you were doing things that you hadn't done in previous books.

MAILER: Except for entering a woman's mind. I barely tried that before: maybe Elena's letter in *The Deer Park*. I've always been afraid to try. In *The Executioner's Song* I was able to get into a great many women's minds, but I didn't feel I had *done* it — I felt it had come about, you know, just because they were wonderful subjects for interview. And so I'd say that the nearest I'd come before on my own was April's mind in *The Executioner's Song*. Practically everything she said was in interviews, but I had to put it together.

That was the only thing I felt was new in *Elegance*. I confess I wanted to do one book where I wasn't stretching. It had been a big stretch on *The Executioner's Song*, and my book about Egypt is a huge stretch, so huge that I walk around winded most of the time in relation to it. And I thought, "I want a little vacation." And it may be that the book suffers from that.

ATTANASIO: You dismiss the whole fact/fiction debate. Do you think any of it is useful, or just a lot of wind?

MAILER: I think it's a dumb debate. If a novelist can take someone who's a legendary figure and invent episodes for them that seem believable, then they've done something wonderful. There's that meeting between J. P. Morgan and Henry Ford in *Ragtime* — I think it's one of the best chapters in American literature. It told me an awful lot about Morgan and an awful lot about Henry Ford, and the fact that it obviously never took place made it even more delicious. When you know the kind of bias and warp with which historians write their history — they're dealing with 10,000 facts and they select 300 very careful ones to make their case, and call that stuff history when we all know it's fiction. The mark of a great historian is that he's a great fiction writer. Very few novels are ever true works of the imagination — I mean, how many Kafkas have there been?

I'm not trying to avoid the fact and fiction argument to protect myself. There's one thing that did worry me in the book with Marilyn. I invented an episode for her that was possibly more extreme than anything in her life. And that gave me pause; I'm worried about it, I'm still worried about it, I think I'd feel less bad about it if I'd done it with a man. I start thinking, "Well, my God, what if after I'm dead somebody writes about me and they put me in a homosexual orgy, which I've never been in, I would detest that, wherever I'd be." And I wrote it — this'll sound incredibly demented — but I wrote it with the idea that Marilyn, wherever she is, would accept this treatment of her. But it's a large assumption.

So I do have a continuing uneasiness about that part of the book. On the other hand I do feel that there's no portrait without it.

ATTANASIO: As far as I can tell, no major figure has appeared in American fiction to provide the sort of Oedipal relationship that you've said you had with Hemingway, nobody to beat out and admire at the same time.

MAILER: Well, it could be said that, on the face of it, he had more talent than anyone coming afterwards, which I think is true. I think Hemingway *and* Faulkner were immensely talented men. I've always felt that way about Faulkner — he just stands out. Hemingway I've had my ups and downs. But I must say after *The Executioner's Song* I realized how very talented he was.

It's obvious why Faulkner had that huge influence on Southern writers. I think that the only metaphor that you can use is that Southern writers are on a rockface, and at the very top of the climb there's that dreadful overhang, Mr. Faulkner.

Hemingway's different. Hemingway occupied the center in every way, not only coming from the Midwest, but he occupies the very center of writing itself. Anyone who's ever read a newspaper can feel how good a writer he is — he uses a vocabulary that if anything is smaller than the average newspaperman's vocabulary. And he does wonderful things with it. So no matter how serious or superficial a reader you are you sense very quickly that you are in the hands of someone who truly can write well. Then, of course, he wrote about things that are very, very interesting to men. There aren't very many women going around saying Hemingway is a great writer. I'm willing to bet more American women who are good writers have been influenced by Proust than by Hemingway. But for men he's central: the anxieties he feels about being a man cover all our anxieties; it's almost impossible *not* to identify with his work.

I just think that nobody has come along since who occupies as much terrain as he does. There were stages in my life when I had something remotely resembling his ambition, but that man had it from the time he was twenty to the time he died. I think he finally packed it in because he wasn't going to sit around and be the Shah of Iran of American letters.

ATTANASIO: Tom Wolfe suggested in his introduction to *The New Journalism* that journalism has sort of usurped the novel since the mid-'60s.

MAILER: I think it's self-serving of Wolfe to say that, because he's a journalist. I've said a hundred times that I think journalism is easier than novel writing because you know the story. I mean, give me a good story that history wrote for me, and I'm content — all I've got to do then is write it. The difficulty of writing a truly impressive novel is equal to asking a singer of the stature of Pavarotti to compose his own music. Journalism makes opera singers of novelists. We've got the story, now all we've got to do is go in and show our vocal cords.

ATTANASIO: What about Vietnam? Do you think it's significant that great movies were made out of the war, but not great books?

MAILER: I haven't thought about it before. If a great war novel's to be written again — and it may be that the great war novel is a form that's now past, it could come fifty years after the war in Vietnam as *War and Peace* came after the Napoleonic Wars. Because I don't think that war will finally be comprehended until we have that perspective. The Second World War accelerated America into a direction it was trying to get into anyway — America was trying to move from one form of capitalism into another; and the government was trying to get into the act.

Vietnam, however, either injured America permanently, so that we may never be the most important nation in the world again, or it may have been an incredible crucible in which the national character shifted and changed. That perspective awaits us yet. But when it comes, I think there may be some incredible stuff done about it, and we may have great novels about Vietnam. And they may be great the way *War and Peace* was great, because the Napoleonic Wars changed Russia forever.

ATTANASIO: What do you look for in a novel or short story when you read?

MAILER: Well, I look for something that's probably different from what anyone else would. I'm searching for very special little tools that I can add to my toolbox. After all, I've been a working craftsman for thirty-five years, and any mechanic or carpenter who works that long acquires a great many tools. I'll also read for other things — to stimulate my flagging interest in narrative. For instance, I reread all of Chandler last summer because he's got such narrative drive.

ATTANASIO: I think there's got to be a new aesthetic of fiction now, a new generation of writers. Do you have any idea —

MAILER: What the direction will be? I think we're lumbered right now in fiction. There are many too many ideologies that prevail. The women are pleasing the Women's Movement much too much to ever let loose and really write; the men are trying to strike stances; nobody's free of the aftereffects of psychoanalysis yet — there's no confidence among most young novelists that they know more about human nature than psychiatrists. I just read a little bit of Ann Beattie — it's not fair, because I didn't read that much of her — but on the basis of those two short stories, it did remind me that whenever fiction doesn't know where it's going, then there's a tendency to return to the novel of manners. And for a very good reason: Manners are always changing, and it's fascinating how they change, and we can always tell a great deal about society itself if we study manners.

That's the fallback position. But it's a dead end — it gives pleasure, but it doesn't give knowledge. My idea finally is that fiction is a noble pursuit, that ideally it profoundly changes the ways in which people perceive their experience. You know, one Tolstoy, in my mind, is worth maybe 10,000 very good writers.

ATTANASIO: I have an idea that *The New Yorker* is probably the most pernicious single influence on American fiction writers.

MAILER: Well, it is if one would like to see things bust loose. They were a million miles away from Kerouac and Ginsberg when the Beat Movement started. So they're awful at such periods. But on the other hand, they hold the act together when nothing's happening. They're kind of like those actors of the second category who keep repertory companies going forever, and without them there might not be theater.

ATTANASIO: I wanted to talk a little bit about your personal life —

MAILER: Good luck!

ATTANASIO: It just strikes me that whenever I bring you up, people don't say "Oh, I read *Why Are We in Vietnam?*, it's a great book," they say, "Did you see that thing about the marriages? Mailer's up to his old shenanigans." Something like your marriages is used as a lever against your work.

MAILER: It is. I don't argue with you. Every time I appear in a newspaper I injure myself professionally. But I don't think there's anything I can do about it. One of the reasons I'm in the papers all the time is that they just keep using the same people, over and over again. It's a game, and there are something like forty players on the board. If I were in a Tarot deck, I'd be the Fool. I used to keep a stern separation between the public legend and myself, but you know, you get older, and after a while, you start to feel like some old slob in Miami, with slits in his sneakers so his feet won't hurt so much. At that point it's harder to fight the legend.

ATTANASIO: One thing about your life that was distressing to admirers of yours: during the '60s, whenever there was a march on Washington, your name was mentioned, and now it seems that whenever there's a society article, you're mentioned.

MAILER: I'm a novelist and I want to know every world. And I would never close myself off to a world unless it's truly repulsive to me. I don't think it means anything if I go to certain kinds of parties, because society is nothing if not fashion. There've been a few homes that invite me for dinner from time to time. If it comes to the point where there's something to fight for and I'm not fighting for it because I don't want to lose my position in society, then there's something to be concerned about. But what's there to march for these days? I just can't get excited about stopping those nuclear plants — I think they're the enemy, yes, but I don't think they're the real enemy. I think big oil and plastics are.

Suppose the Reagan Administration gets us to the point where we're marching on the Pentagon again, and at that point I'm not marching because that might lose me my ticket at certain dinner parties — then I've turned. But up to that point, my feeling is: "Hey, man, that's my wad you're talking about."

ATTANASIO: I guess I was just wondering how important a part of your life this sort of thing was.

MAILER: What's very important to me is knowing how the world works. I think what ruins most writers of talent is that they don't get enough experience to learn, so their novels always tend to have a certain paranoid perfection which isn't as good as the rough edge of reality. If *The Executioner's Song* had a big effect on people, it was because it wasn't a paranoid work. It had all the rough edges of reality. If I had conceived that book in my imagination, it would have been much more perfect and much less good.

If there's a theme that obsesses me, it's how much of the history that's made around us is conspiracy and how much of it is simple stupid fuckups. And you have to know the world to get some idea of it. You know, how much does the Mafia control, how much do they luck into? How much does the Jewish community affect the mentality of government, and how much are they accused of?

On the other hand, it's very dangerous to live in society too much, because it's a world of very rigid rules. You cannot be yourself completely. There's a marvelous game in society, which is: If you are completely of society, then you're totally uninteresting. If I have any entree at all it's because society is always fascinated with mavericks. Till the point where they'll become bored with me, and then, boom, I'm out. But on the other hand, even as a maverick there are certain rules that I have to obey. If you start obeying those rules past the point where you want to go along with them as part of the game, then you are injuring yourself.

I don't think it's basic to me. For one thing, I could never cut a figure in society the way, say, Truman did. So I don't really think about it that much. I think if I had had these experiences twenty years ago, I might have saved myself a lot of time as a writer.

ATTANASIO: I know you gave speeches earlier in the year for Kennedy. How do you feel about the Reagan victory? Does it scare you? Maybe not just Reagan himself, but the people who put him in office?

MAILER: I think we're going to have the biggest money-grab since the Grant Administration. Beefing up the defense plants is the health of any major economy, no matter how glutted and wasteful it is. You can't go wrong on a war economy for five or ten years. So I think they're going to go in that direction, because it'll solve every problem they've got.

Then they're going to try to increase states' rights; all those lobbyists won't have to run through the tough work of having to push something through Congress, they'll be able to buy up state legislatures. And then the ecology business is going to be a disaster, because there's an awful lot of money to be made if we can just violate nature a little more. So there could be incredible scandals, and if that happens, and the thing looks like it's in danger of falling apart, then that again is a move toward getting more militaristic. The military covers everything. At that moment the trade unions can't beef, and obviously the threat of bringing in martial law everywhere tends to tone things down.

But if it keeps building that way, and the ghettos don't take it passively, we're going to have a hell of a situation.

ATTANASIO: Do you think there'll be that sense there was in the '50s? I know you've said that in the '50s, there was a sense that there was a war going on, for the writers.

MAILER: I think it'll clean up the left a lot; I think they'll start examining themselves. You know, the left has been guilty of overweening vanity for the last twenty years. First the left was too militant and too programmatic and took itself much too seriously and thought it was creating vast revolutions when in fact it was only creating small middle-class revolutions. Then the Women's Movement came along and — I'll say one good thing about it: The Women's Movement did alert us to the notion that women systematically were being brought up to be cowards, and that was onerous. To this extent the men have learned a lot, and the women have learned . . . something. Less than men have. Because we've changed our view of women; I don't think the women of Women's Liberation have changed their view of men, which isn't worth printing anyway. But you know the women on the left have just been abominable, guilty of infantile leftism of the worst sort, as Lenin defined it.

ATTANASIO: Which is — ?

MAILER: Pushing for one's own demands to the exclusion of all else. Refusing to see the total picture, the total need. A great inner discipline, perhaps, within the enclave, but no interface with other leftist disciplines.

I think now, if the left is threatened from the outside, that might be healthy. The '70s have been a disaster period for the left, which culminated in the Carter Administration. The blandness, the lack of ideas that anyone was even remotely willing to die for. I think the left functions best on adversity. But I think we've got to open our horizons. Marx would've been appalled at the narrowness of his followers.

1980

A Brief Exchange

with Anita Eichholz*

~

ANITA EICHHOLZ: You said that the Women's Movement tends to become totalitarian and that you don't like that. Don't you think the male system in America is totalitarian?

NORMAN MAILER: Yes, but I always thought women had more sense than men.

EICHHOLZ: Why is that? Why should women be better than men?

MAILER: Because they have been forced to suffer our brutalities and our stupidities and our dominance and people that are on the bottom should always be smarter than people on top, or there is no hope for humanity.

EICHHOLZ: But you don't get better by suffering.

MAILER: You don't get a better person, but you should get a smarter one. I think that the average black knows more about life than the average white in America. I've never met — this is a remark that I've made before and people think I'm blowing smoke — I've never met a stupid black man. I've met any number of black men I couldn't speak to, who wouldn't talk to me or I couldn't talk to them, but I never met a black who I felt was stupid. Because stupidity is a choice. It's not a choice that black people can afford.

EICHHOLZ: But you can't compare blacks in every respect to women.

---

* This was not an interview but a dialogue in a classroom at the University of Munich.

MAILER: Well, but the women in America do. They say: We are your blacks.

EICHHOLZ: This isn't true in all respects.

MAILER: No, of course not. That's one of the troubles with the Women's Movement. They say a great many things that are not true in all respects but they say it as if it is.

EICHHOLZ: But why can't you answer my question with respect to women? Why should women be smarter than men and do everything better than they and be more clever than they are?

MAILER: There's no reason why they should be better. On the other hand, they should not be worse. Men over the centuries have acquired, willy-nilly, a certain rudimentary sense of fair play. The women have yet to learn it. I think they may. I'm not saying that it is impossible for them. But the Women's Movement over the last ten years has not gained respect among those men who are willing to give it. The general attitude among the women in America by now — I do not pretend to speak for them, it's my impression — is that many mistakes were made ten years ago when the movement first came into prominence, great excesses, and the problem is much more difficult than they ever realized. I think there was a certain optimism, almost a manic optimism, among the women back in the early Seventies. They thought they were going to have a quick breakthrough and change the world very quickly and I think that what they've come to recognize is — and I think this is all to the good — they've come to recognize the profound and serious problems that men who are trying to change the world also have. I think that out of all this we may yet arrive at a certain community of agreement that changing the world is a problem that goes beyond sexual gender.

EICHHOLZ: But you could start with that.

MAILER: You could start with that, but you could start with other notions as well. You could start with the idea that the most evil substance on earth today is plastic and that the way to improve society is to tax plastic heavily and reduce all other taxes. If you could remove plastic from human existence, things might be better because people's senses might be more lively. If people's senses were more lively — for instance, if we were in a room with chandeliers instead of these goddamn fluorescent lights overhead — we might all have a little more communion with one another.

EICHHOLZ: Yes, but that's exactly the problem. The women's question is postponed to all other questions.

MAILER: Well, that's your point of view and I respect it. That the women's question does not have enough prominence. My feeling is that the women have had a huge amount of prominence because the nature of their question was such that television loved it. It made good television — the women having a revolution. But in fact, in America all the women revolutionaries stayed in New York where they were comfortable and safe and very few went down to Texas. It's one thing to be a revolutionary, it's another to be a brave revolutionary. I just say they're not quite as good as they pretend to be.

1980

Waste

An Interview with Michael Lennon

❧

MICHAEL LENNON: Do you think the election of Reagan might clarify the conflict between right and left?

NORMAN MAILER: Well, I've felt for a long time that liberalism is bankrupt. I think it was trying to do something, let's say from Roosevelt on, that was unique in human affairs. It attempted not only to take care of the top, but to lubricate the bottom. After the Second World War, out of the great guilt many Americans felt at what had been done to black people for two hundred years or more, a decision was made to ameliorate the black condition. A part of the surplus now began to go down to the blacks. Of course, it was still not a tenth of the amount that was being wasted at the top. Nonetheless, America had become the first super-society to attempt, on a major scale, to pay off the top and bottom while allowing the middle to support the ends. Of course, the middle had no cause for complaint. They had chosen the middle precisely because security was there. All the same, the onus of paying was on them. So it created vast resentment, and it was kept focused toward the bottom. Corporate capitalism succeeded, I believe, in convincing Americans that the Democratic Party was supporting people who didn't work, and in a sense, that was true. There were a lot of people in black areas and poor white areas who were ripping off welfare. But they didn't make up a tenth of that patch who were feeding off American society at the top. Just think of the needless expense that goes into products that don't need to be surrounded with romantic appurtenances. You know we don't have to fall in love with our soap. Maybe we do have to love our automobile, but we certainly don't have to admire any number of basic products that have no character to distinguish them. Money that could be put into increasing true competitive quality instead goes into contests with other producers to have zappier advertising. All the while, there has been a tacit agreement between black power and liberal power: "You guys (you blacks) keep the ghettos relatively quiet, and the money will keep coming in." Now the American voter has thrown that out. The resentment they've felt for the last ten years — it's been building all through the '70s — is that blacks are getting away with murder, not working and getting too much. Reagan came in on that wave. He said, in effect, "Let's keep all the waste for ourselves."

When I was running for mayor in '69, a number of people took me aside and said, "Look, welfare is the biggest single problem in New York City. The blacks are ripping it off. Why don't you talk to some of them? If you could ever work out a plan that looks like it makes a little sense, it would be your best chance to show people that you are doing something the other candidates are not doing. Maybe you'll have a chance to get into real contention." So Breslin and I went up to Harlem and met some mothers who represented a welfare organization. One black woman got up to speak: "Mrs. Richbucks over on Park Avenue, she says I'm taking my welfare check and riding around in a Cadillac and you know what I say? I say: 'Fuck her.' My Cadillac is five years old and I have a lot of trouble meeting the payments on it, and she's riding around in a brand-new Cadillac. Mrs. Gold-ass over on Fifth Avenue says, Look at her, she's been married four times and she's got eighteen children and is drawing welfare for each one of them. She's ripping off the government, I say, 'Fuck her.' I may be lying about five of those children but I got the other thirteen to take care of, and I been married three times. Mrs. Gold-ass over on Fifth Avenue, she don't have to get married because she's got lovers all over the place and furs and diamond rings." The black woman finally glared at me and said, "We want our share of the waste," I thought, "Madam, your argument is unanswerable." I came back to headquarters and said, "Fellows, we got no welfare program." Because I knew we weren't going to tell black people, "Please stop taking things you're not entitled to," when they knew the rich were skimming ten times as much. I think this is the key problem the Democratic Party has to face. If they are truly interested in having a country where everybody has something roughly approaching equal opportunity. To get there, we have to re-think every aspect of American politics and American life, but not in the old radical way of "Let's rally the unions." I mean that is crap beyond crap. By now, America is one vast middle-class consumer nation. Here in the '80s we've got to get into absolutely new ways of looking at politics. You could begin a purification process that might flush out American politics. For instance, America at this point is glutted with needless products that depend for their existence on advertising. Pure waste. Wouldn't sell without it. Suppose any product that advertises itself has to pay a tax in proportion to its relative budget for advertising? That might open up opportunities for a good small business to grow by word of mouth. The left, instead of paying lip service to small business, and then opting immediately for every big government solution they can find, might recognize that big government is truly the enemy of the people and the secret and ultimate ally of the corporation. The Democratic left could begin to re-form around the concept that the economy can't have more productivity until it flushes its waste.

LENNON: Reagan's going to increase the glut.

MAILER: Oh, I think he is an open invitation to big business to take more of a grab. It staggers me how corporate capitalism is endlessly greedy, even greedier than they need to be for their own good.

LENNON: All the counterculture of the '60s didn't really make a dent in the corporation?

MAILER: No effective dent. The corporation has become more and more powerful, controls more and more. It lowers the real standard of living. We used to have roads where people could have an interesting trip. Now even the most beautiful landscape is rendered monotonous by a superhighway. We put up buildings that are absolutely faceless, without decoration, without character, with flat roofs. They do not exalt us when we look at them, they depress us. Exaltation is also part of our real standard of living. Then we adulterate our food. The average food, not only in America by now, but because we export this crap, the average food all over the world is becoming more and more tasteless, more tortured.

LENNON: TV.

MAILER: TV adulterates human relations. TV does the same thing to human relations that frozen food does to real food. All of this is the blight of corporate capitalism. Corporate capitalism is an incubus on the world quite equal to Soviet Communism.

LENNON: And you say that big government is the enemy of the people?

MAILER: Government bears a resemblance to cell fission. Of a cancerous sort. When a cancer cell can't solve a problem, it divides. That's why they proliferate more quickly than normal cells — they're not equipped to solve problems, only to grow. When in doubt, divide; that's cancer. Government proliferates all the time. It doesn't solve problems.

LENNON: What would you like to hear somebody say on American television that's new?

MAILER: Just once let somebody say we don't have to stand up to the Russians. Let them come here and die of indigestion. Let the Russians attempt to take over America. They will perish. Americans would love the idea of joining an underground. The greatest blow for liberty that's ever been struck would indeed be rung. The Russians would founder on the shores of America. That idea is never discussed in America. Let me suggest the real force of it by showing the opposite. What if the Russians invited us to occupy them? It would exhaust us as a nation.

LENNON: What did you think of John Anderson?

MAILER: I thought he was boring. A third party candidate should be interesting, because he has no responsibility.

LENNON: Do you think there is a chance for a third major party in the United States?

MAILER: I think Anderson created some ground for the possibility. He showed that people were interested in a third party in America, he did show that. To such extent we may honor his name someday. But I thought he was awfully boring.

LENNON: Do you think a lot of people didn't vote for John Anderson because they thought he didn't have a chance?

MAILER: That's always true of a third party candidate. You lose half your vote in the last week. As election day gets nearer, people want their vote to count. There is a fetishism to voting. One wants to be buried in the proper cemetery. So, if you're a third party candidate, you should be interesting. You have no responsibilities, you don't have to worry about losing millions of votes for the wrong remark; you're going to lose them anyway. But Anderson had nothing new to offer. He didn't understand that his simple duty was to be interesting.

1980

The Mad Butler

An Interview with Hilary Mills

HILARY MILLS: Looking back on your career, it seems as if your novel *The Deer Park* was a kind of watershed. It was after that book came out in 1955 that you gradually moved away from the novel and into journalism. What happened at that point in your career?

NORMAN MAILER: I think the watershed book was *Advertisements for Myself*. That was the first to be written in what became my style. I never felt as if I had one until that book, and once I developed the style — for better or for worse — a lot of other forms opened to it.

MILLS: You've mentioned previously that you were smoking a lot of marijuana around this time; do you think this had anything to do with the difficulties you were encountering in your work?

MAILER: No. All it did was consume large tracts of my brain. I was doing to my brain what Barry Goldwater recommended we do to the foliage in Vietnam. I think parts of my head have been permanently sluggish ever since. But I don't think the damage to my head was what was giving me difficulty in writing. It was more timidity. I was a little aghast at what I was trying to do because no one had ever done it before. These days everybody is laying claim to having started the New Journalism. Tom Wolfe has been writing manifestos for the last ten years. But I think if I started any aspect of the New Journalism — and I did — it was an enormously personalized journalism where the character of the narrator was one of the elements not only in telling the story but in the way the reader would assess the experience.

I had some dim instinctive feeling that what was wrong with all journalism was that the reporter pretended to be objective and that was one of the great lies of all time. What this really was, was an all-out assault on *New Yorker* writing, and at the same time I had — as all of us did — a vast respect for *The New Yorker*. So I was a little scared at what I was doing. I thought I was either all right or all wrong. The stakes were high, but by now it's more comfortable to write that way.

MILLS: You also pointed out in *Cannibals and Christians* that after the war American society was changing so rapidly that "the novel gave up any desire to be a creation equal to the phenomenon of the country." Did this have anything to do with your move away from the novel form and into journalism?

MAILER: Well, I wasn't taking journalism that seriously.

The thing that makes the novel so hellishly difficult is that you have to elucidate a story from the material. If you make a mistake then you may not discover it until the book is done and you're looking back on it ten years later. It's very much like chess in a funny way. Good chess players always speak of the best line of continuation. They can analyze a game afterward and replay the points of no return and see whether a knight should have been moved to another square. In the novel, you're left wondering.

MILLS: You've talked a lot about your economic problems in the past. If economic necessity hadn't been a factor in your life, would you have written as much as you have?

MAILER: No. I would have written books that are more literary and more well-rubbed, and I would have spent more time on them.

MILLS: Would all these books have been novels or would you have written journalism anyway?

MAILER: I could have gotten into journalism, particularly with the history we had in the Sixties. I'd never come up with a story of my own that was as good as the things that were happening all through the Sixties.

MILLS: So in a sense there has never been a conscious or premeditated orchestration of your own career; it just happened the way it did?

MAILER: Yes. I've always been reacting to the given.

MILLS: There seems to be a kind of tragic irony in American literary life: The youngest writers with the most brilliant first novels are the ones subjected to the most horrendous pressures. How would you say your early success affected you and your work?

MAILER: It changed my life. For a long time after the success of *The Naked and the Dead,* for seven or eight years, I kept walking around saying nobody treats me as if I'm real, nobody wants me for myself, for my five-feet eight-inches, everybody wants me for my celebrity. Therefore my experience wasn't real. All the habits I'd formed up to that point of being an observer on the sidelines were shattered. Suddenly, if I went into a room I was the center of the room, and so regardless of how I carried myself, everything I did was taken seriously and critically. I complained bitterly to myself about the unfairness of it until the day I realized that it was fair, that that was my experience. It's the simplest remark to make to yourself, but it took me ten years to get to that point.

Then I began to realize the kind of writing I was going to do would be altogether different from the kind of writing I thought I would do. After *The Naked and the Dead* I wanted to write huge collective novels about American life, but I knew I had to go out and get experience and my celebrity made it impossible. I then began to realize that there was something else that I was going to get which hopefully would be equally valuable, and that was that I was having a form of twentieth-century experience which would become more and more prevalent: I was utterly separated from my roots. I was successful and alienated and that was a twentieth-century condition. This went into all my work after that in one way or another and will go on forever because by now I suppose I can say that kind of personality interests me more than someone who is rooted.

MILLS: Do you ever think of an audience when you write?

MAILER: No. I used to have a much clearer idea of who I was writing for — certain friends, certain intellectuals, certain critics, a clearer sense of the kind of audience I wanted out there and who they might be. That was in the Sixties, but in the Seventies there was a stretch where I really didn't know who I was writing for. You go in and out of fashion and your sense of who you're writing for goes in and out of focus. I must say with my Egyptian book I've gotten to the point where I don't care. I wouldn't have a clue who's going to like it. You get old enough and realize there are no literary gods left. That's not bad; there's something demeaning about being in awe of a critic.

MILLS: Is your concentration different when you work on a novel from when you work on journalism?

MAILER: The novel is much more demanding physically. I've found that I can't do serious writing without getting into a depression. The depression is a vital part of the process because, to begin with, it's dangerous beyond measure to fall in love with what you're doing while you're doing it. You lose your judgment and you lose it for the simplest reason — that the words, as you're reading them, are stirring you too much. The odds are, if they're stirring you too much, they are going to stir no one else.

MILLS: Are you one of those writers who build a book painstakingly from page one or do you like to get the material down and go back and revise?

MAILER: I'm not happy if I feel that what's behind me is wrong or needs work. I tend to build my books on the basis of what I have already. I never have a master plan for the entire book. Every time I have — and when I was younger I used to sit down and write out a complete plan for a book — I never wrote the book. Even with *The Executioner's Song* where, after all, I knew the story in great detail, I was very careful not to be versed in too many details of the story way ahead. In other words, I tended to do my research let's say 100 pages ahead of where I was because I wanted to keep the feeling that I didn't know how it was all going to turn out. I wanted to have the illusion that I was inventing each little detail as if I were writing a conventional novel.

MILLS: Do you ever show your manuscript pages to someone while a work is in progress?

MAILER: Oh sure. I do it the way I box: I pick my sparring partners carefully. Usually I'll box with people who are so good that I'm in no danger of being hurt because they consider it obscene to damage me. Or I'll box with friends where we understand each other and are trying to bring out the best in each other as boxers. The same thing with an early stage of a manuscript. I'd no more dream of showing it to someone like John Simon than I would of carrying a kite to the Brooklyn Bridge and jumping off. But I'll show it to Norris or to Bob Lucid, who is a great friend of mine, or to Scott Meredith, my agent.

MILLS: You've worked on a number of other books while writing your big novel. Do you ever find it hard to get back in sync with the novel after doing these other projects?

MAILER: I've often said that this Egyptian novel is nicer to me than any of my wives. I leave it for two years and come back and it says, "Oh you look tired, you've been away, here let me wash your feet." I've been able to go back to it without trouble every time so far. But a novel is very much like that mythological creature: a good woman. You can't abuse her forever. So I think I've finally got to finish the Egyptian novel. The time has come.

MILLS: What is it about?

MAILER: It takes place in the reign of Ramses IX who was pharaoh in the twentieth dynasty. The period is 1130 B.C. That's just the first novel. I'm two-thirds of the way through, and it's 1,000 pages long so far. The second novel will take place in the future and a third novel will be contemporary. I've got a tricky way of tying them up, but I'm not going to talk about that.

MILLS: Can you just say what the original inspiration for the book was?

MAILER: I thought I'd take a quick trip through Egypt. At one point I wanted the novel to be picaresque and have a chapter on Egypt of antiquity, a chapter on Greece, and a chapter on Rome just to show how marvelously talented I was to be able to do all these things. So I dipped into Egypt and never got out. I'm kind of sluggish when you get right down to it.

MILLS: Your work is totally unique, but do you see yourself as a direct descendent of any particular literary line?

MAILER: My taste and my loyalties are all in separate places. My loyalties are to people like Dreiser and Farrell and maybe Steinbeck and Wolfe — all the people who were writing about working-class and lower middle-class people. They were the ones who first got me excited about writing. On the other hand, my taste quickly inclined toward Hemingway and Faulkner and Fitzgerald and I learned many things from them that I didn't from the other bunch. Then, in a way, my actual influences are so peculiar. Henry Adams, for instance, obviously had a vast influence on me but I never knew he did until I started to write *The Armies of the Night*.

MILLS: Are you in the habit of socializing a lot with other writers?

MAILER: I think the literary world is a dangerous place to be in if you want to do an awful lot of writing because it's almost necessary to take on airs in order to protect yourself in that world. In a way you can't handle yourself skillfully unless your airs are finely tuned. Capote has a wonderful set and walks around like a little fortress — at least until lately. There are starting to be some cracks in the wall.

Hemingway committed suicide working on those airs. He took

the literary world much too seriously and he's almost there as a lesson to the rest of us: Don't get involved in that world at too deep a level or it will kill you and kill you for the silliest reasons: for vanity and because feuds are beginning to etch your liver with the acids of frustration.

MILLS: On the other hand, you've put almost as much creative energy into your public performing self as you have into your work. Do you think that public self has helped or hurt your work?

MAILER: It's probably helped my mind and hurt my work. I think I've had the kind of experience that made me equipped to deal with certain kinds of problems that a writer who's more serious about keeping to his study and not venturing out too much — or certainly not venturing out on quixotic ventures — would not have had. I think I have an understanding of the complexity of the world that I wouldn't have if I'd stayed at home. I would have tended to have a much more paranoid vision of how sinister things are. Things are sinister but not in the way I used to think.

MILLS: It's interesting that in your latest books, *The Executioner's Song* and *Of Women and Their Elegance*, Norman Mailer is conspicuously absent as narrator. Is this a conscious attempt on your part to get away from the autobiographical mode?

MAILER: I think I've worn out my feeling that that was the style in which to keep writing. It was so difficult for me to arrive at my own style — I didn't start with an identity. I forged an identity through my experience. Because of that, I think it was easier to give up that style when the time came. I didn't feel as if I were giving myself away.

And then I've always felt as if the way people react to me is not to me but to the latest photograph they've seen of me. So I can change the photograph and have the fun of observing the reactions. The devil in me loves the idea of being just that much of a changeling. You can never understand a writer until you find his private little vanity and mine has always been that I will frustrate expectations. People think they've found a way of dismissing me, but, like the mad butler — I'll be back serving the meal.

1980

An Author's Identity

An Interview with Michael Lennon

&

MICHAEL LENNON: To what do you attribute your ability to move from style to style?

NORMAN MAILER: Some writers have a powerful sense of identity. I think the best American example might be Henry Miller. Hemingway too. Faulkner, Thomas Wolfe. Then you get to people like Steinbeck who kept changing his identity with every book he did. I could add myself or Ed Doctorow as other good examples of this second category. I suppose our personality becomes an index to us of how the world is changing. So the act of writing serves us differently than it does Hemingway or Miller. For them, writing works as an assertion of their existence.

LENNON: Picasso went through many styles and it's been attributed by some to his various marriages. Is that true in your case to any extent? Have your relations with your families had a major impact in some underground fashion?

MAILER: Picasso did work in a new vein for every wife. I could say the same about myself up to a point. I suppose I've written a different book with every wife but then I think you become a different man in each marriage. On the other hand, Miller was married many times and that did not change his identity.

LENNON: So what is the crucial difference between you and Miller?

MAILER: Some people are born with clear roots. They know exactly where they came from and who they are and what they are, but the world is mysterious to them. I've always been the opposite —

sensitive to the world and forever in the course of discovering who I am and what I am.

LENNON: Well, I was also going to say you and Miller are both from Brooklyn and Miller has written some about his early life there. You've said your childhood never interested you very much. You didn't really want to write about it. Could it be that you had no sense of reacting against your childhood the way Miller reacted against his German bourgeois roots? What did he say, "My family were Nordic, which is to say idiots." Of course, you had close ties with your family. You still live there. But you never were reacting for or against Brooklyn. Maybe you were freer to move than Miller, in a sense?

MAILER: Well, I was close to my parents. I didn't have to break away. I never had a sense of fighting my way clear. In fact, the outside world was much tougher. Maybe the difference is right there. Someone like Miller had to establish his identity very early in life. If he didn't, a large part of him would have been ruined for any kind of serious effort later in life. I expect this is true for people who grow up in hostile families — they must establish their identities early. So there is often a rock-hard quality to the personality. Hemingway may have had subtler problems in his family, but he also had to establish his identity. Whereas my mother and my father treated my sister and myself as important people. At home, we were the center of their universe. It was the outside world that was difficult. So I was always terribly alert to the street and took the family hearth for granted. I was free to indulge myself there.

LENNON: You've said that some of your best writing comes out of your worst periods and that you sometimes have to go through the bends to accomplish what you want.

MAILER: I'm a little uneasy when writing doesn't come hard. It's better for me when I have to forge the will to do it on a given day. I find looking back, and I can't even tell you why, that on the days it was very hard, but I finally did succeed, and the same occurred next day and the next and the next, each day writing against great resistance in myself and finishing in great depression, that those became the best things I did. *The Armies of the Night* was written in a towering depression. I did it in two months and those were some of the worst weeks in my life. I would come home each night and think it was terrible.

LENNON: You said that when you were attempting to get started on

Armies, you finally tried the third person and it worked for you. Was that a release of some pressure?

MAILER: No, it merely shifted the pressure. On the one hand, it seemed interesting to speak of a protagonist named Norman Mailer, on the other it was odd. I remained uncomfortable with it for quite a period. I'd say I was halfway into the book before I got used to it. It took me longer than any reader. You may remember how the style felt when you started reading the book.

LENNON: It was a shock.

MAILER: It's a very funny way to look at oneself.

LENNON: Nevertheless, it was like an old shoe by the time you got rid of it.

MAILER: Yes, by the time I was done, I missed it so much I kept going back in book after book. It never worked as well again.

LENNON: I think you said in *The Fight* that you were getting tired of that style. Is that correct?

MAILER: I got less and less interested in myself. In *The Armies of the Night* I was a true protagonist of the best sort, which is half-heroic and three-quarters comic. That makes for a marvelous protagonist.

LENNON: Like a Stendhal hero?

MAILER: No, no. Nothing like. Nothing so large.

LENNON: No, but still, you had a success and you had a failure, you were on top of it, you were sick of yourself. That's a little bit like Julien Sorel, I think.

MAILER: Except he had this vast project. He was going to become one of the mightiest men in France. All I wanted to do, if you remember, was get to a dinner party that night.

LENNON: I always think of *The Armies of the Night* as a nineteenth-century novel.

MAILER: There is no sex. In that sense, it's a nineteenth-century novel. It's courtly, it's deliberate, it's amused with its time and place. It's taken for granted that its characters are all very fine and substantial people. We know it's going to turn out well in the end. I suppose it has the restrained merriment of the early nineteenth-century picaresque novel. I guess I have to agree.

LENNON: Do you think that you can influence society in some way by writing? Or change society?

MAILER: When I was young, I used to believe you could do it with one book, apocalyptically. Now I know one has very little effect. You can't even measure the results of your books.

LENNON: Do you worry about bruising the readers' sensibilities ever?

MAILER: Anyone who worries about whether they are going to hurt somebody's feelings by their work is no more a writer than a surgeon who would say to himself, "In making this incision I'm going to give this young woman a scar on her belly that could injure her love life for the next thirty years." The surgeon says, "Scalpel, nurse," and makes the cut. He may be right or wrong in the need for the operation, but he keeps a certain insensitivity to other parts of the context. Writers also have to have their own kind of blindness. They can't say to themselves, "This portrait of my good friend is going to scar him terribly." If they feel that, they can't write. Indeed, a great many young writers can't. They think of all the people they're going to hurt, or those they're going to make enemies of, and the retribution that will come, and it doesn't seem worth it to them. There has to be something a bit maniacal about a young man or woman who wants to write. He has to be willing to get that book out no matter how many psychic corpses are left en route, or who is coming after him later.

LENNON: But what sort of responsibility do you have?

MAILER: Never to take the immediate advantage. Never to cash those easy checks. It's very dangerous when you are writing to milk it, to say to oneself, I have a prize cow and the price of milk is high now. I'm going to get every last bit of milk out. You have to be very careful of that. Writing may be an instinctive process, but it's not always clear. You often feel no more than a dull pressure from your instinct to go here or go there. You have to try to listen to the faint voice that tells you how to stay true to the work. Very hard to do. A writer's open to every pressure to take the immediate advantage, whatever it is. We all do in various ways.

LENNON: I think Faulkner said at one point, "A good book is worth a thousand old grandmothers, a thousand old women. And if it were necessary to get rid of the old grandmothers to write a good book, then it would be well worth it." Do you agree with that?

MAILER: No, a thousand is too many. Three or four, maybe.

LENNON: Do you believe that a movie has more possibilities to influence modern people than literature?

MAILER: I think good movies are more likely to reach deep feelings in people.

LENNON: Why? Because it's visual?

MAILER: Because movies are more primitive, I would argue, than literature. Film directs itself to more primitive states of consciousness. People who can't read get profound reactions out of movies. I would also say that to the degree that film reaches us in a precise way, it's no good. Film is best when ambiguous. A truly good film will affect two people profoundly, but they'll argue for hours over the message. One might say it is a satire, the other, a tragedy. That's as it should be. Film should reach way inside the psyche and prove truly disturbing. One person can go through horror watching a film, another person laugh their head off. That's good film. Bad film is when everybody laughs on cue. Then they are being manipulated. They have merely entered the engines of manipulation of the great institutions.

LENNON: You talk a lot about manipulation. Is there anything in life that is not in some sense manipulation?

MAILER: Yes. An existential situation.

LENNON: Doesn't everybody manipulate somebody else?

MAILER: If I'm manipulating you and you're manipulating me, that's interesting. That has elements of the game in it. One of us wins, the other loses. But at least we're both doing it on relatively fair terms. When you have huge institutions manipulating us, it isn't fair. Fair play, that's all I ask for.

LENNON: Well, you call yourself an existentialist. You speak of returning to the instinctual self. Yet you take notice of habit, discipline, even pretense and compromise as sort of civilized qualities that are more or less necessary. I'd like to know how one can be an existentialist in the modern world.

MAILER: You're asking me a small question. (*laughter*) To begin with, habit and discipline are absolutely necessary to serious projects. That doesn't mean we can ignore the fact that the habits which enable us to be productive are dangerous to our psyche. They keep us from living existentially. Now, when I say existentially, I don't mean that every day we must jump from the roof of one building to the roof of another. Although this is certainly as existential an experience as one could look for. Especially if the jump is at the very limit of our ability to leap. If we do not know whether we're going to be able to make the jump successfully, that would be a pure existential experience. We're going to feel a great rush of adrenaline and happiness if we complete the leap, or know disaster and death if we don't. Obviously, if I speak of living counter to one's habits, I don't mean jumping across the roof every day. However, it may be that one has to leap across that figurative roof once a month, or once a year, or whatever one's inner rhythm is. If one uses discipline to accomplish serious projects in one's life, there comes a point where one becomes a slave of the habit, and one must look then for an existential encounter. But the idea is not that we all go out and climb the Matterhorn every Saturday. It may be that someone who is timid and gentle and reflective and would much rather spend his or her life reading books can still have an existential life. They need only think seriously of climbing the Matterhorn once, or trying it once, and that's enough. For some people, one existential experience is enough nourishment for ten, twenty, thirty years. Other people, like U.S. Marines, need existential experience three times a night. I'm not a bigot about these matters. I don't insist that everybody live the same way.

LENNON: Who would you today consider to be major American authors from your personal perspective? And why?

MAILER: There are probably twenty American authors who if you asked "Who are the major American authors?" would name one writer first — themselves. John Updike would say John Updike, Bellow would say Bellow.

LENNON: What would Norman Mailer say?

MAILER: Norman Mailer, you may depend upon it, would say Norman Mailer. We have a funny situation at present in American letters. There are no giants around. Once we had Hemingway and Faulkner. Now, we're all like spokes in a wheel. You cannot ask, "Who is the major spoke?" Each spoke will reply, "So far as I can feel it, I am the only one."

LENNON: But who, besides yourself?

MAILER: There are a lot of writers for whom I have regard. I think Saul Bellow is a very good writer. John Updike is very good, John Cheever . . .

LENNON: What about Gore Vidal?

MAILER: Vidal is a wit and a good essayist. Not a good novelist.

LENNON: What about Truman Capote?

MAILER: Capote is a stylist and a very good writer, but he's not done anything memorable lately. Of course, he's been working for years on *Answered Prayers*. We'll have to wait and see.

LENNON: Any authors who are overrated?

MAILER: It's hard for an overrated writer to last. There are many more literary critics in America than men or women who can make a living writing novels. We've all been examined and re-examined for twenty or thirty years. So it would be hard for someone *ersatz* to get through.

LENNON: What about Pynchon?

MAILER: Either a genius or vastly overrated. I've never been able to read him. Just can't get through the bananas in *Gravity's Rainbow*.

LENNON: Are there any Latin American writers you are familiar with?

MAILER: Well, I think Borges and Márquez are the two most important writers in the world today.

LENNON: Why Borges? In political terms he is a reactionary, is he not?

MAILER: Well, he is a conservative, but . . . I detest having to think of a writer by his politics first. It's like thinking of people by way of their anus. Borges has this magical ability to take plots and turn them inside out. I sometimes think Borges may do in five pages what Pynchon does in five hundred. Which is, he shows us the resources of the novel. He's a magician's magician. In that sense, I love his work.

LENNON: Márquez?

MAILER: Márquez is wonderful. In *One Hundred Years of Solitude* he created not one world but a hundred. I don't know how Márquez does it. People come into his books. . . . In ten pages he'll create a family that has eighteen children and they go through ten years, and you know every one of the children, and all the events that occur in their life. In ten pages, I have all I can do to get around one bend in the Nile.

1980

Writers and Boxers

An Interview with Michael Lennon

MICHAEL LENNON: Writers, I've heard you say, are a little bit like athletes. And then you said, you never question your instincts. I question your premise. Aren't athletes really very disciplined people?

NORMAN MAILER: Well, I make remarks off the top of my head that have a kernel of truth. Then I have to think about it afterwards. I believe what I actually said was that when it comes to decide which book I'm going to write next, I generally follow my instincts. But not in everything. Why, if I did, I would end up in jail. I think athletes go through their own particular drama. They tend to trust their instincts for a long time — at least the instincts of their body. When they can't, in other words when they follow their deepest instincts and lose their game, they're in more trouble than us. I think athletes first come into contact with despair when their instincts fail them. So with all these amendments, I'll still support the remark.

LENNON: I'm assuming again that instincts are connected to the unconscious in some way. Why can't the unconscious be as error prone as the conscious?

MAILER: You know the famous story of Shelley? He rushed up to a mother, seized a two-month-old infant out of her arms, held up the infant and said, "Babe, speak. Reveal your immortal truth!" He believed the infant was born knowing everything. Like Plato — he was a great Platonist at that point, was Shelley — he believed that the education you receive when you're young obfuscates the instinctive knowledge with which you're born. Then you spend the rest of your life trying to unmake that education. I also believe we're born with a profound appreciation of the universe and lose it in the first few years of our life, then spend the rest of our time trying to gain it back. By the age of six, the school system makes certain we lose it. I don't think this is so evil. It is rather in the nature of things. It was intended that way. We're supposed to lose it and regain it. I think it is impossible to conceive of any real achievement in knowledge without that fall. Because if knowledge is something we receive merely by opening ourselves to it, well — in the West, we can't conceive of that. Most of us find something repellent about Hindu philosophy. It's the idea that you receive wisdom without a Faustian effort. The more you give yourself to the universe, more passive you become, the closer you will be to the secrets of existence. This is profoundly repellent to the Western mind. We feel you get to the kernel of real secrets by smashing the shell. That's the way we want it. It's what we're built to do.

LENNON: Like Melville peeling away the layers of the onion to reach the inmost center?

MAILER: Well, if you're going to peel the layers of the onion, I think we even secretly believe it helps if you cut off a finger or two while peeling. But you say why do *I* trust *my* instincts? Because like a young professional athlete, I never had to think about earning a living until the last ten or fifteen years. From the time I was twenty-five, I knew I was probably going to have enough money to be a writer the rest of my life, and so I could form a habit of consulting my instincts. Most people don't have the leisure to do that. When you have a nine-to-five job, you can't do much with your instincts because your work is a continuation of the very education that buried the instincts in the first place. Which is another reason why young professional athletes are so different.

LENNON: If you had the advantage as a young man of money coming in, at the same time you had some struggles with shifts in your fame and reputation, didn't you? You were twenty-five and . . .

MAILER: I went through the bends. I find an analogy between my own experience and certain boxers. Occasionally you find a prizefighter like Leon Spinks, who becomes champ before he knows whether he can really fight or not. That's terrifying. It happened to me with *The Naked and the Dead.* I can understand what Spinks went through afterward. I mean all that idiotic behavior after he beat Ali and won the championship came from the fact that he wasn't ready for it at all. He didn't know whether he was just a main-event fighter in a small club, or champion of the world. So he lost all sense of who he was. If you don't have an identity, it's very important to have established elements you can refer to. It's not enough to say to yourself, "I'm Heavyweight Champion of the world," it helps more if you can also say, "Yes, and I beat Joe Frazier, George Foreman and twenty-two other tough guys." Spinks could only say, "I beat Muhammad Ali, I don't know if that's because I am very good, or he is very old." It has to create a double sense of identity. Every time you have a thought about yourself, you have to refer to two separate identities: the Champ and the Fraud. Your psychic economy begins to work twice as hard.

LENNON: After having so much success with *The Naked and the Dead* you felt you were a false champion?

MAILER: Well, I felt two ways at once. On the one hand, I believed my reviews, on the other I knew *The Naked and the Dead* had been influenced by a great many writers who were better than me. By Hemingway, Farrell, Steinbeck, by Tolstoy, by Thomas Wolfe, by Dreiser, very much by Dos Passos. In a certain sense it was not my own book. These literary influences had flowed through me. I also had to digest the experience of being at war. I hadn't been a very good soldier. If you took a company, in my case a short-handed cavalry troop of one hundred men, maybe seventy-five or eighty soldiers could put up a tent better than me. So I was a bit of an impostor. On the other hand, I had all these wonderful reviews. There were times when you could think it was the greatest book written since *War and Peace.* Given all that, I had to carry two views of myself. Same with Spinks. He needed two halves of his mind to receive every compliment. One half said, "You're wonderful," and the other was always telling him: "These people are lying to you." That's the nature of obsession. We feel two ways about one question. So obsessions tend to paralyze, or flake you out.

LENNON: You've compared yourself to Spinks. I've also heard you call yourself in an interview the Ezzard Charles of Literature. I thought you were being enormously modest.

MAILER: No, I'd still say that. Compare the true stature of Hemingway and Faulkner to writers like Bellow and Cheever and Updike and myself, name eight or ten writers who might be the best writer in America now, John Barth, Bernard Malamud, Pynchon, Algren, go through the list. Name after name. Out of twenty people, none begin to have, myself included, the stature of Hemingway and Faulkner. In that sense, I'd say to anyone who says I'm the most important writer in America today, well, if I am, I'm still the Ezzard Charles of the heavyweight division.

LENNON: You don't think Hemingway's reputation has slipped in the last ten years? People begin to take a close look at his writing and yours and Pynchon and Bellow? You, Pynchon and Bellow are the three I hear.

MAILER: Well, I don't know. We're all vastly more complex in our preoccupations than Hemingway. But I have to tell you that after I wrote *The Executioner's Song*, I went back and looked at Hemingway again. Cause now I was writing in a simple style. And his style *is* remarkable. The more I know about writing, the more of an achievement Hemingway's style becomes to me. I know his flaws inside out. I've loved and hated him as if he were my own father for years. There is so much he did for one, so much he didn't do. Truly the relationship you have to him is as a father. But he is a remarkable writer. His sense of the English language, I'd say, is virtually primitive in its power to evoke mood and stir the senses.

LENNON: What do you think he would think of *Executioner's Song*?

MAILER: He'd hate it and say, "That is bad Hemingway!" He'd loathe the book. But you know, he was a prick, let's face it.

LENNON: Who would you compare Ali to as a writer?

MAILER: Ali is very much like Hemingway if you're going to look for a parallel. First of all, he dominated his division entirely. Second of all, Hemingway, like Ali, put in a considerable apprenticeship. He just didn't become famous, he spent a number of years writing short stories and working on newspapers. He had not had a tremendous amount of experience before he became prominent, but it was more than people realize. Ali also had a number of tough fights before he beat Liston. Then, like Hemingway, he remained champion for a long, long time and kept dominating his division. Very much like Hemingway, very vain in the way Hemingway was vain. Couldn't bear competition, nor the idea that anyone around him might be remotely as good as he is. I think there is a wonderful study to be made about the similarities between Ernest Hemingway and Muhammad Ali. They come out of that same American urgency to be the only planet in existence.

To be the sun. It goes right back to Egypt. A thousand gods but only one sun.

LENNON: Ali's later career isn't quite as brilliant as his early career. Isn't the same thing true of Hemingway?

MAILER: Roughly true. But Ali still did something Hemingway never quite did. After Ali got old, he still won a couple of great fights. He beat Foreman when he was already over the hill. Foreman was an awesome fighter at the point they met. It's one of the great fights of all time because the weaker man won through vast skill and guile and artistry. Plus a dazzling display of guts.

LENNON: Hemingway, at the end, didn't make the big knockout, to use that metaphor, in his later books.

MAILER: No, he did not.

LENNON: I think you once said that one of the best things Hemingway wrote in his later career was the *Paris Review* interview.

MAILER: Yes, that was the best. That, and *A Moveable Feast.*

LENNON: I'd like to go back to *The Naked and the Dead.* I don't think anyone can deny the brilliance of Hemingway in terms of style. But Hemingway could never write a book like *The Naked and the Dead* in which you're talking about fascism coming to America, technology, and the kinds of themes you have dealt with over the past thirty years.

MAILER: I didn't say Hemingway was brighter than I was. I just said he writes better.

LENNON: But that's not the same as saying his talent is better.

MAILER: Well, I think it is. You can have marvelous character actors like Charles Laughton who could play just about any part. Then you get someone like Marilyn Monroe who, in the technical sense, has a small talent. But she can come out and hold a mandolin in her hand and play a little ditty and wonderful things happen. Let's take an example we would argue about less. In the technical sense, there were limitations, I suppose, to Charlie Chaplin. Any number of actors can do a credible imitation of Charlie Chaplin, and, in addition, play fifty roles Chaplin would never go near. Yet we could never argue that they were greater than Chaplin. Even though they might achieve ninety-five percent of him in an imitation, Chaplin plucked a nerve in us that very few artists reach. What great artists do is so profound, you don't debate with it. Ditto, great athletes.

1980

Literary Ambitions

An Interview with Michael Lennon

❧

MICHAEL LENNON: Norman, once or twice when you were asked which of your books you liked the most, you said, "Oh, I don't know. They're like my children. One day I like one more than the other." Yet this analogy breaks down if you believe that a writer must excel in the art of becoming. Don't you see your books as indices of your growth? Or, do you really agree with E. M. Forster that a writer's works are totally distinct tasks, separate from each other? Like children?

NORMAN MAILER: The advantage of being my age is that you can end up agreeing with everyone. What Forster said is true. On the other hand, I go along with you. It's nice if your books can be looked at as indices of growth. I'm just not certain my work has developed that way. I know a great many people would say that *The Executioner's Song* is my best book. And maybe I'd even agree with them. That doesn't mean it shows the most growth. It might present the most digestion. Maybe, I had assimilated my craft at that point, but I wouldn't take it necessarily as a great indication of growth.

LENNON: The best books of George Orwell were usually about things he despised. Are you like Orwell in this respect?

MAILER: I'm drawn to writing about subjects that I feel comfortable with on the one hand and very uncertain of, on the other. For instance, with *The Executioner's Song*, I felt I understood Gilmore's desire to be executed. It seemed to me that if I were in such a situation, I would also want that. It's very real to me that your soul can die before your body. So I felt I can write about this man in a way other people can't. On the other hand, I knew very little about prison, knew nothing about Utah and absolutely nothing about the particular circumstances of Gilmore's life. That was a good balance for me. Let me put it an altogether different way. Years ago, I was considerably taken with how you never know the sure meaning of a Latin sentence until you hear the last syllable of the last word. In Latin if you want to say, "I drink poison from the glass," you can put it in any order you wish. For example: "Poison from the glass drink I." Then the listener wouldn't know who took poison until "drink I" is spoken. That means people had to be alert. It was very easy to trick your neighbor. Now the Romans were the first nation to live consistently in terms of world conquest, and perhaps there was a certain unconscious conspiracy to construct the language that way. So that only the people who were most alert, most unscrupulous, most tricky, and most concerned with getting their way would be adept in the tongue. It was, goes my hypothesis, a language for people seeking power and ready to use all means to obtain it. With that as a key, assuming my key is correct, Latin might become a more fascinating study. Whereas, to approach Latin cold, without a key, would fill me with dismay. In any novel I might write, I like that same possibility present — that I know something other people don't. Those are the books I'm drawn to write. I'm never attracted to a topic where I have no more to say than anyone else.

LENNON: It's become a commonplace to note that your nonfiction is written novelistically. Why?

MAILER: It's nice to end with a book that reads like a novel rather than the digested contents of the first stomach of the cow. Which latter is what most nonfiction is to me. Someone spends a lot of time studying a body of material, they digest it, and write books. They skip the confusions. That's not interesting. We never know the living origins of the conclusions. What is fascinating to me in another writer is how his mind works. If I obtain clues that way, I can improve my own mind. But to suppose an author can digest a subject so well that there is no need to think about the subject independently is disagreeable. So I don't like the way most nonfiction is done. Whereas the novel changes our lives to some extent. Marriages have broken up, for instance, because someone read a novel and decided the life of the character in the book was more interesting than their own. Good novels are painful to read. That's why few people do.

LENNON: Can nonfiction ever be existential in the sense that you've described it in regard to novels?

MAILER: I think an historian could say, "I start this project with two opposed hypotheses. I'm not sure which is correct. As we explore the material, let me show you the arguments for one, and then for the other. In the course of it, maybe we'll arrive at more of an answer than I have now." Although, to bring that off in truly sustained form is so dangerous, and would so violate the canons of the profession of history, which insist that you go for one stance, not two, that it doesn't often happen. It would tend to agitate exactly what disturbs most people about history in the first place which is that they learn somewhere between high school and college — or is it between graduate school and life? — that history is not history, but a series of immensely sober novels written by men who often don't have large literary talents, and have less to say about the real world than novelists. That's a disturbing discovery. That historians are not dealing with fact, but with the hypothesis they developed in relation to a series of isolated data. The desire to make these facts glow as facets in a mosaic that will enable us to perceive the past is not often done. Once we come to realize that no historians do it more closely than novelists, then all history becomes a novel. Just as any novel is the history of the working of one man's imagination, and so is a real historical artifact to illumine a period for us.

LENNON: How have the metaphors you've used changed over the years?

MAILER: I can tell you a story on that. I had a dear friend, Charlie Devlin, who helped me greatly with *The Naked and the Dead,* and in fact was the model, considerably removed, for the character named McLeod in *Barbary Shore.* Charlie was a quiet saturnine Irishman who was living in a small rooming house where I took a cubicle to finish *The Naked and the Dead.* We used to have long literary conversations. At a certain point I showed him *The Naked and the Dead.* He tore it apart. He was a severe critic. He said, "It's a better book than I thought it would be, but you have no gift for metaphor." Then he said, "Metaphor reveals a man's character, and his true grasp of life. To the degree that you have no metaphor, you are an impoverished writer, and have lived no life." I never forgot this lecture and began to work with might and main on my metaphors. But I can't tell you how they've changed.

LENNON: Many of your characters over the years have carried on negotiations with evil — Marion Faye, D. J., Rojack — I take it that you would not agree with Hannah Arendt on the essential banality of evil?

MAILER: I wouldn't agree with Hannah Arendt at all, not at all. Of course, she can make a case. There are any number of prodigiously evil people who have, from the novelist's point of view, disappointing exteriors. Eichmann, superficially speaking, was a little man, an ordinary man in appearance and vulgar and dull, but to assume therefore that evil itself is banal, strikes me as an exhibition of a prodigious poverty of imagination. You know, one of the paradoxes I always found in the liberal temperament is that they are immensely worshipful of Freud — even though most of his ideas are antipathetic to the notion of liberalism itself. But they go to Freud. The reason is that he is so reductive. Liberals don't like to believe in the vast power of the unconscious, in evil of true murderousness, residing in the most ordinary people. To mistake the surface for the reality, is to perform the fundamental liberal reflex. In effect, liberals are always saying, "I don't see God, so why do you assume God exists?" Out of that has come I think their present bankruptcy. Liberalism has no exciting ideas to offer. I think this enervation comes because it has not been able to deal with the most haunting question of the twentieth century, which is not communism, but nazism. It can't come near to understanding this incredible phenomenon that took over a country of the most decent, hardworking, and *clean* people in the world, this incredible phenomenon of a fascism that went far beyond the normal bounds of totalitarianism into the most extraordinary and despicable extermination of vast numbers of peoples. And this, coming out of a nation which had always been tremendously law-abiding, suggested that the unconscious was truly a hideous place. Liberals, unable to weave that thought into their philosophy, were happy to welcome Hannah Arendt's phrase. But I think to speak of the banality of evil is precisely to point us further in the wrong direction.

LENNON: Didn't Gary Gilmore's story have characteristics that are relevant to this?

MAILER: Probably. I was captured by how complex he was. It seemed to me that it's not the banality or the brutality of evil with which we have to contend, but its complexity, that is, the similarity of evil in others to ourselves. As I got to know Gilmore, and I came to know him better than I know almost anyone in my life,

I began to see that he was a man easily as complex as myself. Naturally, I've always thought of myself as being fairly complicated. Somewhere, in there, I realized that being a murderer was not a final factor, and shouldn't stop all thought. Once we allow ourselves to see Gilmore in his contradictions, the fact that he is a murderer is significant, let's say it's as much as one-quarter of his personality while the potential murderer in each of us might be only one sixteenth or one sixty-fourth of our personality, but fundamentally he is still more like us than unlike us. That is why I wanted to write the book in this way, with its slow accumulation of detail.

LENNON: You didn't have any final judgments on Gilmore?

MAILER: I started with many more opinions than I ended with. I may not be a good intellectual, but my tendency is to create intellections. I put them on like adhesive plasters. In this case I was pulling off the plasters. As I got deeper and deeper into what his nature might be, I decided that every concept I had about Gilmore proved inadequate. So I wanted the reader to confront the true complexity of a human personality that can come from studying one man close enough. The fact that he was a murderer made my task more easy because we're all fascinated with killers. But any person studied in that depth would prove fascinating. It's Flaubert's old idea. You can take any soul alive, including that simple servant girl he wrote about, and make them incredible if you get to know them well enough.

LENNON: *Of Women and Their Elegance* explores Marilyn Monroe's mind and speculates on her ideas, character, obsessions and desires, but does it by way of her inner voice, precisely what you chose not to do for Gilmore. Why? Is Marilyn Monroe less complex than Gilmore?

MAILER: No. A writer has to be ready to gamble when he enters someone's mind. So long as you stay outside, your characters retain a certain integrity, novelistically speaking. There is a mystery about them, a resonance. We can walk around such characters with the same respect we offer people who have a presence in a room. Part of the meaning of charisma is that we don't know the intimate nature of the human force we're dealing with. So, sometimes characters in novels radiate more energy when we don't enter their mind. It is one of the techniques a novelist acquires instinctively — don't enter your protagonist's mind until you have something to say about the interior that's more interesting than the reader's suppositions. The fatal error is to jump in too quickly and then offer banal material. That's the worst of best-sellerdom. Second-rate readers enjoying the insights of second-rate writers.

LENNON: Robert Lucid, the literary critic, once wrote that your writing was based on an implicit — you could almost say, magical — promise to connect the world of Freud with the world of Marx, the public world of politics with the private world of dreams and hallucinations. You called it a "radical bridge." Are you still as committed to this as you were in 1957?

MAILER: I'm no longer particularly interested in Freud. I don't say this disrespectfully. I think Freud had a great deal to say about the nature of the psyche in the nineteenth century. I believe his final importance in intellectual history will be that he gave us more insight into the late nineteenth century than anyone but Marx. Freud is the key to understanding how people put up with the particular kind of lives they led in the 1880s, 1890s, and early 1900s, very much locked up, terribly overstuffed, terrible formal lives. Yet, those lives had a considerable amount of power and energy. In those days the psyche was used like a plumbing system. People were accustomed to living under high pressure. That's not what we have now. Today we know a world in which people act out their anxieties and look to explanations for their conduct all the time. Freud is really not adequate any longer. Marx, for vastly more complex reasons, is also not adequate any longer, not wholly adequate, because corporate capitalism adapted to Marx via Keynes and practically wrapped themselves around some of his ideas. So I don't try to create a bridge from Marx to Freud anymore. I'm not certain I could have.

LENNON: How about other worlds, though? How about the public world of politics and economics, and the private interior world of individuals — hallucinations, surrealism, dream? What about those two worlds? Hasn't your writing always been trying to bridge the inner and outer, public and private?

MAILER: Yes. Always trying. There is a bad sentence I wrote years ago: "Until every manifestation of society from ukase to kiss is comprehended, we will be nowhere." Something of the sort. A most unpleasant sound, "ukase to kiss." I was trying too hard. It was in "The White Negro" and I wrote it at a time when I was coming to realize that everything in society from the largest social institution to those private and intimate personal moments, and the deepest mystical moments such as the onset of death, might all be seen in their connections if one had the courage to begin. In that sense, I'm still trying. But I've come to realize that the task is enormous. Of course, I grew up under the shadow of Marx and Freud. Both men, independently, created an entire world system. They had a vision of all existence. That impressed me immensely. I was nothing if not intellectually ambitious when I was young and wanted to come up with a similar vision that would comprehend everything. By now I've come to realize that it is not only enormously difficult but that I don't have the intellectual discipline to begin to do anything remotely of that sort. But one tries to do one's best with what one's got. I'm still attempting to connect up what I can. Because I do think it's important. Until we understand the ways in which the authorities manipulate us, that is, the ways in which we are obliged to lead our lives in ways we don't particularly enjoy, until we understand all those reasons why so many of us feel dead inside so much of the time, and recognize how much of that is not our lack of imagination but the product of vast institutional systems of greed and injustice that we are schooled to perceive as rather benign manifestations, we are nowhere. The only way I can tell that something terrible is going on is that I feel a little duller than I ought to. Very often that's the end of a very long chain, you might say, of socially intended processes that keeps us malleable, amenable, and short on such powerful emotions as outrage at injustice. In that sense, I'm still trying to find the roots, trace it out, bring in the ultimate indictment against all that's awful and evil in society.

LENNON: That is still a radical bridge, isn't it?

MAILER: Yes, it's just that I don't have these two marvelous mountains — Marx and Freud — any longer. I'm somewhere tracking around in the old lakebeds, kicking up a lot of dust.

LENNON: So you would say that your writing now is less of an exploration than it used to be?

MAILER: Less of an exploration and more of an occupation of territories I reconnoitered years ago. Twenty years ago my mind was so active, I couldn't keep up with it. I had perceptions of all kinds into all sorts of endeavor. I think, not to compare myself, but I believe the same thing happened to Zola. He spoke about how when he was young his thoughts would come so quickly that his hand could not keep up with them as he wrote. As he grew older, the thoughts slowed down, but that was all right, because his hand could now write as fast as his thought. It was the perfect rate. Something of the same sort has happened to me. I now put leaves on the bare branches. It's more satisfying but not as heady as it once was. I'm not as interesting to myself as I used to be.

LENNON: But you've got the card file of all the old ideas to go back to.

MAILER: Well, I live with the old ideas. Part of it is natural. They were so startling when they first came to me that I had to inhabit them, had to grow with them. Maybe I'm bragging, but I think I have a coherent philosophy. I believe we could start talking about virtually anything, and before we were done I could connect our subject to almost anything in my universe.

LENNON: The great book that you hope to write, will that require some new ideas or are you going to be able to use the old ones, the old system, the old philosophy?

MAILER: If I can bring off this three-part novel I'm talking about, I will have to get into places I've never been before. And I'll have to come up with new ideas. I'll have to be bigger and better than I've ever been before. So it is not at all certain to me that I can bring it off. I'm not laying odds.

LENNON: You're off to a hell of a good start.

MAILER: With the Egyptian novel? I hope I am. Practically no one has seen the book, you know.

LENNON: I've heard a few people say it's an amazing work.

MAILER: Well, it's amazing. I mean, chapter for chapter there's extraordinary stuff in it. The question is whether it will hold up. It's one thing to write wonderful chapters, but a great book has to live in other people's minds and change their lives. This book is so ambitious, it's absolutely beyond my measure of anticipation.

After I finish the Egyptian novel, I've then got a second book I want to do about a spaceship in the future, maybe two or three centuries from now, and I'm appalled by the difficulties of the task. I'm going to have to become familiar with science fiction, which I've never read, and get up on the most advanced astro-physics that we have available now. It will be a difficult study for me. Then I'll have to throw that stuff away after I absorb it. The only value it will have for my novel is that the narrator of my book will be able to say, "Yes, back in the twentieth century they believed this was true about the universe. How wrong they were!" That book is going to be staggeringly difficult. Then, of course, the third book, which I look forward to, if I ever get to it, will be contemporary. I've got a couple of tricks up my sleeve that I can't talk about, ways of tying together the Egyptian novel, the novel of the spaceship in the future, and the contemporary book.

So that they will all truly be three parts of the same novel, but in the way a tree might have three trunks growing out of a common root. Or, like the mythical phallus of Osiris which presented itself with three prongs.

1980

A Little
on Novel-Writing

*An Interview with Joseph McElroy
and His Writing Class at Columbia*

⚘

NORMAN MAILER: It might be useful to talk about the practical problems involved in writing a novel, by which I mean the set of psychological stances that you get into in the course of working on one book for a year or two. I remember when I was in college and writing a novel, the great problem I had was (I ran into a phrase by Henry James) "the keeping-up." It's a problem you face when you're young. The novel tends to change too quickly, which is one of the reasons why people in college often tend to write short stories and stay away from longer fiction. Good short story writers often blow up when they start a novel. They'll have a good first chapter, but the second chapter just seems to go off, and they never get it back.

That made me think of the different states I was in when I started each work. Why do I as a voice disappear in one book and appear in another? I found writing some kinds of books to call for this peculiar business of focusing your ego so it becomes literally the hot, burning, highly focused light that underwrites your style.

In other works, your ego tends to disappear completely. You're present as a gentle voice that seems to come in from over the hill — the type of voice that inhabits the third person in most good novels.

In talking about this question of ego and lack of ego, let me make a preface: for reasons that were not very dramatic, I stopped drinking about eight months ago. It's sort of interesting not drinking. I've never been psychoanalyzed, and I thought, this is the closest I'll ever get to it. I know my idea of myself kept changing every day or two. I found that I sort of lost my sense of identity, and didn't know anymore quite who I was in the way that I used to have certain definite assumptions about who I might be. This was sufficiently interesting so that I still haven't gone back to drinking. Because my idea of myself keeps changing. In a way novel-writing is analogous to that — you keep discovering new facets. When you're working on a novel, a variety of motives arise in yourself that shift your sense of identity. That is, honorable reasons and ignoble reasons are both feeding the work. In effect, you have to be writing the book because it's good for you personally, as well as, ideally, for society (or at least your idea of what's good for society).

Apart from that, there are times when one's identity as an author becomes pressing. It's crucial to have some idea then of your own specific density in the social world. How do you impinge on other people? As a result, almost obligatorily, you have to write a novel that has a great emphasis upon the self.

The act of writing has many purposes and many motives, but one of them is a search for one's own increasing sanity. By that I mean one's own increasing effectiveness in the world. Most people start writing out of the curled-up reflex that they're not quite able to contend with the world. They also write in order to become more attractive in the world, more powerful.

JOSEPH MCELROY: To get your own back, Orwell says.

MAILER: Yes. There are those periods when there's a vast absorption in oneself, and in a way, the nicest and happiest and most elegant solution to that is to write a novel in which the protagonist is close to yourself. If you can keep one hand on that high overhead line, that high-voltage line of irony, so that you don't take yourself too seriously, you get to that wonderful land between high seriousness and self-ridicule that is perfectly balanced. Then you've got something awfully good. When you abase and attack yourself, or take yourself too seriously, you have a disaster. You need a marvelous internal navigator to keep bringing you back on course in such a book.

Then there are books where you can no longer deal with yourself — it's too exhausting. You want a vacation from yourself. Sometimes one wants to live like a ghost. Some writers stay in one vein all their lives; other writers keep going back and forth between personal and objective books. You have people who always write out of their own voice, like Hemingway. Then you have writers who never step into their work, like Tolstoy* and James Michener.

STUDENT: You were saying at your reading last night, that at a certain point in your life you went out in the world instead of using that energy in your writing. Could you talk about that?

MAILER: I think most writers do have this problem, particularly if they arrive early. Those of you who don't, can have the fine consolation that your experience will at least remain your own; and that if you have a friend, he's real. People who notice you when you are unknown, notice you because you are in fact a lively protagonist in a given situation, and not because you're walking into the room with a reputation.

The problem of going out and searching for experience, I think, is true for very young writers who just don't have enough to write about. There comes a point where you say, "I want to be a writer, I feel all the equipment of a writer. I feel the livid intelligence of a writer, but I don't really know enough." This is where journalism rears its ugly head. It's very hard to enter strange places and learn a lot about them unless you have clout. Kids get into journalism because the moment they flash a card that says they're a bona fide reporter, people start talking to them. Of course it's a false experience. Hopefully, you develop the sense how to filter this experience, and correct it, refract it into what the experience might have been like if you hadn't had this peculiar advantage of being a journalist.

I discovered this all by myself when I started doing journalism, and realized it was a marvelous way for me to work. It was vastly easier than trying to write novels, and I was discouraged with the difficulty of writing them at that point. I had run into this business of trying to tell a good story and yet say wonderful things about the nature of the world and society, touch all the ultimates, and yet at the same time, have it read like speed. There are so many pitfalls to this. I always had a terrible time with the story. My stories were always ending up begrounded. There I'd be, in the middle of the dunes, no gas in the tank. I loved journalism because it gave me the story, which I'd always been weakest in. Then I discovered that this was the horror of it. Audiences liked

---

* An irresponsible remark! I must have been thinking of "The Death of Ivan Ilyich" rather than *War and Peace.*

it better. They'd all been seeing the same story you'd been seeing, and they wanted interpretation. It was those critical faculties that were being called for, rather than one's novelistic gifts. Under all those temptations, I must say I succumbed, and I spent a good many years working at the edge of journalism, because it was so much easier.

I was asked last night what I'd do if I had it all to do over again, and I said that if I'd had more discipline, I would probably have tried to stick with the novel. Still journalism has its own disciplines. Ideally, you must not only describe the event and bring your own perception to it, but say to the reader, "This is the kind of man or woman I am. This is the way I perceive the event. Now you, having been given me first, and then the event, can see around me into the event, and come away with your own conclusions. They might be different from mine."

In a novel, you do try to create something that exists separately from yourself, even if it's a manifest with yourself as the protagonist. Ideally, at a certain point that novel ought to be able to be separated from you.

STUDENT: How do you write as a novelist when, on the one hand, you have this story that's already been told, and you have all this research, and then you have the act of writing?

MAILER: The trick, as I found for myself, is just to keep from doing it all at once. When I work on a novel — I've had a novel working for years — I don't like to know the end. I'm happier finding things out at the point of the pencil. I think that if you solve the problem of how a chapter's going to end in the shower, then you're not as well off as if you get it while writing. I felt this with *The Executioner's Song*. While I knew the story, I saw this as a hazard. I wanted the book to read as if we did not know the ending. I didn't want to be aware of too many future details, because this would tend to make me curve what was happening to my characters at the place where I had them. I would understand too well their relation to what was going to happen later.

STUDENT: When you're writing about a story that's superficially very well known, there must be some very private experience about what goes into the writing of it.

MAILER: Well, I think *The Executioner's Song*, more than any other book I've ever done, was an exercise in craft. I've never felt close to it. I will say that there were many pitfalls to be avoided in the writing of it, and it did require those many years of experience. What you need is a tremendous amount of lore that'll let you know where all the pitfalls are, and enable you to avoid them.

MCELROY: Can we talk a bit about an earlier book, *Why Are We in Vietnam?* How did you feel when you were writing it?

MAILER: Well, it's the perfect foil to *The Executioner's Song.* I must start with an excursion to the side in answer to your question. Years ago I knew a lot of painters, abstract expressionists, young ones, and I had just begun to understand most of the work they were doing. You'd come in and one of them would have done about twenty window shades. It looked to my untutored eye as if they'd thrown some paint on these window shades and then let it drip down. I knew one of the painters better than the others, and I remember she said, "That's awfully interesting work." I said, "Interesting, what do you mean, interesting? It's horrible." She said, "What he's done is very valuable," and I said, "Why?," and she said, "Well, I'm glad he's done it, because now I don't have to do it." That was the period when they were truly exploring every last way you could put color on a surface, and so she was happy with it, because it saved her some work — she didn't have to go in that direction. You'll find very often in writing, that in the beginning, you have to go in certain directions to find out if they're attractive to you, and if you can do something with them, or also just whether you like them or not. I don't think I could have written *The Executioner's Song* if I hadn't written *Why Are We in Vietnam?*, because there I had the experience of expressing myself without a backward look. I think that *Why Are We in Vietnam?* is interesting to me, because I was able this once to transmute myself and create a somewhat ongoing, rampant, inflamed, sort of mad ego. If there are any forces in the cosmos that ever step in and give a helping hand to a writer, I got it right there.

The Executioner's Song, on the other hand, was another kind of gift, and I was delighted to have been given it. So in effect, two of the best books I've done are not mine. One, from the inside, and one, from the outside. They couldn't be more different, those two books, in every way.

STUDENT: Is your new Egyptian novel mostly research, or is it more of a creative process?

MAILER: There's an awful lot of research, but the trick is to digest it. The most difficult thing about writing an historical novel is to avoid that awful stance where you say, "Hello, I'm Saint-Simon and I'm at the court of Louis XIV and Madame de Maintenon is very angry this morning." You have to get to that point of view in your writing where you say to yourself, "Madame de Maintenon does not quite know that she's the Madame de Maintenon that we know through Saint-Simon. She sees herself as someone other." You have to decide how she sees herself. That's what you're trying to get in an historical novel, and it's very difficult. Anachronisms come in with every phrase. Reading from my Egyptian book aloud last night, I kept thinking, oh my God, there are so many things I like or don't like in terms of style; I felt certain words were reasonable for an Egyptian of the Twentieth Dynasty and others weren't at all. Cleaning up the style is crucial to writing an historical novel. I did a book on Marilyn Monroe which came out last fall, and in that the writing was nothing much — it was easy to write, a question of feeling like a medium — hearing her voice and writing it. Once you begin to discover the ways in which characters talk like themselves and the way they talk like you, you try to write it in their voice, not your own voice. It takes a certain patience to go through and keep weeding out all those traces that don't belong. The problem is magnified in an historical novel.

STUDENT: You once said that form was a substitute for talent or style.

MAILER: I think it's a substitute for inspiration. A perfect example of this is the new journalism. Here the form is delivered to you by the plot of the event. It's a great substitute for the talent to conceive a good story. Of course you still have to flesh it out, but at least the event happened. In novel-writing you have to deal more with time. For instance, putting a story in the first person immediately takes care of the present. I've always found it much easier to write in the first person than in the third person, because in the third person you're making certain philosophical assumptions that the reader may not accept. It is tricky. You're assuming you're God, or some extraordinary observer. In *The Executioner's Song*, the biggest difficulty I had was to get myself knuckled down to the simple point of telling that story flatly, blankly, in the third person.

MCELROY: I think you're right about the first person — the reader will give you that much.

MAILER: Yes, writing in the first person you don't have to jump from one head to another. As I was saying, in *The Executioner's Song*, since I wanted to move through everybody's head, and make no pretty bones about it, I was paralyzed for a month. I just couldn't do it. Finally I thought, "Well, you're going to have to make the jump." To this day I feel uneasy about it. I feel I've violated the fundamental intregrity of the novel.

One thing though, for me, about many novels — I think you have to work as if you're a farmer, and rotate your crops. If you write a novel that's factual and realistic and big, awfully close to what happened, then it's probably a good idea that your next novel be as fanciful as possible. That way you're rotating the crops in your brain.

MCELROY: Do you ever write short stories?

MAILER: Not often anymore, and I have something not awfully attractive to say about that. After you become a working writer, make your living as a writer, then what you write, to a larger extent than you realize, is determined by whether you make your living at it. The sad thing about writing short stories is that you can't. I don't think there are more than four or five writers of short stories in this country who actually do survive that way year after year.

STUDENT: Can we get back to inspiration? It sounds like if something inspires you, because it inspires you, you're willing to justify it ideologically.

MAILER: If you find some theme that keeps you working, don't question it. Let that theme be sufficient to fuel your work. If you start using the value judgments of others, you're never going to get much done. The thing to remember is that there's nobody anymore, not even the President, who can tell us how to live. Nobody knows the answer. If I find something is stimulating me and arousing my energy, that's fine, I'll trust it. If you're a serious young writer and find you are writing, my God, don't listen to what anyone else says, write your book. There probably is a deeper truth than you'll ever know in the fact that you're able to work so well. Of course, you could be writing in absolutely the wrong direction. You could be doing a dreadful book. You could be, let's take an extreme example, flirting with something that justifies Hitler, and you say to yourself, "What am I doing? I'm a monster. Why am I writing this book?" Who knows — in the process of creating such a work you might reawaken the attention of civilization to the fact that they're getting kind of casual, and complacent about Hitler. You see, you won't know the results of your action. The greatest vanity, the thing that has poisoned Marxist literature for decades, is that they assume writers can affect the population profoundly in ways that are foreseeable, and therefore writers should work like scientists.

But, no matter what you find yourself writing about, if it's giving you enough energy to continue then the work bears a profound relationship to you at that point and so you don't question it.

STUDENT: Could you talk a bit about your early career, and the difficulties of writing your first novel, *The Naked and the Dead?*

MAILER: That was probably the easiest and the happiest book I ever wrote. When it came out I was twenty-five. I did it in about fifteen months. I was filled with the war, I'd just come back. This was a relatively peaceful period. The only anxiety I suffered while writing was that my opinion of the book was much higher than it deserved to be. I was young and I thought, "This is the greatest book since *War and Peace.* Maybe it's better." I used to walk around in a rage after reading the *New York Times Book Review,* because of some awful book that was being celebrated. I'd go to my editor and say, "Do you people realize that if they don't treat this book properly I'm going to be forced to go out and write potboilers?" I took myself very seriously. Once, before I'm done, I'd like to get another book that comes through me so quickly. I was getting five good ideas for every bad one, and happily I was oblivious to the faults of the book. At the time of *The Naked and the Dead* I was writing in a style that had very little literary merit to it. The force of the book prevailed over the style. I was lucky. If I'd been even a fraction more concerned with the merits of style, the book would have slowed up and I wouldn't have been able to write it.

STUDENT: What do you think of the way the book turned out — the death of Hearn? It was sure a big surprise.

MAILER: I haven't thought of that in years. Really, it is a shocking death. I must say I stole that directly from E. M. Forster, in *The Longest Journey.* He created a character who was most alive for the reader, and then destroyed him on the next page. Like a rifle shot. You get an idea what a gun is like at that point. In my book it may have been too big a price to pay, because the denouement of the novel was sacrificed. I don't think I was aware of the size of the problem. Today I'd be much more alert to that. If I did the book over again today, I might have kept Hearn alive until the very end, and it might have been a phonier book as a result. It might have been more effective but less true. One of the things you always have trouble with when you talk about "true" or "not true" is, of course, the relative truth of the novel. In a way, if you get a fairly good novel going, then you have a universe functioning, and this universe lives or does not live in relation to its own scheme of cause and effect, of reaction and response. In Kafka's writing, he creates worlds that are absolutely true. You can say practically every sentence in a Kafka story is true to the story.

Looking back on it, I can give you a good and bad motive that I had for killing Hearn at that point. The good motive was that it seemed to me that it was about as powerful a way to show what death is like in war as anything I could do in that book. The shoddy motive was I wasn't altogether sure in my heart that I knew what to do with him, or knew how to bring him off.

MCELROY: You were suspicious even then for the long-range plans of a given book? That is, you'd let where you were going at a given point decide what to do next, right?

MAILER: I think that I truly work on impulse in all of my writing. That's why I don't like to plan too far ahead. It makes it almost impossible to have one of your characters go through a dipsy-doodle bend, because it's going to violate your larger scheme. It's better if the larger scheme comes into focus at the very last moment.

STUDENT: Back to some of the advice you were giving young writers. It seems you're saying that if it feels good, go with it and don't listen to what everybody says. Back when you were young and you were plowing through your stuff, were you aware or was there a mentor around to tell you that if it felt good, go with it; or did you have your doubts and just write your way through it? Didn't you sometimes get your head turned around by all the different forces working on you? Or were you aware, maybe instinctively, of what to do?

MAILER: I think I probably had a certain urgency about writing, because it seemed to me that it was probably the only thing I could do well. There is a great tendency then to follow your own instincts, because that's all you've got. Let me amplify this. Your instinct could be dead wrong. In other words, you could write a book with a powerful sense of inner conviction. You could finish writing it, and a year or two later, look at it and say, "How could I have so deluded myself? This is awful." This inner experience, this instinct can betray you, but you still have to go with it. Very often the instinct sees some light at the end of the tunnel, but that's because you've been trapped in a situation where your creative energies just can't get together. Now, there's become a way to work. You may be writing out some very bad tendencies in yourself, but this can be good, too. Feel happy because (thank God) soon you're going to be done with that stupid side of yourself. That's what the enthusiasm can be about.

STUDENT: How do you go about rewriting?

MAILER: That's where your experience comes in. The more you rewrite, the better you get at it. There comes a point when you may feel on the declining side of your powers. At this point, if you've become one of the best editors in town, then those declining powers will seem much less weak to others than to yourself. That's because you know how to get the maximum out of what you have done. The only way to do this when you're young is to go through your work in every mood. You have to have the courage to look at it when you're in a terrible mood, ready to destroy it. If at that point something still comes through, then at least you have the assurance that it has to be pretty good, at least to you. And then, of course, it's very good to read things at the top of your feelings, way up, to see what the maximum is. If nothing else, all this gives you tolerance for the extraordinary spectrum of reactions you get in the classroom. You realize that the people that hate your work aren't necessarily evil, and the people who love your stuff are not altogether illustrious.

STUDENT: What happens when you find yourself lacking in inspiration or impulse? Do you utilize a problem-solving measure to create inspiration?

MAILER: Well, sometimes you're in the middle of an interesting chapter, but you don't know what the denouement is. You've got interesting people and have aroused certain expectations in your reader and now you don't know what to do with it all. That is the ongoing problem of doing a novel from day to day. As I said, James used that expression, "the keeping-up." How do you keep the level up in such a way that you don't get too dramatic or, equally, don't dissipate a good opportunity? You sit there and you have to solve that problem. Practice is a big part of it. There's a sense of inner timing that develops over the years. There is also the key word, taste. Taste becomes refined. Of course, it can get refined to the point where it ceases to exist.

STUDENT: You're a controversial public figure. I wonder how you feel about your past.

MAILER: After a while you walk around your own life as though it were a piece of sculpture. It depends on where you're looking at it from. Are you thinking of it from the point of view of your work, or your children? Actually, I find I think less and less about myself as I get older. You begin to have the feeling, "Well, I may only have another so many years to write, and write halfway well," and you tend to get more serious. You get practical about your life, and realize that there's going to be more and more work, and less and less fun as you go along. You say, "I'll think about that old part of my life when I'm writing about it, and if I never write about it, I'll never think about it again."

1981

To Pontificate on America and Europe

An Interview with Barbara Probst Solomon

❧

BARBARA PROBST SOLOMON: When Hemingway and Miller went to live and write in Europe, writers were not like governments, they were not nationalistic; they had something to say to each other. Americans and Europeans don't talk to each other very much at this point. Do you feel our novelists have gone in very different directions?

NORMAN MAILER: Yes, I think so.

SOLOMON: European writers have been more influenced by developments in linguistics. American innovators — and you have been a leading force — have gone in another direction. What do you think about this?

MAILER: I think of Borges, who is doing something else altogether. I don't know enough about South America to decide how much Borges speaks for Argentina and South America — but finally, I think of Borges as European because to do what Borges does you need a culture that is profound. Almost none of us in America has that kind of culture. It's possible Saul Bellow is the best read of American novelists; John Barth, maybe. I can think of a few others but none of them has been able to take that culture and use it forcefully in their work. It hardly matters that Bellow is conversant with probably all the great and medium great and small great writers of the Western world since Plato and Aristotle. It doesn't enrich his work, not the way Borges' culture does. Borges poses for us, I think, the difficulty of comprehending reality. He

183

shows us that as we approach reality we are writing scenarios that are the equivalent of propositions and hypotheses in physics. That is, they are correct until the evidence subverts them. But even as they are being subverted we learn a great deal because the next hypothesis, ideally, should be superior.

So in Borges you have this wonderful business of an immensely elaborate hypothesis destroyed by the one fact that turns it inside out. There is this marvelously sinewy dialectical vision of the interplay between culture and history, the two almost being — not artifacts — but separate organisms. Borges reveals to us his immensely vivid inner life which I think is all one finally cares about in another author. It is what I should be able to give others in my own writing. If our inner lives are more alive, we are more able to stand proof against the attacks of the world. And by now the attacks of the world upon our psyche are not so much aggressive as subtle, insidious — we're leached out. We're not destroyed from without, we are sucked out. Our spiritual souls, our social souls, are sucked out of us by the mass media, by information retrievable. I think Borges is the best when it comes to fighting that. Try putting Borges in a computer.

Now, the ways in which the Europeans have been going at it, have come out of a profound weariness with the novel, with plot, with all the impedimenta of writing a book. Everything that is detestable in the best-selling novel comes to visit you every time you try to tell a story. It's getting harder and harder. So you look for ways to get away from it. I suppose I've looked to other fields. To journalism. To historical events that I could write about as they were occurring. Because it's another way of apprehending reality. My fundamental stance in all this is that the attempt to apprehend reality is what is interesting. Because we learn from the attempt. We can't learn that much from the final product. All we can do is argue about how successful it is.

SOLOMON: You wrote, in *The Armies of the Night*, that what saved America was our humor, the belly laugh, "The noble common man was obscene as an old goat and his obscenity was what saved him." The guy who says, "Man, I just managed to take me a noble shit." That cadence is at the heart of the American vernacular. Do you feel all this European weariness comes from their essentially non-democratic society? Where writers feel their connection to the upper rather than lower reaches of society?

MAILER: I think it has a great deal to do with it. I think it's also impossible to live with a culture as rich as the culture of the Western world without being aghast at the poverty of one's ability to write about it. Americans have a saving instinct — we're not that near to European high culture. Sooner or later we suffer from having ignored it; we feel the paucity of our own culture, but at least we're not living in the shadow of the great beauty. Which is the shade, let us say, that sits over the light of European literary endeavor. Americans can live and work on a different street. We don't have to contemplate the beauty every day. In America one can still have the illusion that one is doing something brand new. One can feel like a pioneer.

But it's getting harder; we didn't start with much culture and we never achieved a truly rich American marrow. We're now in terrible trouble because we're getting to the point where we are destroying our culture at a much greater rate than we are creating it. And on top of that, we are exporting it to the rest of the world. Our heritage is in danger of arriving on the main historical stage all but cultureless; and for some time Europe has been attracted by the novelty of America's cultureless culture — taking our architecture, our superhighways, our plastics, our McDonald's, our Coca-Cola and all of it. They're destroying their culture. But in Europe, at least, they have something interesting to burn. So it's going to take them much longer. I make a prediction that European literature is going to get vastly interesting a little further down the road about the time that a great deal of European culture is being destroyed. I think that talented European writers are going to be struck by the tension between the value of what is being destroyed and the ferment of the destruction itself. Some very interesting works are going to come out of it.

SOLOMON: So you think the balance of tension is going to shift because of their fascination with America?

MAILER: Not so much because of America. I think it's going to shift because they won't be living in the shade of their culture any longer. That culture is going to be destroyed to a degree where Europeans will be able to breathe again. At a terrible price to that culture. But they'll be able to breathe again and, of course, breathing again, they're going to value that culture for the first time in decades, rather than feel awe, resentment and reverence for it.

SOLOMON: You were influenced by a European, Jean Malaquais?

MAILER: Yes, very much.

SOLOMON: In *The Armies of the Night*, which was published in '68, you wrote, "Communism would continue to produce heretics and great innovators just so long as it expanded. Between Poland and India, Prague and Bangkok was a diversity of primitive lore which would jam every fine gear of the Marxist." You seem to be proved right.

MAILER: Yes, perhaps.

SOLOMON: That doesn't interest you?

MAILER: I think it would be more Malaquais' idea than mine. Jean Malaquais is the first person I knew who talked seriously and coherently about the inner contradictions of Soviet communism. That is, the very forces that would ultimately destroy communism. But the language in *The Armies of the Night* is not his but mine. I don't know that Malaquais pays as much attention as I do to primitive lore. I can't take credit for the idea, but feel satisfaction as I read it.

SOLOMON: Yes, but you can take credit for the ideas that you choose. We're always choosing somebody else's ideas.

MAILER: I think in choosing some of Malaquais' ideas, I chose well. Better than I usually do.

SOLOMON: In *Armies*, when you are in your Washington hotel room in the Hay-Adams, you reflect on federalist architecture, and suddenly what swam in front of my mind was *The Federalist Papers, Democracy*, and *The Education of Henry Adams*. In that section you mention his influence on you. Did you mean his novel *Democracy* or *The Education of Henry Adams*?

MAILER: The influence of Adams on *The Armies of the Night* was most peculiar. To the best of my recollection, I never read much Adams. I know for certain that I read one long chapter of *The Education of Henry Adams* in my freshman reader at Harvard. I remember thinking at the time, "What an odd thing to do, to write about yourself in the third person. Who is this fellow, Henry Adams, talking about himself as Adams," and being struck with it in that mildly irritable way freshmen have of passing over extraordinary works of literature. It's possible that I then read more of *The Education of Henry Adams* sometime in my freshman or sophomore year although I wouldn't claim that I did. I never wrote about Adams, never thought about him particularly, would never have mentioned his name as one of the writers that were important to me, and yet in *Armies*, one starts reading it, and immediately one says — even I said — "My God, this is pure Henry Adams." What the hell is going on here? It's an absolute take-off, as if I were the great-grandson of Henry Adams. You don't have to posit any other influence but Adams for *The Armies of the Night*.

So look how peculiar is influence: Adams was stuck in my unconscious as a possibility, the way it happens with painters much more than with writers. A painter can look at a particular Picasso, or Cézanne and say to himself, "That's the way to do it." But the work might not pop out for twenty or thirty years. When it does, they say, "Oh yes, there was a Picasso I saw at MOMA twenty-five years ago. I always wanted to try a palette of such and such, and I decided to use it here." In effect, that's what happened to me.

SOLOMON: Adams seems to have been one of the few good American writers who thought of putting Washington, D.C. and an American president at the center of a novel — *Democracy*. I thought of this in connection with you — the protagonist discards Washington and ends contemplating Egypt. So I felt that Adams subliminally was reaching to you on all levels.

MAILER: Well, he is and he isn't. I feel absolutely at a loss before Henry Adams. I mean, on the basis of these facts, it's spooky. I didn't know about Egypt, for instance. Yet one of his books ends with a character going there?

SOLOMON: Madeline Lee in *Democracy* gets disgusted with Washington and then goes off to Egypt at the end of the book. You do seem more like Henry Adams' great-grandson at this moment that you do Hemingway's son.

MAILER: Yes, because here I am going off to Egypt . . . for the last ten years.

SOLOMON: Did any of the elasticity of the Jewish historical experience help you make that imaginative leap into Egypt?

MAILER: I don't know why I started writing about Egypt. I've been working on that book off and on for ten years. I feel only now as if I'm slowly beginning to understand it, that is, the Egypt of antiquity. You can very often write well about matters that you don't understand too well. Most of my life I've written in advance of my comprehension of a subject. Often, years later, I would come to understand the material better and be amazed that I could have done it at all when I did. Oddly enough, now that I have the knowledge, I probably couldn't write about it. There's some potentiality in all of us that we tap when we write. The best writing comes out of that. I don't know that the work I'm writing about Egypt now is better than the stuff eight to ten years ago when I knew very little.

Something in me then was drawn toward Egypt although nothing in my past was even remotely related. All my interests are contemporary. I'm certainly not a man of classical education, in relation to most writers not a man with historical concerns. Yet in this Egyptian book I wish nothing in it to be contemporary. And of course it is a totally different culture. It existed long before Jesus, so there's absolutely nothing of a Christian notion of compassion, which is the very center of all Western thought. There is also nothing of the Judaic tradition. At the time I am writing about, the Jews are a tribe of barbarians who occasionally give a little trouble on the borders. Moses comes into the book for a page. He's mentioned as this fellow who went wild out on the Eastern desert and helped some of the Hebrews pull off a massacre and then took off farther east. That's all we know about Moses in my book. I can't answer why I've been so fascinated with Egypt. I sometimes think that I'm attracted to a subject for literary purposes because I know so little about it — except that I have one deep instinct into the subject.

Let me give you an example. It's more fun to pick up a mystery novel and read it, if early in that book you decide that you and the author share a perception that no one else has. Then you are going to get more out of this book than anyone else, even though you know nothing about the material or the crime. I think something of that sort works in historical research. You have to feel that you do know more than the average historian about one aspect of the subject. I think that I felt I knew more about burial customs than the average Egyptologist. Not more about the details of them, which I hadn't learned, then, but more about the reason for them.

SOLOMON: Did you need a subject of the dimension of Egypt to be able to pull yourself away from America? Up until now America has been a big character in your novels.

MAILER: Yes, but I haven't been altogether successful in pulling away. Sometimes I've gotten terribly tired of this Egyptian book because there's nothing to say in it about America today. *The Executioner's Song* was written as a reaction. It allowed me to immerse myself again in daily matters of American life. I went out to Utah, a place whose inhabitants have hardly heard of New York and where they certainly never have heard of me. I learned again how Americans who don't live in the media do in fact live interesting lives and I steeped myself in all the minutiae of American life. When I went back to the Egyptian book, it was with a certain sense of refreshment. There's been this alternation over the last ten years — writing about Egypt and then writing about matters that are very American: Marilyn Monroe, Muhammad Ali, Henry Miller, Gary Gilmore.

SOLOMON: Do you physically *see* Egypt?

MAILER: Yes, oh yes. I see it so clearly that I can't stand going there. I went once for a visit and said, I have to get out of here. Because it was ruining my vision. It had nothing to do with Egypt of antiquity. I got out fast.

SOLOMON: Language has always been very important in your books. What do you hear in the Egyptian book? What vernacular?

MAILER: I've been studying the Egyptian language a little bit, not in a very serious or concerted way, but I've been using an Egyptian dictionary and I find it fascinating. Ancient Egyptian is a wonderful language, a very dialectical language. Often the nearest cousin to a word means the exact opposite. For example: the word for "dung" also means "the bleaching of linen." And you find this all through the language. The word for "magnetism" is also the word for "you." It's a tremendously sensuous language, rather existential. You feel that the ancient Egyptians had already articulated one highly complex and wonderful and rather magical civilization, and yet they were still close to the primitive. Every word in the language is a revelation. Every word is related to every other word in a fashion that we don't have today. Like "you" and "magnetism." The reason the two words were the same is that when people looked at one another they felt the play of forces between them. Today we have that crude expression, "good vibes," but it's a pale reflection of ancient Egyptian.

SOLOMON: Very few novelists, excepting Saul Bellow, seem to write expansive books.

MAILER: Well, it's hard. It's hard to write well on a large subject. Actually, most large subjects are handled by best-selling novelists. They will have a cast of forty or fifty characters. They'll have stories that cover fifty to one hundred years. They'll have a couple of world wars. They'll have startling changes in the lives of several families. The reason they do all that in a hurry is because they can keep their book moving. What characterizes a best-selling novel is that there's nothing in it that you haven't come across before. At least if you're a reader of some experience. Most serious writers tend to work on smaller and smaller canvases and expatiate upon them with more and more clarity. And that's terribly important. At least they're contributing to knowledge rather than adding to the general cultural sludge that lies over everything. So it's very hard to take on a large topic. At the moment the only living writer I can think of who can handle what I've described — forty to fifty characters and one hundred years — is Garcia Márquez. *One Hundred Years of Solitude* is an amazing work. Garcia Márquez succeeds in doing it, but how, I don't know. In my Egyptian novel — although it's very, very long — not that much happens. As I've said before it takes me ten pages to go around a bend in the Nile.

1981

Acknowledgments

⁂

"Hip, Hell and the Navigator" by Richard G. Stern originally appeared in *The Western Review*, Winter 1959.

"An Impolite Interview" originally appeared as "An Impolite Interview with Norman Mailer" by Paul Krassner in *The Realist*, No. 40, December 1962.

"Craft and Consciousness" appeared as "An Interview with Norman Mailer" from *Writers at Work: The Paris Review Interviews*, third series, © 1967 by The Paris Review, Inc. Reprinted by permission of Viking Penguin Inc.

"Talking of Violence" by W. J. Weatherby originally appeared in *Twentieth Century*, Winter 1964–1965.

"Vices" originally appeared in *Playboy* Magazine; Copyright © 1967 by Playboy. Reprinted by permission of Playboy.

"Norman Mailer on Science and Art" by David Young originally appeared in *Antaeus*, April 1, 1974.

"In Search of the Devil" excerpted from "The Rolling Stone Interview with Norman Mailer" by Richard Stratton from *Rolling Stone* No. 177, January 2, 1975 and No. 178, January 16, 1975. By Straight Arrow Publishers, Inc. © 1975. All rights reserved. Reprinted by permission.

"Existential Aesthetics: An Interview with Norman Mailer" by Laura Adams originally appeared in *Partisan Review*, No. 2, 1975.

"Marriage" originally appeared as "Mailer on Marriage and Women" by Bernard Farbar in *Viva*, October 1973.

"One-Night Stands" originally appeared as "Norman Mailer on Love, Sex, God and the Devil." Interview by Cathleen Medwick. Courtesy *Vogue*. Copyright © 1980 by The Condé Nast Publications, Inc. Reprinted by permission.

"Ethics and Pornography" by Jeffrey Michelson and Sarah Stone originally appeared in *Puritan*, No. 7, published by Puritan Publishing, Inc., Allentown, Pennsylvania.

"Prisoner of Success" by Paul Attanasio originally appeared in the *Boston Phoenix* on February 24, 1981. Reprinted by permission.

"A Brief Exchange" by Anita Eichholz is excerpted from the transcript of *Norman Mailer: The Sanction to Write*, a documentary film produced by Jeffrey Van Davis. Reprinted by permission.

The four "Munich" interviews by Michael Lennon: "Waste": "An Author's Identity"; "Writers and Boxers"; and "Literary Ambitions" are excerpted from the transcript of *Norman Mailer: The Sanction to Write*, a documentary film produced by Jeffrey Van Davis. Reprinted by permission.

"The Mad Butler" originally appeared as "Creators on Creating: Norman Mailer" by Hilary Mills in *Saturday Review*. Copyright © 1981 by Saturday Review. All rights reserved. Reprinted by permission.

"A Little on Novel-Writing" by Joseph McElroy originally appeared in *Columbia: A Magazine of Poetry and Prose*, No. 6, 1981. The interview was conducted under the auspices of The National Committee for the Literary Arts.

"To Pontificate on America and Europe," originally published as "A Conversation with Norman Mailer," © 1981 by Barbara Probst Solomon, is excerpted from an interview dated July 16, 1981 originally published in *El Pais*, Madrid, on October 4, 1981. Reprinted by permission.

EAST HAMPTON LIBRARY

3 0625 00049 2015

813.54   1
Mailer, N.

Pieces and
  pontifications

11/23/82